THE UNITED NATIONS DEVELOPMENT PROGRAMME

The United Nations Development Programme is the central network co-ordinating the work of the United Nations in over 160 developing countries. This book provides the first authoritative and accessible history of the Programme and its predecessors. Based on the findings of hundreds of interviews and archives in more than two dozen countries, Craig Murphy traces the history of the UNDP's organizational structure and mission, its relationship to the multilateral financial institutions, and the development of its doctrines. He argues that the principles on which the UNDP was founded remain as relevant in a world divided by terrorism as they were in the immediate aftermath of the Second World War, as are the fundamental problems that have plagued the Programme from its origin, including the opposition of traditionally isolationist forces in the industrialized world.

CRAIG N. MURPHY is the Historian of the United Nations Development Programme and Professor of International Relations at Wellesley College. He is past president of the International Studies Association and co-founder of the international public policy journal, *Global Governance*. He has written and edited several earlier books, the most recent being *Global Institutions, Marginalization, and Development* (2005).

THE UNITED NATIONS
DEVELOPMENT PROGRAMME

A Better Way?

CRAIG N. MURPHY

CAMBRIDGE
UNIVERSITY PRESS

CAMBRIDGE UNIVERSITY PRESS
Cambridge, New York, Melbourne, Madrid, Cape Town, Singapore, São Paulo

Cambridge University Press
The Edinburgh Building, Cambridge CB2 2RU, UK

Published in the United States of America by Cambridge University Press, New York

www.cambridge.org
Information on this title: www.cambridge.org/9780521683166

First published 2006

Printed in the United Kingdom at the University Press, Cambridge

A catalogue record for this book is available from the British Library

ISBN-13 978-0-521-86469-5 hardback
ISBN-10 0-521-86469-0 hardback
ISBN-13 978-0-521-68316-6 paperback
ISBN-10 0-521-68316-5 paperback

CONTENTS

FIGURES

Unless otherwise acknowledged, all material is from various UNDP offices or the UN Secretariat.

LIST OF TABLES

FOREWORD

While the United Nations Development Programme has been a significant player in the field of international development for more than forty years, its evolution is not widely known nor easily understood.

This is the organization's first published history. It is only one of many possible histories of UNDP that could have been written, and is not an organizational history in the traditional sense. My predecessor, Mark Malloch Brown, who commissioned this project, wanted the book to be a work of genuinely independent scholarship, hence, it is in many ways more essay than chronicle. It could not have been written without the help of many people who have been part of UNDP, who contributed their experiences and insights, knowing full well that what the author would eventually write might be very different than what they would have.

Professor Craig Murphy tells the story building on a truly impressive amount of research and lets an overarching theme emerge. The central argument of the book is that UNDP has increasingly become a learning organization, an approach which may provide models for the larger reform of the United Nations. The key aspect of UNDP's learning achievements has been the wonderful creativity and abiding commitment of the people who work for it. The overwhelming majority of UNDP staff have been people who passionately believe in the goals of the organization, individuals who have overcome daunting obstacles – and often the conventional wisdom of the day – to develop hundreds of initiatives, many of which are cited in this book, as well as countless others. In most cases these initiatives have not been something UNDP staffers have been told or even encouraged to do from Headquarters; indeed, had they required prior approval by some kind of intergovernmental council, they would likely never have happened. Such creative results came about because UNDP has attracted people who not only believe in what they do, but who have been able to be creative in times of crisis, and been willing to put themselves on the line (and had the freedom to do so). In essence, the history of UNDP is about these numerous individuals who come up with smart ways of dealing with situations for which there are no precedents. In the end, a 'better way' consists primarily of finding and attracting these kinds of people; without that, it isn't possible to understand UNDP.

A second major theme of the book relates to how UNDP has creatively engaged in the promotion of democracy – including the democratic legitimacy of international institutions – at the same time as it has served the nation states that make up the United Nations. It is a theme I have argued for elsewhere as being essential for the UN as a whole.

This book reflects our shared commitment to the development of ideas, policies and institutions which contribute to human development and help build a fairer world for all its people. It is my hope that its insights contribute to addressing the many challenges we face, both within the UN system and beyond.

Kemal Dervis
UNDP Admistrator

ACKNOWLEDGEMENTS

I am indebted to UNDP's past Administrator, Mark Malloch Brown, who hired me to write this history. He offered the unbeatable combination of complete scholarly freedom and final editorial control along with a good salary and travel budget, a small but exceedingly qualified staff, unimpeded access to all of UNDP's materials, and the cooperation of the entire organization. I am grateful to Malloch Brown's successor, Kemal Dervis, who maintained that incomparable support (and wrote the book's generous foreword).

The book benefited from the insight of those who have worked on this task before. Many UNDP staffers have written invaluable memoirs of their careers. Others have undertaken histories of specific parts of the Programme's past. Three other people have attempted a task similar to mine, the late Thomas W. Oliver, whose careful manuscript was never published, Pranay Gupte, who combined part of his work into a broader study, and Ruben Mendez, whose major study is greatly anticipated. Gupte, Mendez, and Oliver's widow, Marianna Oliver, have been very generous to me in sharing earlier histories and all their insight.

The research and writing of this book took place over an intense twenty-two months, from June 2004 to March 2006. I am grateful to Wellesley College, its president, Diana Chapman Walsh, its dean, Andrew Shennan, and the endowment of the M. Margaret Ball Chair in International Relations for giving me leave so that I could take on the task full-time and for funding some necessary research assistance and travel that UNDP could not provide.

I was blessed with a wonderfully competent international staff of people half my age whose nationalities and work experience made Cambodia, Chile, China, India, Iran, and Mali places against which my interpretations of UNDP's history were constantly challenged.

Neysan Rassekh assisted me throughout, arranging travel, managing the office and budget, and communicating with the large Advisory Panel and Readers' Group set up by Malloch Brown. Neysan conducted archival research at two sites, substantive interviews in a number of cities, and sometimes acted as my unofficial translator in Farsi, French, Spanish, and Chinese. All that work went well beyond his official job description. The project could not have been completed without him.

From February to July 2005 I had the full-time research assistance of Elizabeth Mandeville, whose research skills are unsurpassed. Liz's diplomacy and editorial finesse are reflected in every chapter of the book. Like Neysan, she worked far beyond her remit. She became my most important critical reader and the person I relied on most to help think through the complex parts of UNDP's story. By the end, we had thousands of pages of interview transcripts and research notes, yet Liz retained a clear picture of everything we had learned and, therefore, was ready and able to challenge any of my hasty conclusions that did not fit the facts.

Many of those thousands of pages of notes were created by one of four part-time undergraduate research assistants, each of whom worked with us for seven or eight months: Lawrence Chow and Stephen Liou from Columbia University, and Katie Ellis and Roopal Mehta from Wellesley College. I am grateful to them all, especially to Roopal, who took on some of Liz's tasks in the last months of the project.

During many of my research trips, I was accompanied by colleagues who offered invaluable help, insight, and companionship. At different times both Neysan and Liz played that role, but I am particularly grateful to those friends who sacrificed work and time with family to join me: Robert Collini, Taylor Mendelsohn, and especially Siti Nurjanah, who made the book's final chapter possible.

In many countries friends who are deeply involved with development, but who have no particular connection to the UN or UNDP, gave me invaluable assistance, including Nurjanah and her husband Christopher Candland (in Indonesia), Florian and Gerdes Fluerant (in Haiti), Victor Gbeho (in Ghana), Esmail Moshiri (in Iran), Paolo Navone (in Burkina Faso), and Diana Tussie (in Argentina).

I am grateful to the many people within UNDP who gave me advice and feedback, especially Malloch Brown and Sakiko Fukuda-Parr. Nada Al-Nashif, Samuel Nyambi, and Mark Suzman also gave extremely important feedback and guidance throughout. At the beginning of my research, they, along with Rafeeuddin Ahmed, Bruce Jenks, and Tim Rothermel were particularly helpful in suggesting ways to approach UNDP's story. I am also deeply grateful to the formally constituted Readers' Group who read every chapter: Margaret Joan Anstee, Garth ap Rees, Robert England, Norma Globerman, Luis Maria Gomez, Trevor

Gordon-Somers, Jean-Jacques Graisse, Michael Gucovsky, Denis Halliday, Zahir Jamal, Basem Khader, Ian Kinniburgh, Carlos Lopes, Khalid Malik, Jan Mattsson, Brenda McSweeney, John Ohiorenuan, Marta Rueda, and Sarah Timpson. Sir Robert Jackson's biographer, James Gibson, also commented on many chapters, at the suggestion of Dame Margaret. Having the input of this group was like participating in a year-long seminar on the history of development with some of the greatest living authorities. The book is much stronger for their attention.

My academic colleagues, Candland, Peter A. Haas, Eric Helleiner, Joel Krieger, and Rorden Wilkinson, gave me thorough critiques of different draft chapters and constantly reminded me of the connections between UNDP's story and the larger issues of development and international relations. I am grateful to them and to Wilkinson, Donna Lee, and Thomas Diez, who gave me the opportunity to receive feedback on my work in progress at the University of Birmingham and to others who arranged similar presentations: Judy Dushku at Suffolk University, Randall Germain at the Patterson School, Carleton University, Nasrin Mosaffa at the Center for Human Rights Studies, University of Tehran, Douglas Nelson at the Murphy Institute, Tulane University, Tim Shaw at the Institute of Commonwealth Studies, Ole Jacob Sending at the Norwegian Institute of International Affairs, Allison Stanger at Middlebury College, Diana Tussie at the Latin American School for the Social Sciences in Buenos Aires, Peter Uvin at the Fletcher School, Tufts University, and Thomas Weiss at the Ralph Bunche Institute, City University of New York.

Weiss also co-directs the UN Intellectual History Project, as does his colleague, Richard Jolly. I am deeply indebted to both of them for letting me use materials collected by the Project, for help in conceptualizing, carrying out, and reporting my own research, and for their recommendation of me to UNDP. They are the models for all of us who are attempting to understand the UN's role in the world.

My editor at Cambridge University Press, John Haslam, also provided excellent feedback. I am obliged to him, to the copy-editor, Philippa Youngman, and to everyone at the Press who produced the book so quickly and so well.

Unless otherwise acknowledged, the photographs throughout the book came from various UNDP offices or the UN Secretariat. I am grateful to all of those who helped me find them.

An author always relies heavily on an intimate network, especially to get through the lonelier parts of the process. I am grateful to my close friends (some of whom have already been mentioned) and to my family, to Max (who insisted on being the second cat acknowledged in a major UNDP study) and most especially to my wife, JoAnne Yates, who, as always, sustained me throughout with her love, humour, and good sense. (She did this despite the fact that, in Boston, January 2005 was the snowiest month on record and I was away in Africa.)

Finally, my greatest debt is to everyone from UNDP and its many partners who gave me their time and support. They trusted me with writing a history that actually belongs to them, knowing that the story I would tell would be partial and incomplete, only one of the many histories of the Programme that could be written and that will be written.

The project involved archival research, extensive interviews, and consultation of materials written by many UNDP staff members. I am indebted to those we interviewed, those who helped us to arrange the interviews, those who helped us in various libraries and archives throughout the world, and the staff members who provided both research materials and guidance. I am sure that we will fail to name many of the people who helped. I apologize for that oversight, but wish at least to acknowledge the following:

Ali Jamma'a Abdalla, Haidar Abdel Shafi, Khaled Abdel Shafi, Eisa Abdellatif, Kwesi Abeasi, Noha Aboueldahab, Hani Abu-Diab, Majid Abu Ramadam, Karen Koning Abu Zayd, Mary Anne Addo, Bisi Adenigba, Vanesa Adreani, William Adrianasolo, K. Adu-Mensah, Albert Aghazarian, Naeem Ahmad, Majid Ahmadi, Joyce Ajlouni, Mericio Akara, Tooraj Akbarlou, Françoise Gruloos Akerman, John Akowuah, Akmel P. Akpa, Anis Alam, M. Nurul Alam, Osama Alfarra, Jonathan A. Allotey, Abdullah Rashid Alnoaimi, Sameer Al Ansari, Qassim Sultan Al Banna, Khalid Ali Al Bustani, Nasser Al-Qudwa, Yousef Abdullah Ali Al Sharhan, Soudabeh Amiri, Suad Amiry, J. Victor Angelo, Clemens D. Anyomi, Naglaa Arafa, Teuku Ardiansyah, William Arthur, Ellen Bortei-Doku Aryeetey, Ernest Aryeetey, Bagher Asadi, Franklin Asamoah-Mensah, K. B. Asante, Hanan Ashrawi, Bo Asplund, Sartaj Aziz, Mihail Bachvarov, Walid Badawi, Justin Badou, Justin B. Bangura, Mualick Abdul Bangura, Zainab Hawa Bangura, Fayyaz Baqir, Kenyeh Barkey, Michael J. Barnett, Kwamena Bartels, Sanjaya Baru, Kayhan Barzegar, Manoj Basnyat, Mohamed Bayoumi, Morteza Beheshti, Raquel Belen, Carol Bellamy, Jose Bello, El-Mostafa Benlamlih, Gilad Ben-Nun, Diana Lina Bernado, Charlotte Bernklau, Julian Bertanou, Douglas Bettcher, John Bevan, Digambar Bhouraskar, Bozena Blix, Pablo J. Boczkowski, Osei Boeh-Ocansey, Riyaz H. Bokhari, Mercedes Botto, David G. Bourns,

Raúl Boyle, Robert Brockman, Oleksandr Brodskyi, Stephen Browne, Neil Buhne, Sarah Burd-Sharps, Urvashi Butalia, Olexandr M. Butsko, Lia Buttenhelm, Yevhen Bystrytsky, Charles L. Cadet, Edmund J. Cain, Lauren Canning, Alessandra Casazza, Roromme Chantal, George Charpentier, Meera Chatterjee, Mohammad Ashraf Cheema, Beatrice Chinapen, Graham Chipande, Jarat Chopra, Refat Chubarov, Hernando Clavijo, Alain Roger Coefe, Aureola Cole, Deidre Colvin, George Conway, Jean Harry Cothias, Aron Critolotti, Barbara Crossette, Brian Cugelman, Emmanuel Cuvillier, Dai Genyou, Ibrahim Dakkak, Pierre-Claver Damiba, Maher Daoudi, Mohammad Hadi Daryaei, Hernani Da Silva, Mireya Davila, Francis Davis, Jane Dawson, Cláudio de Jesus Ximenes, Paul Andre de la Porte, Pamela Delargy, Carlos del Castillo, Valentina Delich, Ceclia Del Rio, Ad de Raad, Leelananda de Silva, Rosny Desroches, Paul R. Deuster, Hani Abu Diab, Djibril Diallo, Léon Diberet, Ding Ying, Carlos Dinis, Laura Dix, Eugénie Djibo-Zongo, Philip Dobie, Hui ('Bob') Dong, Antonio Donini, Ariel Dorfman, Alan Doss, Michael Doyle, Petko Draganov, William J. Drake, William H. Draper III, Du Yuexin, Muchkund Dubey, Arnaud Dupuy, Jacques Dyotte, Nadia Makram Ebeid, Osama El-Farra, Ehab El Kharrat, Hisham El Sherif, Sherif El Tokali, Dede Emerson, Marian Samuel Emil, Douglas Evangelista, Hugh Evans, Mamge Fabien, Sylvanus Joe Fannah, Angela Farhat, Contanza Farina, Paul A. Farmer, Cristina Fasano, Johnson Fasemkye, Charlie Fautin, Alfred Sallia Fawundu, Nader Fergany, Carmen Ferrufino, Simon Fields, Petranka Fileva, Marge Fonyi, Anne Forrester, Walter Franco, Lorna French, Tony French, Fritz Frolich, Fu Li, Micha Gaillard, Hazem Galal, Gao Hong Bin, Tiémoko Marc Garango, Marcela Garcia-Bernard, Guy Gauvreau, Zdravko Genchev, Hamid Ghaffarzadeh, Aramazd Ghalamkaryan, Antoaneta Ginina, Michael Afedi Gizo, Brian Gleeson, Steven Glovinsky, Ivan Gnybidenko, Manu Goel, Ellen Goldstein, Rui Gomes, Carmen B. Gonslaves, Lise Grande, Constancia Grati, Jacques Gruloos, Philomena Guillebaud, Adama Guindo, Samia Guirguis, Inder Kumar Gujral, Hanna Gutema, Eduardo Gutiérrez, Ricardo A. Gutiérrez, George Gyan-Baffour, Ahmed Haggag, El-Balla Hagona, Thomas N. Hale, Ahmad Human Hamid, Nadir Hadj Hammou, Handoko, Heba Handoussa, Ameera Haq, Khadija Haq, Naheed Atiq Haque, Beatrice L. Harding, Frederick E. Hare, Bruce Harland, Nicola M. Harrington, Sukehiro Hasegawa, Walid Hasna, Noeleen Heyzer, Lana Abu Hijleh, Bruce Hillis, Arthur Holcombe, Mark Holzer, Huang Mudong, Miguel Huezo, Rima Khalaf Hunaidi, Tajammul Hussain, Rehana Hyder, Tariq Osman Hyder, Valeria Iglesias, G. John

Ikenberry, Louis Imbleau, Samuel Oluoch Imbo, Dhiman Inderpal, Mohammad Zafar Iqbal, Rajeswary Iruthayanathan, Jad Ishaq, Daoud Istanbuli, William Jackson, Abdoulie Janneh, Rita Janssen, Michael Johnny, Terence D. Jones, El Hassan Jouaouine, Christopher C. Joyner, Mutar Ahmed Abdullah Juma, Alhaji Tejan Kabbah, May Kadkoy, Dominique Kafando, Francis Kaikai, Dimitar Kalchev, Zahera Kamal, Sung-Hack Kang, Soheir Kansouh-Habib, Davesh Kapur, Henning Karcher, Mehtab S. Karim, Mats Karlsson, Peggy Karns, Nina Karpachova, Boriana Katzarska, Inge Kaul, Amy Kay, A. G. N. Kazi, Michael Keating, Stanislav Kedrun, Douglas Keh, Faris Khader, Mojtaba Khalessi, Moshen Khalili, Aftab Ahmed Khan, Mohammed Nawaz Khan, Salman Khan, Shaharyar M. Khan, Bibi Halima Khanam, Nazim Khizar, Jawdat N. Khoudary, George Khoury, Hind Khoury, Üner Kidar, Kiril Kiryakov, Jacqueline Ki-Zerbo, Joseph Ki-Zerbo, Ignas Kleden, Mounir Kleibo, Gideon Klu, Tsutomu Kono, Kona Koroma, Sirkka Korpela, Vasyl Kostrytsya, James Kraft, Jean E. Krasno, Paul Krugman, Carlos E. Kulikowski, Suraj Kumar, Serhiy Kurykin, Clarke Kwesie, Alan Kyeremateng, Yanty Lacsana, Fritz Lafontant, Richardo Lagos Escobar, Chuck Lankester, Wajahot Latif, Gerard Latortue, Nestor Laverne, James A. Lee, Eric Lemetais, Miguel Lengyel, Marc Lepage, Ella Libanova, Moisés Lichtmajer, Bill Lineberry, Steve Lize, David Lockwood, Elen-Magurite Loj, David Long, Long Yongtu, Camilio Lopes, Lu Mai, Luo Delong, Maureen Lynch, Frederick Lyons, Charles Ian McNeill, Majid Maedani, Galal Magdi, Kishore Mahbubani, R. D. Makkar, Klavdia Maksimenko, Shaukat M. Malik, Sanfo Mamadou, Camille Mansu, Bayzid Mardookhi, Sissi Marini, Sarah Papineau Marshall, Carlos Felipe Martínez, Elena Martínez, Alice Mascarenhas, Ali N. Mashayekhi, Marcela Masnatta, Muhammad Mateen-ud-Din, Jane Mbagi, Anthony McDermott, Charles McNeill, Desmond McNeill, Julie Anne Mejia, Luz Angela Melo, J. H. Mensah, K. Adu Mensah, Louis S. Michel, Elaine Michetti, Mark Miles, Yoichi Mine, Mehdi Mirzfzal, Pankaj Mishra, Kalman Mizsei, Khadija T. Moalla, Hamed Mobarek, Osama Mohamed, Mohammad J. Mojarrad, Belin Mollov, Antonio Molpeceres, Roy D. Morey, Michael Morgan, Viola Morgan, Angus Morris, Nasrin Mosaffa, Petra Moser, Hala Mouneimne, Joseph Muana, Hussein Muhder, Njaunga M. Mulikita, Sami Mushasa, Sufian Mushaha, Alphecca Muttardy, Ngila Mwase, Bagher Namazi, Alka Narang, Sunil Narula, Hamid Nazari, Ivan Neikov, Yvon Neptune, Peter Newell, Jenny Nielsen, Shoji Nishimoto, Normala, Nurlaili, Wajeeh Y. Nuseibeh, Francis O'Donnell, Francis G. Okelo, John A. Olver, Richard Olver, Maxine

Olsen, Abdusalam Omer, Joana Opare, Judith Ossom, Hamda Al Otaiba, Georges Ouattara, Barthélémy Ouedraogo, Bernard Lédéa Ouedraogo, M. Harouna Ouedraogo, Sylvestre Ouedraogo, Youssouf Ouedraogo, Roger Owen, Robert L. Paarlberg, G. Padmanabhan, Elena Panova, K. C. Pant, Jane L. Parpart, Hafiz Pasha, Oleksandr Paskhaver, I. G. Patel, Eduardo A. Perez, Charles ('Pete') Perry, Enrique Peruzzotti, Kwame Pianim, Rajeev Pillay, Richard Ponzio, Ion C. Popescu, Nabil Qassis, Cintia Quiliconi, Saeed A. Qureshi, M. B. Radhakrishnan, Vivek Rae, Reza Raei, Abdul Qadir Rafiq, Eleanor Raheem, Jehan Raheem, Majid Rahnema, G. Ravi Rajan, Majid Ramin, Sonam Yangchen Rana, Matt Reeder, Chris Reij, Rini Reza, Akibo Robinson, William I. Robinson, Efrain Rodriguez, Jean-Claude Rogivue, Cristina Rojas de Ferro, Bjoern Rongevaer, Nicholas Rosellini, Alexander Holt Rotival, Jian Ruan, Silvia Rucks, As Alimin Rusdy, Luis Ruy de Villalobos, Nabil Sha'ath, Farhan Sabih, Jeffrey D. Sachs, James Sackey, Nafis Sadik, Jacob Jusu Saffa, Fred T. Sai, Sabri Saidam, Louis Saint-Lot, Ahmed Samatar,Gregory Sanchez, Anjana Sankar, Martin Santiago, Eyad Sarraj, Jerome Sauvage, Jo Scheuer, Eric Scheye, Linda Schieber, Folke Schimanski, Brian D. Schmidt, Wolfgang Scholtes, Lars Schoultz, Eric Sealine, Kordzo Sedegah, Ndapiwa Semausu, Amartya Sen, Kalyani Menon Sen, S. Sen, Jorge Sequeria, Sekou M. Sesay, Shuja Shah, Kaled Shahwan Ehab Shanti, Khalid Hamid Sheikh, Muhammad Asif Sheikh, Ognian Shentov, Alwi Shihab, Patrick Shima, Mehnaz Shiraz, Mukunda Shrestha, Azmi Shuaibi, Ihor Shumylo, Kathryn Sikkink, Peter Simkin, Kristanto Sinandang, Justin Singbo, Hans W. Singer, J. Singh, Mazen T. Sinokrot, Torild Skard, Anne-Marie Slaughter, Daniel Smilov, William C. Smith, Kim Smithies, Margaret Snyder, Ilkin Sodikin, Soeroso, Angelina Soldatenko, Gwi-Yeop Son, Casper Sonesson, Gillian Sorensen, James Gustave Speth, Marylene Spezzati, Hans-C. Graf Sponeck, Charlie Springhall, J. N. L. Srivastava, Bruce Stedman, Ian Stewart, Olav Stokke, Emilda Stronge, Surekha Subarwal, Sugihartatmo, Hardini Sumono, Karin Svadlenak-Gomez, Richard Symonds, Julia Taft, B. Taheri, Pierre Tahita, Naoki Takyo, Andrea Tamagnini, Alizatta Tamboula, Tan Grace Poi Chiew, Valeriy Tantsyura, Hussain Tashakori, Vida Tawia, Andrews Taylor, Leon Terblanche, Majid Tehranian, Rekha Thapa, Graham Thompson, Ngo Thi Bich Thuy, J. Ann Tickner, Robert L. Tignor, Kumar M. Tiku, M. S. Tinauli, Uka Tjandrasasmita, M. Tootoochian, John Toye, Richard Toye, Jose Vincente Troya, Georgi Tsekov, Han Tun, Henadiy Udovenko, Haleem Ul Hasnain, S. Vasu Vaitla, Svetla Velkova, Lenore Verceles-Price, Jean-André Victor, Endre Vigeland, Antonio Vigilante,

N. Vijayaditya, Maryse Villard, Pablo Vinocur, Antonio Vitor, Nataliya Vlasenko, Hannu Wager, Lysbeth M. Wallace, Tim Walsh, Daniel Wang, Wang Yue, Wang Zhe, Lois Wasserspring, Wei Xiaodong, Charles H. Weitz, Robin Welles, Achim Wennman, Mark White, Eduardo Wiesner, Kanni Wignaraja, John Winter, Albert Wright, Wu Yuan-bin, Wu Zhong, Haoliang Xu, Xu Jinjin, Yuxue ('Ian') Xue, Adisa Kansah Yakubu, Oran Young, Amin Mohamed Yousuf, Yu Cong, Önder Yücer, Soetedjo Yuwono, Abdelouahhab Zaid, Aster Zaoude, Zhan Chengfu, Zhang Jing, Zhang Jun, Zhang Zhengwei, Zhang Zhijian, Zhang Zhiming, Zhou Dadi, Zhou Yiping, Mykola Zhulynskyi, Maria Zlatareva-Pernishka, Zou Jiayi, Zuo Ran.

1

Not the standard image

In 1971 two Chilean activists – a literary critic and a sociologist – created a cartoon character, Cabro Chico (the 'Little Kid'), to challenge the comic book monopoly of foreign multinationals and poke fun at the opposition to Salvador Allende's democratically elected Popular Unity government. Allende's overthrow in 1973 brought prosperity (for a few) and a tragic seventeen-year dictatorship. In 1971 Allende's opponents already ranged from entrenched economic elites to international development agencies that withheld loans needed for his programmes of mass education and agrarian reform.

In what became an international bestseller, *How to Read Donald Duck*, the same professors-turned-cartoonists reprinted a Disney strip that made the connection between complicit, incompetent elites and unreliable global agencies just as effectively as the exploits of Cabro Chico had. In the strip, smiling to an absurdly masked 'native' leader, a surprised Donald Duck says, 'I see you have an up-to-date nation! Have you got telephones?' The reply: 'Have we gottee telephone? Of course! Only trouble is only *one* has wires! It's a hot line to World Loan Bank!'[1]

The Disney cartoon conveyed a standard image of international development cooperation in many circles, on the libertarian right just as much as on the egalitarian left. That image makes another comic book, drawn a generation later and a continent away, particularly surprising. Kenyan cartoonist Terry Hirst is known for defying his country's land barons, their official protectors, and their foreign friends, including some of the most powerful international development agencies. Yet, in 2003, Kenyans found the familiar faces of Hirst's ensemble (characters who are as beloved in Africa today as Cabro Chico once was in Latin America) welcoming them to a celebration of the ideas of economics Nobel laureate Amartya Sen, ideas widely promulgated by a global aid organization, the UN Development Programme (UNDP), through its annual *Human*

---

[1] Ariel Dorfman and Armand Mattelart, *How to Read Donald Duck*, trans. David Kunzle (New York: International General, 1975), p. 50.

1.1 The major sources of unfreedom

Development Report. In Hirst's *There is a Better Way!* 'development' is not the business of deluded witch doctors whose magical wires can entangle their countries into hopeless debt traps. Instead, Hirst draws a democratic chorus to tell us, 'development' means *getting rid of* poverty, famine, tyranny, and 'most of all, intolerant, repressive government'.[2]

This book is about UNDP and its approach to development, about the Programme's origins, its structure and growth, its successes and failures, and its different roles in different parts of the world. I am an academic, a sceptic by trade, but I have borrowed my title from Terry Hirst's (albeit with the addition of the sceptic's question mark) because UNDP's story is, ultimately, about a *way* of doing something. It is not just a way of achieving economic development, but also, more broadly, *a way of conducting relations among peoples and nations.*

On balance, I have come to agree with many of the Programme's champions who see its way of doing things as fundamentally better than most of the alternatives. UNDP's champions make three kinds of claim.

---

[2] Anantha Kumar Duraiappah, Flavio Comim, Davinder Lamba, and Terry Hirst, *There is a Better Way! An Introduction to the* Development *as* Freedom *Approach* (Nairobi: International Institute for Sustainable Development and the Mazingira Institute, 2003), p. 4.

First, they argue that the *theory* that has come to underlie UNDP's development practice is superior to other theories of development. That is Hirst's point. This theory is both strategic and it is normative. Today, when UNDP looks for the answers for questions about development, its official (and largely effective) strategy is to 'just ask' the people whom 'development' is meant to serve. Moreover, today, for UNDP 'development' *means* the end of tyranny just as much as the end of poverty, which is the normative point.

Second, those who favour UNDP often contrast the Programme's practice and the theory underlying it to those of other development organizations, claiming that, at many points in time, UNDP has been 'better' than the World Bank, the US Agency for International Development, the Japan International Cooperation Agency, and the like. It would, I believe, be difficult to sustain a claim that the UN Development Programme is inherently superior or that the others have ever been irredeemably worse. After all, these days, most international development agencies see eradicating poverty and fostering substantive democracy as part of their core mission. Nevertheless, UNDP learned many lessons of development before other organizations did, which, one group of historians argues, reflects a larger pattern of the UN being 'ahead of the curve'.[3]

That the UN Programme has often been ahead of the curve is, in part, due to the third, and the earliest, of its claims to know 'a better way', in this case, a better way to conduct relations between nations than what was available before the Second World War, before there was a United Nations.

We are so distant from the Second World War that most of us have forgotten what that original 'better way' was all about. Yet we understand it almost intuitively, even when the argument behind it is presented very quickly, as it was by US Secretary of State Condoleezza Rice in the Senate hearings before her confirmation in January 2005. Rice began her commentary on the unprecedented Indian Ocean tragedy (which had taken place just three weeks earlier) by saying, 'The tsunami was a wonderful opportunity for us.' California's Barbara Boxer chastised Rice for insensitivity,[4] but the senator misunderstood Rice's underlying, sensible point: the outpouring of genuine US concern for the victims of the tsunami – which hit hardest in the Islamist province of the largest Muslim nation,

---

[3] Louis Emmerij, Richard Jolly, and Thomas G. Weiss, *Ahead of the Curve? UN Ideas and Global Challenges* (Bloomington, Ind.: Indiana University Press, 2001).

[4] 'Transcript of Remarks between Boxer and Rice', *San Francisco Chronicle*, 19 Jan. 2005. http://www.sfgate.com/cgi-bin/article.cgi?file=/c/a/2005/01/18/RICEBOXER.DTL (accessed 2 June 2006).

Indonesia – would, Rice argued, help to bridge the division between the United States and some of the people that they most feared.

More generally, expressions of solidarity, even with people with whom one disagrees, can contribute to peace. This was a new principle of international relations, a new and 'better way', when it was adopted by the original organization that was called the 'United Nations', the wartime anti-fascist alliance. That 'better way' was then institutionalized in the Marshall Plan and the reconstruction of Germany and Japan following the Second World War. UNDP's story is about the application of the same ideas to relations between wealthy countries and poorer ones, and UNDP's commitment to that idea helps to explain why it has frequently been able to learn about effective means to achieve development sooner than other organizations.

UNDP's history is significant because, more than most of the other institutions founded at the same time, the UN Programme has retained that commitment, and, as Secretary Rice suggested, the hope that international cooperation between the developed and the developing world will foster peace is still very relevant in today's world of terrorism – fuelled, in part, by 'development frustration' (the *in*ability of much of the 'developing' world to achieve the power and wealth of western Europe, North America, or Japan) and nurtured in 'failed states' (development's disasters).

UNDP's story is important not only because the organization embodies this hope and has often been ahead of the curve, but also because it has *always* been at the centre of the global development effort – not the richest organization in its field by a long way, but usually the one that is the most connected to all the rest. UNDP is the direct descendent of the first major, operational international development organization, a Programme that embraced the 'better way' as its development philosophy at the same time as the Marshall Plan began to aid Europe's reconstruction. Thus UNDP's history can help us to make sense of the entire international development enterprise. It is, therefore, a history relevant to all of us simply because development cooperation is our primary way of dealing with one of humanity's greatest problems, our seemingly intractable division into two interdependent and potentially hostile worlds, one of wealth and one of poverty.

The Programme and what it does

UNDP describes itself as 'the UN's global development network, an organization advocating for change and connecting countries to knowledge, experience and resources to help people build a better life'.[5] Its job is to confront poverty, give a voice to the voiceless, and to begin to reverse the growing global economic and political gaps.

Today's UNDP came into being in January 1966 as a combination of two predecessor organizations. One, the Expanded Programme of Technical Assistance (EPTA) – under David Owen, the British diplomat who was the first person hired by the post-war United Nations – provided 'technical assistance' to less privileged nations (connecting countries to 'knowledge' useful for development). The other, the United Nations Special Fund – under Paul Hoffman, the American businessman who had run the Marshall Plan – performed surveys and investment analysis to help to identify large, economically feasible development projects (connecting countries to 'resources').

This early development work helped to create institutions and infrastructure fundamental to the transformation of economies, governments, and societies, particularly in newly independent countries. In India in the 1950s the UN network helped to design the campuses and curricula and then to staff the major universities of technology that are now engines of their countries' growth. In the 1970s UNDP followed up by supporting the pilot projects that became India's National Informatics Centre, the world's most complex 'e-government' initiative. In Brazil in the 1960s the Programme financed an unprecedented study of the country's hydroelectric potential by an army of full-time expatriate experts, part-time international consultants, and national advisors. All of the capacity the country has since built – scores of billions of dollars' worth of investment in an essential element of the country's development success – was identified by that one project.

However, UNDP has always been more than just a provider of technical assistance and what was once called 'preinvestment' services. It and its predecessors have provided the most extensive and most consistent presence of the entire UN system throughout the world. The system of UNDP 'Resident Representatives' and country offices in national capitals began more than fifty years ago. (Today the Programme has offices in more than 150 countries.) Most of the UNDP 'Res Reps' have also been charged with coordinating, at a country level, the development work of the entire UN family of organizations, which includes the functionally 'Specialized Agencies' such as the Food and Agriculture Organization (FAO), the International Civil Aviation Organization (ICAO), and the International

---

[5] This standard description appears prominently in recent documents, paper or electronic, including the UNDP home page, http://www.undp.org (accessed 12 Jan. 2006).

Labour Organization (ILO), as well as other major providers of development assistance, UNICEF (the UN Children's Fund), the World Food Programme, and even the Washington-based 'Bretton Woods'[6] agencies, the International Monetary Fund (IMF) and the World Bank. Moreover, in some countries, UNDP has played an explicit, *de jure* role as the coordinator and promoter of all external assistance, whether from individual governments ('bilateral' assistance) or from the international agencies. Even in countries where UNDP has no responsibility for convening such 'Round Tables', the office of the Resident Representative often, de facto, becomes the one place where any harmonization of external assistance can happen.[7]

UNDP's role in coordinating development work in the field has sometimes been matched with a parallel responsibility to coordinate the development activities of the UN family's often fractious headquarters' offices. Thus, as a result of a long UN reform process, UNDP's recent Administrators (the title brought by Hoffman from the Marshall Plan) also chaired the UN Development Group of more than thirty separate agencies. The last Administrator, Mark Malloch Brown, also spearheaded the broader programme of achieving eight 'Millennium Development Goals' adopted in 2000 by all the (then) 189 member states of the United Nations. These targets include reducing the instance of extreme poverty by half and eliminating gender disparities in education by 2015.

UNDP played a part in the origin of many of the agencies that the recent Administrators have coordinated, and it played a critical role in making development a priority of most of the rest. This is one of the Programme's most significant, and least well understood, functions: it nurtures new organizations with specific roles to play in the process of global development.

The standard organization chart of the United Nations[8] – a nightmare to contemplate – includes almost ninety different entities: Specialized

---

[6] Named for the New Hampshire resort where the 1944 conference creating the IMF and the World Bank took place.

[7] For more than fifty years, in specific situations, the EPTA or UNDP Resident Representatives have played the role of the representative, in-country, of all UN agencies, de facto and sometimes *de jure*. In this case some of the non-resident agencies reluctantly allow the Representative to discharge all of their functions unimpeded, in other cases they are given responsibility without authority. This latter sometimes includes those delicate socio-economic and political functions that are in the domain of the UN Secretariat. The inter-agency support work comes with varied responsibilities, from managing staff and funds to overseeing operations and managing the technical issues as well as the programmes of those agencies. The Representative is expected to attend all the relevant in-country activities and meetings of the non-resident UN agencies.

[8] Organization Chart of the United Nations, http://www.un.org/aboutun/chart.html (accessed 12 Jan. 2006).

Agencies, 'departments and offices', 'subsidiary bodies', 'programmes and funds', 'institutes', and 'commissions'. At least one-third of them were nurtured by UNDP. That is, they began as part of UNDP, their development activities were originally funded by UNDP, they are jointly governed bodies controlled in part by UNDP, or they were initially staffed largely by men and women from UNDP.

UNDP and its predecessor, EPTA, dramatically shifted the agendas of many of the original Specialized Agencies by funding their initial development work, work that then became a major focus of every agency, in many cases, its primary focus. Later, new organizations often found temporary homes within UNDP. Some split from the Programme in significant ways, as was the case with UNFPA (the UN Population Fund). Others have remained more embedded within UNDP, but in a variety of ways, as the very different cases of the Capital Development Fund (CDF, which facilitates small-scale investment in the poorest countries), UN Volunteers (UNV), and the UN Development Fund for Women (UNIFEM) suggest.

UNDP has also long been a source of new information and ideas about development, including, of course, the ideas underpinning the new development organizations that it has fostered. The Programme publishes annually a global *Human Development Report* that tracks global and national progress relative to a set of indicators of the capacity of people to direct their own lives. It is perhaps even more significant that, over the years, the *Report* has regularly introduced new indicators to help monitor the kinds of issues raised by the democratic chorus in Terry Hirst's comic: eliminating poverty, providing access to clean water, reducing government repression, and the like. The Programme has also sponsored the production of scores of local, national, and regional *Human Development Reports* that have allowed different communities, at all levels, to set and monitor the goals that are relevant to *them*.

The intellectual and social processes that go into making the various *Human Development Reports* are one part of what was once considered a somewhat revolutionary programme of 'advocacy' that UNDP first took on explicitly in 1986. 'Advocacy' in this instance means promoting the concerns of women, the poor, minorities, and other disadvantaged people to the governments of developing countries and their many partners. It also means promoting specific approaches to development – environmental sustainability, working with the private sector, and democratic, participatory, and transparent forms of planning – without turning adherence to them into ideological litmus tests that governments must pass in order to receive UNDP support.

Advocacy was 'revolutionary' only because in the first forty years of the UN's development network under different names, UNDP had become 'the development programme *of* the developing countries', the intergovernmental organization most trusted by governments in the developing world because it was the most responsive to them. UNDP, for example, had assisted both Marxist Cuba and anti-Marxist Singapore. Nevertheless, embracing 'advocacy' actually just made explicit a role that UNDP had long played informally, a role that it could only play successfully because it was trusted throughout the developing world.

In fact, as extensive as any list of official UNDP functions may be, it will not cover many of the important things done by the Programme and its precursors over more than sixty years. Perhaps the most important of UNDP's less official functions has been to act as an incubator not just of other international development organizations, but of states themselves. The staff of UNDP's predecessors helped the United Nations as a whole in its temporary provision of effective government in places like Libya and Congo-Kinshasa. In many of the other newly independent nations of Africa, Asia, and the Caribbean – especially in those abandoned by embittered colonial powers who ripped out telephones and removed typewriters along with their colonial staff – the UN development network did much of the early technical work of government, creating new postal systems, health ministries, civil aviation organizations, and the like. Most significantly, UNDP and its predecessors worked to develop the capacity of nationals of the new states to take over all these tasks as quickly as possible.

This state-building work never completely disappeared from UNDP's portfolio. While it was less common in the late 1970s and throughout the 1980s, it became central once again in the 1990s, after the collapse of the Soviet system, a decade of financial crises, the emergence of protracted social conflicts no longer contained by the superpowers, and, finally, the violent conflicts and reconstitution of governments that have resulted from the 'war on terrorism'. In this recent era, more than in the era of decolonization, UNDP has directly promoted *democratic* institutions, organizing and helping to set up parliamentary systems, monitoring elections, and supporting the evolution of new political parties and the strengthening of older ones. In 2002, with the creation of UNDP's Bureau for Crisis Prevention and Recovery, part of this role (when it is performed in the most dire circumstances) was made a central focus of the Programme, while, only slightly earlier, UNDP's explicit concern with 'good governance' evolved into what is, today, the first of six priority areas: 'democratic governance'.

One critical role UNDP has played in state building could be called 'granter of last resort', in contrast to the role of 'lender of last resort' that the Bretton Woods institutions were designed to play so as to help avert global financial crises. UNDP does not lend money to governments. It is neither concerned with the Bank's 'bankable' projects nor with the short-term balance of payment problems that were the original concern of the IMF. Rather, UNDP has provided grants in aid to help with almost everything that contributes to development. Such grants can be especially important to newly democratic states saddled with the enormous debts often accumulated by waning authoritarian régimes. The new governments often cannot get loans; there is a catch-22 to the 'last-resort' loans available from the Bretton Woods institutions: you have to be able to pay back the old government's debt before you can borrow more.

Margaret Joan Anstee (one of the main characters in the early part of the UNDP story) writes about this granter role played by the EPTA in Bolivia after a profound social revolution took place in 1952. Immediately, Hugh Keenleyside (another significant actor in the same era) headed a UN mission to the country. As a result, many UN experts were appointed to key ministries with line functions. 'For Bolivia in the 1950s the contribution of these men (no women!) was a godsend to a government struggling with huge problems, among them the traditionally poor quality of Bolivian public service.' Parts of their salaries were covered by grants provided by EPTA. These were especially critical because the World Bank refused to lend to the government since it had defaulted on its external debt.[9]

Even when democratic transitions are not marked by complex economic and social crises or the threat of violence, UNDP sometimes ends up playing a central role at an even earlier stage. Ravi Rajan, who was Resident Representative in Indonesia during the collapse of Suharto's long-lived authoritarian régime, says that this is because the Res Rep, if also acting as UN Resident Coordinator, is often the only person 'two phone calls away from everyone in the country'.[10] Only one person may stand between the head of the country office and a frightened and besieged leader of the old régime. Yet, at the same time, a Res Rep can also be 'two phone calls' – or, more probably, one phone call and an exhausting drive over bad roads – away from many of the leaders who now have

---

[9] Margaret Joan Anstee, *Never Learn to Type: A Woman at the United Nations* (Chichester: John Wiley & Sons, 2003), p. 177.

[10] Ravi Rajan, interview with the author (CNM), 4 June 2004.

the support of a disgruntled population. The Res Rep is likely to have their trust as well, due to the record of UNDP advocacy (however quiet) and due to the impact of projects that have helped the country's least advantaged. A wise and unpresuming Res Rep can use the power temporarily created by his unique position – and by the United Nations' access to a wide range of emergency equipment, resources, and expertise – to help the country towards a more peaceful and democratic future. Many heads of UNDP country offices have done just that, especially in the last ten years, even though they would be hard-pressed to point to that role in their job descriptions.

Sally Timpson, who worked in increasingly influential positions within UNDP from 1967, points out that helping countries towards a more peaceful and democratic future has been as much a matter of offering some protection for democratic forces when authoritarianism is in the ascendant as it has been one of facilitating peaceful transitions and elections when dictatorships are weakening. Much of Timpson's career focused on Latin America. Her first decade in UNDP was a time when many of the region's populist or democratic governments were replaced by means of a coup. (Chile's story is far from unique.) This was also the era of 'disappearances' – non-judicial, government-sponsored kidnappings and murders used to control dissidents. As a matter of compassion and, initially, in a purely incremental way, some UNDP staffers took on a long-term task that Timpson calls the 'recycling' of many democratic political leaders and professionals connected to the governments that had been toppled. Country offices and staff at UNDP headquarters in New York helped many Latin Americans find jobs in the UN system and, in many instances, saved their lives. Some officials received grants for education abroad or became UN experts providing technical assistance or joining research teams in relatively safe countries like Costa Rica or Mexico. Others found more permanent employment in the Specialized Agencies.

As a result, in many Latin American countries when the authoritarian grip loosened in the 1980s the people who could make the democratic state work effectively were available to cycle back.[11] UNDP played a role in this second phase of 'recycling' by helping the new democratic governments bring back many of the professionals who had been forced to flee. Programme officers helped to provide the bureaucratic means and the funds for the renewed democracies to attract and keep the needed personnel.

[11]　Sarah Timpson, interview with CNM, 8 Aug. 2004.

In Latin America, and in other parts of the world, those who directly benefited from this work include presidents and senior ministers, famous names in what has been called the 'Third Global Wave' of democratization. They also include many people, perhaps equally important, who are not necessarily in the global limelight, as I learned when I went to Argentina to carry out part of the research for this book. (It was one of the sixteen developing countries where I was able to conduct extensive interviews and archival research.) In each country I tried to spend time with knowledgeable people who had no personal connections to the UN, people who could give me an independent perspective on UNDP's work. In Argentina, my first thought was Diana Tussie, a senior research fellow at FLACSO (the Latin American School for the Social Sciences) and a colleague through a mutual mentor at the London School of Economics. After I outlined the events that interested me most, Diana mused,

> But I realize, *I* was one of those UNDP helped. I was a graduate student who knew finance and computers. It was one of those projects that brought me back to the country in 1983, right after the Dirty War, to help figure out just how much debt the generals had accumulated, something the government had to know to even begin to talk to the IMF and World Bank about debt relief or new loans.[12]

John Olver, a robust and good-humoured eighty-something, someone who has been part of the UN development network since the beginning, laughs when I recount this. He says that that is the problem with telling the story of UNDP: many of the most interesting things done by those in the UN network either are not documented or else the people involved have forgotten UNDP's role. Many were things UNDP officials were *able* to do because of their jobs, but they were not *required* to do them. In other cases, they were 'official' duties that still did not fit well with any of the simple 'official' descriptions of the mission of the Programme as a whole.

Olver's favourite case of the latter is the Programme of Assistance to the Palestinian People (PAPP), which he started and supervised for its first dozen years. Since 1980 PAPP has helped to reverse the deterioration of schools, health facilities, housing, roads, and utilities that began in the territories when Israel occupied Gaza and the West Bank in 1967. Olver jokes about the then new Administrator, Malloch Brown, taking a tour of PAPP's work in 2000. The boss kept noting things that did not fit with the way UNDP was supposed to work, or with the direction in which he

---

[12] Diana Tussie, interview with CNM, 3 Aug. 2004.

wanted to take the Programme: there was this strange funding mechanism. UNDP was providing capital assistance – bricks and boards – when its real forte was technical assistance – brains and books. Usually UNDP does not implement its own projects; it delegates implementation to other UN agencies or to the government of the developing country involved. In Palestine there was no national government. None of the other international agencies had the trust of both Israel and the Palestinians in the way in which UNDP did. (Olver is one of the few people to have received testimonials from both Yasser Arafat and Yitzak Rabin long before Bill Clinton got them to shake hands.) Malloch Brown could see that UNDP staff on the ground had certainly worked out what to do with bricks and boards, and, while the funding mechanism may have been strange, it got the job done. By the end of the tour, after considering roads and hospitals, classrooms and sewage plants, fish markets and power stations that otherwise would not have existed, the new Administrator agreed, 'Even if it doesn't fit, it's something that needs to be done and we are the only ones who can do it.'[13]

For John Olver, that is what the UN's development network has always been about: getting things done to better people's lives, things that no one else can do. The special virtue of the Programme, according to Olver, is the trust it has gained by supporting the entire range of visions of development embraced by different states. That trust is the reason UNDP can do those things that no one else can do.

Yet, even in the examples of PAPP and the long-standing UNDP activities that really are not in anyone's job description, the Programme may have more focus than Olver's characterization would suggest. Over the years, EPTA and then UNDP concentrated on developing the capacity of states, public and private organizations, and individuals to set their own goals and to achieve them. This sort of 'capacity development' is more about brains and books than it is about bricks and boards, and it is a theme that runs from the UN's initial concern with 'technical assistance' right through Amartya Sen's 'capabilities approach' to human development and to UNDP's recent concerns about 'good governance' and then 'democratic governance'. It is even a theme central to UNDP's role as the coordinator of international development assistance. Adriano Garcia, who was one of the first Resident Representatives, writes, 'It is the UNDP's official policy that coordination is a sovereign responsibility of the governments. The task of the Resident Representative is to assist the

[13] John Olver, interview with CNM, 27 Sept. 2004.

Government in this effort, to the best of his ability.'[14] In other words, UNDP's coordination work is also about building the capacity of governments, the capacity to take on the task themselves either individually, within each country, or collectively, through the United Nations.

Nonetheless, the story of UNDP is more than the story of an organization finding its permanent niche as the leader in capacity development. John Olver's broader version of UNDP's mission is a better starting point for the larger story. Olver is, as he says, a bit ruefully, 'truly one of the last of the "Mohicans"', the name taken by the association of the United Nations' original staff members.

When the group started, the joke was just that the nineteenth-century novelist James Fenimore Cooper had named his title character (the last member of the Mohican tribe of Native American 'Indians') 'Uncas'. That sounded like one of the ever growing list of acronymed UN agencies of the 1950s.[15] Moreover, many old UN hands vacationed in upstate New York where Cooper's novels were set.

In 1946, when the United Nations began, the Mohicans shared many things, but perhaps the most important was that fundamentally new vision of world politics: a desire to create an international system of pragmatic solidarity among nations, a system whose goal would be to improve the lives of citizens in all countries. What we now call 'development' was just one part of that vision; it was the realization of solidarity between the materially advantaged group of countries and the group of countries that were not as advantaged. Moreover, 'capacity development' or, in the first incarnation, 'technical assistance' was only part of a triad of the transfer of *skills*, the transfer of *resources*, and the establishment of global *institutions* that, together, would make up the international development enterprise. UNDP's story is the chronicle of that vision, how it originated, how it became institutionalized within the UN network, and how it was transformed.

Learning and its sources

It is the transformation of that vision – the learning that has taken place within UNDP – that provides the most important lessons from the

[14] Adriano Garcia, *International Cooperation and Development: The United Nations Development Programme Resident Representative System* (Quezon City: University of Philippines Law Center, 1982), p. 288.

[15] There was, eventually, a United Nations Common (or 'Coordinated') Air Service (UNCAS) in Somalia beginning in the 1990s.

Programme's history. After all, we live at a time when many thoughtful observers have concluded that the vision of the UN Mohicans was absurdly idealistic and the goals of development illusory. One standard image is that sixty years of international development cooperation has taught us only that 'There is not much we can do directly that works in any lasting way. We would be better off by going home and closing down all projects that do not directly save lives.'[16]

What has been learned

Nevertheless, many who have worked with UNDP are convinced that it has achieved its much loftier goals of spreading prosperity and peace. Singapore's founding father, Lee Kuan Yew, credits the Programme with guiding his country's first steps along its path from the 'Third World to the First'. Fidel Castro, the last of the old-style communist titans, sees UNDP as an essential partner in Cuba's signal achievements in science, education, and public health. Former US President Jimmy Carter considers UNDP to be a key to 'mainstreaming' the catalytic efforts towards global democratization and sustainable human development undertaken by the Carter Center and other innovative non-governmental organizations.

Of course, what was attractive about the Programme to Lee and Castro – whose first contacts with the UN network were in the 1950s and 1960s – was quite different from what Carter found appealing in the 1990s. In between, UNDP had learned to respond to a persistent criticism that its original vision of 'peace through solidarity' really could be achieved only through solidarity with the *people* of other nations, and not through solidarity with non-democratic *governments*. The Programme had learned to make the original theory more coherent by attaching commitments to democratization and to promoting global norms to non-status quo powers to the original imperative that states have material responsibilities to other states whose people are less advantaged.

The 1986 embrace of 'advocacy' and the introduction of the *Human Development Report* (both were innovations of another of the Programme's US businessmen Administrators, William H. Draper III) began UNDP's formal embrace of democratization. Even earlier UNDP had begun to play the socialization role with China, when Deng Xiaoping turned to it to help with his new economic policy. PAPP did the same

---

[16] Thomas W. Dichter, *Despite Good Intentions: Why Development Assistance to the Third World Has Failed* (Amherst: University of Massachusetts Press, 2003), p. 9.

with the major Palestinian political movements and the Programme has done something similar with revolutionary Iran and Vietnam (all of which are highlighted in chapter 7).

In Iran, where this work is still ongoing, UNDP was the first intergovernmental agency to return to the country after the 1979 Islamic Revolution and one of the few to stay active throughout the decade-long war with Iraq in the 1980s. Regular negotiations with the revolutionary government over access to the funds that could be allocated to the country under UNDP rules built trust between the new leaders and an ever growing set of international partners. As one Iranian familiar with the Programme's work explained in early 2005, much of what is positive in today's Iran came

> ... from UNDP giving experience abroad to so many Iranians, and in bringing Iranian experts back to the country to help with reconstruction. If, in this decade, we avoid war . . . and continue along our reform path, much of the credit should go to the UNDP staff who worked until midnight behind windows taped against bomb blasts, twenty years ago.[17]

In addition to this learning that gave greater coherence to the strategic and moral theory underlying UNDP's work, the programme has also been 'ahead of the curve', ahead of other international development agencies, in at least four instances.

First, as early as the 1950s some of the UN network's leaders – most significantly, Paul Hoffman's deputy, W. Arthur Lewis – became sceptical of the grand development schemes – the giant dams and massive resettlement projects – that were typical in the middle of the century. This made UNDP open to the argument that development should be environmentally sustainable as well as relatively democratic.

Second, in the 1970s and 1980s UNDP was one of the first major development organizations to accept the central role of women in development, a fact connected to its role as the incubator of UNIFEM.

Third, in the 1980s, along with many other parts of the United Nations, UNDP was an early sceptic of 'the Washington Consensus' on development policy, a set of ideas originally embraced by the Bretton Woods organizations but later amended as experience proved the validity of many of the sceptics' criticisms.

Finally, in the 1990s UNDP was one of the first organizations to see that substantive administrative reform across the entire UN system

---

[17] Confidential interview with CNM, March 2005.

would be essential if the original UN vision for development was to survive.

The impact of UNDP's ability to learn can be seen in the contrasting actions of the Programme and the World Bank in Chile in the days of Cabro Chico. The deepest moral convictions of the officers of the two organizations were the same. Paul Hoffman worked closely with his World Bank counterpart, Robert S. McNamara. (Similar relationships have existed between most UNDP administrators and World Bank presidents.) McNamara's belief that combating poverty was the essence of development was just as strong as Hoffman's, and it was the one-time head of McNamara's brain trust (and close friend of Amartya Sen), Mahbub ul Haq, whom Bill Draper would bring to UNDP to start the *Human Development Report*.

In 1971, at the request of Allende's beleaguered government, Hoffman held an unprecedented UNDP Governing Council meeting in Santiago rather than New York or Geneva 'as a matter of principle',[18] to demonstrate solidarity with Chile's egalitarian policies. This angered US National Security Advisor Henry Kissinger and his political allies who had begun to 'oppose Allende as strongly as we can and do all we can to keep him from consolidating power'.[19] Most historians contend that Kissinger's stance led to the World Bank's withdrawal of support from Chile. At the time, however, World Bank officials justified their actions by pointing to the questionable 'economic soundness' of Allende's policies. Privately, ul Haq told McNamara that the Bank approach was ultimately counterproductive:

> We failed to support the basic objectives of the Allende régime [with which McNamara was sympathetic] . . . If we had done that, we could have been freer to make the legitimate point that 'economic' costs of these objectives were unnecessarily high and could be reduced by proper economic management. We could have gone further and shown what set of economic policies would have been consistent with these objectives. Instead, we mumbled about exchange rates, fiscal balances, and price distortions, without ever trying to establish a link between our theology and Allende's concerns.[20]

---

[18] Hoffman's words recalled by Alexander H. Rotival, interview with CNM, 14 Sept. 2004, and Francis Okelo, interview with CNM, 29 April 2005.

[19] Kissinger (5 Nov. 1970) quoted in Jim Lobe, 'Kissinger Document Shows Preemption in Practice', *InterPress Service*, 5 Feb. 2004.

[20] Quoted in Devesh Kapur, John B. Lewis, and Richard Webb, *The World Bank: Its First Half-Century* (Washington, D.C.: Brookings Institution Press, 1997), p. 301.

The historians of the World Bank at 50 say that the same commitment to a single, narrow understanding of economics caused the Bank to take an unusually long time to realize that confronting poverty should be at the centre of its work.[21] The Bank's first history, written after its first twenty-five years, mentioned poverty only three times in its 900 pages.[22]

Reducing poverty and promoting democracy directly confront the global pattern of inequality that is the central problem that gave rise to the entire enterprise of 'development' in the first place. Nevertheless, like the World Bank, the UN Programme began in the 1940s without an explicit focus on those goals, but UNDP moved towards them more rapidly, and came to focus on them more explicitly.

A new kind of organization

Whenever those of us who study international organizations find one that has learned a great deal and has learned it quickly, we are a little surprised.[23] After all, bureaucracies are rarely creative. Most seem to learn only when threatened by extinction, which is the key to the creativity of private companies in a competitive marketplace and of democratic governments held accountable by voters. In contrast, international organizations rarely have to worry about survival. They have usually been set up to serve some lofty purpose and they do not cost that much. That makes their members reluctant to cut an international organization off completely, no matter how irresponsive or out of date it may have become. It took the outbreak of the First World War to kill off the International Association of Public Baths and Cleanliness and to begin to merge similar organizations, including the International Commission on Revision of the Nomenclature of the Causes of Death, into a single global health body, something that remained controversial for another thirty years.[24]

Those international organizations that *do* learn tend not to be standard bureaucracies. That is the case with UNDP.

---

[21] This is a central thesis of Kapur, Lewis, and Webb, *The World Bank.*

[22] Martha Finnemore, 'Redefining Development in the World Bank', in Frederick Cooper and Randall Packard, eds., *International Development and the Social Sciences: Essays on the History and Politics of Knowledge* (Berkeley: University of California Press, 1997), p. 207.

[23] The best summary of the problem is Peter M. Haas and Ernst B. Haas, 'Learning to Learn', *Global Governance*, 1, 3 (1995): 255–84.

[24] Craig N. Murphy, *International Organization and Industrial Change: Global Governance since 1850* (Cambridge: Polity Press, 1994), p. 83.

In the early days this difference was partially a matter of necessity: EPTA contracted with the Specialized Agencies to provide technical assistance through a network of 'experts' on short-term contracts. Thus, around a core of permanent staff in the New York headquarters and the various country offices grew a much larger periphery of people with deep ties to various professions and to the countries in which they served.

It was also a matter of choice. The dedication of the Programme's founders to an international relations of solidarity made them responsive to the entire range of actual development priorities of UN members; that is what saved UNDP from ever adopting a single 'theology' like that of the World Bank criticized by ul Haq, following its failure to support Allende. The same dedication committed UNDP to a style of interaction with the developing countries that, in the words of MIT (Massachusetts Institute of Technology) management professor Thomas W. Malone, is one of 'coordinate-and-cultivate' rather than 'command-and-control'.[25] The usefulness of this management style was reinforced by the fact that UNDP's financial resources are the voluntary contributions of member states. Unlike bilateral development programmes, UNDP does not rely on a regular stream of tax dollars, and, unlike the World Bank, it does not float bonds to underwrite its own investments. Instead, UNDP relies on and nurtures an ever growing network of donor partners, many of whom are previous, or current, recipients of the Programme's support.

To put the issue even more broadly: to accomplish the work that they set for themselves, UNDP's founders had to create a type of organization that was, in the 1940s and 1950s, something fundamentally new. UNDP's internal documents always call the Programme a 'network', a system of 'partnerships', and a centre of 'cooperation'. The Programme is just that, which means that, unlike most development agencies, UNDP (broadly understood) is *not* simply a bureaucratic hierarchy of nested roles and their related obligations. It is, instead, a decentralized complex of relatively autonomous (and creative) people and organizations involving independent experts, short-term alliances, and joint projects. It is at once public and private, international and national, bilateral and multilateral. This complex organization is held together by personal bonds, by professional norms and the external professional associations in which they are embodied, and by complex multi-directional webs of communication

---

[25] Thomas W. Malone, *The Future of Work: How the New Order of Business Will Shape Your Organization, Your Management Style, and Your Life* (Cambridge, Mass.: Harvard Business School Press, 2004).

linking every corner of the globe. Its glue is not just messages going up and down simple chains of command, nor is it primarily money, either as an incentive to staff members or as a conditional promise to clients.

This, it turns out, is a kind of organization that can learn. As Sally Timpson explains, UNDP's 'coordinate and cultivate' mode

> allows for flexibility to adapt to varying needs and to learning from experience. This is essential in an infinitely complex world where there can be no universally applicable 'solutions' or formulas, or even a full understanding of the nature of the problems. In fact, it may reflect an unconscious realization of the need for a certain humility in the face of the difficulties presented by partial knowledge.[26]

Fabians and Republicans: allies of the Third World, depending on the First World

If the type of organization that UNDP became contributed to learning, it was the relationships between UNDP staff members and people whom they served in the developing world that provided the specific impetus for most innovations. The Programme's founders gathered around themselves a group that was open-minded and idealistic. Many were pragmatic socialists, Fabians just like David Owen (who recruited much of the first generation) and W. Arthur Lewis (who shaped the way in which UNDP would disperse its funds). They identified with the struggles of people within the developing world. The first generation created an organizational culture, in Timpson's words, 'a tone that attracted other, likeminded people'.[27]

Each new generation learned that, compared with the World Bank or UNICEF, UNDP was relatively unknown in the developed world, except among a 'development cognoscenti' of people like former President Carter. Back in 1976, when Dede Davies made the first T-shirts emblazoned 'U N D P' for herself and fellow staffers in the Programme's Manhattan headquarters, none of the railway commuters who waited with her in suburban Westchester, New York asked what the acronym meant. They were, she says, 'secure in their belief that the initials obviously stood for "one of those Midwestern colleges"'.[28]

In contrast, each new generation found that throughout the developing world UNDP was well known and respected. In 1974 Adriano Garcia,

---

[26] Sarah Timpson, letter to CNM, 18 Sept. 2005.   [27] Ibid.
[28] Dede Davis, 'Tale of a T-Shirt', *UNDP News*, November/December 1976: 1.

then the head of the Programme's Indonesian office, was travelling in a remote part of the country with his boss from UN headquarters:

> one of the district policemen . . . asked who the very important visitor was . . . I carefully replied . . . in village terms [and in a language over which Garcia had only limited command] he was the 'headman' of . . . 'Program Perserikatan Permbaggunan Bangsa Bangsa'.

The policeman looked quizzically . . . 'Oh, you mean *U N D P*?'[29]

Garcia was overjoyed. 'Now we know that UNDP does not take a back seat to any other international acronyms – at least in Irian Jaya.'

In the same year I had a similar experience as a very young US social science student in Ghana. My tutor, Peter Osei-Kwame, was about to pair me up with a Ghanaian graduate student to conduct household surveys in agricultural villages around the city of Kumasi. He looked me up and down, sceptically, and said, 'When you introduce yourself to a chief, if he assumes you are from the Peace Corps, interrupt him and explain that you are from the University. If he assumes you are a "junior expert" from UNDP, you may be more polite; it won't harm to wait to explain that you are only a student.'

One additional set of factors – beyond the type of organization that UNDP became and the nature of the relationships between staff members and their clients – contributed to the Programme's ability to learn. The international public policy literature contends that 'The quality of executive leadership may prove to be the most critical single determinant of the growth and scope of authority of international organization.' Leaders are, of course, constrained by their context; they are made more or less creative by the constraints and opportunities that they face. Nevertheless, as one of the leading twentieth-century scholars of international organization, Robert W. Cox, has argued, an executive head with excellent 'sailor's skills', using available 'winds and currents' to advance a direction of choice, can transform the interest and aspirations of even the most hidebound states.[30]

Leaders of this sort are rare, because the executives of major intergovernmental organizations tend to be chosen through highly political processes. Governments either identify the person who is the 'least offensive' to the most powerful state members or else leave the choice

---

[29] Garcia, *International Cooperation and Development*, p. 472.
[30] See Robert W. Cox's 1969 article, 'The Executive Head: An Essay on Leadership in International Organizations', repr. in Robert W. Cox with Timothy J. Sinclair, *Approaches to World Order* (Cambridge: Cambridge University Press, 1996), p. 317.

to the patronage system of one of their number; many top UN system positions have long 'belonged' to one country or regional group. Until 1999, the man nominated by the US President became UNDP's Administrator. It was a matter of coincidence that when the post became vacant, the President, who always nominated someone from his own party, was on most occasions a Republican.

While, on the surface, the way in which UNDP administrators have been selected does not suggest that they would be any more (or any less) creative than other executive heads, the context in which they have had to operate has encouraged innovation. UNDP's commitment to the original UN development idea gains it the trust of developing governments, but it also means that the trust of donor governments is rarely complete because the Programme can never simply be an instrument of any donor's foreign policy. The United States, for example, could veto World Bank loans to Allende's government, but could not change UNDP's commitment to serve Chile. To win over donors, ADMINISTRATORS have had to be unusually creative. Moreover, because successive ADMINISTRATORS have (out of loyalty as much as out of necessity) engaged the most conservative wing of the US Republican Party – a group consistently opposed to the UN visions of international relations and of development – these executive heads have honed their 'sailor's skills' on the roughest of seas.

Each Administrator has also had to face the problem that UNDP creates its own competition, a consequence (initially) of being the first major intergovernmental development organization within a 'functionalist' structure of global governance, a structure in which governments create a new organization for each new task undertaken at a global level. UNDP has always had to worry about 'losing its mission' even if, at the same time, it has been in a better position to understand 'the overall development mission' than the newer organizations with their narrower mandates.

Assessing UNDP's impact

UNDP's learning has been far from continuous. In 2004 UNDP hired me to recount that uneven history and to provide 'a candid overview and assessment of successes and failures'.[31] They guaranteed scholarly independence and gave me access to all the material that is still under the UN's control, as well as the resources needed to consult other archives and to interview informants throughout the world.

[31] UNDP History Project – Terms of Reference, January 2004.

Throughout my research I asked the people with whom I spoke to evaluate UNDP's role, both in the past and today. Many of the Programme's partners, and many people who have worked inside the institution, say that it has not succeeded, that it began with great promise that it no longer fulfils. One of the Programme's oldest hands, Basem Khader, remembers the 1950s as a 'phase of hope and expansion when everyone was excited and people had the best of motives'. Today, Khader fears,

> UNDP is being phased out. It is not a priority for the major donors. The US is certainly not interested and the Europeans are losing interest, whether as a response to their own economic situation or due to a change in the international community as a whole.[32]

Philomena Guillebaud, one of the handful who remain from Hoffman's original staff, says something similar:

> In the early days, when our resources were also small, we were told that the role of the organization was to be marginal but decisive. In the last few years before I retired in 1986, I felt that UNDP became steadily more and more marginal and less and less decisive.[33]

In this book's last chapter I come to a different conclusion, although one far from the enthusiastic assessment offered by Edmund Cain, the UNDP career officer who headed Jimmy Carter's Global Development Initiative, 'Everything is set in place for UNDP, now, to play the role it was designed to play from the beginning.'[34]

The more negative assessments reflect, in part, a misunderstanding of the structure of the UN development network. MIT's Malone observes that 'most of us still have – deep in our minds – models of management based on the classical, centralized philosophy of command and control'.[35] Even if we have helped to create an organization of a different type, our desire to understand our everyday world using the older, and increasingly inappropriate, paradigm is strong.

Understood as the type of organization UNDP has always really been – more like a global consulting firm or a multi-campus university than a monastic order or a traditional army – the competence and effectiveness of the UN network has at least remained constant. Its founders may now seem larger than life – the first person from the developing world to win

---

[32] Basem Khader, interview with Neysan Rassekh (NR), 10 Nov. 2004.
[33] Philomena Guillebaud, 'Special Fund Memoir', unpublished ms., 7 Nov. 2005.
[34] Edmund Cain, interview with CNM, 8 Sept. 2004.
[35] Malone, *Future of Work*, p. 11.

the Nobel prize in economics, the man who commanded the largest relief effort ever mounted, the first woman to run a comprehensive peacekeeping mission – but the Programme's most important work – coordinating and cultivating the network of relationships that allow people in the developing world more and more control over their own lives – has been done just as effectively in UNDP's last decade as it was in its first.

Ultimately, it is the people doing that coordination and cultivation, idealistic and deeply committed people across four generations, who make UNDP's story fascinating. Throughout the two years that I worked on this book, I told friends about having one of the best jobs around. I went to work each day with extraordinarily admirable people from every part of the globe, people whose experience goes back to the first quarter of the last century and whose vision goes forwards to the end of this one. I met most of them only through letters and official documents or the reminiscences of others, but their commitment and passion has kept them very much alive. They jumped out of the yellowed pages stored in archival boxes and they commanded attention even when speaking through the soft and cracking voice of a surviving friend. These compassionate and hopeful men and women did things over sixty years that were sometimes triumphantly brilliant and, at other times, horribly foolish, even if motivated by impeccable intentions.

As the next three chapters explain, despite the rosy memories that many Programme officers have of the 1950s, the outbreak of the cold war and the scepticism about development assistance of the historically isolationist, conservative faction in the US Congress ensured that the founders' vision was only partially fulfilled. Many of the global institutions originally intended to be part of a UN system were stillborn, and the function of providing financial resources to the developing countries was transferred to institutions that were not patterned on the principle of solidarity that underlay the Marshall Plan and the United Nations. Yet the Programme remained, as the agency funding the technical assistance work of the UN system, as the system's coordinator, and as the incubator of new development institutions. It recruited a global cadre of women and men committed to the same core ideals who were able to react with surprising agility and success to the relatively unexpected rush of decolonization in the early 1960s.

At the same time, throughout the 1950s and 1960s, many EPTA, Special Fund, and UNDP staffers shared the limited vision of almost all the early international development efforts. Many had been so energized by the success of the Marshall Plan that they began to see development as something relatively straightforward and easy: just apply the right ideas and enough money and the whole world will be as peaceful and prosperous as western Europe was becoming. The early generation was also too ready to see knowledge as something originating in the wealthy North that could be easily transferred to the poor South, rather than seeing that knowledge has to be acquired and that, for development, relevant knowledge is *always* a combination of *local* understanding with the experience brought from other places. In addition, the early UNDP was surprisingly blind to most of the ultimate clients of development – to women and to many others who were marginalized.

Chapter 5 provides an extended vignette from the 1950s and early 1960s that illustrates how these attitudes began to change. In that chapter, as in many other parts of the book, the stories of a few individuals and of one or two countries have to stand for dozens of similar stories that took place in many other places. I chose this particular one because one of the key characters, Arthur Lewis, played a unique role in UNDP's history that began with the events recounted here. Yet, in this particular story, Robert G. A. Jackson, another man who had a uniquely positive impact on what UNDP became, appears primarily as a representative of what was then the (somewhat limited) mainstream of development thinking, a role played by hundreds of other men and women at the same time.

One of Jackson's unique and positive roles was to set in motion a process of reform throughout the UN development network at the end of the 1960s. In the 1970s UNDP suffered three major institutional shocks, the main topic of chapter 6. The first was a planned, orderly reorganization in response to recommendations that Jackson had made, while the second was an unexpected financial crisis, something that Khader, reflecting the general consensus, calls 'an internal bungle of the first order'.[36] The third was also a financial problem of a different sort: a crisis of unmet expectations. At the beginning of the decade, UNDP's founders imagined that its funds at the decade's end would be three or four times what they actually turned out to be.

Throughout the decade, new funding was much more likely to go to bilateral programmes or to other multilateral agencies, including many that UNDP had nurtured. The World Bank, the major international provider of development resources, even began to take over some of UNDP's technical assistance role, and to do so quite effectively. However, despite the disappointment, the late 1970s was a period of

---

[36] Basem Khader, interview with NR, 10 Nov. 2004.

relative prosperity for UNDP, one of slowly rising income. Moreover, because the entire decade was marked by an increasingly vocal and assertive developing world that called for a 'New International Economic Order', UNDP's continued adherence to the principle of solidarity made the Programme ever more popular with its main clients. It was in this decade that UNDP cemented its reputation as the development programme *of* the developing countries.

The Administrator who ushered in this period, F. Bradford Morse, maintained and expanded the reach of the Programme, leaving his successor an unwieldy, incoherent organization. Yet hidden within the bric-a-brac of UNDP's expanding programmes was Morse's lasting achievement: the critically important relationships with liberation movements and states that had been outside the global mainstream. At the same time, separate parts of UNDP began to give it the characteristics of a learning organization. Chapters 7 and 8 focus on these progressive changes.

It is in the late 1980s and the 1990s, under Morse's successor, Bill Draper, and the man who followed him (Gus Speth, a Democrat like the man who nominated him, Bill Clinton), UNDP became what it is today, the sponsor of the *Human Development Report*, the organization focusing on democratic governance, reducing poverty, empowering women, aiding countries in crisis, and promoting environmental sustainability. Chapters 9 and 10 discuss this period of rapid learning and increasing global visibility. Unfortunately, for those who championed the UN's 'better way', the period ended with years of declining donor support for development and increasing demand from the many states of eastern Europe and the former Soviet Union that were transformed by the end of the cold war from nominal providers of international assistance to major aid recipients.

Chapter 11 focuses on the period from 1999 to 2005, the era when, Ed Cain believes, everything was 'set in place for UNDP . . . to play the role it was designed to play from the beginning'. It is the period of the Programme's first Administrator not chosen by the US President. Mark Malloch Brown put the Programme back on sound financial footing and brought an additional focus on HIV/AIDS – a central concern of country offices not only in Africa, where the crisis was the greatest, but also in countries where the epidemic had yet to take off. UNDP gained a new international prominence, took on the role of promoting and monitoring the global development goals set by UN members in 2000, and became the showpiece of UN reform.

Yet, as I argue in the final chapter, it would be difficult to claim that UNDP is now in a position to fulfil the vision of the founders of the UN development network. Chapter 12 takes a series of interrelated stories that best illustrate the Programme's persistent patterns of success and failure. The chapter begins with UNDP's involvement in Indonesia after the 1997 Asian financial crisis, moves to East Timor (which had been occupied by Indonesia for a generation), and back to the separatist province of Aceh and UNDP's role there after the Indian Ocean tsunami (with short detours to Haiti and Ghana).

Many of UNDP's failures have to do with organizational pathologies that also characterize other, more traditional, intergovernmental agencies. Others involve the increasingly Byzantine (and difficult to reform) UN system as a whole. Nevertheless, the greatest impediments to fulfilling the original UN development vision have to do with the traditional structure of the international system, with the powers and the interests of nation-states, and with the dynamics of the kind of world politics that existed before the United Nations.

This should not be surprising. The United Nations – in fact, all of what we call 'global governance' – is, at best, a transition between an older system of governance (a system of states and state systems) that we know is no longer effective, and a future form of substantively democratic global governance that we do not yet know how to create. What is most hopeful about UNDP's history is that its first sixty years suggest one path by which we may be able to move from one to the other.

2

Development and the United Nations

UNDP's story begins in the first days of the United Nations, and not just the first days of the organization whose General Assembly convened in London on 10 January 1946, but at the outset of the anti-fascist alliance that took the same name four years earlier. To set the stage, we have to go back even further, to the Industrial Revolution, when the problem of 'development' arose, and then to the last days of the Great War, when the Allies made decisions that many would later believe encouraged fascism and led to the Second World War.

A problem of the industrial age

In 1986 I was reminded of the modernity of 'development', as we now understand it, while visiting Cape Verde to study responses to the devastating West African drought. The country's location, 500 km off the coast and in the path of the major Atlantic currents, helped it to become one of Europe's first colonies (the Portuguese arrived in 1456). It was also one of the last. When I visited, Cape Verdeans had just celebrated their ninth year of independence.

I began with a standard government tour for development professionals. My companions included an Italian from the United Nations Food and Agriculture Organization (FAO), an officer from the Cuban mission, and a teacher from the United Kingdom. He was working on human rights issues, but also pursuing his hobby of visiting all the places sacked by the sixteenth-century British privateer, Sir Francis Drake.

Our first stop was a project where the impoverished descendents of runaway slaves were piecing together the elegant mosaic of a dazzling, snaking road-bed out of the tens of thousands of hand-sized rocks that littered the mountainside. The workers' reward was food for their families, courtesy of some international donor, and a tiny salary, the funds for which were raised by selling some of the donated food at the local market.

'Philip II,' the Italian said, 'must have started this about 400 years ago.'

We all nodded. We had read similar histories: Cape Verde's denuded landscape, already nearly treeless when Drake attacked the old capital, subjected the country to periodic famine. The best of the overseas rulers would import food and set up road works that let some live.

'But,' said the Cuban, 'this is *not* "development".'

At the time, I was not sure. When I saw a similar scene in 2003, in Kanha National Park in Madhya Pradesh, I finally understood. In Kanha, India's national government was giving displaced tribal people food and small stipends to head-carry basketfuls of dirt as they widened the road through land on which they no longer had a right to forage or farm. Because I had just been in Sarnath, where Asoka, the third-century BCE emperor, had erected a giant stupa to commemorate the Buddha's first teaching, I realized that same scene had been played out thousands of years *before* Philip II. This certainly was not 'development'. It was, instead, a standard practice of what the political historian S. E. Finer liked to call, simply, 'government', an invention of the agricultural age.[1] 'Government' helped solve some of the problems presented when the discovery of farming first allowed human communities to settle and grow. One problem was what to do with marginalized populations when crops fail. I was watching the solution: the controlled exchange of food for labour on public projects goes back to Egypt's First Dynasty, which was as ancient to Asoka as he is to us.

'Development' responds to a more recent problem, but one triggered by something just as dramatic as the Neolithic Agricultural Revolution. Fig. 2.1 suggests how to date the problem and the practice. According to historical demographer Massimo Livi-Bacci, the graph 'describes schematically (on a double logarithmic scale and simplifying dramatically the complexities of history) the evolution of population as a function of the three great technological–cultural phases' of human history: the hunter-gatherer, the agricultural, and the industrial.[2] Each curve hints at social, economic, political, and ideological changes much greater than the demographic transitions that are directly depicted. Just as 'government' was part of the solution to the problems of the Neolithic Agricultural Revolution, 'development' is part of the solution to the problems of the Industrial Revolution.

---

[1] S. E. Finer, *The History of Government from the Earliest Times* (Oxford: Oxford University Press, 1997).

[2] Massimo Livi-Bacci, *A Concise History of World Population*, trans. Carl Ipsen, 2nd edn (Oxford: Blackwell Publishers, 1997), p. 29.

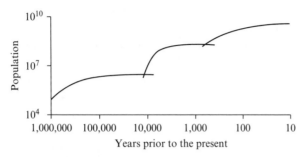

2.1 Cycles of demographic growth

'Development' can be understood as the complex of social practices designed to ameliorate the post-Industrial Revolution problem of inequality across societies in a sustainable manner. Modern industry has linked together a global community with large areas of wealth and poverty unlike anything that existed from one agricultural empire to the next.[3] Ecological and social historian Mike Davis, looking in depth at the experience of China, India, and Brazil (and less extensively at the history of many other countries, including Cape Verde), argues that today's massive differences between the poor global South and rich global North originated only in the last century and a half. Industrialism allowed material abundance to spread, first throughout north-western Europe and the United States. At the same time, colonial governments and those independent governments in the South that followed the economic orthodoxies of the day deepened the immiseration of the poor. In response to a generation of drought (something outside human control), these rulers ignored the solutions sometimes adopted by Catholic princes and Buddhist saints; they let the poor starve, and thus cemented an inequality that is with us still.[4]

In 1700, before the Industrial Revolution, the difference between the incomes of the richest and poorest fifths of the world's population, based on a comparison between rich and poor countries, was only two to one. At the end of the nineteenth century, after the famines that Davis says 'created the Third World', the difference was three to five to one.[5] By

[3] Paul Bairoch, 'Was There a Large Income Differential before Modern Development?', in his *Economics and World History: Myths and Paradoxes* (Chicago: University of Chicago Press, 1993), pp. 101–10.

[4] Mike Davis, *Late Victorian Holocausts: El Niño Famines and the Making of the Third World* (London: Verso, 2001).

[5] Gilbert Rist, *The History of Development, from Western Origins to Global Faith*, trans. Patrick Camiller, 2nd edn (London: Zed Books, 2002), p. 45; W. Arthur Lewis, *Racial Conflict and Economic Development* (Cambridge, Mass.: Harvard University Press, 1985), p. 116.

1985, economics Nobel laureate W. Arthur Lewis estimated a similar figure at eight to one.[6] The 1992 *Human Development Report* declared, 'In 1960, the richest 20% of the world's population had incomes 30 times greater than the poorest 20%. By 1990, the richest 20% were getting 60 times more.'[7] As the World Bank's Lant Pritchett puts it, 'The basic fact of modern economic history is massive absolute *divergence* in the distribution of incomes across countries.'[8] Because we live in a world where income translates into power, into the ability to control one's own life, growing income inequality is a sign of growth in a deeper inequality in the freedoms that different groups of people enjoy. *This* is the problem development solves: 'development' is the set of practices that increase the capacity of people to control their own lives.

Let me go back to Cape Verde and Madhya Pradesh to amplify the point. Twenty years ago, when I was in Cape Verde's compact capital city, Praia, I would sit on the roof of the guest house every evening and watch children climb a few kilometres into the dry, grey moonscape on the north and the east of town. Each carried a small bucket or old cooking-oil can filled with water. Each had a target: one specific tiny seedling tree planted on the side of the rock-strewn hill. This was *development*, a collective action reversing one of the earliest repercussions of modern colonialism. Reforestation was a priority of the country's first independent government. Every day the radio urged, 'Plant, plant, plant. Don't cut the trees . . . plant a million trees.' If the scheme succeeded, trees would capture the clouds that the winds had been rushing out to sea, rains would become regular, and the food-for-work programmes, needed since the days of Drake and Philip II, would be history. It is too soon to see significant changes in the climate, but as early as 1997 the Cape Verdean Minister of Agriculture and the Environment, Jose Antonio Monteiro, reported to the UN General Assembly that reforestation had multiplied the country's vegetation twenty-fold. Fully one-fifth of the country was covered by forest.[9]

Reforestation is also an issue in Kanha National Park and in all the other remaining habitats for tigers, the park's most famous and

---

[6] Lewis, *Racial Conflict*, p. 117.

[7] United Nations Development Programme, *Human Development Report 1992* (New York: Oxford University Press, 1992), p. 1.

[8] Lant Pritchett, 'Divergence Big Time', World Bank Policy Research Working Paper No. 1522 (Washington, D.C.: World Bank, 1995), p. 1 (emphasis in original).

[9] UN General Assembly, Press Release GA/9270, Nineteenth Special Session ENV/DEV/436 7th Meeting (AM) 26 June 1997.

privileged residents. In Kanha, as in many other places, a desire to protect the forest makes governments keep marginalized people off the land. When I was in Kanha, I kept thinking, 'What a strange world where a few hundred tigers can displace thousands of human beings.' Not that I begrudge the tigers, I am an even bigger fan of the charismatic animals than are most other citizens of the United States. Yet the relevance of that comparison points to the problem: the displacement of people from the tigers' habitat is not really about the relative power of tigers and humans. It is about the power of the tigers' allies (people like me) relative to that of the men and women who live around the tigers' homes, people who, on average, have 1/200th or 1/300th of the market power, the income, that I have. The whims of those of us whom money has made powerful, our consumer tastes, and even our ideas about right and wrong can reach out and change the lives of people on the other side of the world about whom we know nothing.

Before practical solidarity

European governments, Europe's princes, and privateers began to have that power derived from wealth in the sixteenth century, but the common people of the privileged world have only been granted it by the abundance we have accumulated since the beginning of the industrial age.

The first generation of the Industrial Revolution also gave us visionaries who imagined a cooperative end to this global inequality. Condorcet foretold a final stage of history marked by 'the abolition of inequality between nations, the progress of equality within each nation, and the true perfection of mankind'. Europe's colonies would be freed, 'These vast lands . . . need only assistance from us to become civilized [and] wait only to find brothers amongst the European nations to become their friends and pupils.'[10] Later, in 1851, an Anglo-Irish promoter of Illinois' railroads (probably a colleague of Congressman Abraham Lincoln) offered a less paternalistic vision of global equality achieved by the universal extension of railways through public–private partnerships: governments would grant land to entrepreneurs willing to build segments of the system, in the way it was being done in the United States. Anticipating twentieth-century arguments about development, John Wright promised Africa, India, East Asia, and Latin America that this plan, 'cannot fail to soon place all alike on an equality with the advanced kingdoms of the

---

[10] Quoted in Rist, *History of Development*, p. 39.

world, and in many instances, render their sources of wealth superior'. He acknowledged that the promise of

> producing such mighty results . . . may at first appear speculative, even impossible. But when we reflect how the United States, less than two centuries ago a mere penal settlement of diverse European nations, has acquired a degree of power and importance, bidding fair to surpass that of Greece or Rome . . . in less than four score years . . . should we hesitate?[11]

Yet governments *did* hesitate to work on the problem of global inequality *together*. It took another century before they established *international* institutions concerned with placing all nations 'on an equality with the advanced kingdoms of the world'. Until the end of the Second World War, what we now call 'development' was primarily the task of national governments attempting to catch up with the first industrial nation, Great Britain, or of political movements attempting to unify *nation*-states that would be able to do so, as in nineteenth-century Germany and Italy.

Initially, the few governments that were effective all followed relatively similar plans: they built modern transport and communications infrastructure, encouraged industrialists to steal advanced technologies from abroad, and erected trade barriers to protect their infant industries. Unfortunately this relatively simple development plan could not be followed for long. Industrialism has a logic of market expansion and innovation that prevents small states (and, increasingly, *all* states) from establishing the latest generation of industries on their own. Economies as small as those of the north of England, New England, or Belgium were big enough for the development of the early industrial economies of the cotton mills. More extensive, 'national' economies were needed for the mid-nineteenth-century railway age. The new lead industries of the end of the century's Second Industrial Revolution (the chemical, electrical, and branded consumer products industries) grew within the larger market areas of extended nation-states. These included the British Empire of the 'new' imperialism, the 'German' market area that had been expanded to, and beyond, continental Europe through the economic integration encouraged by late-nineteenth-century international

---

[11] John Wright, *Christianity and Commerce, the Natural Results of the Geographical Progression of the Railways or A Treatise on the Advantage of the Universal Extension of Railways in our Colonies and Other Countries, and the Probability of Increased National Intercommunication Leading to the Early Restoration of the Land of Promise to the Jews* (London: Dolman, 1851), pp. 12–13.

organizations, and the pan-American market area centred on the United States.

The imperialism of the industrial powers before the First World War certainly integrated the entire world into huge industrial economies, but the inter-imperial system of international relations did nothing to create equality across the world, even if it did involve practices that were called 'development'. The World Bank's historians remind us that until the Second World War 'development' meant something like 'the duty of the landlord to develop his estate'. The duty colonial powers understood was the duty to extract wealth and raw materials from their colonies, the duty to make them paying ventures.[12] As one leading historian of Africa puts it, 'development', initially, was designed to create a more productive and legitimate empire, 'something to be done *to* and *for* Africa, not with it'.[13]

The lesson of the First World War

That approach began to change, not because the great powers rethought their relations with their colonies, but, rather, because some rethought their relations with one another. In August 1940 a defiant Winston Churchill, facing invasion, with no great power allies, anticipated what would be the Second World War's actual endgame:

> We can and we will arrange in advance for the speedy entry of food into any part of the enslaved area, when this part has been wholly cleared of German forces and has genuinely regained its freedom. We shall do our utmost to encourage the building up of reserves of food all over the world, so that there will always be held up before the peoples of Europe – I say deliberately – the German and Austrian peoples, the certainty that the shattering of the Nazi power will bring them immediate food, freedom, and peace.[14]

Five months later, Franklin Delano Roosevelt spoke of a post-war 'world founded upon . . . freedom of speech and expression . . . freedom of every person to worship God in his own way . . . freedom from want . . . [and] freedom from fear . . . [not in] a distant millennium . . .

---

[12] Devesh Kapur, John B. Lewis, and Richard Webb, *The World Bank: Its First Half-Century* (Washington, D.C.: Brookings Institution Press, 1997), p. 95.

[13] Frederick Cooper, 'Modernizing Bureaucrats, Backward Africans, and the Development Concept', in Frederick Cooper and Randall Packard, eds., *International Development and the Social Sciences: Essays on the History and Politics of Knowledge* (Berkeley: University of California Press, 1997), p. 65 (emphasis in original).

[14] Quoted in George Woodbridge (Director), *UNRRA: The History of the United Nations Relief and Rehabilitation Administration*, vol. 1 (New York: Columbia University Press, 1950), p. 7.

in our own time', 'everywhere in the world', the world of the 'Four Freedoms'.[15]

In January 1942, in the multilateral Declaration by United Nations, many of which were from the group that we now call 'developing' nations (China, Costa Rica, Cuba, Dominican Republic, El Salvador, Guatemala, Haiti, Honduras, India, Nicaragua, and Panama) embraced Roosevelt's cause. Most accepted the immediate collective goal of providing 1 per cent of their national income for the recovery of the liberated areas as long as that was needed. Soon Bolivia, Brazil, Chile, Colombia, Ecuador, Egypt, Ethiopia, Iran, Iraq, Liberia, Mexico, Paraguay, Peru, Philippines, Saudi Arabia, Turkey, Uruguay, and Venezuela joined them.[16] When the Allies finally landed in western Europe, Roosevelt ordered his Supreme Commander, Dwight Eisenhower, to assure the liberated populace that 'No one will go hungry or without the means of livelihood in any territory occupied by the United Nations' alliance, if it is humanly within our powers to make the necessary supplies available to them.'[17]

In 1943 the Allies created an organization, the UN Relief and Rehabilitation Administration (UNRRA), to carry out the order. UNICEF's historian, Maggie Black, describes the system of practical solidarity on which UNRRA was based.

> It was a general international partnership, in which even countries which received its help provided whatever they could spare in surplus foodstuffs and commodities for the relief of others. The guiding principle of the financial plan was that countries which had not been invaded would contribute 1 per cent of their national income: 'to each according to their needs; from each according to their resources'.[18]

The 1 per cent figure was the inspiration of the architects of the Bretton Woods system, the American Harry Dexter White, in consultation with

[15] Franklin D. Roosevelt, 'The Four Freedoms', speech delivered 6 January 1941, http://www.americanrhetoric.com/speeches/fdrthefourfreedoms.htm (accessed 7 Sept. 2005).

[16] 'Declaration by United Nations' (Subscribing to the Principles of the Atlantic Charter), signed 1 January 1942, *Pillars of Peace: Documents Pertaining to American Interest in Establishing a Lasting World Peace, January 1941–February 1946* (Carlisle Barracks, Pa.: US Army Information School, 1946), pp. 4–5 (this particular compilation puts the documents in a useful historical context).

[17] David Halloran Lumsdaine, *Moral Vision in International Politics: The Foreign Aid Régime 1949–1989* (Princeton: Princeton University Press, 1993), p. 206.

[18] Maggie Black, *The Children and the Nations: The Story of UNICEF* (New York: UNICEF, 1986), p. 24.

John Maynard Keynes,[19] the famous economist and frequent contributor to British policy whom many also credit for first recognizing the desirability of an international system based on such principles.

At the end of the First World War, a young Keynes had served as an economic advisor to the British delegation that negotiated the peace. He was horrified with the results, which had proceeded from the traditional international practice of forcing the defeated parties to compensate the victors. In *The Economic Consequences of the Peace*, Keynes demonstrated the practical, sometimes even physical, impossibility of Germany paying the reparations owed under the Treaty of Versailles.[20] Moreover, because the country's democratic political leaders, both of the right and of the left, had been forced to subscribe to the treaty, Keynes worried that Germans would be forced to elect a party outside the democratic mainstream to abrogate it, a militarist party under whom the Great War would continue in a second, more horrible, phase.

Other Allied leaders, in business as well as government, drew similar lessons as they attempted to renegotiate Germany's unsustainable reparation obligations after the sudden downturn of the world economy in the late 1920s: the Allies themselves, their greed at Versailles, and their callousness towards the German people, contributed to the looming war. Churchill's Battle of Britain pledge to aid Germany, Austria, and Italy after their defeat signalled that a lesson had been learned: after *this* war, things would be different.

As Roosevelt's 'Four Freedoms' speech made clear, this new post-war vision was meant to apply to the entire world. Sir Robert Jackson, the man responsible for much of the success of UNRRA's relief efforts, points out that Churchill's speech was aimed, in part, at Argentina and similar countries that could become allies of either Germany or Britain, countries vitally concerned to know the contrasting British and Nazi visions of the post-war world.[21]

Churchill's still unofficial partner, Franklin Delano Roosevelt, was already giving Latin America a practical demonstration of the vision he shared with the British. Even before the war began (with Germany's invasion of Poland in 1939), US officials feared growing Nazi influence in the

---

[19] Robert G. A. Jackson, *A Study of the Capacity of the United Nations Development System*, vol. 2 (Geneva: United Nations, 1969), p. 4.

[20] John Maynard Keynes, *The Economic Consequences of the Peace* (New York: Harcourt, Brace & Howe, 1920).

[21] Robert G. A. Jackson, Transcripts of interviews, 1990, mainly concerning UNRRA, Oxford, Bodleian Library, MS Eng. c. 4678, fo. 2.

hemisphere where leading US companies had, for decades, relied on strategic raw materials, profitable investments, and key export markets. The
Roosevelt administration reacted by offering financial support, technical
assistance, and international backing for Latin American experiments in
state regulation that the US administration saw as reflecting the same principles as the New Deal. The new US approach to regional affairs was
designed, as Roosevelt put it, 'to give them [Latin Americans] a share'.[22]

Isolationists in Congress and some business leaders, including a few
with extensive interests in the hemisphere, objected to the new approach,
but Roosevelt dismissed them as short-sighted. Almost all of the key
figures in the administration embraced the new policy. They included
Sumner Welles (the powerful Assistant Secretary of State for Latin
America and primary author of the 1941 'Four Freedoms' speech), Harry
Dexter White (one architect, recall, of the Bretton Woods system), Henry
Wallace (Vice President after 1940), Robert Triffin, the lead economist in
the Federal Reserve, and Roosevelt brain-truster Adolfe Berle.[23]

In 1941 Berle contrasted the new policy to previous US attempts to
secure private investment by providing 'technical assistance' that was
limited to demanding 'sound' (that is, pro-foreign investment) economic
policies, financial support that was limited to US firms, and an institutional environment that favoured only US investors:

> [W]e have shifted our entire point of view. Instead of being anxious to find
> a place where a group of people who have privately saved money can secure
> a private stream of profits, we are anxious rather to find opportunities for
> sound development which may add to the general safety, security, and well-
> being of the Western Hemisphere.

Moreover, Berle concluded, the new US policy in Latin America was
the model of international economic cooperation for the world after the
war.[24] Peace between the richer and poorer nations would be achieved
through the principle of practical solidarity, a principle that demanded
international cooperation for development.

Even in the short time between the articulation of the new policy and

---

[22] Quoted in Lloyd Gardner, *Economic Aspects of New Deal Diplomacy* (Madison, Wis.:
University of Wisconsin Press), p. 109.

[23] Eric Helleiner, 'Reinterpreting Bretton Woods: International Development and the
Neglected Origins of Embedded Liberalism', *Development and Change*, 37, 5 (2006): forthcoming.

[24] David Green, *The Containment of Latin America: A History of the Myths and Realities of the
Good Neighbor Policy* (Chicago: Quadrangle Books, 1971), pp. 82–3.

the narrowing of the United States' foreign policy focus after the Japanese attack on Pearl Harbor (in December 1941), the new approach had a significant impact. The US Export-Import Bank began pre-investment studies and project lending associated with Latin American government plans for industrialization.[25] The United States pushed to create an inter-American development bank and a permanent regional financial advisory committee. US technical assistance expanded in scale, with some 1,200 expert missions sent from 1939 to the end of the war,[26] and it expanded beyond the preaching of a laissez-faire economic orthodoxy embraced by some US firms. 'Indeed, in preparing his [wartime] advice for Paraguay, [the Federal Reserve's Robert] Triffin even went out of his way to consult extensively with, and acknowledge his debt to the ideas of Argentine economist Raúl Prebisch who was emerging as the leading Latin American theorist of a more inward-looking "structuralist" approach to economic development.'[27] When the 'United Nations' began, with that declaration by the anti-fascist nations shortly after Pearl Harbor, most of its members imagined that the peacetime relationship between all richer and poorer countries would be something like this, the most recent, version of US economic policy towards Latin America. The relationship would be influenced, of course, by the UNRRA precedent that states should be expected to give something like 1 per cent of their income to those that were less advantaged.

The Middle East supply centre, UNRRA, and the post-war United Nations

Although Roosevelt's 'Good Neighbor' policy provided the only strategic precedent for the development policy of the post-war United Nations, the UN's initial tactics and personnel came from other parts of the wartime alliance, from UNRRA, and from the organization that provided much of its leadership.

Early in the war the British created the Middle East Supply Centre (MESC) to transform the economies of a large part of what we now think of as the 'developing' world. The Centre solved a problem discovered

---

[25] William H. Becker and William M. McClenahan, Jr, *The Market, the State, and the Export-Import Bank of the United States, 1934–2000* (Cambridge: Cambridge University Press, 2003), pp. 48–9.

[26] Hugh L. Keenleyside, *International Aid: A Summary with Special Reference to the Programmes of the United Nations* (New York: James H. Heinemann, 1966), p. 119.

[27] Helleiner, 'Reinterpreting Bretton Woods'.

when the Allies began operations in the Middle East in 1940: local ports could not process the massive influx of weaponry and men needed to secure the region and open a southern European front without disrupting the complex flows of essential food and fuel that had linked and sustained the region for centuries. In response, the British began planning a vast expansion of harbours and inland transport, something that would have taken many years to complete. Luckily, an impossibly young (29-year-old) Australian officer, Paymaster-Commander Robert Gillman Allen Jackson, had a better idea. The Allies could 'make the entire area involved – from Turkey to South Africa and from Cyrenaica to India, with a population of about 100 million – as self-sufficient as possible in essential agricultural commodities and industrial output as quickly as possible, and thus reduce civilian imports to a minimum'.[28]

Despite his youth, Jackson was able to convince the top brass because he had already proven his uncanny logistical skill. He had demonstrated how to supply and defend Malta, an operational base crucial for the Allies' victory in North Africa that the Royal Air Force had considered undefendable. The former Paymaster-Commander (by then, deservedly, *Sir* Robert) later explained that the MESC

> naturally involved every aspect of every economy in the region – agriculture, industry, health, infrastructure, education, science, etc. – and the establishment of a watertight import licensing system. Schemes to achieve greater productivity and import substitution became the order of the day . . . Within 15 months, 90 per cent of the civilian imports which previously had occupied 90 per cent of the total port capacity of the Red Sea and Persian Gulf had been replaced by local production. As a result, the flow of military supplies to the Allied armed forces in the Western Desert was vastly increased, and also the USSR via the Persian Gulf.[29]

The Centre quickly became a model for the first international development efforts: technical assistance to war-ravaged countries designed to minimize waste, improve the flow of goods, and otherwise uncover new efficiencies, not to make room for the instruments of war, but to better the lives of those who still suffered its effects.

Initially it was the temporary agency, UNRRA, that did this work, and its first director, New York Governor Herbert Lehman, hired Jackson to be his senior deputy. MESC also nurtured dozens of other key figures in the UN development story, including Charles Malik, the Lebanese diplo-

---

[28] Jackson quoted in UNDP, *Generation: Portrait of the United Nations Development Programme 1950–1985* (New York: UNDP, 1985), p. 10.   [29] Ibid.

mat who was an early head of the UN Economic and Social Council (ECOSOC), and David Owen, a Welshman who was the Whitehall liaison to the MESC, the first civil servant hired by the post-war United Nations, and the principal architect of UNDP.[30]

UNRRA provided still more of the UN's early personnel, as one of them, Richard Symonds, a long-time director of UNDP's Geneva office, explains:

> Working together in UNRRA were a number of people, particularly British and American, who were shortly afterwards to be appointed to key administrative posts in the United Nations and the specialized agencies. With this shared background of mistakes as well as achievements, they were able to agree on common personnel, salary, pension, and other arrangements which have been an important element in holding together the UN system.[31]

By summer 1947 David Owen, the new UN's chief economic officer, and Jackson were in a lively personal correspondence about how various UNRAA staff members could be deployed throughout the post-war United Nations and the Specialized Agencies.[32]

The story of UNRRA's demise and of the dispersion of its resources and personnel into new agencies guided by similar principles foreshadows some key themes in UNDP's history. Jackson considered Churchill responsible both for UNRRA's life and for its death. His Battle of Britain speech brought it to life. His 'Iron Curtain' speech in 1946, when he delineated that part of the world to which the principle of solidarity should not apply, killed it.[33] By late 1946, some conservatives in the US Congress were demanding that UNRRA impose an anti-communist litmus test or else cease to exist. President Truman, egged on by the conservative former president, Herbert Hoover, who was widely respected for his organization of relief work after the First World War, supported UNRRA's detractors. Lehman, who had been appointed by Roosevelt, disagreed and resigned. Truman filled his place with New York City's

---

[30] *Generation*, p. 10. Brian Urquhart, 'Owen, Sir (Arthur) David Kemp (1904–1970)', in H. C. G. Matthew and Brian Harrison, eds., *Oxford Dictionary of National Biography* (Oxford: Oxford University Press, 2004), http://0-www.oxfroddnb.com.luna.wellesley. edu:80/view/ article/35346 (accessed 3 November 2004).

[31] Richard Symonds, 'Bliss Was It in That Dawn: Memoirs of an Early United Nations Career, 1946–1979', Oxford, Bodleian Library, MS Eng. c. 4703, p. 26.

[32] Box 1 of the David Owen Papers, Columbia University Library, New York (hereafter Owen Papers).

[33] Robert G. A. Jackson, Foreword to Black, *The Children and the Nations*, pp. 7–9.

charismatic Republican mayor, Fiorello LaGuardia. In December 1946 LaGuardia found himself defending UNRRA and its principles (impartiality and 'to each according to their needs from each according to their resources') against Adlai Stevenson, the US representative in the UN General Assembly's Second Committee and the future Democratic Party presidential candidate. Stevenson loyally embraced the political conditionality and unilateralism (for the sake of 'efficiency' in the allocation of aid) that were the hallmarks of the approach advocated by Hoover and the congressional conservatives.

LaGuardia tried to explain why UNRRA's was the better way. True, in 1946 the world's greatest economic needs were in central Europe, where people were starving and without shelter, and that is why UNRRA operated there, despite the communist leanings of some of the new governments. When those needs were met, there would be other jobs to do, contributing to 'public works projects and industrialization' in places like Latin America, where many states had been especially generous to UNRRA. That is why he hoped new UN agencies governed by UNRRA's principles would succeed it.[34]

In failing health, LaGuardia lost that particular battle, but he won the war. As UNRRA disbanded, the UN used its funds and much of its expertise to nurture the earliest development work of the FAO, the UN Educational, Scientific, and Cultural Organization (UNESCO), and two agencies opposed by congressional conservatives to whom Stevenson was responding: UNICEF and the World Health Organization (WHO).[35] What may have been LaGuardia's greatest vindication came just three months before his death in September 1947. In June, US Secretary of State George Marshall announced an even broader programme for European recovery, the Marshall Plan, the most massive international assistance programme ever undertaken, before or since. The plan embraced impartiality, inviting eastern European countries to participate as long as they '"abandoned [the] near-exclusive Soviet orientation of their economies" in favour of European-wide integration'.[36] In fact, the United States limited conditionality to that one demand: Europeans had to work cooperatively to reconstruct a *continental* economy; the compet-

---

[34] United Nations, *Summary Record of the Meetings of the Second Committee of the General Assembly First Session, Second Part* (Lake Success, N.Y.: 1946), pp. 127, 136–7.

[35] Jackson, Foreword to Black, *The Children and the Nations*, pp. 7–10.

[36] Michael J. Hogan, *The Marshall Plan: America, Britain, and the Reconstruction of Europe* (New York: Cambridge University Press, 1987), p. 43, quoting summaries of State Department discussions, 29 May 1947.

itive national and imperial economies of the early industrial eras had to go. Of necessity, the Marshall Plan embraced multilateralism, creating a multilateral agency to coordinate that work. It, in turn, spawned a surviving successor, the OECD (Organization for Economic Cooperation and Development), as well as the economic communities which eventually were to become the European Union.

The 'better way', UNDP's trajectory, and other paths to development

The Marshall Plan had only one chief executive in its decade-long history, the former Studebaker chairman, Paul G. Hoffman. When Hoffman saw his work in Europe with the Plan ending, he helped his friends in the Eisenhower administration extricate themselves from a protracted conflict over the future of the UN development system by promoting 'pre-investment', the justification for the Special Fund. Hoffman moved to the UN as the head of the Fund. Then, in 1966, he took his Marshall Plan expertise, and his unassuming Marshall Plan title, 'the Administrator', to the new UNDP.

Throughout his life, Hoffman explained his UN work in the same way in which he explained the Marshall Plan work. He reiterated the lesson his generation took from the First World War. One of his favourite catchphrases was Eisenhower's, 'an investment in peace'. Hoffman said that he 'could think of no two words that handicap a programme more than *foreign* and *aid*'.[37] Not 'foreign', because we are in it together; it is a matter of solidarity. Not 'aid', because it is more like an investment, and not just in development. (In fact, we do not yet know how to make sure-fire investments in 'development'; that is one of the reasons why the 'pre-investment' work of the Special Fund was so important.) UNDP was an investment in peace.

It is worth anticipating the direction in which these ideas were going to take the UN's development work in the 1950s and 1960s. To begin with, it is important to recognize that Hoffman's generation was probably right: even today, we may actually know more about how to achieve 'peace' (at least of a temporary kind) than we do about assuring 'development'. The problem that 'development' aims to solve has only been with us for 200 years, whereas the kind of international systems that give us war go back as far as the first of those separate 'governments' that humans invented to solve problems created by the Neolithic Agricultural Revolution. Moreover, it is only since the last years of the League of Nations that we

---

[37] Kapur, Lewis, and Webb, *World Bank*, p. 149.

have had systematic *global* analyses of the problem of bringing all nations 'alike on an equality'. The League was the first body with an institutional commitment to understanding the global political economy in its entirety. The League's chief economic analyst, Folke Hilgerdt, undertook a series of massive historical studies that 'anticipated a good deal in the post-war prescriptive literature on development', according to one of the early giants in the field, W. W. Rostow, but Hilgert's work did not influence global policy making until after the war had ended.[38]

The slow emergence of our understanding of development should not be surprising. It took our ancestors 5,000 years to come up with 'government' as a workable solution to some of the problems generated by settled agriculture. Yet, as both pundits and serious scholars like to remind us, space and time have become remarkably compressed since the Industrial Revolution. That explains the logarithmic scales used on the graph near the beginning of this chapter. (Really, they are not there to rekindle first-year maths anxieties!) If we compare the central curve (representing the consequences of the agricultural age) to that on the right, the figure suggests that we might be able to discover the equivalent of 'government' in this generation or the next, as early as 250 years after the start of the Industrial Revolution, but it was unlikely, even with the time compression caused by 'globalization', that the problem would be solved in the generation that spanned the world wars.

The triangle in fig. 2.2 suggests the degree to which understandings of development have begun to converge since then. Most of today's theories, programmes, and practices aimed at diminishing inequality across the world's countries can be located inside a space whose extreme points represent three distinct approaches: 'development as efficiency', 'development as growth', and 'development as freedom'. To understand the history of UNDP, we have to understand a bit about these three approaches to development, which is why I briefly explain them here.

'Development as growth' may be the most familiar. Here, greater global equality is to be achieved by ensuring that the disadvantaged have opportunities to earn incomes equal to those in the privileged world.

---

[38] W. W. Rostow, *Theorists of Economic Growth from David Hume to the Present, with a Perspective on the New Century* (New York: Oxford University Press, 1990), p. 320. See especially Folke Hilgerdt, *Industrialization and Foreign Trade* (New York: Columbia University Press for the League of Nations, 1945). Hans W. Singer outlines Hilgerdt's role in establishing the agenda for the UN's policy analysis, 'The Terms of Trade Controversy and the Evolution of Soft Financing: Early Years in the UN', in Gerald M. Meier and Dudley Seers, eds., *Pioneers in Development* (New York: Oxford University Press for the World Bank, 1984), p. 280.

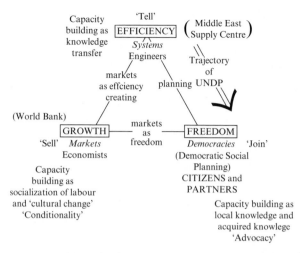

2.2 Approaches to development

'Development as freedom' is the approach highlighted by the Kenyan comic strip at the head of chapter 1. The aim is to ensure for each of us the ability, the freedom, to pursue our individual and collective goals. This is the approach associated with the *Human Development Report,* and with the work of Mahbub ul Haq and Amartya Sen.

'Development as efficiency' may be the least familiar approach, but it was the first to have an impact on international development efforts and on UNDP through the work of the MESC and UNRRA, and Sir Robert Jackson acting in a time of crisis. 'Efficiency' can serve many ends, but, for development specialists, the goal usually has been to help a state become equal to the most powerful states in the world. This was the goal that animated Ghana's first prime minister, Kwame Nkrumah, and Jackson's dedication to that goal made them fast friends. Jackson was a military man and his father started an engineering firm. Jackson brought the intellectual virtues of those fields to his development work, including his help with Ghana's monumental Volta River Project. Engineering, operations research (the mathematical field developed by Second World War tacticians to deal with complex problems like Jackson's), and systems dynamics are the disciplines most compatible with this approach. It requires understanding the sources and flows in complex, real-world systems, and creating interventions, fabricated systems (such as incentives for import substitution), designed to move goods to where they are most needed.

Those who focus on 'development as growth' emphasize different techniques and have different disciplinary inclinations. Their field of preference is economics, the economics of Adam Smith that sees the incentives provided by unregulated markets as the best way of ensuring that natural resources, human labour, and capital will be combined to produce the most goods. It is the abundance of those goods that promises to eliminate destitution, and with it, the deepest of human inequalities. This is not the promise offered by managerial systems efficiently allocating goods to those who need them most.

If MESC was the institutional embodiment of the 'development as efficiency' approach, the World Bank's historians tell us that their institution (in the past, at least) was the international institution closest to the 'growth' pole. 'If rhetoric is put aside, the Bank for the most part and throughout its history has seen the promotion of economic growth as its principal means of bringing about poverty reduction ... Underlying these activities is the unwavering assumption that a rising tide lifts all boats.'[39] Moreover, when it comes to making programmatic recommendations to governments, the Bank's most frequent counsel has been that of the neoclassical economists: set up markets and then let them alone.

In contrast, the most characteristic institutional advice of the third approach – 'development as freedom' – goes more directly to the heart of the problem of unequal power: set up systems of egalitarian collective decision making; create democracies. If development is what the people want it to be, its characteristic means will be techniques for reaching joint agreements on long-term goals and the collective action needed to achieve them – 'democracy' or 'democratic social planning'. Moreover, the primary source of the knowledge needed for development does not come from some discrete discipline. That knowledge must come from citizens themselves, even though they may seek more expert partners from whose experience they can learn.

Disciplinary knowledge can still be relevant. Historian Mamadou Diouf writes about the ideas that energized Senegal's populist development practices in the 1960s. He explains the resulting difference between the francophone 'development economics' of the day and the narrower discipline of 'economics' associated with the growth approach. Practitioners of the relevant discipline of development economics considered it an integration of *all* the social sciences through direct

---

[39] Kapur, Lewis, and Webb, *World Bank*, p. 54.

observation and fieldwork.[40] To the extent that the discipline retains those characteristics, it continues to be relevant to the 'development as freedom' approach.

Another way to think about the differences between the three poles is to consider the different notions of 'capacity building' that are the most relevant to each. In the 'development as freedom' approach, capacity building involves a combination of local knowledge with acquired knowledge, people taking concepts, theories, procedures, and skills from abroad and remaking them as their own, remaking them as something contextualized and embedded within their own lives. In the 'efficiency' approach, capacity building is a more traditional form of knowledge transfer: people in the developing world adopt procedures and skills that originate elsewhere, whether they be plans for building sweeter-smelling latrines or model legal instruments protecting the autonomy of the central bank.

For the 'development as growth' approach, the issue is a little different. The primary capacity at stake here is the ability (and desire) of societies to create and to work within a market economy that initially may be culturally alien. That is why the first generation of international development theorists were attracted to arguments about cultural 'modernization', about the conditions under which people acquire the personalities and the mindsets that are necessary if a market economy is to do its magic. Thus one of the earliest development journals, established in 1952, took the title *Economic Development and Cultural Change*.

Adherents to this approach see a great deal of power in the market mindset itself. Not surprisingly, they are apt to see international development assistance, the provision of resources or technical assistance (bricks and boards or brains and books), as an *exchange*. (This was Adlai Stevenson's argument back in 1946.) Donors make aid conditional upon the recipient country's taking certain market-nurturing actions. Thus the donor uses aid as a means of convincing the recipient to adopt particular ideas or take particular actions from which it expects eventually to benefit.

Another way of looking at these three approaches to development is to consider the way in which they are promoted. Business school professors sometimes refer to three ideal types of management based on three different means of persuasion: 'sell', 'tell', and 'join'. Adherents to the

---

[40] Mamadou Diouf, 'Senegalese Development: From Mass Mobilization to Technocratic Elitism', trans. Molly Roth and Frederick Cooper, in Frederick Cooper and Randall Packard, eds., *International Development and the Social Sciences: Essays on the History and Politics of Knowledge* (Berkeley: University of California Press, 1997), p. 300.

'development as growth' approach tend to be the most comfortable with 'sell', with convincing clients by pointing out the advantages of a particular course of action.

The 'development as freedom' pole is more conducive to the 'join' style of persuasion. 'Joining' is not equivalent to accepting all the views of your partners. Rather, donors taking this approach, which is compatible with the kind of advocacy that UNDP has pursued since the 1980s, simply believe that recipients should define their own goals and are capable of making good decisions. Management gurus contend that within organizations, especially within the kind of complex, multifaceted networks that are involved in development, this style of persuasion (as compared with 'selling' or 'telling') gains the highest commitment of all involved and is particularly useful for gaining commitment to tasks that can be done in a number of ways.

'Tell' is the persuasive style of the 'development as efficiency' pole. It is the 'top-down' management style of traditional bureaucratic organizations and of the military. A key to the success of the Middle East Supply Centre was the fact that almost the entire region was under the direct colonial command of the British government. The region could become self-sufficient so rapidly because its commanders could just tell everyone what to do, and – given the enemy – they all had good reason to comply. In other contexts, the characteristic virtues of this approach can become liabilities. J. H. Mensah, one of Ghana's elder statesmen and someone who knew Robert Jackson over many decades, chortles over the Australian's way of sometimes treating development projects as if they were military campaigns. 'Jackson,' Mensah says, 'always wanted just to roll over things to make things happen!' He was superb in emergency situations when it was necessary for someone to take command.[41]

Jackson, was, however, more complex than Mensah suggests. Even in Ghana much of his success rested on his empathy with the country's elected leaders and on his diplomacy, a persuasive style that was much closer to the 'join' pole. Within UNDP, especially through his leadership of the organization's first major internal review, the 1969 'Capacity Study', Jackson gave the Programme a major push towards 'development as freedom'.

As Jackson's example suggests, a combination of the three approaches usually proves the most effective; most development theories, and most development practices, can be located somewhere inside the triangle and,

---

[41] J. H. Mensah, interview with the author (CNM) 21 Jan. 2005.

if there is anything like a 'best' development strategy, it, too, is likely to be found *inside* the triangle rather than at one of the corners. Remember that, as economists remind us, markets can contribute to efficiency, and colonial administrations certainly established and nurtured many for just that purpose. Similarly, the 'development as freedom' approach embraces markets as a way to expand human opportunities, especially choices for work and education. At the same time, the idea of 'democratic social planning' takes adherents to the 'development as freedom' approach back towards the goal of efficiency. Even a democratically arrived upon plan dictates a limited range of collective action over a particular period of time; 'join' has to become 'tell'.

The history of the UN development network tends to trace an irregular path from the 'tell' of the MESC to 'join'. The path was opened by the philosophy embraced by Hoffman, LaGuardia, Roosevelt, Churchill, and, most significantly, David Owen. That philosophy asserted that it was the 'right of each requesting government itself to decide what help it needs and in what form'.[42] 'Join', at least with *governments*, was always the UN mode. A 1965 analysis (for which Owen provided the preface) argued that the UN was unique among the then burgeoning clan of international aid providers in holding this view. Richard Symonds, who often held diplomatically sensitive UNDP posts, writes about telling the South African apartheid government that political conditionality was not part of *his* mandate, no matter what the most powerful members of the UN might think it should be. He was 'glad to talk of "shoes, and ships and sealing wax, and cabbages – but not Kings"'.[43]

'Joining' with *governments* is hardly the same thing as embracing 'development as freedom', as the South African case illustrates, and the lesson from the First World War was one about the Allies' lack of solidarity with the German *people*, not about the Allies' lack of sympathy for the German government. Churchill and Truman's opposition to UNRRA came from their perception that the organization served only the governments, and not the people, of eastern Europe (a conclusion that LaGuardia and Jackson thought was gravely mistaken). From the beginning, officials at the centre of the UN development network hoped for an international system dedicated to this broader kind of solidarity. One of only a handful of reports written by an expert outside the UN that David

---

[42] James Avery Joyce, *World of Promise: A Guide to the United Nations Decade of Development* (Dobbs Ferry, N.Y.: Oceana Publications, Inc., 1965), p. 44.

[43] Symonds, 'Bliss Was It in that Dawn', p. 93.

Owen bothered to save in his professional papers makes the point. In 1950, George Masselman, a historian of modern imperialism argued, 'The aim of any development programme should be to narrow the economic gap and so reduce the envy and inferiority which is now so evident throughout the world.' The problem, he argued, was not the envy and inferiority felt by undemocratic elites, but that felt by the masses who enjoyed neither prosperity nor 'full employment'.[44] Similarly, another of Owen's correspondents in the 1950s, a UNESCO expert supported by the Expanded Programme of Technical Assistance (EPTA), A. Nicholas Gillett, writing from the Philippines,[45] made the case that the new UN development system was a manifestation of the larger advance of 'liberty, equality, and fraternity'. So far, it had been achieved mostly 'by the establishment of trade unions and by nationalization and by co-ops'.

Yet Gillett also worried about those who believed that international solidarity demanded adherence to any one economic vision. Rejecting knee-jerk anti-communism and the market theology of those on the 'growth' pole, he argued, 'We must not achieve group feeling by the suppression of individual thought on the pattern of the Nazi Youth Group. Indeed, Nazism should be a perpetual warning against one of the diseases of Fraternity.' Yet the EPTA expert worried even more about the idealism of the enterprise of which he had become a part, about whether the sacrifice needed for international fraternity was sustainable, 'The man in the street whose head aches with the emotional constipation of the films . . . cannot be expected to believe in much . . . His ancestors were scared into being good by fear of Hellfire: Maybe he will be scared into doing good by fear of atom bombs.'

Fifty years later Gus Speth, the UNDP Administrator of the 1990s, would describe his tenure as, 'the greatest experience, at a personal level', due to the qualities of the people within the organization. They were, he said, 'the last great concentration of idealists on the planet', women and men who, nonetheless, were practical enough to have 'an incredible capacity to do good'.[46] It is that practical idealism, and the embrace of a larger democratic agenda, that pulled EPTA, the Special Fund, and UNDP towards the pole of 'freedom', and towards a direct confrontation with the unequal power that is at the heart of the post-Industrial Revolution problem of development.

[44] George Masselman, 'Point Four: An Appraisal', typescript, Owen Papers, Box 2.
[45] A. Nicholas Gillett to unnamed recipient, Oxford, Bodleian Library, MS Eng. c. 4671, fos. 255–6. [46] James Gustave Speth, interview with CNM, 24 Sept. 2004.

Writing about the World Bank trajectory over the last decade, Sebastian Mallaby argues that the practical part of a practical idealism – learning that development cannot be achieved by staying at the 'growth' pole – has also pulled the Bank more and more in the direction of placing democracy and the equalization of power at the centre of its mission.[47] In the longer history of the movement in the same direction by UNDP and its predecessors, practicality also pulled just as strongly. W. Arthur Lewis, the British Nobel laureate from St Lucia brought by Paul Hoffman to the Special Fund as his number two, recalled having 'had the misfortune' of reading dozens of project reports and development plans in the late 1940s when he disbursed funds under Britain's Colonial Development and Welfare Act. The Act had been designed to do things 'to' and 'for' the colonies, not 'with' them. Whether perfunctory, unctuous, or merely dreadfully written, the reports reflected the unequal power relationship and the fact of the colonizer's lack of interest in the real progress of its 'development' clients.[48] Later, in one of the reports that would define the EPTA and Special Fund's approach to development, Lewis argued for something very different:

> Men learn administration by participating in it. They therefore learn fastest in countries where self-governing institutions are most widespread, embracing central and local government, right down to the level of the village, the cooperative movement, trade unions, and the hundred and one other voluntary or official groups in which free peoples love to foregather.[49]

Similarly, to return to the stories at the beginning of the chapter, UNDP references to the unequal relationship between the displaced human residents of India's Kanha National Park and the tigers' powerful global allies tell us that the big cats will not survive without the deep involvement of those I saw working along the road.

On the Vietnam country office's environmental practice area electronic bulletin board, in 2001, Vern Weitzel suggested that Kanha's most significant innovation is a system for tracking the elusive predators. The system involves sophisticated software (to analyse pugmarks, each tiger's

[47] Sebastian Mallaby, *The World's Banker: A Story of Failed States, Financial Crises, and the Wealth and Poverty of Nations* (New York: Penguin Press, 2004).

[48] A. F. Robertson, *People and the State: An Anthropology of Planned Development* (Cambridge: Cambridge University Press, 1984), p. 19.

[49] *Measures for the Economic Development of Under-Developed Countries* (New York: United Nations, 1951), p. 32, quoted in Louis Emmerij, Richard Jolly, and Thomas G. Weiss, *Ahead of the Curve? UN Ideas and Global Challenges* (Bloomington, Ind.: Indiana University Press, 2001), p. 32.

fingerprints), but relies on the knowledge of people who live on the park's perimeter and have good reason to know each cat very well.[50] Two years later, UNDP initiated and funded a census of one of the world's largest tiger populations in the immense mangrove forest that straddles India and Bangladesh. It used the Kanha system, but involved local residents even more as primary stakeholders.[51] At the same time, the Programme began working with the World Wide Fund for Nature and the government of Bhutan to create another huge habitat, a 'green corridor' where deforestation, poaching, and the illegal trade in tiger parts are discouraged through investments in 'alternative energy sources, improved health services, and cottage industries'.[52]

UNDP's way of dealing with the tiger problem – empowering the people who live with them – should not be surprising. It reflects the policy direction in which the Programme and its predecessors had been moving for sixty years. It reflects the trajectory of UNDP's 'better way', the way in which the lesson of the First World War was gradually transformed into the UN network's distinctive approach to development.

---

[50] http://www.undp.org.vn/mlist/envirovlc/082001/post85.htm (accessed 8 Nov. 2004).

[51] UNDP News Bulletin, 'Bangladesh and India Start Joint Tiger Census', 14 Jan. 2004, http://www.undp.org/dpa/pressrelease/releases/2004/january/14jan04.html (accessed 8 Nov. 2004).

[52] Five Tigers, the Tiger Information Center, 'WWF, UNDP Join Forces to Conserve Nature, Reduce Poverty', 30 April 2003, http://www.5tigers.org/news/2003/April/03_4_30w.htm (accessed 8 Nov. 2004).

3

Institutions for practical solidarity

Despite the widespread agreement on the lesson of the world wars and on its applicability to relations between rich and poor countries, when the post-war UN started, few imagined that its Secretariat – the central bureau with headquarters in New York – would become so focused on development. The most powerful governments saw the institutions in New York as concerned, primarily, with matters of international high politics, in contrast to the World Bank (officially named the International Bank for Reconstruction and *Development*, IBRD) and the UN Specialized Agencies, where global inequalities might well be addressed. Yet, while it would take more than fifteen years for the Bank to put development at the centre of its portfolio, the UN Secretariat immediately started to focus on the issue, bringing the Specialized Agencies along. That is how UNDP became the centre of the UN's development network. This chapter is about the construction of that network from the end of the Second World War until the late 1960s.

The network grew through the efforts of the UN representatives from Asia and Latin America who worked alongside the economic staff of the Secretariat itself. Men and women in both groups had been schooled through participation in the Good Neighbor policy, the Middle East Supply Centre (MESC), UNRAA (UN Relief and Rehabilitation Administration), and, in a few cases, the League of Nations. In 1946, David Owen, UN Assistant Secretary-General and chief of the Economic Department of the Secretariat, brought the League's Folke Hilgerdt (one of the grandfathers of development economics) to head the department's major division concerned with 'economic stability and development'. At the first meetings of the Economic and Social Council (ECOSOC) and of the General Assembly, the Chinese delegation, conscious of how China had benefited from the League's only comprehensive technical assistance programme (a set of missions to China in the 1930s), joined Lebanon's Charles Malik (ECOSOC head and MESC alumnus) to propose the first UN technical assistance programme.

A multilateral approach, they argued, would help developing countries to resist the 'real danger for their economic independence' of relying solely on assistance from either of the increasingly hostile cold war superpowers.

This was the year when Truman, in response to congressional conservatives, pronounced UNRRA's death sentence, when the United States was focused on the 'efficiency' of the UN's few development operations. Truman's representatives in New York joined the Soviet Union's ambassador to water down the technical assistance resolution and give the Secretariat only a coordinating role, insisting that it rely on the Specialized Agencies to provide actual advice. Australia, Canada, Norway, and other countries that would become important aid donors also worried about giving ECOSOC too many functions for it to be effective and about the risk of duplicating the mandates of the Specialized Agencies within new bureaux of an expanding Secretariat.[1]

Because none of the Specialized Agencies was designed to provide technical assistance that might have been the end of the story. However, UNRRA's demise gave some of the agencies an injection of funds that led them to an interest in development.[2] The Secretariat also convinced the majority of members that it needed its own technical assistance capacity in order to provide for 'the continuation of the urgent and important advisory functions in the field of social welfare' to the countries that had previously received assistance under UNRRA.[3]

The coalition in support of a larger UN role included the persuasive voices of governments that had experienced Roosevelt's Good Neighbor policy and then became significant contributors to UNRRA and the early work of the UN. When the Brazilian ambassador rose at the November 1946 session of the General Assembly's economic committee to support a

---

[1] Mahyar Nashat, *National Interests and Bureaucracy versus Development Aid: A Study of the United Nations Expanded Programme for Technical Assistance to the Third World* (Geneva: Tribune Editions, 1978), pp. 8–10.

[2] Sixten Heppling, *UNDP: From Agency Shares to Country Programmes, 1949–1975* (Stockholm: Ministry of Foreign Affairs, 1995), pp. 13–15, surveys the extent to which the Specialized Agencies were prepared to do technical assistance. WHO was the first with a constitutional mandate to do so, but only beginning in 1949. Hugh L. Keenleyside, *International Aid: A Summary with Special Reference to the Programmes of the United Nations* (New York: James H. Heinemann, 1966), p. 111, notes that FAO sent advisory missions to Greece, Poland, Thailand, and Nicaragua in 1946. These increased in 1947 when FAO received funds from the disbanding UNRRA.

[3] Yonah Alexander, *International Technical Assistance Experts: A Case Study in UN Experience* (New York: Praeger, 1966), p. 5.

Secretariat-based technical assistance programme to Asia and the Americas, he represented a country that had, for two years, given nearly 1 per cent of its national income to UNRRA for war-ravaged Europe, a record of solidarity that few states have ever matched.[4] Similarly, relying on his own prestige and the new interest in development of some of the agencies, Haiti's Emile Saint-Lot, one of the drafters of the 1948 Universal Declaration of Human Rights, worked with the Secretariat throughout the same year to organize the UN system's first multiple-agency technical assistance mission. Experts from Owen's division, the Food and Agriculture Organization (FAO), the International Monetary Fund (IMF), UNESCO (the Educational, Scientific, and Cultural Organization), and the World Health Organization (WHO) travelled to Haiti to pilot the kind of programme that had been debated in the UN's first sessions.[5] When the Soviets, the United States, Australia, or the Europeans complained about the explosion of programmes in the developing world, many of the original 'United Nations' responded, as Brazil's Roberto Oliveria de Campos did in 1948, that Latin Americans had supported UNRRA, but 'European recovery meant that their own children's needs were now as, or more pressing than those in Europe'.[6]

Over the summer that year Owen's office gave UN members a book detailing ten sources of *Technical Assistance Available through the United Nations and the Specialized Agencies*. The publication was as more an act of agenda-setting than a reflection of real capacity. The FAO and International Labour Organisation had yet to return to Europe from their temporary headquarters in Washington and Montreal respectively. The IMF was in the book, due to its role in the Haiti mission. The World Bank (IBRD) was listed, even though, up to that point, its attention remained fixed on its first task, reconstruction. Even the International Trade Organization, which never came into existence, was

[4] United Nations, *Summary of the Meetings of the Second Committee of the General Assembly, First Session, Second Part* (Lake Success, N.Y.: United Nations, 1946), p. 89 (actual debate: 20 Nov. 1946), hereafter, listed by session and sub-session number, date of the actual debate, and page number. Earlier, Brazil claimed that its government had given 10 per cent of its national income to UNRRA, a claim not challenged in the debate, *Second Committee* 1.1, 25 Jan. 1946, p. 12. Authoritative figures can be found in UNRRA, *Report of the Director General to the Council* (Washington, D.C.: UNRRA, 1947), p. 55.
[5] United Nations Mission of Technical Assistance to Haiti, *Mission to Haiti: Report* (Lake Success, N.Y.: United Nations, 1949).
[6] Maggie Black, *The Children and the Nations: The Story of UNICEF* (New York: UNICEF, 1986), p. 75.

listed as one of the nine Specialized Agencies ready to provide assistance![7]

A few months later the General Assembly provided a legal foundation for this vision in Resolution 200 (III) of 4 December 1948. Sixten Heppling, one of the early champions of Sweden's generous aid policy (one of those who helped secure his country's commitment to the original 1 per cent aid target), describes the support for this resolution and the one, eight months later, that created UNDP's predecessor, the Expanded Programme of Technical Assistance (EPTA) as 'a personal triumph for David Owen'.

Heppling describes Owen as EPTA's 'midwife',[8] yet, Truman, by reversing his immediate post-war policy of resistance to multilateral aid programmes, also played a lead role. His address at his January 1949 inauguration gave Owen and other advocates of a major UN technical assistance role the opportunity they had not had before. The US president outlined a four-point programme to tackle what he perceived as the major global problems, especially the growing assertiveness of the Soviet Union. Truman's celebrated 'Point Four' was a pledge to assist the underdeveloped countries through 'a co-operative enterprise in which all nations work together through the United Nations and its Specialized Agencies wherever practicable'.[9]

What led to Truman's change of mind? One official close to the drafting of the speech says that Point Four was put in as a rhetorical afterthought, something to make the whole new cold war programme sound more coherent and weighty, 'a public-relations gimmick, thrown in by a professional speech-writer to give the speech more life'.[10] Even so, Truman's desire for an additional plank to his global platform gave long-serving members of his government a chance to revive some of Roosevelt's policies to which they had been so committed. In the more than two years since Churchill's 'Iron Curtain' speech, it had become clear that 'The policy of getting along with Moscow would no longer work, and the effort to make it work threatened disaster. China was turning hostile. In Latin America the bloom was off the Good-Neighbor

[7] *Technical Assistance Available through the United Nations and the Specialized Agencies* (Lake Success, N.Y.: United Nations Department of Economic Affairs Division of Economic Stability and Development, September 1948), pp. 100–1.

[8] Heppling, *UNDP*, p. 20.   [9] Quoted in ibid., p. 23.

[10] Louis J. Halle, 'On Teaching International Relations', *Virginia Quarterly Review*, 40, 1 (winter 1964): 17. The article's title is unrevealing. Halle was a State Department official and co-author of the idea of providing technical assistance world-wide.

Policy.' US policy planners were at a loss over how to shape a new grand strategy in the face of the unexpected conflict with their wartime ally.[11] The opportunity to add a 'Point Four', like the commitment to European recovery that led to the Marshall Plan, allowed the lesson of the First World War, the lesson behind the Good Neighbor policy and UNRRA's 'better way', to continue to shape US policy even in the context of its growing hostility to the Soviet Union. As the same State Department officer put it, 'In 1948, the [US] Government had for some years been conducting programs of technical assistance in Latin America, and only there. It seemed reasonable that this novel way of conducting international relations might have its uses elsewhere in the world.'[12]

In 1949 Truman's UN delegation 'quickly took and retained an initiative in the process' of creating the EPTA, while Owen used the opening created by US interest to push through his idea for a centralized voluntary fund within the Secretariat that would then contract out both to the Specialized Agencies and to the Secretariat's own technical assistance group.[13] Coordinating everything at the country level would be a representative, in residence, of the Secretary-General. That is to say, each Resident would actually represent the Secretary-General's deputy, Owen, a role already being piloted in Haiti by his British colleague, Arthur Wakefield.

Robert Jackson would later claim that this innovation was something that Owen borrowed from the Middle East Supply Centre, 'Resident Representatives, what were they? Nothing more than my country representatives of MESC. I mean, they're merely carrying on that concept.'[14]

This may sound like an overstatement, but it is clear that Jackson had been helping Owen to think about what structures for an expanded UN development role would be feasible and effective from the first days of the organization. A '"strictly confidential" note on the possible reorganization of the Secretariat', written by either Owen or Jackson (who also served directly under the Secretary-General) probably in mid-1947, points to the lack of effective coordination among the Specialized Agencies and between New York's economic and social departments. In the note two alternative structures are suggested; both have Jackson in charge of social and economic affairs, with the power to corral the Specialized Agencies to support a development agenda. Owen would be

[11] Ibid., at 12.   [12] Ibid., at 15.   [13] Heppling, *UNDP*, p. 23–41, quotation from p. 23.
[14] Robert G. A. Jackson, Transcripts of interviews, 1990, Oxford, Bodleian Library, MS Eng. c. 4678, fos. 58–9.

the UN's chief executive officer under Secretary-General Trygve Lie as a sort of weak chairman of the board. That was wishful thinking, but that kind of speculative planning made it easy for a vacationing Owen to respond when he received Lie's urgent post-'Point Four' cable:

TECHNICAL ASSISTANCE DEVELOPMENTS HERE MAKE DAVID OWEN'S IMMEDIATE RETURN IMPERATIVE — STOP —[15]

Just a year after Truman's speech, an operational EPTA was a reality. ECOSOC and the General Assembly had passed enabling resolutions. The United States had agreed to provide more than half the funds. The UN had raised the rest from other wealthy nations, and had launched programmes in a score of countries and Resident Representatives in Iran and Pakistan (as well as in Haiti). By 1952, there were Res Reps in fifteen countries. Due to a slight restructuring of the Secretariat, by then they reported jointly to Owen, in his new role as executive chairman of the Technical Assistance Board (UNTAB, the governing body for the EPTA), and to Hugh Keenleyside, the head of the Secretariat's original technical assistance programme. By 1958 there were Res Reps in forty-five countries and by 1966 there were seventy-two, and the numbers continued to grow as more nations gained their independence.[16]

In May 1949 the UN Secretariat's programme had grown large enough (and it was sure to expand, given the Point Four initiative) that Owen had sought out Raúl Prebisch, the Argentine economist who had so impressed architects of the Good Neighbor policy, to be the UN technical assistance head. Prebisch, who had already been tapped by Owen's boss to head the new Economic Commission for Latin America (ECLA), said to Owen, 'Tell Trygve Lie that I would accept whatever he likes. If he wants me to come to New York, to this new institution, I would go. If he likes me to stay as ECLA Executive Secretary, I will accept.' Lie quickly (and typically, for Lie was not the greatest of managers) chose to keep Prebisch in Latin America.[17] Arguably, this was one of the most unfortunate decisions in the history of the UN's development network: Lie's decision

[15] Both documents are in Box 1 of the David Owen Papers, Columbia University Library, New York (hereafter Owen Papers).

[16] Adriano Garcia, *International Cooperation and Development: The United Nations Development Programme Resident Representative System* (Quezon City: University of the Philippines Law Center, 1982), p. 209. Alexander, *International Technical Assistance Experts*, p. 20.

[17] David Pollok, Daniel Kerner, and Joseph Love, 'Raúl Prebisch on ECLAC's Achievements and Deficiencies: An Unpublished Interview', *CEPAL Review*, 75 (December 2001): 12.

meant that the UN failed to set the precedent that Prebisch's appointment would have set. Owen soon found the competent and genial Keenleyside, a Canadian diplomat, to take the job, and he, like Owen and their successors, was a smart manager, creative, and deeply committed to development, from one of the most important donor countries. But his appointment meant rejecting the principle that the UN's development chief should be one of the most respected economists from the developing world.

Development finance and the Special Fund

Owen had sought Prebisch out because of the similarity of Owen's own views to those expressed in Prebisch's hastily written Introduction to the first ECLA *Economic Survey of Latin America*. Officially, the Secretariat had distanced itself from the report. Headquarters quickly informed ECLA that 'The report is a document with a great content. But it speaks about development, industrialization, terms of trade, and many other things that ECLA is not supposed to deal with.'[18]

Unofficially, Owen saw in Prebisch a kindred spirit. The Introduction made the same arguments that his office had been making since the UN began: the Secretariat needed to be able to focus on the problem of development, and the solution to that problem had at least three elements: *skills, resources,* and *institutions* or, in other words, *technical assistance* (providing the brains and books needed to transform less industrialized societies); *financial assistance* to pay for the necessary infrastructure (the bricks and boards); and a proper *institutional environment* both domestically and globally (including a global trade system that would maintain or improve the terms of trade enjoyed by the developing world).

From the late 1960s until the end of the century, much of the intergovernmental debate about development focused on the failure to develop proper institutional environments, first at a global level (the issue that would become Prebisch's overriding concern), then at a national one. However, in the 1950s the question of inadequate financing was the one that sparked the most discussion.

At the beginning, Owen and the Secretariat played a central role in the debate. Later, UNDP's first Administrator, Paul Hoffman, played the

---

[18] Ibid., at 11. Prebisch notes that the original cable he is quoting 'does not exist [either] in New York or Santiago [at ECLAC headquarters]', a consequence of a UN policy of regularly destroying key documents, one of the banes of anyone who attempts to write the history of the organization.

decisive part in ending the debate, and in the process created the Special Fund, which he headed until it merged with EPTA to form UNDP in 1966.

The end of the debate was also marked by the creation of the International Development Authority (IDA), the 'concessional' or 'soft' (that is, lower-than-market-rate) loan facility within the World Bank, an agency dominated by the developed countries and, ultimately, by the United States. In fact, creating the Special Fund contributed to Hoffman's larger goal of gaining US support for a well-endowed development finance facility, even if it was within the World Bank, a goal Owen's part of the Secretariat had also been pursuing throughout the 1950s. However, it was that same power structure within the Bank that had led developing countries to push, instead, for a financing authority within the one-nation, one-vote United Nations, a 'Special United Nations Fund for Economic Development'– SUNFED.

At UNDP's birth Hugh Keenleyside called the earlier IDA/Special Fund compromise a 'sop' for those who had championed SUNFED.[19] Similarly, in Owen's announcement of the Special Fund to the directors general of the Specialized Agencies he pointedly noted that the United States and most of the other powerful aid donors 'see the proposed new development as an extension of technical assistance'.[20] Owen wrote even more candidly to his Resident Representative in Iran, one of EPTA's largest offices,

> Doubtless you have heard of the new US initiative which is, of course . . . a tactical alternative to SUNFED . . . The question now arises whether the SUNFED crusaders are willing to hold off for a little while in view of the new US offer.[21]

The adamant view of the major donors, the immediate and deep collaboration between EPTA and the Special Fund, and contemporary statements by Keenleyside, Owen, and Hoffman suggest that the Secretariat's view, from the beginning, was that the two programmes would become one, that the Special Fund would simply expand EPTA's capabilities. The seven-year delay between the resolution establishing the Fund in late 1958 and that establishing UNDP in late 1965 was only a matter of waiting for a decent interval to save the face of those who regarded the Fund as 'SUNFED in embryo'.[22]

---

[19] Keenleyside, *International Aid*, p. 263.   [20] 31 Dec. 1951, Owen Papers, Box 27.
[21] Owen to Arthur Goldschmidt, 14 Nov. 1957, Owen Papers, Box 7.
[22] Owen in the same letter to the Executive Directors, Owen Papers, Box 27.

Nonetheless, it was the SUNFED coalition in the General Assembly, working in collaboration with Owen's group within the Secretariat, that kept an international development financing agency on the agenda long enough for the World Bank's IDA to be created and, therefore, for the second plank of the multilateral development system imagined by Prebisch, Owen, and many others to be put in place.

The Special Fund's story begins at the end of 1948, when a precocious 33-year-old West Indian economist, W. Arthur Lewis, who had recently been awarded a chair at the University of Manchester, introduced himself to Owen.[23] Like Prebisch, Lewis had been writing about the *skills, financing,* and *institutions* triad for almost a decade, as a small part of his larger work for the British government and the Fabian Society on social policy and colonial development.[24]

A little more than a year later, under pressure from the Asian and Latin American UN members, Owen put together a team charged with suggesting what the UN could do about the global problem of underdevelopment. He made George Hakim, one of the Lebanese MESC alumni, and Lewis responsible for drafting the report. As Lewis later explained,

> We were informed that many member nations of the United Nations view with great uneasiness the increasing disparity between the developed and the undeveloped world . . . They would like to see the gap between income per capita in say, Western Europe, on the one hand, and say, India on the other hand, narrow instead of widen every day as it does at present. This is why we asked what it would cost to bring about a rate of increase in the underdeveloped world comparable with that in Western Europe.[25]

The answer was to have incomes in the developing world grow rapidly, and more rapidly in (say) India than in western Europe. That would require more than just technical assistance, Lewis's report argued. It would require financing, at least US$10 billion a year, money that was unlikely to come either from private direct investment or from commercial lenders.

This conclusion was far from unexpected. It was the reason why India's V. K. R. V. Rao, one of Keynes's students, had put the issue of creating

---

[23] Letter from Folke Hilgerdt to W. Arthur Lewis, 28 Dec. 1948, W. Arthur Lewis Papers, Box 6, Seeley G. Mudd Manuscript Library, Princeton University. Used by Permission of Princeton University Library.   [24] See chapter 5.

[25] W. Arthur Lewis, 'United Nations Primer for Development: Comment', *Quarterly Journal of Economics,* 67, 2 (May 1953): 267.

a soft-loan facility on the UN agenda in 1949.[26] Others working on the problem had come up with figures in the same range. Walter Reuther of the North American United Auto Workers union, an important collaborator in the Good Neighbor policy, concluded that US$13 billion was the US share that needed to be given in aid to narrow the global gaps. The range, from a variety of sources, was from 2 to 5 per cent of the income of the developed countries.[27]

Armed with these astonishing figures that suggested needs in the order of five or ten times the amounts transferred annually under the Marshall Plan, Lewis and another expert from the UN team (another future economics Nobel laureate), Theodore Schultz, went to the IBRD president, Eugene Black. They argued that the Bank should expand development lending to at least US$1 billion a year. Black brushed them aside. Radically increasing the financing available to the developing world would, in one way or another, have to mean lending at concessional rates. That would jeopardize Black's primary goal: ensuring that Wall Street saw the Bank's bonds as sound investments.[28]

With that, the debate moved back to the United Nations. In the autumn 1951 General Assembly session, a two-to-one majority approved a resolution empowering a panel to determine how to create SUNFED. Mike Mansfield, one of the US delegates, who would later become Speaker of the US House of Representatives, told his UN colleagues,

> As a member of the Congress of the United States, I am positive that I am correctly reflecting the prevailing opinion in that body when I say that the United States is not prepared to commit itself to any such action either now or in the foreseeable future.[29]

Yet, at the same time, Richard N. Gardner (who would become John F. Kennedy's Deputy Assistant Secretary of State for International Organization Affairs after writing what is still the classic history of the creation of the UN's economic institutions[30]) called the SUNFED resolution the

---

[26] John Toye and Richard Toye, *The UN and Global Political Economy: Trade, Finance, and Development* (Bloomington, Ind.: Indiana University Press, 2004), p. 172.

[27] Devesh Kapur, John B. Lewis, and Richard Webb, *The World Bank: Its First Half-Century* (Washington, D.C.: Brookings Institution Press, 1997), p. 91.

[28] Kapur, Lewis, and Webb, *The World Bank*, p. 11.

[29] Robert E. Elder and Forrest D. Murden, *Economic Cooperation, Special United Nations Fund for Economic Development (SUNFED)* (New York: Woodrow Wilson Foundation, 1954), p. 5.

[30] Richard N. Gardner, *Sterling–Dollar Diplomacy: Anglo-American Collaboration in the Reconstruction of Multilateral Trade* (Oxford: Oxford University Press, 1956).

'most serious UN defeat' that the United States had ever suffered, a significant challenge to its global leadership.[31]

The debate over creating a multilateral institution for financing development remained heated throughout the early 1950s, especially in the United States. In spring 1953 the new US president, Dwight Eisenhower, argued that funds saved through disarmament if the cold war wound down should be transferred to development assistance, while an article by the US Chamber of Commerce and the National Association of Manufacturers referred to 'SUNFED – Your Name on a Blank Check'.[32]

At the autumn session of the General Assembly, three of the governments that had benefited the most from the first few years of UN technical assistance – Greece, Haiti, and Pakistan – attempted to find a compromise. At one meeting, Haiti's Ernest Chauvet turned to the US representative and said that the UN had become

> a club in which sixty members were playing poker . . . one winner remained in the game . . . the only way to continue was for the winner to redistribute some of the chips to the other players. The United States, at present, . . . had all the money and the underdeveloped countries had none. Obviously, the winner could get up and walk out.

However, if the United States still believed in the 'gospel' of Roosevelt's Four Freedoms, it would ensure that the game would go on.[33]

If nothing else, the debating game *did* continue. The outlines of an effective compromise did not appear until 1956. Earlier, the General Assembly had authorized an intergovernmental committee to analyse a variety of questions about SUNFED, including identification of the broad areas in which its investments should be made. In that context Argentina proposed a plan for regional training centres and special surveys of natural resources, 'a special fund for regional cooperation'.[34] The Argentine proposal, in turn, reflected a 1955 mid-decade evaluation of EPTA, the 'Forward Look Study', which concluded that EPTA, to date, had been 'essentially a long-range educational programme'. What was needed, in addition, was a programme of larger grants-in-aid based on 'needs arising from EPTA', a programme that could build on the

---

[31] Elder and Murden, *Economic Cooperation*, p. 5.   [32] Ibid., p. 13.

[33] United Nations, *Summary Record of the Meetings of the Second Committee of the General Assembly Eighth Session* (New York: United Nations, 1953), pp. 127, 131.

[34] James Patrick Sewell, *Functionalism and World Politics, A Study Based on United Nations Programs Financing Economic Development* (Princeton, N.J.: Princeton University Press, 1966), p. 111.

capacities that EPTA had created in many countries. The programme would fund geological surveys, training institutes, and other long-term activities.[35]

In the meantime, the US-led coalition of developed countries opposing SUNFED was showing sign of strain. The Netherlands, the Soviet Union, and Czechoslovakia, which were by that time significant contributors to UN technical assistance, had all become part of the SUNFED bloc.[36]

Into the breach stepped the Marshall Plan's former Administrator, Paul Hoffmann. Long a friend of Eisenhower (he had been the chief fundraiser for his first campaign) and immensely optimistic about the prospects for development in Asia and Latin America (based on the Marshall Plan's remarkable success in Europe), Hoffman joined the US delegation to the UN from 1956 to 1958.

By early 1957 he had developed a plan. He placed an article in the *New York Times Magazine*. It elaborated on (without crediting) the Argentine proposal and the 'Forward Look'. 'Blueprint for Foreign Aid' called for an experimental fund to be used for raw material surveys and for a limited number of financial projects.[37] At the same time, Hoffman began lobbying those fellow Republicans in Congress and in the business community who were reluctant to establish a multilateral financing agency. He urged them to support a soft-loan facility (the IDA) within the World Bank, whose voting procedures would give the United States a preponderant voice in the allocation of any loans. Finally, as part of his lobbying effort, Hoffman appealed to congressional representatives from farm states, many of them traditionally conservative and isolationist, with the suggestion that international versions of the ancient food-for-work programmes be greatly expanded, both the United States' own programmes and a new multilateral programme. This had been an attractive part of the original SUNFED proposal. The expansion would, not incidentally, also justify the maintenance of high US farm subsidies, which were beginning to generate huge, politically troublesome, food surpluses.[38]

[35] Adriano Garcia, *International Cooperation and Development: The United Nations Development Programme Resident Representative System* (Quezon City: University of the Philippines Law Center, 1982), p. 158.

[36] Sewell, *Functionalism and World Politics*, p. 289.

[37] Paul G. Hoffman, 'Blueprint for Foreign Aid', *New York Times Magazine* (17 Feb. 1957): 9, 38–43.

[38] Ibid.; Sewell, *Functionalism and World Politics*, p. 113. Hoffman's biographer, Alan R. Raucher, provides a concise account of Hoffman's work on SUNFED, the Special Fund, and the IDA, *Paul G. Hoffman: Architect of Foreign Aid* (Lexington, Ky.: University of Kentucky Press, 1985), pp. 125–32.

3.1 Paul G. Hoffman at the Special Fund

Working parallel to Hoffman, but with greater influence on the Democrats rather than the Republicans, was the Secretariat's Hans W. Singer. He had been Keynes's student (working alongside V. K. R. V. Rao), became Lewis's friend, and was Owen's confidant. (They had worked together in the 1930s and Singer was the first person Owen asked to join him at the UN.[39]) Singer's primary accomplishment in the 1950s is often considered to be his design of the World Food Programme (WFP), whose political engineers were the later US presidential candidates George McGovern and, to a lesser extent, Hubert Humphrey.[40] However, Singer was also involved with the Secretariat's side of the SUNFED debate from the beginning, and he helped Dag Hammarskjöld, the second

[39] Hans W. Singer, interview with the author (CNM), 8 July 2005.
[40] D. John Shaw, *The UN World Food Programme and the Development of Food Aid* (Houndmills: Palgrave, 2001), pp. 6–18, 32.

UN Secretary-General, when he lobbied the World Bank to expand its development facilities.[41]

Singer was also a seemingly inexhaustible fountain of ideas pouring over Owen from 1946 (when the UN economic chief convinced his pre-war employer, the University of Glasgow, to second Singer to New York) until both men left the organization in the late 1960s.

Characteristically, when the Special Fund was in its infancy Singer sent Owen a paper linking 'pre-investment', the concept Hoffman used (and Singer invented[42]) to distinguish the role of the nascent organization, with the new theory of development articulated in a series of Cambridge lectures by W. W. Rostow, an advisor to Senator Kennedy. At the first of Rostow's five 'Stages of Development', 'Traditional Society', Singer argued that governments needed broad assessments of resources to help shape sensible requests for technical assistance. At the next stage (the 'Transitional Stage'), surveys of specific resources and the development of large industrial projects, the basis of requests for large investment, would be desirable. At the stage of 'Take-off', investigations into potential macroeconomic bottlenecks and the design of critical investments to reduce them were essential. In short, the combination of Singer's and Rostow's ideas would provide a persuasive argument for building on EPTA's capacity and for convincing major donors and the World Bank that extensive development financing could be used soundly.[43]

John and Richard Toye's history of UN contributions to global economics argues that Singer's attempt to link Rostow's modernization theory to the work of EPTA and the Special Fund was a way of making the best of the 'Pyrrhic victory' that 'the developing countries and their supporters within the UN Secretariat' won with the IDA/Special Fund compromise.[44] The limited 'victory' may have been especially bittersweet to Singer, who, as one of the most public of the Secretariat's advocates of SUNFED, had been made the subject of 'a campaign of character assassination' by the 'extreme right wing' of Congress and some in the US press. Singer confided to Owen,

> The devil of it is, of course, that one not only *feels* defenceless, but *is* defenceless. Having given one's soul and 10 years to the UN and the problems of poor countries, there is probably little else that one can now do.[45]

---

[41] Hans W. Singer, Foreword to Shaw, *The UN World Food Programme*, p. ix; Shaw, p. 27.

[42] Hans W. Singer, Interview for the UN Intellectual History Project, 26 Aug. 1997, Graduate Center, City University of New York.

[43] Hans W. Singer, 'Stages of Development and Preinvestment Activities', mimeo, n.d., Owen Papers, Box 24.   [44] Toye and Toye, *The UN and Global Political Economy*, p. 174.

[45] Quoted in ibid., p. 173 (emphasis in original).

Singer would be far from the last Secretariat official to feel the same way.

Nevertheless, the Secretariat and the developing nations *had* succeeded in creating a multilateral development financing facility. As the World Bank's Eugene Black readily admitted, the IDA was 'an idea to offset the urge for SUNFED'.[46] Moreover, the Special Fund's 'preinvestment' activities would shape much of the investment carried out by the IDA. The Special Fund, in turn, was very much a reflection of the ideas and people that had been part of the Secretariat's development work from the beginning. When Hoffman, the inevitable choice as the Special Fund's chief executive, first assembled his core staff after the passage of the enabling General Assembly resolution in October 1958, he introduced his deputy, W. Arthur Lewis. '*My job*,' Hoffman told them, 'is to *raise* the money. *Your job* is to *spend* it, the way *Lewis* tells you to.'[47]

Money, people, and skills: how the programmes did their job

Hoffman's original *New York Times Magazine* article envisioned the preinvestment fund as an extension of EPTA, which is largely what it became. Large-scale development finance was handled elsewhere, by the IDA and by the bilateral aid programmes of major donors. The question of establishing the proper global and domestic institutional environments for development would continue to engage the UN for decades, but the UN's operational activities would be limited to influencing domestic institutional environments, largely indirectly, through the technical assistance it provided via UNDP.

The 'Special Fund', with its name that echoed SUNFED, certainly served an important rhetorical purpose, but much of what Hoffman did at the beginning of his seven-year transitional administration anticipated the Fund's merger with EPTA. Hoffman began his tenure with a gracious letter to Owen saying that a major consideration in accepting the Special Fund job was 'the opportunity afforded to work in close association with you in assisting the emerging nations'.[48] The Special Fund chief made Owen, Dag Hammarskjöld, and the World Bank president Eugene Black his 'Consultative Board',[49] a relationship that, in operational terms, affected Owen much more than the others. The Fund shared EPTA's New York headquarters and a 'Joint Administration Division', under Bruce Stedman

---

[46] Quoted in Kapur, Lewis, and Webb, *The World Bank: Its First Half-Century*, p. 155.
[47] Hoffman's words recalled by Bruce Stedman, interview with CNM, 3 Feb. 2005.
[48] Hoffman to Owen, 1 Dec. 1958, Owen Papers, Box 8.
[49] Garcia, *International Cooperation and Development*, p. 163.

who had been with EPTA since the early 1950s. In 1961 the Resident Representatives formally became 'Directors of Special Fund Programmes' at the country level, a role many already played in an ad hoc way.[50]

The main difference between the two programmes was that EPTA assigned a target funding level to each country, which the Resident Representative, the government, and, ultimately, the Technical Assistance Board then allocated to a range of projects that brought foreign experts into the country or sent nationals abroad for training. In contrast, the Special Fund had no system of predetermined authorizations to specific countries or regions. The Fund's more costly resource surveys and background studies for capital investments involved groups of experts. They could be managed centrally, with the UN country offices serving as agents for country proposals rather than as shapers and evaluators of a particular country's whole technical assistance programme.[51] Nonetheless, because (as Singer's 'Pre-investment' paper had anticipated) many Special Fund projects arose out of earlier, EPTA-financed, technical assistance work, the centralizing tendency of the Fund and the decentralizing tendency of EPTA were never pure and rarely led to conflict.[52]

By 1962, the decent interval had passed and ECOSOC and the General Assembly began discussing the merger. The Specialized Agencies (which had a vested interest in decentralization, as discussed at the end of this chapter) tended to oppose the merger, as did the Soviet bloc (fearing the domination of the combined agency by the United States). Many developing nations demanded that the possibility of a UN-based development financing facility be kept alive, which led to the establishment of the symbolically significant UN Capital Development Fund (CDF) at the same time as UNDP.[53] In 1964, ECOSOC and the new UN Secretary-General, U Thant of Burma, endorsed the merger and embraced the expedient of having a group of 'objective experts' recommend what should be done. They returned their report in February 1965, the General Assembly passed the enabling resolution in November, and UNDP officially came to life on 1 January 1966.[54]

---

[50] Sewell, *Functionalism and World Politics*, p. 185.

[51] Alexander, *International Technical Assistance Experts*, p. 46.   [52] Heppling, *UNDP*, p. 66.

[53] The CDF only became operational in the 1970s and has remained a small, but more than just symbolically important, part of the UN development network. See p. 165, below.

[54] Heppling, *UNDP*, pp. 66–71. Gerard T. Mangone, coordinator, 'Maxwell School Recommendations on the Merger of the UN Special Fund and Expanded Programme of Technical Assistance', Maxwell School of Citizenship and Public Affairs, Syracuse University, 15 Feb. 1965, Owen Papers, Box 27.

Money

Paul Hoffman, soon to turn 75, became UNDP's 'Administrator' (reviving his Marshall Plan title) while the younger David Owen, as Margaret Joan Anstee complains, 'had to play second fiddle, a poor reward for having created the network of Resident Representatives and built the Programme from scratch'.[55] Owen was given the title of UNDP 'Co-administrator', but had little specific authority after the two programmes were fully merged, a process that took about three years. In 1969 Owen left the UN, and died shortly thereafter, of an unexpected and tragic heart attack in the summer of 1970.

Co-administrator was, indeed, a strange place for Owen to end up. However, as one of UNDP's most reflective senior officers, Robert England, reminds us, 'The golden rule applies to the international community, as elsewhere: "Whoever has the gold makes the rules".'[56] There are important exceptions, but the rule does explain the choice of Hoffmann, who had one set of outstanding skills, over Owen, who had another. US contributions financed more than half of EPTA outlays from 1949 until the merger, and at least an equal proportion of the outlays of the Special Fund.[57] In that context it made sense to have someone from the United States as Administrator. Contributions to UNDP were voluntary, and its Administrator's first job, like that of the president of a private foundation or university, was to secure those contributions. It was important to have someone trusted by the chief donor, and Hoffman, the Marshall Plan hero, had the trust of the US Congress and of President Johnson.

[55] Margaret Joan Anstee, *Never Learn to Type: A Woman at the United Nations* (Chichester: John Wiley & Sons, 2003), p. 216. Anstee recalls Hoffman to have been 'in his eighties', an overestimate.

[56] J. K. Robert England, 'Caught in the Crossfire: The Continuing Conundrum of UNDP', typescript, 24 July 2003, p. 3.

[57] Calculated from Tables 3 and 5 in *The UN in Iran, a Compendium of United Nations Activities in Iran 1950–1965* (Tehran: Office of the United Nations Development Programme in Iran, January 1966), pp. 25, 27. Accurate statistics on the actual outlays and revenues of UNDP and its predecessors are notoriously difficult to come by. The Programme's long-time official historian, Ruben Mendez, 'was unsuccessful in getting the data, and the finance people said they had records only going back to recent years'. Mendez 'found this hard to believe', but could discover few figures that matched across a series of tables beyond those for the 1940s (personal correspondence, Mendez to CNM, 27 Jan. 2005). In the compilation cited above, US contributions to the Special Fund during 1965, from Table 5, would be equal to more than 100 per cent of outlays, from Table 3. This may be correct. A recurrent problem of EPTA, the Special Fund, and UNDP has been the inability to 'programme', to make expenditures in the field, as rapidly as funds have been pledged. This is the flipside of the Programme's recurrent financial crises. See pp. 142, 158.

Nevertheless, while Hoffman may have become UNDP's most effective fundraiser, it was Owen who, before Hoffman arrived, had figured out the basic mechanisms that would assure the Programme's financial survival.

First, it was essential to remain in constant dialogue with the US Congress, not just the executive branch, something Owen learned from the Programme's first financial crisis in 1953. At the time congressional conservatives had got wind of the fact that EPTA had assigned thirteen technicians from Iron Curtain countries to countries outside the Soviet bloc. 'US money', the representatives concluded, was being used to 'spread doctrines inimical to this nation', hence EPTA's funding had to be cut. While the seditious technicians turned out to be refugees with no interest in returning to their home countries and the Eisenhower administration convinced Congress to restore the appropriation, doing so took a long time, and Owen was faced with the unpleasant task of cutting EPTA's administrative costs by some 20 per cent almost overnight.[58] Such misunderstandings were not worth risking in the future.

Given the funding gap that temporarily remained even after the problem had been resolved, Owen became even more convinced of a second lesson: EPTA needed to find alternative, reliable, and growing sources of funds. The United States had even set a timetable. It had pledged to provide 60 per cent of EPTA's funds through 1953, but the figure would gradually decrease to 50 per cent in 1958. Moreover, in 1955, a US official with great sympathy for the Programme had pointed out that while,

> . . . on the basis of relative strength and ability to pay, the United States might expect to be assessed one-half of the budget of the United Nations, one-third has been accepted by the General Assembly . . . on the principle that . . . no permanent international organization should be unduly dependent for its financial support on any one nation.[59]

The General Assembly precedent ensured that the US contribution would continue to decline. (In 2004, it stood at 11.7 per cent of UNDP's core resources.[60])

In searching for new, reliable contributions that were likely to grow, Owen targeted the Scandinavian countries, especially those that had been

---

[58] Kathleen McLaughlin, *New Life in Old Lands* (New York: Dodd, Mead, 1954), p. 263. Memo from David Owen to Trygve Lie, 16 Nov. 1953, Owen Papers, Box 11.

[59] Johanna von Goeckingk, *United Nations Technical Assistance Board: A Case Study in International Administration* (New York: Woodrow Wilson Foundation, 1955), p. 17.

[60] Calculated from *United Nations Development Programme Annual Report 2005* (New York: UNDP, 2005), pp. 40–1.

occupied by the Nazis: Denmark and Norway. He paid less attention to donors to EPTA that ranked immediately behind the United States: the United Kingdom, Canada, and France, whose proportions of UN voluntary funding were less likely to grow. Owen first visited Denmark, Norway, and Sweden in 1952.[61] He took with him the 'better way' argument: that the war had been fought to create a more decent world where states whose people were rich took on material responsibilities towards those whose people were poor. Moreover, the extent of a state's commitments to others was a sign of recovery, strength, and success.

This turned out to be a good strategy. Arguments about international solidarity were extremely salient in Scandinavia in the early 1950s, and they remained so long after reconstruction.[62] Those arguments were constantly reinforced by the main political parties, the Church, and many secular institutions. Over time, democratic states with high domestic social welfare expenditures (for example, those whose core political contests pit a welfare-oriented Christian democratic party against an equally welfare-oriented socialist or social democratic party, as is the case throughout Scandinavia) proved to be those that give the most generously to poorer people in other lands.[63] By 1963, citizens of Denmark, the Netherlands, Norway, Sweden, and Switzerland were already giving more to international development efforts on a per capita basis than the United States.[64] Sweden, the Federal Republic of Germany, and the Netherlands were three of the Special Fund's top five donors, and in EPTA's last year as a separate programme, West Germany and Denmark had become two of its top five.[65]

Moreover, since the 1940s there has been what social scientists like to call a 'strong socialization effect' that regularly adds new donors to the club of the most generous. Some of the most open-handed donors of the 1990s included 'Ireland and Finland [who] started giving foreign aid

---

[61] Peter Brunbech, 'UN Policy, New Markets, Burden-Sharing, and Altruism: Danish Development Policy and Aid from 1949', unpublished paper, University of Aarhus Institute of History and Area Studies, August 2004, p. 11. The paper was not written for publication; the research in the paper will appear in the author's forthcoming doctoral dissertation.

[62] In Sweden, at the beginning of the 1970s, 84 per cent of survey respondents agreed with the statement, 'We should help the developing countries because it is a matter of showing solidarity with other people', which was by far the most widely agreed justification. Stig Lindholm, *The Image of the Developing Countries: An Inquiry into Swedish Public Opinion* (Uppsala: Dag Hammarskjöld Foundation, 1971), pp. 56–9.

[63] David Halloran Lumsdaine, *Moral Vision in International Politics: The Foreign Aid Régime 1949–1989* (Princeton, N.J.: Princeton University Press, 1993), pp. 122, 166.

[64] Keenleyside, *International Aid*, p. 198. [65] *The UN in Iran*, p. 27.

partly to feel that they were members of the peer group of nations they used in defining their own identity'.[66] They wanted to be like their egalitarian, prosperous, well-respected Scandinavian neighbours, so they acted like them. Arguably, the same may have been true of West Germany and even of Sweden and Switzerland in the 1950s. (The Swedes and Swiss had been neutral in the war against fascism.) It has certainly been true of New Zealand, Japan, and Italy (other more recent additions to the club of major donors), of many of the newer members of the European Union, and perhaps even of India, which, after the 2004 tsunami disaster, pointedly positioned itself as an aid giver, not a recipient.

Working with the Scandinavians and others, Owen contributed to such socialization by making a virtue out of the ways in which individual countries tied their own contributions to those of others. The United States, initially, matched the contributions of all other countries, dollar for dollar, but only up to a fixed maximum. That meant that EPTA needed to lobby other governments to get to that maximum. With their initial pledge in 1950, the Danes set a similar limit, either a specific figure or else an amount equal to the contribution of its less war-ravaged and twice as populous neighbour, Sweden, whichever was lower.[67] This link made Stockholm a major object of Owen's attention.

The EPTA chief was also perfectly willing to cut special deals in order to get maximum funding, as he did with Denmark in the mid-1950s. In order to reach the United States' maximum, he allowed the Danes to donate funds to EPTA that they had earmarked for specific purposes. This placated those Danish lawmakers and civil servants who wanted an identifiable Danish effort under the programme and those who hoped for an economic benefit from the aid, for example through the placement of Asian and Latin American students in Denmark who 'might develop personal connections which might prove valuable for Danish exports'.[68]

That arrangement – a violation of the spirit, if not the letter, of the rules applied to other donors – had the unintended and probably, in the long run, positive effect of encouraging the government that replaced Stalin after his death in 1953 to reverse Soviet policy and begin supporting the multilateral aid system. Even though it started late, the Soviet Union became one of the top five donors to EPTA. However, the funds it gave, in non-transferable roubles, could only be used to pay for services

---

[66] Lumsdaine, *Moral Vision in International Politics*, p. 25.
[67] Brunbech, 'UN Policy, New Markets, Burden-Sharing, and Altruism', p. 5.
[68] Ibid., pp. 17–18, and quotation from p. 5.

within the Soviet sphere. That encouraged the employment of Soviet experts and the placement of African, Asian, and Latin American students in Soviet universities and technical colleges (even so, large amounts of unused roubles continued to accumulate).[69]

Despite the bias *towards* Soviet experts that this funding mechanism created, eastern European governments regularly complained about how few of EPTA's experts came from their countries: fewer than 1 per cent of the total came from the USSR. This, in part, was a matter of developing-country preference, and of language. Developing governments favoured experts who needed no translators, so EPTA quickly developed three linguistic subcultures, of Spanish-speaking technical assistance workers (primarily in Latin America), francophone workers (in the former French colonies), and anglophone workers (in the Commonwealth).[70] School curricula in the Nordic countries, the Netherlands, and the Federal Republic of Germany promoted fluency in English, giving their citizens access to the largest of EPTA's subcultures.

An additional, perhaps less benign, reason why nearly two-thirds of EPTA's experts came from western countries exists. In connection with its fund-raising strategy, EPTA encouraged the formation of national technical assistance committees throughout western Europe. Belgium, Denmark, France, the Netherlands, Norway, Sweden, and the United Kingdom set up the first in 1951. The committees helped to funnel their own nationals into UN technical assistance jobs, some 21,000 of which were filled in the 1950s. A full-time public official in regular contact with universities, professional associations, and corporate leaders chaired each committee. Each maintained 'some kind of roster, file card index, or list containing data about national experts whose qualifications meet standards required, and against which the job description can be checked'. Moreover, from their beginning, Owen stayed in regular contact with each of the committees. He was able to learn of any difficulties their clients might encounter in gaining positions within any of the Specialized Agencies carrying out technical assistance. Neither the Soviet Union nor the United States created such committees, and EPTA apparently did not press them to do so.[71]

---

[69] *The UN in Iran*, p. 27; A. F. Robertson, *People and the State: An Anthropology of Planned Development* (Cambridge: Cambridge University Press, 1984), p. 38.

[70] Alexander, *International Technical Assistance Experts*, pp. 87–8, 98.

[71] Ibid., pp. 121–6, quotation from p. 123.

People

Given the way in which EPTA and the Special Fund operated, by subcontracting their work to the Specialized Agencies and to the UN's own operational technical assistance branch, it was the agencies that made the key decisions about the thousands of men and women employed as technical assistance experts. The influence of EPTA's New York office and the Resident Representatives was a matter of 'coordinate-and-cultivate', not 'command-and-control'. The smaller (but still extensive) network of personnel at headquarters and the country offices were part of a more traditional bureaucracy, although, at least at the beginning, it was not the rational, objectively meritocratic kind of organization that is described in textbooks.

John and Richard Toye argue that David Owen played the major role in building EPTA's professional staff, relying 'heavily on his past professional network of contacts . . . recruitment was thus mainly of the patrimonial rather than the modern bureaucratic variety'.[72] Richard Symonds concurs: 'It is only after David's time that the Resident Representatives really became a service', with rules about necessary qualifications and a transparent system of recruitment. In the early years the majority of the heads of the Specialized Agencies, who made up the UNTAB, had to approve each of those nominations. 'On the whole, however', the UNTAB chair decided, 'David Owen's recommendations were respected'.[73] Whether in the field or at headquarters, the MESC, UNRRA, the University of Glasgow (where Owen had been a lecturer), and the 'non-doctrinaire socialist[s] of the old school' with whom he had worked on 'social and economic planning in the post-depression years'[74] all appear to have been sources of key staff members. This, in part, explains the large number of British, Commonwealth, and Near Eastern staff members in UNDP's early years.

Yet Owen's recruitment pool was never confined to those he had met before he came to the UN. He also drew on the host of idealistic young men and women, mostly Americans, who showed up at UN headquarters – often fresh from combat – shortly after the organization

---

[72] Toye and Toye, *The UN and Global Political Economy*, p. 61.
[73] Richard Symonds, 'Bliss Was It in That Dawn: Memoirs of an Early United Nations Career, 1946–1979', Oxford, Bodleian Library, MS Eng. c. 4703, pp. 45–6.
[74] Ibid., p. 26. The quoted parts are from Brian Urquhart, 'Owen, Sir (Arthur) David Kemp (1904–1970)', in H. C. G. Matthew and Brian Harrison, eds., *Oxford Dictionary of National Biography* (Oxford: Oxford University Press, 2004), http://0-www.oxfroddnb.com.luna. wellesley.edu:80/view/article/35346 (accessed 3 Nov. 2004).

opened its doors. Bruce Stedman describes sitting on a destroyer in the Pacific, reading E. B. White's *New Yorker* dispatches from the UN's founding conference in San Francisco and resolving to make the organization his life work. Shortly after he was discharged, he found himself sitting on the edge of a table in a barely furnished office at New York's Hunter College (the UN's first temporary headquarters) being interviewed for a 'very temporary' job. Six years later, never having left the UN, he was seconded to Owen, and remained with EPTA, the Special Fund, and UNDP until retirement.[75]

Owen recruited more internationally in a variety of ways. Convenience, moving a proven technical assistance expert into a long-term job, was certainly one. The point was driven home to me in summer 2004 by the affable acting prime minister of Haiti, Gerard Latortue, whose twenty-two-year UN career was largely in UNIDO (the UN Industrial Development Organization), in UNDP-funded projects,

> I tell you, never turn down a UN contract, no matter how short, three months, six months; it doesn't matter. If you do well, there are always other contracts and likely that permanent job in New York, Geneva, somewhere. It's been that way from the beginning.[76]

Sometimes Owen relied on the suggestions of TAB members, as was the case with the unfortunate selection of Sir Mirza Ismail, a retired Indian political figure with no UN experience, to be the first Res Rep in Indonesia. His position

> ... ended dramatically when he gave a party in honor of Dr. Hugh Keenleyside ... who was visiting Indonesia. Keenleyside refused to shake hands with Dr. [Hjalmar] Schacht, who was advising the government and who had been Hitler's finance minister. Sir Mirza resigned because his guest had been insulted.[77]

Keenleyside fumed at the idiocy of honouring Schacht in the first place, 'now, having learned nothing, he is advising the Indonesian government to adopt the Nazi labor laws of the 30s, to start forced migrations, and so on'.[78]

More successful were people Owen met in his own travels to country offices, including Rajendra Coomaraswamy, the brilliant Sri Lankan who would later become the first head of UNDP's Asian Bureau.[79]

[75] Interview with CNM, 3 Feb. 2005.   [76] Interview with CNM, 29 July 2004.
[77] Symonds, 'Bliss Was It in That Dawn', p. 46.
[78] Keenleyside to Owen, 28 March 1952, Owen Papers, Box 1.
[79] On his recruitment see Coomaraswamy to David Owen, 10 Sept. 1958, Owen Papers, Box 8.

3.2 David Owen (with white hair) and UNDP Staff in Guyana, 1967

The 'patrimonial' hiring practices of the Programme throughout its first twenty to twenty-five years probably did little to undermine the effectiveness of UNDP. Then, as today, the pool of qualified and idealistic people ready to work for the United Nations is many times greater than the number of jobs available. The Programme's patrimonialism, instead, resulted in a particularly distinctive and strong organizational culture. Consciously or unconsciously, Owen created the Programme in his own image, choosing from among the pool of potential Programme officers a group of men and women who shared orientations and values similar to his own. They were, largely, 'non-doctrinaire socialist[s] of the old school', people deeply concerned about social welfare and convinced that the state had a central and positive role to play. And they were men and women who shared a particular understanding of the meaning of the Second World War and the events that led to it, people to whom any attempt to forget (let alone honour) the makers of fascism was anathema, people who would react as Keenleyside had when confronted with Schacht.

In the mid-1970s, at one of the low points in relations between the United States and the UN, the US ambassador to the UN, Daniel Patrick Moynihan, considered the UN's Third World majority to be spouting a kind of misguided Fabianism.[80] Many African, Asian, and Latin American ambassadors could have politely pointed out that there were other, more relevant (if less intellectually coherent) sources of the positions that united them: the breakdown of some of the global economic institutions established at the end of the world wars, the failure of the UN's 'First Development Decade'. Yet had Moynihan turned his gaze across the street, from the General Assembly to UNDP's headquarters on the other side of New York's First Avenue, he would have found what looked very much like a community of Fabians, the community Paul Hoffman inherited from David Owen. Ironically, it had been, was in the 1970s, and would largely remain, a community of 'Fabians' serving under an internationalist Republican from the United States.

Skills

The primary job of EPTA, the Special Fund, and UNDP was to provide expertise to developing countries. When the UN first undertook technical assistance, it placed equal emphasis on fellowships (sending people

---

[80] Daniel Patrick Moynihan, *A Dangerous Place* (Boston: Little, Brown, 1978).

from the developing world to institutions in the industrialized countries for training) and sending 'experts' to the developing world. Over time, the preference of headquarters staff shifted to the provision of experts over fellowships. Keenleyside explains some of the growing suspicion about the value of the fellowship programme:

> The number of government nominees who turned out to be the sons or nephews of ministers, or otherwise 'well-connected', was statistically astonishing. So was the percentage of applicants who indicated that their intellectual needs could be satisfied only by a year or two in Paris![81]

However, a bias towards providing the rather expensive skills of foreign experts to the developing world arose throughout the UN system.

Recall that EPTA, the Special Fund, and UNDP did not provide their own experts. They were required to contract that role out to the UN Specialized Agencies and to the small operational technical assistance programme that Keenleyside oversaw within the Secretariat. In fact, until January 1955, each of the Specialized Agencies received an automatic allocation of Programme funds, but even then, when EPTA began to move towards a system of country programming consonant with the principle of responding to the specific needs of each developing country, each agency was guaranteed 85 per cent of its previous year's allocation. Change also would be very slow, in part because each of the Specialized Agencies tended to develop mutually supportive relationships with their parallel ministry within each developing country (UNESCO with the education ministry, FAO with agriculture). Even under a 'country programming' format, the ministries would ensure that each specialized agency would get its 'traditional' share.[82]

The agencies preferred maintaining experts in the field, because they received an overhead of up to 14 per cent of the expert's salary for each man or woman they put in the developing countries. 'For every seven people they maintained in the field using EPTA funds, they could hire one additional staff member in Geneva, Paris, or Rome.' This was the main way in which the agencies grew throughout the 1950s and 1960s. Their core budgets, provided to them by their members, tended only to keep up with inflation. Technical assistance provided an opportune way of expanding staff, taking on new programmes, and expanding the

---

[81] Keenleyside, *International Aid*, p. 191.   [82] Heppling, *UNDP*, pp. 49–57.

headquarters' physical plant – all the things that every bureaucracy, no matter how idealistic, tends to want to do.[83]

The headquarters of EPTA, the Special Fund, and UNDP also had a bias towards putting as many experts as possible in the field, 'in order that there should be a convincing case to appeal for further contributions from [donor] governments'. Richard Symonds, the long-time chief of Programme operations in Geneva, where meetings of the governing Technical Assistance Board usually took place, recalls Owen urging the heads of the Specialized Agencies, 'Get experts into the field; I don't mind what they do.'[84] Bruce Stedman, the finance chief under Hoffman, recalls similar admonitions made by his boss.[85]

The same pressures led to a tendency to renew experts' contracts or to shift the same expert from one country to another. This is why Gerard Latortue could feel so confident advising people interested in a UN career to take on any expert contract, no matter how short.

Where did the agencies go to look for the experts they put in the field? Sometimes they went to their own headquarters' staff, often to the parallel ministries within the industrialized countries (with whom the agencies had strong relations, as they had in the developing world); the European Technical Assistance Committees provided a ready pool, as did universities and professional associations in the United States. Yet in the early decades of the Programme, perhaps the most important sources of expertise were the colonial civil services and the pools of recent retirees from various ministries throughout the governments of the United Kingdom and France.[86]

There was not just an irony, but also a logic in this. The original 1949 General Assembly resolution setting up the Programme demanded that experts be chosen not only for their 'technical competence, but also for their sympathetic understanding of the cultural backgrounds and specific needs of the countries concerned, and for their capacity to adapt methods of work to local conditions, social and material'.[87] Most colonial civil servants had proved their adaptability, and many had developed that kind of sympathetic understanding. As a result, even a generation later, development specialists could observe, 'one of the striking features of

---

[83] Richard Symonds, interview with CNM, 23 March 2005. Bruce Stedman provided a similar analysis, interview with CNM, 3 Feb. 2005.

[84] Symonds, 'Bliss Was It in That Dawn', p. 139.   [85] Interview with CNM, 3 Feb. 2005.

[86] Alexander, *International Technical Assistance Experts*, p. 97.

[87] Symonds, 'Bliss Was It in That Dawn', p. 142.

Table 3.1. *Country of origin and number of EPTA experts, 1950-64*

United Kingdom 4,811	Canada 1,157
United States 3,966	Denmark 856
France 3,215	Switzerland 821
Netherlands 1,675	Australia 803
India 1,336	Sweden 791

development personnel is how frequently they are the children of colonial civil servants, military personnel, missionaries and so on'.[88] Symonds, the author of the summary of the 1949 Resolution, was a perfect example of the best of the class, a cherished friend of Gandhi's who had worked for the British Quakers throughout India's violent partition.

Still, both the sources of experts and the bias towards keeping them in the field could lead one to question whether UNDP and its predecessors had found the best possible way to do its main job – transferring needed skills to the developing world. However, two positive things about the Programme's technical assistance were certain. First, the multilateral programme could draw on a larger pool of experts than could any bilateral aid programme. Second, and more significantly, the Specialized Agencies relied, in part, on experts from the developing world, whom governments often preferred, as they were able to take lessons from one relatively similar context and apply them to another. For example, in the early 1950s, relatively successful Haitian and Thai fish farming projects were developed by Indonesia, at the same time that Haitian experts took the lessons of an early WHO project that eradicated the debilitating disease, yaws, to Java and Thailand.[89] Since the time of UNRRA, the whole point of the UN development system, as Keenleyside argued in the year UNDP began, was to be a system of 'mutual' or 'reciprocal' international aid. It was that characteristic, he believed, that made the UN development system the most 'important' and 'encouraging' innovation, perhaps since the

---

[88] Emma Crewe and Elizabeth Harrison, *Whose Development? An Ethnography of Aid* (London: Zed Books 1998), p. 87.

[89] *Sharing Skills: Stories of Technical Assistance* (New York: United Nations, 1954), pp. 17–19. *The War Against Want* (New York: United Nations, 1953), p. 5. Black, *The Children and the Nations*, p. 93.

Industrial Revolution, something that might help secure humanity's somewhat doubtful future.[90]

Cooperation with governments in the developing world

It is hard to explain just how critically important to development the governments of the developing world were perceived to be by the founders of the UN system. This was true not only of the Third World UN representatives who had ensured that the UN would have a technical assistance capacity and that a multilateral development financing agency would exist, but even more so of the men and women within the Secretariat from all parts of the world. In part, this was because, from the 1940s to the 1970s, the standard model of how development could be achieved had a central role for the state. States needed to plan, to have clear economic goals and to have a clear sense of what skills and financing, whether private or public, would go towards achieving those ends, even without state intervention. Then governments needed to create an environment of enabling domestic institutions that would ensure that other resources would be directed towards those ends. Finally, they needed to work with the international agencies, and bilateral donors to fill any remaining gaps.

The entire evolution of UNDP 'country programming' was based on this need to match the flow of external inputs with needs outlined in a coherent national economic plan. This was not just a 'Fabian' concern (although Lewis's early Fabian Society study provided one of the clearest statements of the specific needs in developing countries[91]); Hoffman was even more likely than Lewis was to rail against the 'prejudice against planning' that had been prevalent in some circles throughout the 1950s.[92]

For the UN, planning was always a matter for governments themselves. Arthur Wakefield, the first Resident Representative, set the tone for others who followed by working with the Haitian government to clarify its own development plan, since it was only within the context of such a plan that much impact could come from the relatively inexpensive forms of assistance that the Specialized Agencies could provide. In order to work, the plan had to reflect the energy and ambition of the Haitian people; it could not be the UN's handiwork.

[90] Keenleyside, International Aid, p. 35.
[91] W. Arthur Lewis, The Principles of Economic Planning: A Study Prepared for the Fabian Society, 2nd edn (London: Dobson, 1952), pp. 121–2.
[92] Paul G. Hoffman, World Without Want (New York, Harper & Row, 1962), p. 121.

This was the first of 'Wakefield's principles': 'help people help themselves'. The contrast he made was with the top-down and, at best, paternal 'development' policy undertaken by the United States when it had occupied the Caribbean country from the beginning of the First World War until the end of Franklin Roosevelt's first year in office.

Wakefield's second principle – 'avoidance of publicity' – followed from the first. The Secretariat, ECOSOC, the General Assembly, and especially the major donors all wanted 'success stories' to brag about. However, in many developing countries, spectacular results would be impossible and extravagant claims about what had been achieved would just lead to cynicism. Moreover, when outstanding results were achieved, the accolades should go to the government and people of the country. It was their accomplishment; the international community had only assisted in the ways the country had requested.[93]

By the time Hoffman joined the UN, Wakefield's principles had become second nature. W. Arthur Lewis told his staff in his earliest letter to the field, 'The Special Fund will not operate in the dark, but it will usually operate in twilight.'[94] The spotlight, if it came on, would be for developing countries themselves.

Arthur Holcombe, one of the longest serving Resident Representatives, says that David Owen's greatest accomplishments include the establishment of the UN field offices and the network of Resident Representatives. This is the usual assessment – the one made by Margaret Joan Anstee, Robert Jackson, Adriano Garcia, most of the UN Mohicans, and much of the scholarly literature on international development – but Holcombe adds the critical point that Owen negotiated and established the basic agreements with recipient countries that defined a set of country obligations as well as expectations about international support.[95] Owen's agreements 'remain the basis for current assistance provided by UNDP', and (for Holcombe, perhaps the most important point) they cleared the ground for the kind of advocacy – of democracy, civil society, the status of women, and other goals – that would become such a central part of UNDP's work a generation later. It may seem paradoxical that that ground was cleared by means of Owen's embrace, in those early country agreements, of Wakefield's principle's of country ownership and the

---

[93] Marian Neal, 'United Nations Technical Assistance Programs in Haiti', *International Conciliation*, 468 (February 1951), pp. 99–100.

[94] Symonds, 'Bliss Was It in That Dawn', p. 158.

[95] Arthur Holcombe, *Running on Two Tracks* (no city [probably New York]: UNDP, n.d. [probably 1998]), p. 7.

avoidance of undue publicity. Yet trusted friends are often the only ones whose criticism we are able to hear, they rarely make a public show of their criticism, and we know that – despite whatever they advocate that we should do – they will support us in our own choices.

Perhaps only one thing should be added to Holcombe's assessment: the peculiar 'patrimonialism' with which Owen built the UN's global development network ensured that, when UNDP did begin a conscious programme of advocacy, UNDP's culture, the values shared by its staff over more than a generation, would largely be a reflection of Owen's own. Advocacy of democracy and of egalitarian principles, more broadly, would come naturally to the Programme's staff, while other goals, such as promotion of the private sector, would be treated with scepticism and misunderstanding.

4

Decolonization and economic transformation

On a crisp autumn day in 2004, David Owen's son, Roger Owen, a Harvard professor of history nearing 70, fondly recalled visiting his father's office on a similar day forty years before. The then Technical Assistance Board (UNTAB) executive chairman beamed as he pointed out to his son a map of the world rapidly filling with pins.[1] Each large coloured pin represented a UN expert, the colour indicating 'whether he was an agronomist, an engineer, a meteorologist, a malariologist or other specialist'. Smaller pins 'denoted the award of a fellowship to the national of a developing country'. In 1965, David Owen wrote about his 'growing satisfaction . . . from the story that map has told', with its 'bands of colour' growing 'denser as Governments have requested more UN assistance, and becoming brighter as more international Agencies have entered the field'.[2] If the pins had accumulated from year to year, there would have been more than 60,000 when Owen wrote about them with such pleasure.[3]

The map exemplifies the way in which the UN technical assistance officers of the 1950s and 1960s judged themselves – by their ability to help to build ever greater expert capacity within the developing nations. Later, the generation that replaced the staff first assembled by David Owen would want to know more, especially whether and how the transfer of expert knowledge really did contribute to *most* people's abilities to make the most out of their own lives.

The *Human Development Reports*, launched by UNDP in 1990, help to answer this question by providing three indicators, three reliable signs, of that much more complex capacity: improvements in health, in education,

---

[1] Roger Owen, interview with the author (CNM), 7 Sept. 2004.
[2] David Owen, Introduction to James Avery Joyce, *World of Promise: A Guide to the United Nations Decade of Development* (Dobbs Ferry, N.Y.: Oceana Publications, 1965), p. xi.
[3] Calculated from Tables 7 and 8 in *The UN in Iran, a Compendium of United Nations Activities in Iran 1950–1965* (Tehran: Office of the United Nations Development Programme in Iran, January 1966), pp. 29–30.

and in income, the last of which also points to the questions of economic growth that preoccupy other approaches to development.

Much of UNDP's early history remains bright when summarized by this larger, yet still simple, set of maps.[4] Some of it does not. Moreover, much that had been intended in the 1940s was not accomplished, so that even Owen's and Paul Hoffman's satisfaction was far from complete when they left the UN in 1969 (Owen) and 1972 (Hoffman), at the height of a period of intensive self-evaluation and reform within the organization that they had initiated. Unfortunately, despite that critical attention, some of the sources of the early failures of UN technical assistance would remain hidden for many years more.

Health, education, and economic growth

There are a few remarkable places where the Expanded Programme of Technical Assistance (EPTA) and the Special Fund dramatically improved the lives of whole populations along many of the dimensions of human development. For example, the Special Fund led the UN system in supporting a massive reconstruction of Skopje, the capital of Macedonia (then a republic of Yugoslavia), after a 1963 earthquake, which, according to contemporaries, was as devastating as the Nazi onslaught on Warsaw. The physical structure of the revitalized city, its hospitals, schools, houses, markets, and industrial parks, all reflect the work of UNDP's predecessors and the commitment of the UN member states that insisted an extraordinary effort be made.[5]

Nonetheless, most of the UN's early development work was both more circumscribed and more global than the restoration of Skopje. Most projects influenced only one aspect of life, yet many projects took innovations piloted in one or two places to countries all around the world. Typical was EPTA's role in the control of yaws, in the 1940s, a devastating disease for 100 million people, mostly in the tropics, in the western hemisphere, and among the poor. By the 1980s, fewer than 500 cases remained across the Americas. Arthur Wakefield, whose experience in Haiti as the first Resident Representative led to the principles guiding EPTA's work, describes the early UN programme to combat yaws:

---

[4] Chapter 9 outlines the greater complexity of the Human Development approach as a whole.

[5] *Skopje Resurgent: The Story of a United Nations Special Fund Town Planning Project* (New York: United Nations, 1963).

It's practically unbelievable. One morning I went to a tiny clinic well up in the mountains. That day I saw there a boy of about ten, who had been unable to stand for the last few years, because the soles of his feet were covered with sores. This youngster crawled along the ground like a serpent, hitching himself along on his little backside, and digging in with his elbows. He was given a single injection of penicillin. One week later I saw that same child – walking normally. There was a laborer there too, that morning, a man of thirty-two. He had been unemployed for three years, the palms of both hands being so cracked and swollen that he could not hold any tool. He also got a single injection of penicillin. Ten days later I saw him swinging a scythe in a field nearby, once again earning his own living.[6]

The yaws eradication campaign, in which the World Health Organization (WHO) and UNICEF collaborated with EPTA, represented the kind of activity that only a global network could accomplish. EPTA-funded experts developed a plan under which medical workers visited every household in Haiti. It took two years, but, at the end, the disease was all but eradicated. WHO took a second important island – Indonesia's much more populous Java – for the next project. The success there allowed protocols to be refined so that the disease could also be eliminated in less confined territories: Thailand, Mexico, and the rest of the world.[7]

Throughout the 1950s and 1960s, EPTA and UNDP helped to control other diseases including malaria, smallpox, and polio. Moreover, the same network connections, and many of the same countries involved in the anti-yaws campaign, contributed to the greatest source of improvements in human health in the third quarter of the twentieth century: agricultural transformations, including 'the Green Revolution'.

Actually, some of the earliest (and most often repeated) projects to end malnutrition and protein deficiency had nothing to do with plants. They came from an EPTA-funded FAO (Food and Agriculture Organization) network of fish-farming experiments. Haitians brought Indonesian techniques to the western hemisphere at the same time that the Haitian lessons in yaws eradication were arriving in Java.[8]

---

[6] Kathleen McLaughlin, *New Life in Old Lands* (New York: Dodd, Mead, 1954), p. 206.

[7] Maggie Black, *The Children and the Nations: The Story of UNICEF* (New York: UNICEF, 1986), pp. 92–4.

[8] *United Nations Work and Programs for Technical Assistance* (New York: United Nations Department of Public Information, 1951), p. 27; *Sharing Skills: Stories of Technical Assistance* (New York: United Nations Department of Public Information, 1953), pp. 17–19.

Meanwhile, also in the early 1950s, the Programme began funding the network of research institutes in Mexico, India, the Philippines, and other countries that would become the places where Green Revolution seed and cultivation methods were developed, as well as the nodes from which knowledge about those innovations would be dispersed throughout the world.[9] EPTA and UNDP were far from the only players in the drama of the Green Revolution, but they were major players, even though their role has long remained in the twilight created by Arthur Wakefield's principles and Arthur Lewis's commitment to having the developing countries stand out. There were individual projects with remarkable results. For example, the history written for EPTA's fifteenth anniversary in 1965 cites a single Chinese expert who had been key to Egypt's 75 per cent increase in rice yields from 1953 to 1962.[10] Nonetheless, EPTA's and UNDP's more important roles were the larger ones of providing critical resources to the nodes in the global research networks, using country offices and the network of Res Reps to facilitate the flow of information to places where it could be employed effectively, and modelling the kind of organization that would be needed to routinize these linkages.

Not surprisingly, many UNDP staffers cite this work as some of the most significant in the UN's first twenty-five or thirty years, as Paul Hoffman did in his farewell address as Administrator in 1971.[11] It demonstrated mankind's ability to 'take full control of our technology and consciously turn it to more humanistic ends'.[12] Also not surprisingly, Hoffman and a handful of UNDP's senior staff members played central roles in the establishment, in that same year, of CGIAR (the Consultative Group on International Agricultural Research), the alliance of private foundations, governments, and intergovernmental organizations that supports the global agricultural research centres and links them to farmers' associations, agribusinesses, and national extension services. Thus, UNDP helped

[9] *United Nations Work*, p. 26; *Sharing Skills*, pp. 28–30.

[10] *15 years and 150,000 Skills: An Anniversary Review of the United Nations Expanded Programme of Technical Assistance* (New York: United Nations Economic and Social Council, 1965), p. 79.

[11] Adriano Garcia, *International Cooperation and Development: The United Nations Development Programme Resident Representative System* (Quezon City: University of Philippines Law Center, 1982), pp. 509–12; Arthur Holcombe, *Running on Two Tracks* (no city [probably New York]: UNDP, n.d. [probably 1998]), p. 25; Richard Symonds, 'Bliss Was It in That Dawn: Memoirs of an Early United Nations Career, 1946–1979', Oxford, Bodleian Library, MS Eng. c. 4703; Paul G. Hoffman, 'No Time Like the Future', *International Development Review*, 13, 4 (1971): 4.

[12] Hoffman, 'No Time Like the Future', 8.

to spin off a UNDP-like network to focus specifically on developing and disseminating agricultural innovations throughout the world.[13]

UNDP's early impact on educational attainment has been similar, even in a country like Haiti, where people see little positive result from more than fifty years of extensive UN involvement, as I learned when I visited the country in 2004. During my visit, Gerdes Fleurant, the director of the cultural centre in Mirabelais, organized a long meeting with local leaders – teachers, judges, and heads of local NGOs (non-governmental organizations).

Mirabelais is a few miles from the site of the ecological devastation caused by the country's largest development project of the 1950s, the Peligre hydroelectric dam, and a few miles further from Cange, the town where Fleurant's boyhood friend, Fr Fritz Lafontant, and the noted Harvard physician, Paul Farmer, work among the families displaced to the steep hills above the dam's artificial lake. Farmer later echoed the views of almost everyone around the table. He hoped that the history of UNDP could explain 'how the "international community" (not UNDP per se) can have accomplished so little in Haiti with so many resources'.[14] The hulks of fifty-year-old construction equipment – originally state-of-the-art, and very expensive – stand abandoned at the base of the dam, up against a shanty town scavenged from the elaborate structures built for foreign engineers.

What *development* came from interventions like this? Beyond the early health programmes, the Haitians around the table remembered one intervention with long-lasting, positive impact: UNESCO's development of an orthography for the language spoken by the country's vast major-ity and its publication of the first materials in Creole for a mass literacy campaign.

That early literacy initiative, with its basic readers that 'attempted to deal with other problems by addressing yaws, malaria, house-building, and land-terracing in story form', was originally deemed a failure by a Carnegie Endowment study of 1951,[15] but immediate assessments of development projects can often be faulty. (In fact, initial evaluations of most of the UN's projects in Haiti said that they were completely successful!) Not only is the literacy campaign remembered positively in Haiti, but its principles, refined over time in other contexts, were taken into UNESCO's successful

---

[13] Michael Gucovsky interview with CNM, 23 Sept. 2004. Alexander H. Rotival, interview with CNM, 14 Sept. 2004.   [14] Electronic mail to CNM, 23 Aug. 2004.

[15] Marian Neal, 'United Nations Technical Assistance Programs in Haiti', *International Conciliation*, 468 (Feb. 1951): 109–10, quotation at 106.

UNDP-funded 'Experimental World Literacy Programme' of the late 1960s, which operated in more than a dozen countries. Hallmarks of this approach included offering training in people's everyday language (for example, in Haitian Creole rather than French) and making reading relevant to everyday life. The approach is related to that of the visionary Brazilian educator, Paulo Freire, whose most important international sponsor was the non-governmental World Council of Churches, but it was UNESCO, with UNDP's backing, that first made Freire's human-development-oriented approach a part of governmental literacy campaigns in many of the countries that have been the most successful.[16]

In Tanzania, for example, the first project enrolled half a million people and eventually certified nearly 100,000 of them as literate, at a cost of only US$32 for each person who successfully completed the course.[17] Tanzania expanded the experiment, relying on former staff of the UN system project to train thousands of voluntary literacy teachers. 'Building on the UNDP/UNESCO experience in designing and evaluating material, twelve different primer sets were used . . . Subjects covered were cotton, bananas, home economics, fishing, cattle, tobacco, maize, rice, cashew nuts, coconut, political education, and wheat.' By 1977, 73 per cent of Tanzanian adults were literate, up from 33 per cent in 1967, when the UNDP project began.[18]

UNESCO executed other education projects at all levels and in every part of the developing world. As UNESCO's official history points out, it is a small organization whose own budget 'could be compared to that of a medium-sized university'. Therefore UNDP 'became the main source of funding for [UNESCO's] operational programmes', supporting basic, primary, secondary, and tertiary education across the developing world.[19]

Industrial change

UNDP's work in education empowered societies as well as individuals. Support for scientific and technical education, through UNESCO and other executing agencies, has had a marked, long-term impact on economic growth in many countries. Before 1970, UNDP and its predecessors were

---

[16] *UNESCO: 50 Years for Education* (Paris, UNESCO, 1997), http://www.unesco.org/education/educprog/50y/brochure/tle/124.htmp (accessed 24 June 2005).   [17] Ibid.

[18] UNESCO Institute for Education, 'The Tanzanian Literacy and Post-Literacy Efforts in the 1970s' (Hamburg: UNESCO Institute for Education Documentation Centre, 2005), http://www.rrz.uni-hamburg.de/UNESCO-UIE/literacyexchange/tanzania/tanzaniadata.htm#alpha (accessed 24 June 2005).

[19] *UNESCO: 50 Years for Education*, http://www.unesco.org/education/educprog/50y/brochure/tle/226.htm (accessed 24 June 2005).

the midwives of the major engineering institutions of India, Mongolia, Thailand, Trinidad, Turkey, and many other countries, institutions that became engines of growth for their countries and regions.

In the 1950s EPTA and the Special Fund supported the creation of the Indian Institute of Technology (IIT). EPTA supported the initial curricular design (and some of the physical planning) for what eventually became a network of seven campuses, using the Massachusetts Institute of Technology (MIT) as its model. EPTA and UNESCO then played a particularly pivotal role in the early history of the second of the campuses, opened in what were then the outskirts of Bombay (now Mumbai) in 1955. Over ten years, the UN agencies equipped the metallurgical, mechanical, chemical, and electrical engineering laboratories and helped to recruit and pay for many of the Institute's faculty members, many of whom came from the Soviet Union, which proved an excellent way to use some of the non-transferable roubles that EPTA was accumulating from the USSR. It also allowed a kind of arms-length East–West cooperation, with Soviet experts carrying out a design taken from the United States' premier school of engineering.[20]

Res Reps tended to take special interest in the foundation of the engineering and scientific institutions that eventually had such a profound impact. Charles Weitz, the young American whom Owen sent to Turkey in 1954, recalls how he fought to ensure that the government would be able to structure the Middle East Technical University (METU) in the way in which *it* wanted, which meant cutting UNESCO *out* of much of the project. (Due to some early spectacular failures, UNESCO had a bad reputation in Turkey at the time.) This earned Weitz a *persona non grata* letter from the Director-General of UNESCO, Weitz's former employer, to David Owen, who seems to have ignored it.[21]

Weitz says that he was able to push UNESCO's unwanted help aside in part because 'David Owen created a situation in which, with cultivation and a low profile, the UNTAB Resident Representative in Turkey became de facto the [UN system's] country representative.' Owen encouraged Weitz to build personal relationships with the technical assistance chiefs at the agency head offices, and provided Weitz with opportunities to visit their European headquarters. Weitz initiated regular meetings among the six UN agencies in Turkey along with their national counterparts, rotating the meetings from ministry to ministry. Thus, a respected, unified

---

[20] *Assignment to Everywhere: The United Nations Programme of Technical Assistance* (Geneva: United Nations, 1954), p. 16; *15 years and 150,000 Skills*, p. 92.

[21] The quoted parts of this and the next paragraphs come from a series of four letters from Weitz to CNM written between 11 Feb. and 14 March 2005.

4.1 The Indian Institute of Technology (Powai, Mumbai (formerly Bombay)), 1964

UN presence already existed when a group of ' "young Turks", in the 1950s meaning of the term [men dissatisfied with the country's unimaginative urban policies]' asked EPTA to bring Charles Abrams, an influential, egalitarian US town planner, to the country to stir things up.[22]

At the end of his UN mission, Abrams did not want to talk about city planning. 'It is hopeless', Weitz recalls him insisting,

> In the old Maine saying: 'You can't get there from here.' You have universities . . . hopelessly mired in the past, teaching leftover French and German

[22] A. Scott Henderson, *Housing and the Democratic Ideal: The Life and Thought of Charles Abrams* (New York: Columbia University Press, 2000), pp. 179–89, discusses Abrams's UN missions to Turkey, Ghana, and Singapore.

approaches, and in Turkish! Very little modern technology is translated into Turkish . . . If you are really serious, you must start at the beginning. You must establish your own university, here in Ankara, where it will become a national monument . . . There is no other way for you to catch up with the world. Start with architecture and town planning, if you think that is important, but add engineering, mathematics, all the other sciences, as quickly as possible and a liberal arts school so you get new librarians, social thinkers, etc.

Abrams's audience was stunned, but receptive. They presented his ideas to the prime minister, who gave his full support.

The whole UN mission then went into full swing (with UNESCO taking a back seat), finding experts, suggesting designs (curricular and physical), pointing to other models around the world. The results were rapid, impressive, and fully embraced by the Turkish government, even if the young Res Rep was not above tweaking Wakefield's principle that the UN should take little credit for a project's success. Weitz remembers the groundbreaking ceremony, with ministers, members of parliament, and 'all of the Ankara diplomatic corps'. There were to be three flags (four, if you include the new flag of METU, cut out and sewn by the Res Rep's wife, Gretchen). There would be the flags of

> Turkey, the United Nations, and the US [Turkey's cold war ally] . . . It was summer – hot, often without wind. So I telexed New York to send me the appropriate size UN flag, but in silk, and I was right. There was a slight breeze that memorable afternoon and while the wool Turkish and US flags hung limp from their poles, the silk UN flag stood out by itself, flapping in the breeze.

As METU approached another celebration, its fiftieth anniversary in 2006, it had become one of Turkey's main sources of innovation and economic growth. There have been small, specific victories that those who recall the university's founding like to remember: the thousands of companies that have benefited from METU's teaching and research, one, Koc Holdings, recently took over Grundig,[23] the quintessential German, high-tech consumer brand of the 1950s, a symbol of what many Turks then felt would be hard to achieve; and METU's tens of thousands of former faculty members and students, one of whom, Kemal Dervis, started his career in its Department of Economics and became in 2005 the first UNDP Administrator from a country that had been a recipient of UN development support.

---

[23] 'GRUNDIG Consumer Electronics "Official" Under New Management, 1 May 2004.' http://www.grundig.com/presse.grundig/unternehmensmeldungen/grundig_consumer_ electronics_/ (accessed 22 June 2005).

The first Administrator, Hoffman, would have been pleased by the long-term impact of the educational institutions that UNDP's predecessors helped to found. Hoffman took particular pride in the ways in which the Special Fund and UNDP created the conditions under which scientific and engineering knowledge could be used to transform societies. He believed that one of the organizations' greatest accomplishments (already visible thirty-five years ago) was their role in demonstrating the practicality of investment in large-scale electric power projects. After all, the leading analysts of the Industrial Revolution – from Babbage to Marx to Rostow – all saw machines (complex tools linked to artificial sources of power) and the rapid expansion of the sources of that power, as *the* key to the unprecedented prosperity that some parts of the world began to enjoy in the nineteenth century.

Searching for investment opportunity, Hoffman would often repeat, was the UN's real development forte. Increasingly, the World Bank and the bilateral donors had much greater resources, but the UN knew how to find the best ways for those resources to be used. 'I have found that a ratio of 100 to 1 between investment opportunity' and cost of 'pre-investment' work, Hoffman said, 'is not unusual; indeed, it is the average'. It can be even greater. Consider, he wrote, the Special Fund's first project in Argentina. It cost US$300,000 and identified US$735 million of profitable investments,[24] many of them in the electric power field. Similarly, Walter Franco, an Ecuadorian whose UN career spanned almost thirty years, including stints as Res Rep in Bolivia, Brazil, and El Salvador, speaks about how, decades later, most Brazilians involved with riparian conservation and the power industry keep a copy of the original Special Fund pre-investment study near their desks. That study was similar to the first Argentine project: it uncovered Brazil's vast hydropower potential and provided an authoritative guide for its exploitation. It provided the map that located the turbines that would power the machines throughout Brazil's industrial take-off.[25] Similar studies exist for other Latin American countries, in Africa, and across Asia.

This early pre-investment work was linked to four additional, often overlooked, effects of the UN agencies directed by Hoffman. First, in many countries they were instrumental in convincing the World Bank to take on its development role. In the early 1960s the Bank first entered many countries not as a lender, but as an executor of Special Fund

---

[24] Paul G. Hoffman, *World Without Want* (New York, Harper & Row, 1962), pp. 84–5.
[25] Walter Franco, interview with CNM, 4 June 2004.

pre-investment studies, studies that often led to investments in the huge hydroelectric projects for which the Bank became famous.[26] Second, the power projects often led to larger, UNDP-funded regional development planning, to industrial schemes as well as integrated rural development programmes like that begun in the flood plain below Ghana's Volta River dam, one of the world's largest hydroelectric schemes (and one of the subjects of the next chapter). Third, this planning, in turn, often triggered a country's first national programmes to deal with environmental issues. Finally, this work often encouraged regional cooperation throughout the developing world, which was one of Hoffman's major goals.

Recall that the one major condition placed on Marshall Plan aid was that its recipients cooperate in the reconstruction of the European industrial economy. The lesson of that cooperation informed Hoffman's conviction that international economic solidarity – aid from almost every country to societies where people were less advantaged – would contribute to peace.[27]

Some of the seeds Hoffman planted, including projects for cooperative exploitation of the Mekong River by Cambodia, Laos, Thailand, and Vietnam, took years to bear fruit. Only an organization that did not take sides in the cold war or the conflict between China and the Soviet Union could maintain cooperation throughout the region's wars and the difficult reconstruction that followed. This is one reason why the project was long championed by India's C. V. Narasimhan,[28] who first served under UN Secretary-General Dag Hammarskjöld in the 1950s, then as U Thant's *chef de cabinet*, and then doubled up as UNDP Deputy Administrator in the early 1970s.

Narasimhan remained committed to a process begun in 1955, when 'Teams of experts traveled up and down the [Mekong's] mainstream and its tributaries in boats, in jeeps, on foot, and on the backs of elephants to map, measure, sample and catalogue a rich diversity of resources.'[29] They

[26] See the Bank's official chronology, http://web.worldbank.org/WBSITE/EXTERNAL/ EXTABOUTUS/EXTARCHIVES/0,,contentMDK:20035660~menuPK:56316~pagePK: 36726~piPK:36092~theSitePK:29506,00.html (accessed 24 June 2005).

[27] Norma Globerman (interview with CNM, 29 Sept. 2004), Michael Gucovsky (interview with CNM, 23 Sept. 2004), and Alexander H. Rotival (interview with CNM, 14 Sept. 2004) all emphasize the importance of this UNDP role.

[28] Hugh L. Keenleyside, *International Aid: A Summary with Special Reference to the Programmes of the United Nations* (New York: James H. Heinemann, 1966), pp. 181–2.

[29] Mekong River Commission for Sustainable Development, 'The Story of Mekong Cooperation', http://www.mrcmekong.org/about_mekong/history_6.htm (accessed 24 June 2004).

collected data for irrigation, flood control, and hydropower projects, some of which sat on the shelves for twenty years, but now guide the strategies of the powerful intergovernmental Mekong River Commission for Sustainable Development, formed in 1995.

Hoffman's UNDP gave even broader support to regional economic integration by providing financial backing to the various UN regional economic commissions when they attempted to create 'an infrastructure of regional institutions'.[30] These included common markets and free trade areas with markets large enough to encourage the growth of the industries that had yet to be established in Africa, Asia, or Latin America. After all, the challenge of catching up with the countries that first experienced the Industrial Revolution is more than one of building machines and finding ways to power them. For more than 200 years the industrial system has generated new lead industries as it expanded its geographic scope from the cotton mills of the north of England, to the national economies of the railway age, to the imperial economies of the Second Industrial Revolution in the late nineteenth century.

For the developing nations of the 1950s and 1960s, the challenge was not only to find the power for and build the industries of earlier eras. It was also to find some way to play an active part in the industries of the late-twentieth-century 'automobile age' or 'jet age'. Establishing larger regional trade areas would not, by itself, be enough. Developing nations needed access to new technologies and new skills. Here EPTA, the Special Fund, and UNDP played a particularly crucial role in their support of projects executed by the International Civil Aviation Organization (ICAO). They established training centres for civil aviation personnel – from aircraft mechanics to air traffic controllers – in every region of the world. They also supplied technical assistance key to the establishment of most of the successful national airlines in the developing world. Tourists and executives today criss-crossing South-east Asia on Garuda Indonesia, or any of us who understand that the motto of Ethiopian Airlines, 'Bringing Africa together', is not mere hype (the airline has long had the continent's most extensive internal network) are the beneficiaries of ICAO/EPTA projects of the 1950s.[31]

---

[30] Leelananda de Silva, 'From ECAFE to ESCAP: Pioneering a Regional Perspective', in Yves Berthelot, ed., *Unity and Diversity in Development Ideas: Perspectives from the UN Regional Commissions* (Bloomington, Ind.: Indiana University Press, 2004), p. 137.

[31] *Generations: Portrait of the United Nations Development Programme 1950–1985* (New York: UNDP, 1983), p. 15; *Seeds of Progress: Stories of Technical* Assistance (New York: United Nations Office of Information, 1955), pp. 36–40; *Technical Assistance: What? How? Why?* (New York: United Nations Office of Information, 1958), p. 54.

EPTA and UNDP played on the competition between the two aero-space powers, the cold war rivals, to ensure that developing nations had access to technologies and skills that may not have been available had there been only one centre of innovation. In some cases the results were especially dramatic. Michael Gucovsky, whose thirty-year UNDP career focused on Latin America, argues that Embraer, the Brazilian manufac-turer of civilian aircraft (now the world's third largest, behind Boeing and Airbus) was 'not likely to have been successfully established without UNDP strategic support', that is, the transfer of skills and technologies to Brazilian civil aviation through UN projects in the 1960s.[32]

Throughout Latin America, UNDP and its predecessors also sup-ported the transformation of one of the other critical industries of the late twentieth century, telecommunications. A typical project in the early 1960s involved one International Telecommunications Union expert in Chile who drew up 'a multimillion dollar telecommunications modern-ization plan which was later implemented and financed' by the govern-ment and larger international donors.[33]

In other middle-income countries, the support most often sought from the UN was technical training for workers in the newest industries, such as aviation and consumer electronics. The former Yugoslavia was one of the major beneficiaries of such training, usually provided by the International Labour Organisation (ILO).

That important relationship between one agency and one country led to one of the droller incidents that Richard Symonds remembers from his long career. In 1958,

> there was the ILO expert in Zagreb who with his wife occupied a lavish suite in the main hotel. Eventually the hotel raised the rent and the expert gave notice that he would have to move to humbler quarters. About this time, the former head of the trade unions of Yugoslavia died and was buried in Zagreb. The expert, on the instructions of ILO headquarters in Geneva, sent a wreath on behalf of the organization labeled, 'in memory of our dear comrade who did so much for his fellows.' The wreath was accidentally transferred to the coffin of a waiter from the hotel, which was being escorted to the cemetery by his colleagues. Moved to tears by this tribute from the ILO to such a humble worker, the hotel management committee held an urgent meeting at which it was resolved that the ILO expert should be allowed to retain his suite at the former price.[34]

[32] Michael Gucovsky, electronic mail to Elizabeth Mandeville (EM), 19 June 2005.
[33] Garcia, *International Cooperation and Development*, p. 145.
[34] Symonds, 'Bliss Was It in That Dawn', p. 66.

Decolonization and support for new states

The humour Symonds could find in other assignments was much darker. He was serving in Geneva in July 1960, when the Force Publique in Congo mutinied, and Belgian officials, who still occupied all the new country's government posts requiring a secondary education, fled. Dag Hammarskjöld committed the UN to clear up the mess. He sent a representative to speak to the Specialized Agency heads in Geneva. 'Each of you,' the representative said, 'is needed in Leopoldville immediately to arrange the assistance of your agency. But take care to wear a UN armband when you get out of the plane or you may be mistaken for a Belgian and massacred.' Symonds went to the cellar of the Palais de Nations where 'motherly ladies used to sit around a revolving table assembling documents. Pleading life and death, I persuaded them to stop their work and knit UN armbands which were handed out to our departing colleagues with a kiss.'[35]

The EPTA and Special Fund role in Congo was much greater than is often remembered. Their network of Res Reps and country offices provided Hammarskjöld with his largest pool of civilian personnel for the tasks to which he had committed the UN: temporarily running the country and training a new civil service. Ralph Bunche, the distinguished Under-Secretary for Special Political Affairs from 1955 to 1967, described the Congo Civilian Operations Programme as 'the most massive technical assistance effort in human history, and certainly in the history of the United Nations', and the US ambassador to the UN, Adlai Stevenson, told radio listeners in January 1963 that 'the 1,200 UN experts have been for all practical purposes, the national administration of the country'.[36] At the time, Winifred Tickner, the wife of the EPTA officer who served as the Secretary-General's Resident Representative in Kasai Province, wrote:

> [All] who could be spared were wafted to the Congo at the shortest notice . . . Never before had the demand been made for so many people for the same project at the same time, and the pioneers in that operation, moreover, had suddenly to face dangers, deprivations, fatigues, frustrations and unsuspected hazards, and to cope with immense and bewildering problems almost without warning.[37]

[35] Ibid., p. 76.
[36] Yonah Alexander, *International Technical Assistance Experts: A Case Study in UN Experience* (New York: Frederick A. Praeger, 1966), p. 172.
[37] Winifred Tickner, 'A Spectator in the Congo', used courtesy of J. Ann Tickner, Oxford, Bodleian Library, MS Eng. c. 4704, p. 4.

In 1961 Hammarskjöld himself would be killed while on a Congo peace mission, but the Programme's extraordinary commitment remained. In 1963 EPTA took over many of the coordination tasks undertaken there earlier by the Secretariat.[38] In 1968 UNDP's international staff in the Congo still numbered forty-eight. The next largest of its country offices had twelve international staff members and the total international staff across the Programme's ninety-six country offices numbered fewer than 400.[39]

It would be difficult to argue that the role of Programme staff and Specialized Agency experts in the Congo was effective. More than forty years later, the UN is still attempting to help build a state. The strongest claim of UN success that Fred Tickner reports any of his colleagues making is that it kept banknotes and fuel flowing, the things needed according to a bizarre sort of humanitarian-crisis-Keynesian 'theory of economics . . . [U]sually the army loots the banknotes, so more must be substituted. The gas is needed to get the banknotes to pay the workers, who use them for consumer goods and food whereas the soldiers use them for liquor.'[40] There were, of course, some more lasting accomplishments. For example, there were no Congolese doctors in 1960. By 1970, WHO projects (funded by the Programme) had trained 200.[41]

Much more positive things could be said about an earlier case in which the EPTA staff and the experts it funded played such a central role in managing and building a new state. In 1950 the UN began setting up an independent government in Libya, a former colony of Italy, which had been defeated in the Second World War. In 1951 EPTA assigned to Libya one of the first Res Reps and took on much of the task of building a civilian administration there. Three years later, the Libyan office still accounted for almost 20 per cent of EPTA's total field office budget.[42] In 1962 Paul Hoffman devoted a chapter of his book on international solidarity to the Libya case, noting that it had been one of the poorest of the self-governing countries when it became independent, with a per capita income of well

---

[38] 15 years and 150,000 Skills, p. 26.

[39] 'Staff of the United Nations Development Programme', DP/STAFF LISTING/2, 19 Jan. 1968. The ratio of international staff, foreign UNDP employees in a country office, to experts (people working for the Specialized Agencies but funded by UNDP) was about 1 to 10 in those days, so the UN civilian presence had probably declined by 60 per cent since its height, but it was still vast.

[40] Letter from Fred Tickner to Winifred Tickner, 17 March 1961, used courtesy of J. Ann Tickner.   [41] Joyce, World of Promise, p. 60.

[42] Memo from David Owen to Trygve Lie, 16 Nov. 1953, Box 11 of David Owen Papers, Columbia University Library, New York.

under a dollar per day (at the 2005 US dollar rate). EPTA helped change that. WHO projects attacked Libya's chronic diseases. ILO and UNESCO education programmes dramatically increased literacy. FAO experts helped to push back the desert, revive Libya's leather exports, and start a citrus industry. UN technical assistance supported new civil service, tax, and statistical systems. All of which put the country in a strong position to use its natural wealth effectively when oil was discovered in 1958.[43]

Basem Khader, whose EPTA and UNDP career began in Libya in the same year, argues that two factors explain the success of the technical assistance programme there. EPTA insisted on having national counterparts working alongside all the foreign experts assigned to the various fledgling ministries. In addition, it had an excellent Resident Representative, Harold Caustin, an economist who had a clear understanding of which sectors should be given priority. 'Of course, we started the process whereby we would respond to requests of government, but the advantage of having a good economist at the head of the mission was that you really weighed the merits of each proposal.' Caustin emphasized the productive sectors, but also health and education, fundamental social sectors that had been ignored throughout years of 'war and colonialist rule'.[44] Khader remembers that soon after oil was discovered Caustin gently dissuaded the prime minister 'from spending the bulk of its new found wealth on large infrastructure projects, as it intended to, emphasizing instead the need to invest in people – mind you this was in the early sixties, way before Human Development Reports came into being'.[45]

Even though Libya, like Congo, enjoyed an extraordinary level of UN financial commitment, it was more typical of the Programme's role in most newly independent nations. Initially the technical assistance programmes provided a few experts who carried out particular state functions while training national counterparts. Some of this was done through a programme called OPEX (provision of OPerational and EXecutive personnel), based on an experiment initiated by Hugh Keenleyside in Bolivia during the crisis there in the early 1950s. Hammarskjöld had a similar idea, an 'International Administrative Service' of experienced and versatile administrators who could be seconded to states that needed them. In 1958 the UN General Assembly approved the programme as a separate part of the Secretariat, but it

[43] Hoffman, *World Without Want*, pp. 98–110.
[44] Basem Khader, interview with Neysan Rassekh (NR), 10 Nov. 2004.
[45] Basem Khader, letter to CNM, 20 Sept. 2005.

always relied on EPTA's recruitment network and was managed, in country, by the Res Reps. From 1964 onwards, EPTA funds could officially be used for the same purpose.[46]

In fact, as has often been the case with UNDP activities, this programme was carried out long before there was an official mandate. W. Arthur Lewis, for example, was acting as Ghana's chief economic planner under an EPTA contract before OPEX was established. In 1961 there were eighty-one official OPEX officers, mostly in Africa, 'with titles like "Air Traffic Controller", "Chief Engineer", "Telecommunications Manager", "Chief Statistician", and "Finance Officer" ',[47] and many more 'standard experts' playing similar roles under EPTA contracts.

The same flexibility demonstrated by EPTA staff in finding and supporting key personnel for the new nations allowed the Programme to open new country offices as rapidly as states became independent. In the same year that EPTA Res Reps took over coordination of the Special Fund at a country level, twenty new country offices were added. Many of their programmes were paid for by contingency reserves that Owen had placed in EPTA budgets after the first financial crisis in the 1950s.[48]

With the funds the technical assistance programme built postal services and public communications systems; for example, EPTA helped to link geographically divided Pakistan by telephone and radio.[49] The Special Fund and UNDP helped to establish schools of public administration in Ethiopia and Ghana, and supported similar schools throughout the developing world.[50] It provided the seed money for planning agencies and development boards. In Singapore, for example, where the Economic Development Board focused on promoting foreign investment, the Special Fund's assistance created a system for the rapid evaluation of investors' proposals, set up industrial estates, and created a technical service department to determine standards for manufacturing products, directly supporting more than 600 firms between 1960 and 1965.[51] In most other new states, where national plans called for building *government* capacity to establish, finance, and manage new enterprises, UNDP and its predecessors supported that role just as vigorously.

Bernard Chidzero, the late Zimbabwean finance minister who spent much of his career at the UN, including UNDP (in exile from the

---

[46] Keenleyside, *International Aid*, pp. 61–2. Alexander, *International Technical Assistance Experts*, pp. 15–16.   [47] Joyce, *World of Promise*, p. 63.

[48] *15 years and 150,000 Skills*, p. 25.   [49] *Technical Assistance: What? How? Why?*, pp. 56–7.

[50] Alexander, *Technical Assistance Experts*, p. 171.

[51] *40 Years of World Development* (New York: UNDP, 1989), p. 8.

white-settler government), but who was known as one of the organization's sharpest internal critics, saw this capacity-building work as very
different from much of what emanated from New York and Geneva.
UNDP's predecessors played 'a most constructive role . . . in promoting
the independence or decolonization process rather than simply talk,
preach, make resolutions, or leave the process to take its own course'.[52]

Richard N. Gardner, a key figure in the Kennedy administration's
Bureau of International Organization Affairs, agrees. The unprecedented
wave of decolonization that crested during Kennedy's short tenure
(1961–3) was both unexpected and unstoppable. The new governments
needed support, and it was better that it came multilaterally. When the
United States was out there alone, 'putting down conditions, then rocks
started going though the American embassy windows'. Moreover, there
was 'a multiplier effect of getting other countries to contribute', especially
when Hoffman 'refashioned' Kennedy's idea of making the 1960s a
'Development Decade' in ways that attracted commitments of funds from
other nations that Kennedy was willing to match with 80 cents of new US
money for every new dollar contributed to UNDP by other countries.[53]

Like Chidzero, Kennedy was primarily concerned with 'the political
side' of development.[54] Yet decolonization involves more than building
local capacities to take over the apparatus of the colonial state. As India's
renowned social psychologist, Ashis Nandy, argues, it is sometimes a question of preaching and talking, at least to the extent that new words can aid
in the decolonization of the mind, the obliteration of the sense of inferiority inculcated not only by colonial schools, but by the entire culture of
inequality enforced by the colonizer.[55] Obliterating the remnants of that
colonial culture has been a focus of Uka Tjandrasasmita's life work. An
eminent Indonesian archaeologist now in his seventies, Tjandrasasmita
smiles when he thinks about just how important the restoration of a ninth-
century Buddhist temple complex was to developing his own specialty, the
architectural history of his country's Islamic period, beginning some 500
years later. The modern restoration of Borobudur, in central Java, began
with an EPTA/UNESCO study in 1955, the first of UNESCO's projects
(with support of UNDP) aimed at preserving major world cultural sites.

---

[52] Louis Emmerij, Richard Jolly, and Thomas G. Weiss, *Ahead of the Curve? UN Ideas and Global Challenges* (Bloomington, Ind.: Indiana University Press, 2001), p. 184.
[53] Richard N. Gardner, interview with Thomas G. Weiss, UN Intellectual History Project, 29 Feb. 2002, pp. 16–18.   [54] Ibid., p. 16.
[55] Ashis Nandy, *The Intimate Enemy: Loss and Recovery of Self Under Colonialism* (Delhi: Oxford University Press, 1983).

4.2 Borobudur (the surrounding vegetation provides a sense of scale)

(Others include saving Egypt's Abu Simbel from the rising waters behind
the Aswan dam in the 1960s and 1970s and a current programme to restore
Cambodia's war-ravaged Angkor Wat temple complex.) In 1968 a plan to
rebuild the lower terraces of the Borobudur complex and stop further
erosion was completed. In 1971 a UNESCO/UNDP resident director of the
project was put in place. In 1975 the most concentrated phase of work
began. It was completed eight years later, in 1983.

Thus throughout Tjandrasasmita's fifty-year career, Borobudur has
been the laboratory and training ground for a growing cadre dedicated to
reconstructing and remembering every aspect of Indonesia's precolonial
history. It was the place for the students to learn field skills, for archaeol-
ogists in charge of their first major projects to recall lessons about
complex restorations, and for old men to impart their wisdom to another
generation. 'We know now that Borobudur was a place of learning, a university of the Buddhist world. It has become that again', even after the
restoration. The archaeologist points to a weathered briefcase from a
recent international conference, one in a long series that have engaged
Borobudur alumni in the reconstruction of all corners of pre-colonial
Asia – animist, Buddhist, Hindu, Islamic – 'in words' as well as in stone.
Then he talks about the UNDP-sponsored global conferences on heritage
that began in Borobudur in the early 1990s. Of course, the people in the

immediate neighborhood of world heritage sites benefit from the tourism they generate, but 'everyone' gains from the new 'confidence about our past'.[56]

When some old UNDP hands think about the sense of confidence within the developing world to which the Programme contributed, the first place that comes to mind is not Java's Borobudur, but nearby Singapore. When the British ceded control over internal affairs, in 1959, they left a four-year-old development plan appropriate to a medium-sized English county seat with a large rural hinterland, a place where economic and social change was expected to be almost imperceptible. The automobile age was considered so far off that bicycle rickshaws were still at the centre of the transport plan.

Instead, what the new native government inherited was a fractured community in the middle of a population explosion, rampant unemployment, and constant industrial unrest. The new government faced the almost certain prospect that Singapore would be separated from its natural regional market in the rest of British Malaysia. (Integration was anathema both to Malays, who feared the hegemony of Singapore's non-Malay business and professional elite, and to Indonesia, the already fully independent regional power.) Growth through import substitution was out of the question.

Singapore turned to EPTA for advice and received two industrial planning missions, in 1960 and 1961, led by a Dutch economist, Albert Winsemius, who regularly returned to the country and remained one of its main economic architects for the next twenty-five years. In 1984 Winsemius argued that his missions had convinced Prime Minister Lee Kuan Yew's People's Action Party to pursue 'a capitalist policy of free enterprise on the economic plane, for the purpose of spending the money thus earned according to its social principles'.[57] UNDP remained Singapore's major source of technical assistance throughout the entire period. Denis Halliday, who served as deputy Res Rep to the city state,

---

[56] Uka Tjandrasasmita, interview with CNM, 25 May 2005. A more critical analysis of the specific impact of Borobudur can be found in Heidi Dahles, *Tourism, Heritage, and National Culture in Java: Dilemmas of a Local Community* (London: Routledge, 2001). While the restoration served the end of reclaiming the pre-colonial past by meticulously reconstructing the region as a textbook of national history, it also served the government's political goal of repressing potential separatist interpretations of the Indonesian past, especially those generated by the poor.

[57] Speech to the General Electric International Personnel Council Meeting, 19 June 1984, quoted in Chow Kit Boey, Chew Moh Leen, and Elizabeth Su, *One Partnership in Development: UNDP and Singapore* (Singapore: United Nations Association of Singapore, 1989), p. 1.

notes that Singapore received the highest per capita UNDP support of any country, and that the government used it wisely, 'focusing heavily on education, industrial development, and the urban planning, on every aspect of the now successful industries'.[58]

Lee Kwan Yew's party also sequenced its interventions well. When Charles Abrams, the urban planner whose EPTA mission triggered the establishment of the Middle East Technical University, arrived in Singapore in 1963, there was no talk of not being able to 'get there from here'. Earlier decisions about the industrial trajectory of the country, and about the educational infrastructure needed to keep the country on that path, allowed Abrams's UN mission to focus on its assigned tasks: dealing with population growth, housing, traffic congestion, and urban decay.[59] In 1978 the country's former finance minister, Sui Sen, emphasized the effect of that sequencing:

> In retrospect, I can fairly describe Singapore's evolution since 1960, when the UN team on Economic Development led by Dr. Winsemius first studied us, as the prototype of economic development promoted by international institutions such as the World Bank, IMF [International Monetary Fund], and GATT [General Agreement on Tariffs and Trade]. We have followed policies which developed countries have urged all developing countries to pursue, that is, to start with simple manufactures (which the developed countries helped by opening markets . . .) and then to upgrade our economic skills and go on to more skill intensive manufacture. Eventually the hope is that we, like the industrialized countries, can go on to capital intensive, high technology industries,[60]

which, in fact, have become the engines of Singapore's growth in the twenty-first century.

Sui Sen shared the view of virtually all of Singapore's political and economic leaders that the country's development would have been much slower without UNDP. The Programme had the technical knowledge and contacts to find appropriate experts and the best overseas training more quickly than the government on its own, and it provided those knowledge resources at a low cost.[61]

---

[58] Denis Halliday, interview with NR, 4 Dec. 2004.
[59] Boey, Leen, and Su, *One Partnership in Development*, p. 60; Henderson, *Housing and the Democratic Ideal*, pp. 187–9.
[60] Sui Sen, quoted in Boey, Leen, and Su, *One Partnership in Development*, p. 19.
[61] Kishore Mahbubani, interview with CNM, 26 July 2004.

Many of Singapore's leaders were recipients of EPTA/UNDP fellowships to study abroad. Others worked on UNDP projects, including
the country's fifth president, Ong Teng Cheong, a government architect
who was seconded to the UNDP project that followed Charles Abrams's
recommendations about transport and land-use planning in the
city's core.[62] Denis Halliday, imbued with Wakefield's principles, would
have us remember the wisdom of Ong and officials like him as the real
source of Singapore's decolonization and development. UNDP's role, as
always, was just to provide the means of achieving a vision articulated by
national leaders.

What of other former colonies? Sui Sen emphasizes that Singapore's
choices were, in part, a matter of good luck, including some element of
luck in getting *good* advice from a UN expert at the beginning. Others are
less charitable. Kishore Mahbubani, Singapore's long-time ambassador
to the UN, notes that in the 1950s per capita income in Singapore and
Ghana was similar and Ghana's resource endowment and education
institutions were better. Today, incomes in Ghana, one of sub-Saharan
Africa's relative success stories, are much what they were in the 1950s,
while Singapore has become part of the First World. Mahbubani believes
that this was the result of 'bad policy choices over the years'.[63] It might
also have had something to do bad advice from foreign experts at the
beginning, as we shall see in the next chapter. Yet even if that is true, there
still may be reason to praise the accomplishments of many African governments and the role played by UNDP in helping to build their capacity.

Victor Angelo, a career UNDP officer from Portugal who has served in
some of Africa's most troubled countries (Angola, São Tomé and
Príncipe, Tanzania (dealing with refugees from the Rwandan genocide),
Zimbabwe), gets exasperated at those who dismiss the continent's development. Tired, squeezing in time for a conversation with me into the wee
hours of Saturday morning at the end of a difficult week in Sierra Leone
where he worked as Res Rep, he insisted that 'Certainly things are better
than they were under colonialism. Under colonialism, [as far as their
colonial governments were concerned] these people did not even
exist . . . We don't know what happens in the mind of someone who is
colonized. The Zimbabweans, for instance, twenty-four years ago they
were several notches below the white man's dog.'

---

[62] 'Mr. Ong Teng Cheong: Fifth President of the Republic of Singapore', http://www.istana.
gov.sg/history.html (accessed 15 July 2005).
[63] Kishore Mahbubani, interview with CNM, 26 July 2004.

Decolonization is 'about human dignity', about treating people as equals, letting them 'succeed, and letting them *fail*'. That is why the approach *must* be, 'This is your country. You are in charge. And you are the ones who will be assessed by your population and history. Do it. We will help, but you have to take the lead – it is your call.' There is no particular reason for us, for Europeans or North Americans, to think that we could do it any better.

> I always remember a report that the Chamber of Commerce of London wrote after travelling to a country at the end of the nineteenth century. They came back, a trade mission to explore trading [opportunities] – came back with a terrible report. [The locals] spend their time drinking, don't work, lazy, spend their time making children, brutish – better to forget that. This country was Norway. [Even] . . . in the 1950s, Norway was a backwater.[64]

His point struck home. I had lived in Norway as a child in the early 1960s, before oil was discovered there. 'Backwater' may be too harsh, but Norway then was very different from the country that is now regularly at the top of the Human Development Index. Angelo's argument reminded me of a point made by Sandy Rotival, one of the earliest Res Reps in francophone West Africa. Rotival explained that Administrator Paul Hoffman was always reminding international staff (in those days, primarily British, US, and French nationals) to think about their own countries' not so distant pasts, and about their backward regions, today. That is why Hoffman pushed for UNDP to be 'universal', to be 'ready to offer assistance to Mississippi, if asked'.[65]

Learning and blind spots

Hoffman and his colleagues also increasingly recognized that many of their original assumptions about the capabilities of developing countries – many of which were based on the western European experience of the Marshall Plan – were painfully off-base. For example, in the early years, UNDP technical assistance placed a significant burden on many national governments; they were supposed to provide housing, transport, and salaries for national counterparts of every UN expert. Writing about Rwanda immediately after independence, Richard Symonds complains, 'Regulations which made sense in New York made none in a country as

---

[64] J. Victor Angelo, interview with CNM, 8 Jan. 2005.
[65] Alexander Holt Rotival, interview with CNM, 14 Sept. 2004.

poor as this. The Government was required to provide transport for our experts, but the total transport at its disposal was the Presidential Volkswagen.' Symonds convinced New York to make exceptions, and then found that the only people in Kigali who could maintain the vehicles were European missionaries, the White Fathers, who also became the major source of briefings for new experts, 'for the Ministers in Government had almost all been their pupils'.[66]

Under such conditions, one of the basic assumptions of the original UNDP approach was almost always violated: national governments rarely had the capacity to develop comprehensive forward-looking indicative plans that identified the critical inputs of expertise and capital that needed to be provided by international donors. When Margaret Joan Anstee was Resident Representative in Bolivia in the 1960s, she addressed this problem by bringing in a team led by a Chilean, Pedro Vuskovic, to create the kind of development plan that had been identified by both Arthur Lewis and her close friend Raúl Prebisch as essential if a country were to get the most out of its resources.[67] Ironically, in 1965, when EPTA began its first comprehensive evaluation of the UN contribution to development in a handful of countries, it decided that it could not do so because the combined programmes of the UN were not prepared within an overall framework. Even in Chile, where indicative planning was the most advanced, the government had only begun to plan and coordinate technical assistance from all sources in 1964.[68] Perhaps even more ironically, over the next decade the capitalist country that would plan its use of foreign assistance most effectively was Singapore, yet it had abolished its Economic Planning Unit in 1968. Nevertheless, 'economic planning continued at the highest levels of the Ministry of Finance with major support from the Economic Development Board, the country's (UNDP supported) investment promotion agency'.[69]

Singapore's choice not to draw attention to its economic planning actually made sense in the cold war world, where 'planning' was increasingly treated as anathema among both centrist politicians in the United States and international investors. (It was like accepting Winsemius's

---

[66] Symonds, 'Bliss Was It in That Dawn', p. 87.

[67] Margaret Joan Anstee, *Never Learn to Type: A Woman at the United Nations* (Chichester: John Wiley & Sons, 2003), p. 87. Anstee adds, 'With due modesty, this was not my initiative, but that of Prebisch. It was intended as a pilot project to see if the approach would work.' Letter to CNM, 27 Sept. 2005.

[68] Garcia, *International Cooperation and Development*, p. 170.

[69] Boey, Leen, and Su, *One Partnership in Development*, p. 16.

recommendation that the statue of the British colonial leader, Raffles, be left standing as proof of the country's interest in working with foreign business and governments.) That growing antipathy to planning also helps to explain why UNDP itself became more reticent about emphasizing its centrality to any rational approach to development. In 1962 Hoffman would forcefully argue that market economies needed comprehensive planning to ensure that resources would be used efficiently, and that (contrary to some academic arguments) this was something that *democratic* societies could do quite well, as the Marshall Plan had proved. By 1971 the theme had almost disappeared from his set speeches, even though every other part of the original 'better way' argument remained.[70]

In explaining the development failures of the 1960s, Hoffman, like most of the founding generation of the UN's development network, tended to point to failures on the part of the developed nations to live up to their part of the bargain. Recall that the original concept involved not just the sharing of skills and resources, but also the creation of a conducive environment of domestic and international institutions. Yes, it may have been the case that few developing nations had created the institutions that allowed them to get the most out of the technical assistance and investment provided by the international community. Nonetheless, Hoffman would remind audiences, the 'international community' had not provided the institutional or structural environment in which most countries could advance. He cited his former deputy, Arthur Lewis, who argued that before forcing developing countries to compete in the global marketplace (a panacea that was becoming fashionable in Washington), it was essential to fix the international trading system so that they had a level playing field on which to contend.[71] Singapore's Sui Sen is correct in concluding that his country had been successful in following the economic orthodoxy taking hold in Washington because 'developed countries helped by opening markets' to Singaporean goods, but few other countries enjoyed the same international trading environment. Developed countries had not opened their markets to goods produced by most developing countries.

Hoffman's and Lewis's arguments echoed a 1968 report by Prebisch, a mid-term evaluation of the 1960s 'Development Decade' that had been declared by John F. Kennedy in 1961. Without agreement on a global strategy, and without agreement on the institutions that would make such a

---

[70] Cf. Hoffman, *World Without Want*, pp. 42–50, with Hoffman, 'Development Cooperation: A Fact of Modern Life', *Virginia Quarterly Review*, 47, 3 (1971): 321–33.

[71] Hoffman, 'Development Cooperation', 323–5.

strategy feasible, the world had been left with 'A Development Decade without a development policy . . . no wonder its results are so meager'.[72] In a 1971 account of the UN's development work, begun by Owen but completed by a colleague after Owen's death, Prebisch's argument provided the central explanation for those places where UNDP had failed.

Yet even if members of the founding generation placed the blame for the decade's limited success on the governments of developed countries, they recognized many flaws in the UN technical assistance system itself. The most widely recognized problems came from the execution of all projects by the Specialized Agencies, which received overhead payments of one-sixth or one-seventh of the cost of every expert they placed in the field. Because the agencies' regular budgets were no larger than that of a 'medium-sized university', technical assistance funds were like manna from heaven. For every six or seven experts an agency put in a field, a new regular staff member could be hired in Paris, Geneva, Rome, or Montreal, which helped to explain why the agencies tried to keep so many people in the field, even when their contribution to development was marginal.

When Hoffman asked Sir Robert Jackson to write an independent study on the capacity of the UN development system to take on more tasks effectively, as part of the evaluation at the end of the Decade, Jackson thought about having

> a Swiss artist . . . who draws very good animals, draw me a coloured plate . . . there were about 22 agencies and we would have had 22 dogs and FAO would have been the biggest dog. He would have been a Saint Bernard, and ILO would have been an Airedale and so on and so forth . . . But in every case, the tail, which is technical assistance, would have been much bigger than the dog.[73]

It had become a bureaucratic imperative to provide as much technical assistance as possible. Agencies fought to protect their pieces of the technical assistance pie, and combined to exclude other potential executors of UNDP projects. This led to inflexibility and thus an inability to respond to many of the needs for expertise that governments identified.

Often, the self-interest of the agencies reinforced prejudices within the UNDP culture. When the UN's regional economic commission surveyed

---

[72] Prebisch quoted in Vernon Duckworth-Barker, *Breakthrough to Tomorrow: The Story of International Cooperation for Development through the United Nations* (New York: United Nations, 1971), p. 23.

[73] Robert G. A. Jackson, United Nations Oral History Project Interview, 10 Feb. 1986, Dag Hammarskjöld Library.

Asian governments regarding their needs for technical personnel, the list included the electrical engineers, statisticians, and planners that the agencies were ready to provide. Yet some of the most critical needs – for experts in managing private firms, commercial attachés, trade promotion officers, marketing personnel, and entrepreneurs[74] – were for the kinds of people that no agency could provide and who were, in any event, considered a little suspect by many on the staff that Owen had built in his own image.

Equally, despite the generally egalitarian commitments of UNDP staff, in Owen and Hoffman's day the notion that the imposition of 'expertise' could be part of the *problem* of underdevelopment, rather than part of its solution, was never considered, even though some of the earliest independent critiques of the UN development system pointed to just that issue. Recall the very different vision of international development cooperation proposed in the nineteenth century by the Anglo-Irish railway promoter who wanted the whole developing world to follow the lead of the North American west (page 32, above). In 1964 Harvard economist (and Kennedy's ambassador to India) John Kenneth Galbraith wrote,

> A hundred years ago the development of the trans-Mississippi plains in the United States called, above all else, for a land policy which would get the land settled and plowed and a transportation system which would get the products to market. . . It was our unquestioned good fortune that community education experts, grain marketing analysts, home economists, vocational counselors, communication specialists, or public safety advisors had not been invented. Had these existed, attention would have been drawn away from the strategically central tasks.[75]

So as to make the point perfectly clear, in 1966, development economists I. M. Little and J. M. Clifford noted that this was just the sort of expert 'assistance' that UNESCO, the FAO, the ILO, and the ITU were providing to Africa, Asia, and Latin America.[76]

The UN network's uncritical reliance on 'expertise', well into the 1970s, reflected the slow movement of its governing ideas from the colo-

---

[74] United Nations Commission for Asia and the Far East, *Fields of Economic Development Handicapped by Lack of Trained Personnel in Certain Countries of Asia and the Far East* (Bangkok: United Nations, 1951).

[75] John Kenneth Galbraith, *Economic Development* (Cambridge, Mass.: Harvard University Press, 1964), pp. 27–8.

[76] I. M. Little and J. M. Clifford, *International Aid* (Chicago: Aldine, 1966), p. 46.

nial, 'development as efficiency' pole towards the democratic pole of 'development as freedom', outlined in chapter 2. Similarly, African, Asian, and Latin American staffers remember colonial attitudes, paternalism, and racism that pervaded parts of the organization. The acting Haitian prime minister, Gerard Latortue, has only a few bitter memories of UNDP. They are about a series of interactions with former French colonial officers in UNDP and a German expert under contract who denigrated the West Africans they served and tried to treat Latortue in the same way.[77]

Ahmed Tejan Kabbah, who became Sierra Leone's president in 1996 after a twenty-five year career with UNDP, remembers encountering fewer specific instances of racism, but there was the case when the Programme turned down a man with a degree from Congo's Kinshasa University out of hand, 'because no one believed Kinshasa was capable of giving a Master's degree'. More typically, what looked like racism, Kabbah argues, was really just a matter of the donors, especially the United States, exercising their indirect control over things.[78]

R. D. Makkar, who joined the EPTA office in India in 1964 and rose to the highest rank ever achieved by an Indian 'national' officer, recalls the same pattern. Unlike Latortue or Kabbah, he turned down the opportunity to stay in New York as a more highly paid 'international' UN staffer, largely because of this problem. When he was first brought to headquarters, he noticed a more intense version of a pattern he had seen in Delhi,

> Some brave Johnny was always dictating to me from behind my shoulder as to how to write my project formulation [to reflect] the orientation of certain major donors who wanted the country to move in a particular direction, not the direction the country itself would have liked to go. This deprived people like me . . . of a certain sense of satisfaction in not being able to give honest opinions, views about these things. I was getting a bit suffocated.[79]

A further sign of how far the early UNDP still had to move towards the democratic pole has to do with its almost astonishing lack of attention to the role of women in development. This was not unconnected to the sexism that pervaded some UN activities. Recently, the United Nations has been rocked by the scandal of sexual abuse by peacekeepers and the

---

[77] Gerard Latortue, interview with CNM, 29 July 2004.
[78] Ahmed Tejan Kabbah, interview with CNM, 10 Jan. 2005.
[79] R. D. Makkar, interview with CNM, 14 Dec. 2004.

UN reacted swiftly. Forty years ago, things were a little different: male staff simply billed the UN for the costs of the sexual favours they demanded from local women. The provincial Resident Representative, Fred Tickner, wrote of one (not unique) case one group of bluehelmets who 'rendered an account as follows: "une maison et 4 demoiselles – à frs. 42,000 pour chaque demoiselle par mois".'[80]

More telling for the work that UNDP was expected to accomplish was how often reports aimed at showing EPTA's involvement in the promotion of women describe fortuitous accidents rather than planned interventions. Typical was a 1953 account billed as 'Reviving Cottage Industries in the Philippines', after the influx of cheap US products had destroyed the market for local cloth. The key figures were a weaver (the unnamed wife of a diplomat at the US embassy) and an EPTA social welfare consultant (identified only as 'Mrs Murphy') from another project. The diplomat's wife, 'being very much interested in weaving . . . intended to spend the two years [of her husband's assignment] weaving and experimenting particularly with Philippine fibres'. There was little information about that among the diplomatic set, but Mrs Murphy introduced the American to local hand-weavers. That led to personal interest in the welfare of Philippine women.

The two foreigners found ways of producing better thread at local plants, changing traditional looms to reflect the widths of cloth coming from the States, giving women weavers access to credit to boost production, convincing dressmakers to buy the new local cloth, and even cajoling the wife of the US ambassador into wearing a local cloth dress: 'Everyone, of course, thought it was imported, and they were very much interested when it was found to be locally made.'[81]

The project was far from inconsequential, but that is not the point. It is rather that something that initially involved the volunteer work of women who happened to be in the country, a project that began with no material support from the UN, was one of the best that EPTA could find to show its commitment to women. Even as the project ramped up, with significant UN funding and with expansion into other craft fields, some dominated by men, women remained in the background. The 1953 report includes a photograph of 'one of the [female] United Nations experts in cottage weaving who is supervising the research and training programme',[82] but again, no name is given.

---

[80] Letter from Fred Tickner to Winifred Tickner, 28 March 1961. Used by permission of J. Ann Tickner.   [81] *Sharing Skills*, pp. 11–15.   [82] Ibid., p. 15.

Margaret Joan Anstee, who was in the Philippines at the time, clearly remembers the unnamed expert. She is Lysbeth M. Wallace, a celebrated craftswoman who arrived in Manila with a fresh Master of Fine Arts degree from the prestigious Cranbrook Academy and left, two years later, the author of the definitive *Hand-Weaving in the Philippines*, and the mentor to scores of the women who created a new, competitive industry.[83] Unfortunately, the name of the diplomat's wife who initiated the project is still lost.

Over the last twenty years feminist scholars of international affairs have documented the critical role that seemingly fortuitously placed women – wives, secretaries, nannies, and the like – have always played, long before women had an official place.[84] The UN development network benefited from that in the Philippines. Similarly, Fred Tickner's wife, Winifred, calls her memoir, 'A Spectator in the Congo', even though it is full of evidence that belies the title. A better one might have begun, 'An Unpaid UN Worker . . .'

Even the best of the UN's technical assistance leaders wore the same blinders. Anstee remembers Hugh Keenleyside as being supportive of women (he was also one of Winifred Tickner's friends) and Anstee's autobiography lionizes Keenleyside for his early work in Bolivia.[85] He only partially returned the compliment. In 1966 he wrote,

> [T]he Resident Representatives have been men with two exceptions, first, Joan Anstie [*sic*] in Bolivia. It is probable that there will be very few opportunities of this kind and that discrimination against women will indefinitely continue. Governments . . . are hesitant about accepting such nominees . . . The nomination of Barbara Ward . . . would, of course, be a compliment to any country, but the number of such women is extremely limited.[86]

Ward was Robert Jackson's wife, a celebrated writer on development, an extremely close friend of Kennedy's UN ambassador, Adlai Stevenson, and

---

[83] Margaret Joan Anstee, letter to CNM, 27 Sept. 2005. A brief biography and recent photograph of Wallace can be found in 'Lysbeth M. Wallace Named 2004 Rude Osolnik Award Winner', *The Blue Moon*, 11, 4 (July/August 2004). http://artscouncil.ky.gov/whtsnew/bmoon/julaug04/06.htm (accessed 5 Oct. 2005).

[84] One of the important early analyses was Cynthia Enloe, 'Diplomatic Wives', in her *Bananas, Beaches, and Bases: Making Feminist sense of International Politics* (Berkeley: University of California Press, 1989), pp. 93–123. J. Ann Tickner, the daughter of Winifred, is one of the pioneering scholars in feminist international relations. See her *Gender in International Relations: Feminist Perspectives on Achieving Global Security* (New York: Columbia University Press, 1992).

[85] Margaret Joan Anstee, interview with CNM, 6 July 2005. Anstee, *Never Learn to Type*, p. 177.

[86] Keenleyside, *International Aid*, p. 179.

a dining partner of Kennedy, the Pope, and hundreds of other luminaries. She was not, however, someone with the extensive day-to-day administrative and field experience of Anstee or, for that matter, of Winifred Tickner.

If the culture of the times explains some of the blind spots of the early UN development network – its sexism and its racism – others were a matter of its particular practices. As its leaders recognized, the early UNDP, like many international development agencies, had no effective evaluation system. A 1971 study concluded,

> for the most part, the lessons of experience repose in the memories of programme managers, in project files, in the experience and reports of experts and in the minds of national officials. This situation has prompted the Administrator of UNDP to state that the agencies 'have no memory'. There is very little collated knowledge about the factors and conditions which make for success and those which make for failure.[87]

For many years even project evaluation was just a matter of asking the expert assigned, the executing agency, and the developing country government whether they were 'satisfied' with the project. The bias of such a process should be clear: experts were likely to be rehired if they were proved 'successful', the agencies' interest in posting the largest number of experts has already been discussed, and governments – the group most likely to provide an honest opinion – could also have perverse reasons for considering most projects a success. Symonds observed that 'there were even cases where the extension of an expert appeared not unconnected with the desire of national counterparts to retain a source of duty free whisky'.[88] The limited evaluation that took place was recognized as likely to yield biased results.

Yet, Keenleyside, Hoffman, and most of the UN development network's founders remained unaware of how their own unrealistic preconceptions helped create a culture in which serious evaluation and the slow accumulation of lessons from experience were unlikely to emerge. The problem of world development seemed, at the same time, both too urgent and too easy to solve. Marge Fonyi, who worked beside the first Administrator almost every day, remembers Hoffman's constant refrain, 'If we do our jobs well, we will be out of business in twenty-five years', which should not be too hard, if you went by the experience of the Marshall Plan.[89]

---

[87] William Leonard, Béat Alexander Jenny, and Offia Nwali, *UN Development Aid Criteria and Methods of Evaluation* (New York: Arno Press, 1971), p. 48.
[88] Symonds, 'Bliss Was It in That Dawn', pp. 127–8.
[89] Marge Fonyi, interview with CNM, 22 Sept. 2004.

When I asked Roger Owen about the aspects of his father's work and time that it is essential to understand if we are going to get UNDP's history right, he slightly changed the subject, 'I met Walt Rostow once, in Texas. He leaned across his desk and said, "I'm worried about Africa" – this is how they talked. They were "worried" about large parts of the world, which they then would propose to reform in totally naïve and simplistic ways.' David Owen, his son said, was very sensibly proud of UN technical assistance:

> The request comes, you send in an expert, they are provided with a counterpart, and the counterpart learns. Sometimes, remarkable things happen – yaws and malaria are eradicated. It's when it got 'grand' that it got much more complicated.

His father tried to cling 'to the TA bit', but that was 'very difficult to remain steady' among the

> flashy, flamboyant dead men of those days. . . . It *had* to work, it had to work *quickly*, it had to be *shown* that it worked. If it *didn't* work quickly, you *had* to try something else . . . Somebody always has to come forward with a new plan and say the old plan doesn't work, this is the way to do it, there's some inbuilt dynamic there, which means that it [the international development system] can never consider itself properly, so it's always the next thing, the next thing, the next thing.[90]

When David Owen began to document the history of UN technical assistance with the coloured pins that came to crowd his map of the world, it is unlikely that he expected them eventually to make a picture of a universally prosperous, technologically sophisticated, 'developed' world. The goal then was only to show the dissemination of one, modest 'better idea' about the conduct of world affairs, the idea, in Hoffman's words, that

> There is no country so rich that it cannot profit from an expanding world economy and a more progressive world society. By the same token, there is no country so poor that it cannot help itself and its neighbors by contributing to the attainment of such goals.[91]

For better or worse, by 1971, when Hoffman wrote those words, the expectations of the UN's development network had become much higher.

90 Roger Owen, interview with CNM, 7 Sept. 2004.
91 Hoffman, 'Development Cooperation', 328.

5

Lewis in Ghana and after

This chapter recounts one story about how expectations grew, about how the modest idea of UN technical assistance, perhaps inevitably, 'got grand'. It is also a story about how one man, associated with much of the rest of UNDP's history, began to see beyond the 'grand' ideas of the 1950s and to anticipate the ideas that would govern UNDP a half century later. Bill Draper, the Administrator in the early 1990s, argues that the first *Human Development Reports* 'showed how national budgets could be redirected from . . . prestige projects into priority areas . . . such as basic health and universal primary education'.[1] This is the story of how one man began to learn that lesson.

It is a story about the way in which people from the UN's development network played a central role in the economic transformation of a new country; in that sense, it is one story that could stand for many more, one instance of the roles that UNDP and its predecessor played in scores of countries. Thus, it is the story of a country where the UN's early role paralleled its role in Singapore, but this story has a very different outcome. It is a story about the archetypal development project of the time: a giant hydroelectric dam at Akosombo, Ghana, behind which rose what was intended to be the world's largest man-made lake, stretching more than 200 miles up the Volta River.

The central players in the story are just as big as the project itself. First, there is Robert G. A. Jackson, one of the real heroes of the Second World War and, even more, of the immediate reconstruction, a man for whom running a quarter of the British empire as a command economy was not too daunting a job. He was later lionized by Frank J. Davidson, the engineer and philanthropist who coined the phrases 'big is beautiful' and 'global infrastructure solutions' to describe the kind of work for which Sir

---

[1] William H. Draper III, 'Foreword', *Human Development Report 1992* (New York: Oxford University Press), p. iii.

Robert was famous.[2] Jackson epitomized the best of the grand view of development. He once declared that

> great and imaginative macro-engineering projects, schemes that would benefit tens of millions of people (just think, for a moment of making adequate supplies of water available in the Sahel), are already available on the drawing boards, and the technical means to carry them out are at hand, yet they languish. Why? Because only a tiny minority of the architects of the schemes possess the diplomatic and negotiating skills . . . to convince governments and people that they should be brought to life. Many examples of this failure can be found all over the world, as a result, mankind is the poorer, and large parts of the globe remain underdeveloped.[3]

Second, there is Jackson's wife, Barbara Ward, a moral philosopher, brilliant journalist, and more than competent economist, someone who could summarize the fundamental critique of neoclassical economics 'in four persuasive sentences' and speak with the greatest moral authority to the most devout religious leaders, Christian or Muslim,[4] all the while captivating them with her stunning good looks and elegant style.

And then there is the largest of the larger-than-life characters, Kwame Nkrumah, Africa's George Washington[5] and more.

Nkrumah was an acute social analyst and philosopher who, in 1957, brought independence to Great Britain's Gold Coast colony, which he renamed 'Ghana', after a West African empire that had flourished a thousand years before. *Life* magazine, in its issue celebrating the millennium, named Nkrumah one of the 100 most influential people of the last 1,000 years, alongside Martin Luther, Christopher Columbus, and Kublai Khan.[6] Nkrumah was not a modest man; he probably would have agreed, and he may have been right to do so.

---

[2] Davidson helped to endow MIT's Systems Engineering Division and is the author of *Macro: Big is Beautiful* (London: Anthony Blond, 1986) and co-editor of Davidson and C. Lawrence Meador, eds., *Macro-Engineering: Global Infrastructure Solutions, the MIT Brunel Lectures 1983–1992* (Chichester: Ellis Horwood, Ltd., 1992).

[3] Robert G. A. Jackson, 'Isambard Kingdom Brunel: Engineer-Manager and Engineer-Diplomat of the Nineteenth Century', in Davidson and Meador, *Macro-Engineering*, p. 7.

[4] Sartaj Aziz, interview with the author (CNM), 10 Dec. 2004. The four sentences are in Barbara Ward, 'Foreword', in Sartaj Aziz, *Hunger, Politics and Markets: the Real Issues in the Food Crisis* (New York: New York University Press, 1975), p. xi.

[5] At least, considered that by many black people in many parts of the world during his lifetime, Roger A. Davidson, Jr, 'The Question of Freedom: African American's and Ghanaian Independence', *Negro History Bulletin*, 60, 3 (1997): 6.

[6] 'Millennium: Top 100 People', *Life*, http://www.life.com/Life/millennium/people/01.html (accessed 22 July 2005).

The least assuming actor in this drama was W. Arthur Lewis, who, nonetheless, had a well-founded, if prickly, faith in his own professional talents. Lewis was the first person born outside Europe or North America to receive the Nobel Prize for economics and was, of course, the man Hoffman chose to be his first UN deputy and to set the broad outlines of the development policy that his organizations would follow.

The story of Ghana's early relationship with the UN development network explains how Lewis ended up working at Hoffman's side. It also helps to explain why Lewis brought a particular set of ideas to that work. These ideas were not necessarily at the centre of his theory of development economics, nor were they the reason he received the Nobel Prize. Nonetheless, they help to explain why, despite the ever grander conceptions of UNDP's role that many officials held throughout the 1960s and 1970s, the Programme's approach moved in the modesty-making direction of 'development as freedom'.

The Volta River project

The story begins with the Gold Coast and the ninety-year history of plans to dam the Volta River. At the beginning of the twentieth century Britain gained control over the Asante kingdom, which covered much the same territory as contemporary Ghana. The colony was unusually prosperous. More important than the gold emphasized by its British name, was cocoa, a cash crop raised by local entrepreneurs, most of whom began as small, migratory farmers. At independence, Ghana produced more than half the world's supply. As early as 1915 the British began thinking about further 'developing' the colony (that is, 'making it even more profitable') by building a hydroelectric dam on the Volta. By 1938 some plans included the construction of a massive aluminium smelter powered by electricity from the dam and supplied by the country's bauxite deposits to the far west of the river crossing at Akosombo.

The Second World War, reconstruction, and a non-violent nationalist revolution in Ghana intervened. In January 1951, the colonial government, two foreign companies (one British, one Canadian), and a compliant board of local chiefs were ready to begin construction when the country's first real elections gave a decisive victory to the nationalists. The new government leader, Nkrumah, whom the British reluctantly released from prison, reopened the entire question of building the dam. He wanted an independent international expert to consider the proposed arrangement and, perhaps, come up with a larger plan for the development of the entire Volta basin, from a new deep-water port on the coast to irrigated agriculture for the former floodplain and inland fisheries throughout the massive lake that would form behind the dam.

The project became the centrepiece of Nkrumah's plan for the country's economic future, even though, as time went on, projections of the strictly economic benefits of the projects declined. For years Nkrumah could find no international financing; nonetheless, 'in a supreme act of faith', he called for construction tenders in 1960, concluding that 'if worst came to the worst, Ghana could just afford to pay for it from the government's own resources'.[7] Eventually, Nkrumah secured loans from the United States and the World Bank. This, in part, required sacrificing the plan to establish Ghana's own bauxite industry (and the network of rails and roads that would connect mines to the dam and port) and awarding two US aluminium companies a long-term contract for very cheap electricity, the key cost in the production of the metal.

What Nkrumah gained in these arrangements were loans. As Jackson, the person with the greatest influence over the final form of the Project, emphasized, 'Not one penny is being *given* to Ghana.'[8] Ultimately the project's costs would be borne by Ghana's citizens in anticipation of the transformation of industry, transport, agriculture, fisheries, and even tourism that the project promised.

The actual consequences have become the stuff of legend for students of development. One-time World Bank economist William Easterly laments that 'The saddest part was that the Volta River Project was the most successful investment project in Ghanaian history.'[9] Nkrumah had expected the project to ensure that Ghanaian incomes would grow at a rate close to that which Singapore actually experienced. Instead, the taxes needed to support the project depressed the incomes of cocoa farmers (already reeling from a general fall in commodity prices) and none of the economic objectives of the project were fully met.

Nor were its political objectives. Nkrumah was overthrown by military men with ties to the country's cocoa regions in 1966, just days after he inaugurated the dam. Yet, neither that military government, nor any of those that followed over the next thirty years, was willing to give up on the fiscal expedient that Nkrumah had discovered: using the easily taxed

---

[7] Robert G. A. Jackson, *The Volta River Project* (London: United Africa Company, 1965), p. 10.
[8] Ibid., p. 11 (emphasis in original).
[9] William R. Easterly, *The Illusive Quest for Growth: Economists' Adventures and Misadventures in the Tropics* (Cambridge, Mass.: MIT Press, 2001), p. 28.

cocoa farmers as a cash cow, milking them to nourish decreasingly far-sighted development schemes.

In response, farmers smuggled their crops outside the country, or stopped producing altogether. When I was a student in Ghana in 1973, the port that the project built was thriving, electricity seemed plentiful, and most of the country's aluminium pots and pans were local products, but the roads to the lake were already in disrepair. Ghana's cocoa exports were falling rapidly as farmers illegally shipped their goods to better markets in neighbouring countries. There were fish from Lake Volta, but, even twenty years after that, in the mid-1990s, UNDP would be funding projects to revive that industry among the farming communities the lake had displaced twenty-five years before.[10]

Rather than increasing agriculture in the Volta basin, as had been the goal of a big rural project of Hoffman's UNDP, the dam reduced crop yields and destroyed shrimp, clam, and river fishing industries. This led, in turn, to 'very intense poverty . . . widespread migration of the popula-tions, particularly of the young and energetic men and women', and increases in crime, prostitution, and 'sexually transmitted diseases, to the extent of becoming a common phenomenon'.[11]

In 2003 the aluminium companies were still consuming 60 per cent of the electricity produced by the dam, yet their contract meant that they only had to pay half the cost of the electricity's production. At the same time that Ghanaians continued to be taxed to cover this huge subsidy, 60 per cent of the country's electrical needs had to be met from other, more expensive, sources.[12] The port remained, aluminium production contin-ued, and a few tourists came each year to gape at the dam and, very occa-sionally, to sport on the lake – meagre results for 'the most successful investment project in Ghanaian history'.

Lewis before Ghana

W. Arthur Lewis enters the Volta River project story in the middle, when Nkrumah, freed from prison, first asks for his advice. To understand why Nkrumah would turn to Lewis, we need to go back to 1915, for the year

[10] Andrew Taylor, interview with CNM, 20 Jan. 2005.
[11] Julius Najah Fobil, 'Remediation of the Environmental Impacts of the Akosombo and Kpong Dams', Volta Basin River Project, University of Ghana, 16 Aug. 2000, http://www.solutions-site.org/artman/publish/article_53.shtml (accessed 24 July 2005).
[12] Government of Ghana, 'The Position of Ghana on the Arrangements with VALCO', 7 May 2003, http://fr.allafrica.com/stories/200305070811.html (accessed 24 July 2005).

the Volta Project was conceived was also the year of W. Arthur Lewis's birth on the small Caribbean island of St Lucia. Lewis was four years younger than Jackson and six years younger than Nkrumah. Like both of them, he was an extremely talented young man from the periphery of the British empire. Like Nkrumah, he became an ardent anti-colonialist. Despite his relative youth, Lewis was the first to do so, attending meetings of followers of Marcus Garvey (one of the fathers of Pan-Africanism) as a young boy.[13]

Lewis was always a precocious child. He completed school at 14, but could not attend university until he reached the normal age, in 1932. He spent the intervening years in the St Lucia civil service, where he learned 'to write, to type, to file and to be orderly. But this was at the expense of not reading enough history and literature, for which these years of one's life are the most appropriate.'[14] In 1935, as a 19-year-old student at the London School of Economics, he offered his services to the leader of the socialist Fabian Society to write a comprehensive policy document on the British West Indies for the 'next Labour government', which seemed a not-too-distant prospect then, at the height of the Depression. Leonard Woolf, a leading Fabian who with his wife, the novelist Virginia Woolf, was at the centre of the Bloomsbury Group and the most prominent theorist of international organization in the first half of the twentieth century, became Lewis's champion, recommending that the proposed pamphlet was 'just what was wanted in the Party'.[15] The result was only the first of a long series of influential studies that Lewis wrote for the Fabian Society.

Lewis continued at LSE until 1948, earning a Ph.D. and then becoming a lecturer. Throughout the Second World War and immediately afterwards he also worked for the government, helping to implement the welfare-oriented Colonial Development and Welfare Act of 1940, a very late, and largely inadequate, British attempt to do something akin to Roosevelt's Good Neighbor Policy.

[13] Yoichi Mine, 'The Political Element in the Works of W. Arthur Lewis: The 1954 Lewis Model and African Development', *The Developing Economies*, 44, 3 (2006), forthcoming.

[14] W. Arthur Lewis, 'Autobiography', from Assar Lindbeck, ed., *Nobel Lectures, Economics 1969–1980* (Singapore: World Scientific Publishing Co., 1992) and http://nobelprize.org/economics/laureates/1979/lewis-autobio.html (accessed 24 July 2005).

[15] Mine, 'The Political Element'. Woolf's signal contribution to the study of international organization was, *International Government: Two reports by L. S. Woolf prepared for the Fabian Research Department, together with a project, by a Fabian committee, for a supranational authority that will prevent war* (Westminster: Fabian Society, 1916).

It was in connection with his work with both the Fabian Society and the government that Lewis first met Nkrumah, at a 1946 conference on British colonial relations. The West African leader had been invited to speak as a critic of government policy, but he also lambasted the Fabians' timid anticolonialism. Lewis took the podium immediately afterward, defending the Fabians' concern with the nitty-gritty of public policy, but, like Nkrumah, attacking the racism still perpetuated by the post-war Labour government.[16]

In 1948 Lewis moved to the University of Manchester, becoming a full professor at the remarkably young age of 33. He also began his correspondence with David Owen at the United Nations and he completed the most influential of his Fabian tracts, *The Principles of Economic Planning*, a pamphlet that laid out the role of government in a mixed, but still fundamentally capitalist, economy.[17] The chapter 'On Planning in Backward Countries' presented Lewis's version of the formula of skills, resources, and institutions (international and domestic) that dominated early UN discussions of the subject.

In September 1950 Owen, in a letter very similar to the one he had written to secure Hans Singer's secondment from the University of Glasgow, wrote to Manchester's Vice-Chancellor requesting that Lewis be assigned to the UN for one year. In November Owen asked Lewis to chair the committee that would write a report on ways 'to promote employment in under-developed countries by means of their development', and Owen broadly hinted at what the conclusion of the report should be, that 'unemployment can be caused by a lack of capital equipment or other complementary resources'.[18]

Lewis, undoubtedly, was sympathetic. Since his first Fabian pamphlet, all his work on development had emphasized the need for much higher levels of international capital assistance than was being contemplated by any of the colonial governments or by the UN. In an often reprinted 1940 article, for example, he had argued that significant economic growth in British Africa would require foreign capital assistance, in today's money, of somewhat more than US$100 per capita, two or three times the annual level of assistance that has ever been achieved.[19] Lewis accepted this, his

[16] Mine, 'Political Element'.
[17] W. Arthur Lewis, *Principles of Economic Planning: A Study Prepared for the Fabian Society* (London: D. Dobson, 1949).
[18] Both letters are in the W. Arthur Lewis Papers, Box 9, Seeley G. Mudd Manuscript Library, Princeton University. Used by permission of the Princeton University Library (Lewis Papers).
[19] W. Arthur Lewis, Michael Scott, Martin Wight, and Colin Legum, *Attitude to Africa* (Harmondsworth: Penguin Books, 1951), p. 71. Lewis's chapter is reprinted from *Three Banks Review*, 1940.

first, UN assignment and continued at the centre of the debates over the creation of a capital development fund until the establishment in 1960 of the World Bank's International Development Association (IDA), even though he spent much of his time away from UN headquarters and in the developing world.

Ghana

Shortly after completing his first assignment for Owen, Lewis was contacted by Nkrumah, who wanted him to come to the Gold Coast capital, Accra, to advise him on the colonial authority's planned Volta Project and on the possibility of extending it to a monumental 'TVA type' regional development scheme. (TVA – the Tennessee Valley Authority – oversaw the massive series of dams, reforestation, flood control, and agricultural projects, initiated by Roosevelt in 1933, that eventually transformed the poorest region of the United States.) The job would take one and a half to two years.

Lewis refused. He could not, he said, resign from Manchester at that point, and, in any event, he had already been asked to take on a short-term UN assignment in India.[20] Nkrumah then turned to Robert Jackson, who, after a number of years working for the UN, had had a falling-out with Secretary-General Trygve Lie and was now employed by the British Treasury and seconded to the UN on a more flexible basis as a high-level consultant. (Jackson, too, had just been in India.)

Jackson was a brilliant choice – certainly, at the time, a more prudent one than Lewis, who had neither designed nor overseen any system as complicated as the project Nkrumah envisioned for Ghana. Recall (from chapter 2) that Jackson had contributed to the Allied victory in the Second World War first by solving the problem of the defence of Malta, which led to victory in Mediterranean and in turn to control of North Africa. Then the Middle East Supply Centre, which Jackson designed and helped run, cleared North African ports for all the military equipment needed to open a second front in Europe. Jackson became the key leader of 'UNRRA [the UN Relief and Rehabilitation Administration] – the biggest relief operation ever – which put the world on its feet after World War II'. Brian Urquhart, who was at the centre of the UN Secretariat for its first forty years, concludes that 'Jacko . . . was the best international

---

[20] Nkrumah to Lewis, 1 April 1953; Lewis to Nkrumah, 7 April 1953; Lewis Papers, Box 9.

5.1 Lewis at the United Nations, 1984

operator I have ever seen.'[21] By 1955 Jackson was not only a man of action who knew how to get done whatever was asked of him, he had a reputation as a real friend of the developing world. He believed that countries should be able to dictate their own futures, and, if asked, was ready to be there and help them do it. He broke with Trygve Lie over Middle East policy in a way that made Jackson a hero to some Arab nationalists, including some of Nkrumah's closest international allies.

That Nkrumah even considered Lewis is a sign of the esteem in which he held the economist. Two and half years later, in November 1955, Nkrumah again asked Lewis to come to Ghana, this time to help to evaluate Jackson's completed report. Jackson followed up on Nkrumah's invitation, graciously offering Lewis his digs: 'A bed, books, two Siamese cats and a gramophone are at your disposal.' Jackson would be back and forth to Britain with Ward, who was expecting their first (and only) child in the spring.

---

[21] Brian Urquhart, interview with Thomas G. Weiss, UN Intellectual History Project, 6 Jan. 2000.

Lewis turned down the hospitality, 'It is important that you and the P.M. [Prime Minister Nkrumah] and others be able to emphasise my complete independence in my assessment of the project, and fear some of its opponents might interpret my staying with you wrongly.'[22]

Much of the scholarly literature on Nkrumah's economic policy treats Lewis's and Jackson's influence on Nkrumah as similar or complementary,[23] but their letters show that, from the beginning, the two men saw things differently. Lewis' independent assessment of the proposals in Jackson's report turned out to be: 'it depends'. The project made sense if financing could be secured from Britain and the World Bank (which was still in its early mode of supporting only commercially viable projects, and of charging standard commercial rates of interest). No concessions, Lewis argued, could be made to the British and Canadian companies that would also have to give Ghana half the profits of their aluminium operations for the project to be bankable. Privately, he warned Nkrumah about Jackson's less-specific recommendations: 'I feel reluctantly compelled to advise you against leaning too heavily on Commander Jackson . . . his chief concern is that the project should go forward at all costs.' Jackson, Lewis argued, had no real influence with the companies, the British government, or the World Bank.

> His present position is awkward. If the project does not come off, he will have to return to his post in the UK Treasury, at a salary less tax which is only a fraction of what he receives in the Gold Coast, and his return would be as embarrassing to the UK Treasury as to himself. Hence, although he begins most of his suggestions with the formula, 'Being the only neutral in this setup . . .', you should treat his suggestions with exactly the same scepticism as if they originated [at the aluminium company headquarters] in Montreal . . . Given his over-riding personal interest in seeing the project started at any cost, any influence he may acquire in the formulation of the Gold Coast policy at this stage is likely to be unfortunate for the Gold Coast people.[24]

Two comments on this peculiarly harsh assessment are in order.

First, although Lewis certainly understood the financial advantage that a British citizen might gain on secondment to the United Nations – which

---

[22] Nkrumah to Lewis, 24 Nov. 1955, Jackson to Lewis, 2 Dec. 1955; Lewis to Jackson, 22 Dec. 1955, Lewis Papers, Box 9.

[23] For example, Evan White, 'Kwame Nkrumah: Cold War Modernity, Pan-African Ideology and the Geopolitics of Development', *Geopolitics*, 8, 2 (Summer 2003): 105.

[24] Lewis to Nkrumah, marked 'secret and personal', 12 April 1956, Lewis Papers, Box 9.

in those days provided a higher income – he just assumed that this was Jackson's status without verifying it, and Jackson's ambition for a long-term, well-paying job with the Volta Project was pure speculation. Later, Lewis would write to Owen with an amended hypothesis.

> My first task was to explain to Jackson that I considered the development of the country to be more important than the Volta River Project . . . To my complete surprise, he agreed. Apparently Jackson doesn't much care about what the policy is so long as he is given the task of carrying it out – perhaps this is due to his training as a sailor.[25]

A better way to put it is that Jackson was a problem solver who supremely enjoyed the complex task of building systems of people and machines that transformed things in major ways. It is a bit dismissive to treat this as the habit of 'a sailor'. But the letter to Owen was private, something among trusted colleagues accustomed to sharing their prejudices without fear that they will be held to account for them if, on reflection, the original judgement proves to be wrong. Lewis and Jackson, and their wives remained friends for some time, which suggests, perhaps, that Lewis moderated his views, at least temporarily. The fact that Lewis kept a copy of the letter, however, suggests that his initial judgement may have become relevant to how he eventually understood what had happened in Ghana.

Second, and more significantly, Lewis was incorrect about Jackson's influence with the major financers. J. H. Mensah, who worked with Lewis in Ghana as a young national counterpart, points out that Jackson's secret weapon in the campaign for the Volta Project was always Barbara Ward, who had excellent relations with the World Bank's successive presidents and whose close connections with Adlai Stevenson and John F. Kennedy helped to secure US support for the project.[26] Convincing the US president of the value of the dam would have been relatively easy. After all, one of Kennedy's biographers credits Ward with getting the male chauvinistic president 'to appreciate the quality of a woman's mind'. A Kennedy family friend, Marian Schlesinger, recalls that Ward 'was an intellectual, good-looking woman who dressed well and was a great expert who intrigued all those guys.'[27]

Ward's intellectual skills were just as much on display in Accra as in

---

[25] Lewis to Owen, 3 Feb. 1958.   [26] J. H. Mensah, interview with CNM, 21 Jan. 2005.

[27] Sally Bedell Smith, *Grace and Power: The Private World of the Kennedy White House* (New York: Random House, 2004), p. xxviii.

Washington, and they served the Volta Project well. For much of the time the extraordinary couple lived apart, with Ward circling back from the far corners of the world to their rooms in Nkrumah's compound. Often, shortly after she did so, Mensah recalls, Jackson would appear with revised proposals that answered Nkrumah's economists' latest objections.[28] She was very much Jackson's partner in ensuring that the project that he made physically and logistically feasible would also work politically and economically.

Nonetheless, even with continuing refinements, the plan proposed in the first Volta Project report failed. It relied on commercial financing from the World Bank, which the Bank refused. Bank president Eugene Black broke the bad news to Nkrumah in March 1957, just a month after the country gained full independence, citing the fall in cocoa prices since the end of the Korean War and the rise in the country's official expenditures after the native government had come to power. The expected economic return from the project was not high enough, given that Ghana would shortly 'have to face a serious readjustment of the economy'.[29]

Nkrumah was under enormous pressure at that moment: the popular but inexperienced leader of a new country, sub-Saharan Africa's first modern nation and the hope for the continent's independence and unity. He felt a terrible responsibility to live up to what he saw as his image, and his country's, in the eyes of his people, the world community, the opponents of Pan-Africanism, and the opposition at home. At the moment of decolonization, the leaders of many countries faced similar pressures, but perhaps none so acutely.

Nkrumah then asked Lewis to return to Ghana for two years to serve as his economic advisor. Lewis agreed and the two worked out an arrangement with Owen and Keenleyside for Lewis to be paid as an EPTA (Expanded Programme of Technical Assistance) expert.

The relationship between the prime minister and his new economic advisor was rocky from the start, in part due to Lewis's renewed animus towards Nkrumah's other, long-trusted advisor, Robert Jackson. Lewis arrived at the end of October 1957 and three months later was writing to David Owen that Ghana's development expenditure had mysteriously dropped by a third in two years, 'I suspect, because Jackson persuaded

28 J. H. Mensah, interview with CNM, 21 Jan. 2005.
29 Letter from Eugene Black to Kwame Nkrumah, 15 March 1957, enclosed in Nkrumah to Lewis, 2 April 1957, Lewis Papers, Box 9.

Ministers to hoard all their reserves . . . for the Volta River Project'.[30] (This was an odd comment; the fall in cocoa prices, noted by the World Bank's Eugene Black, would also provide sufficient explanation.)

Lewis kept few documents from his first few months as Nkrumah's advisor, yet one was a memo that he neither wrote nor received, nor was it enclosed in a letter sent to him by someone else. For that reason, it jumps out of the files of Lewis's voluminous correspondence. It had been sent to Jackson before Lewis's arrival, apparently by one of his staff. It concerned project financing: 'In any case, the most important contributor is the Cocoa Marketing Board and the General Manager has agreed that my picture of its accounts and prospects is about right as far as one can tell.'[31]

What did Lewis think was this memo's significance? Why did he keep it? Ghana's Cocoa Marketing Board was the outfit set up by the colonial administration to purchase the country's entire crop and sell it on the global market. The original aim of this plan was to protect farmers from usurious middlemen and to keep their incomes steady despite the endemic rapid fluctuations in the world price of the commodity. The Board became, instead, a simple means of collecting taxes, the centre of Ghana's system of public finance. The marketing board would regularly pay farmers less than half of what the government had earned from the previous years' crop. The resulting 'surpluses' did not become an insurance fund against bad harvests; they were returned to the state for development projects that rarely served the country's rural majority. Given the analysis of Ghana's economic trajectory emerging in Lewis's mind, perhaps he thought of the memo as a sort of smoking gun, evidence of Nkrumah learning the fiscal secret that would become his country's economic ruin.

Throughout 1958 Lewis argued with Nkrumah over many aspects of his development programme: prestige projects at home, a lavishly endowed diplomatic corps, massive investment in the nation's capital and the economically unviable dam. In August, at the height of his distress, Lewis gave the prime minister a long hand-written note begging him to change his priorities:

> I plead first on behalf of the common people of Ghana, who love you and who will trustfully accept whatever you give them, whether it be an international conference hall or water supplies. This trust is all the more reason why it is your duty to see that not a penny is spent for mere ostentation, or swank, or 'politics', until their essential needs are cared for.

---

[30] Ibid., Lewis to Owen, 3 Feb. 1958.   [31] Ibid., J. Ilett to Jackson, 12 July 1957.

I plead secondly on behalf of all black people everywhere. White people have always said that we do not know how to spend money economically; that we make ourselves ridiculous by spending on showing off, instead of essentials. They are saying so in Ghana today. Africans in every continent look to you to prove them wrong.

Finally, I plead to you as a fellow socialist, to whom the idea of spending money on embassies, airforces, yachts, 'making Ghana's voice heard all over the world' and other such boastfulness is downright sinful, so long as 80 per cent of the people still have no water, and so long as one baby in every three still dies before it is five years old. You belong to the class of great world leaders of small nations, like Masaryk, Ben Gurion, Munoz, Marin, Cardenas or U Nu, none of whom would for one moment consider spending £18 million on such baubles.[32]

Nkrumah walked to Lewis's rooms and returned the note the same evening, saying nothing more than, 'That's all right, you and I must be completely frank with each other.'[33]

Nkrumah's reasons for the embassies, the air force, and the 'politics', his reasons for all the 'swank', are well known. He did not think of himself as the leader of a small nation. Czechoslovakia's Masaryk and Israel's Ben Gurion were not his models. China's Sun Yat-sen and India's Nehru and Gandhi were more relevant. Nkrumah hoped for Africa to be united as one economic and political space, an entity of sufficient size to create a market area large enough to make even the newest industries cost-effective: an Africa with its own automobile industry, its own electronics industry, its own aerospace industry, its own science, its own technology. Like many Chinese and Indian nationalists, Nkrumah feared the 'Balkanization' that could turn his society into a place of tiny antagonistic nations. Like Gandhi – who opposed the partition of British India and who lambasted the British plan to have all India's little princely states become separately 'sovereign' and, thus, remain divided and weak – Nkrumah would have preferred sub-Saharan Africa to have become independent as one nation. That was impossible, but second best would be that Africa's *first* new nation begin the diplomatic and political work of uniting the continent. That may not have required 'swank', but it did require embassies, an international conference centre, and 'making Ghana's voice heard all over the world'.[34]

---

[32] Ibid., Lewis to Nkrumah, 1 Aug. 1957.
[33] As reported by Lewis in a letter to Hugh Keenleyside, 11 Dec. 1958, Lewis Papers, Box 9.
[34] Of the many political biographies of Nkrumah, Basil Davidson's, *Black Star: The Life and Times of Kwame Nkrumah* (New York: Praeger Publishers, 1973), is one of the most interesting and sympathetic.

After Lewis's plea, some of the prime minister's priorities changed, but three months later Lewis was again writing an exasperated memo to the prime minister about the Volta Project. 'Cheap power', Lewis said, 'is not the key to industrialization.' Nkrumah returned the memo with a handwritten note, 'My mind is finally made up and irrespective of anybody's advice to the contrary, I am determined to see that at all cost the dams . . . are built.'[35] Six weeks later, after completing a draft of the national economic plan that was his major task, Lewis sent a long letter to Hugh Keenleyside outlining all that had happened in his thirteen months as economic advisor, and asking his immediate boss to find him another assignment, but, Lewis pleaded,

> the last thing I want to do is to make a public issue of my departure . . . which could only comfort the enemies of Africans everywhere . . . announce that, 'The Second Development Plan having been completed, the United Nations has asked the Prime Minister to be good enough to release Professor Lewis, whose services are urgently required for an assignment in _____.'[36]

The new assignment need only be temporary. Lewis had already accepted the post of Principal of the University College of the West Indies, to begin when his contract with Nkrumah was scheduled to end, in late 1959.

Five days later Lewis received a cable from Paul Hoffman asking him to come to New York as his deputy in the new Special Fund, a job that would begin immediately.[37] A few hours after that, Keenleyside cabled, diplomatically, 'Your letter of 11 December received after despatch of Hoffman's cable.'[38]

On 18 December Lewis told Nkrumah of Hoffman's offer, emphasizing the importance of the UN job, but saying that he would prefer to stay in Ghana, but only under the condition that the prime minister abandon more of his luxury projects and limit government investment in the Volta project to £25 million.[39] (In the end, Ghana invested £165 million, excluding interest payments.[40]) Nkrumah rejected Lewis's conditions:

> The advice you have given me, sound though it may be, is essentially from an economic point of view and I have told you on many occasions that I cannot always follow this advice as I am a politician and must gamble on the future.[41]

[35] Lewis to Nkrumah, 31 Oct. 1958, Lewis Papers, Box 9.
[36] Ibid., Lewis to Keenleyside, 11 Dec. 1958.   [37] Ibid., Hoffman to Lewis, 16 Dec. 1958.
[38] Ibid., Keenleyside to Lewis, 17 Dec. 1958.   [39] Ibid., Lewis to Nkrumah, 18 Dec. 1958.
[40] Jackson, *Volta River Project*, p. 2.   [41] Nkrumah to Lewis, 18 Dec. 1958, Lewis Papers, Box 9.

The last cable Lewis saved from Accra was one he wrote to Keenleyside the next day, 20 December: 'Ask Dr [Hans] Singer to meet my plane, Pan American 151, at Idlewild on Sunday 28th at 8 pm, to put me up for the night, and to book me at the Tudor City Hotel from the following day.'[42]

In the summer of 2005, I asked Singer – still incredibly sharp at the age of 94 – if he remembered any harsh words about Ghana from his friend when he got off the plane. He did not. He was on mission in Ethiopia, and therefore unable to honour Lewis's request.[43] For many years, at least until after Nkrumah's ouster in 1966, it is possible that only Keenleyside and Owen (and perhaps Hoffman) knew the full story.

Lessons?

In fact, Lewis never published the *full* story. He presented his old friends from Ghana in a relatively good light, even if he was not above remembering himself as a little more quick-witted than he had actually been. In 1967 he recalled Nkrumah's justification for spending half of the development budget on Accra, home to only 5 per cent of the country's population: 'Why not?' Nkrumah had said, 'When you think of England, you think of London; when you think of France you think of Paris; when you think of Russia, you think of Moscow.' Lewis wrote that he replied, 'No, sir. When I think of England, I do not think of London because I live in Manchester, and this is also why I know that capital cities exploit the rest of the country.'[44] When the events actually occurred, he had written to Keenleyside, '[I]t took me two days to realize that I should have said, "But when *I* think of England, I think not of London, but of Manchester."' As the distinguished Africanist, Yoichi Mine, notes, the original point was probably meant to be sarcastic; Lewis would have liked to have reminded his old socialist friend of Nkrumah's own first triumph on the world stage. It had been at the 1945 Pan-African Conference, held at the centre of the world-historically-important Industrial Revolution, Manchester![45]

Lewis took some clear lessons from his experience in Ghana, and those lessons influenced the course of UNDP's history. But what lessons should *we* take from the case? Was it just a matter of Nkrumah listening to the 'wrong' international advisor? If so, then why did he listen to Jackson

---

[42] Ibid., Lewis to Keenleyside, 20 Dec. 1958.
[43] Hans W. Singer, interview with CNM, 8 July 2005.
[44] W. Arthur Lewis, 'Unemployment in Developing Countries', *World Today*, 23, 1 (1967): 16.
[45] Mine, 'Political Element'.

rather than Lewis? Did Nkrumah's own 'colonized mind' lead him to credit the advisor who was slightly older, spoke more forcefully, had greater practical experience, and was white? Or was it just that Nkrumah's advisors offered him two incompatible things, both of which he wanted: the international prestige and political connections assured by the Volta Project, or the slow economic progress that might have come from Lewis's plans.

Yoichi Mine, who shares the view of many other Africanists, would have us discount Lewis's contemporary critique of the Volta Project because 'the economic policy of Ghana was not formulated only in terms of Nkrumah's personal preferences but strongly influenced by mainstream economic thinking in the West and the East at that time'.[46] Mine's argument is that believing in 'big projects', in physical and sociological transformations as massive as the TVA, had become the order of the day in the late 1950s. The success of the TVA, and of the Marshall Plan, had convinced many economists and policy makers that the right combination of large inputs of technology and money could transform any society.

But Ghana's policy *was* a matter of Nkrumah's preferences – his party had an unbreakable hold on parliament. Moreover, there were examples (albeit, very few) of states with greater financial resources than Ghana that followed the kind of human-development-oriented policy that Lewis recommended to Nkrumah. Recall Libya, where the Resident Representative, Harold Caustin, convinced the government to forgo huge projects and invest in its people.

Basem Khader recalls that Caustin, like Lewis, 'belonged to the Fabian circle',[47] but you did not have to be Fabian to be suspicious of at least *some* 'grand' projects. One of Nkrumah's allies, K. B. Asante, remembers widespread support among 'mainstream' and social democratic economists in Ghana for the alternative that Lewis proposed. That was, in fact, part of the problem.[48] Nkrumah developed greater faith in the advice that Jackson offered in part because he accepted the prime minister's goals, something the economists did not. J. H. Mensah remembers a typical interaction: he, Lewis, and Nicholas Kaldor (a distinguished Keynesian on a short EPTA consultancy) had presented Nkrumah with a complex (and, I would argue, unlikely to succeed) strategy for securing reasonable

[46] Ibid. He cites Tony Killick, *Development Economics in Action: A Study of Economic Policies in Ghana* (London: Heinemann, 1978), as supporting this view.
[47] Basem Khader, letter to CNM, 20 Sept. 2005.
[48] K. B. Asante, interview with CNM, 21 Jan. 2005.

contracts from the aluminium firms when Jackson burst in. 'These economists are dreamers,' he said, 'Let's get things done!' That kind of talk, Mensah says, was what made Nkrumah appreciate Jackson so much.[49]

Both Mensah and Asante recall that Jackson's appreciation of Nkrumah was reciprocal. Jackson and Nkrumah both understood the context of the cold war, which made Ghana's economic policy inherently political, something that Lewis either discounted or failed to understand. Given Nkrumah's views about Africa's role in the world, Asante argues, Ghana was almost forced to play off the Soviet Union against the United States; the only question was whether he could do it well enough to survive and to be able to achieve some of his larger, Pan-Africanist goals. Nkrumah's socialism and his quasi-Leninist writings on imperialism (going back at least to 1945) could easily have led the United States to brand him as being in the enemy camp. The Volta Project, Jackson, and Ward – even the mere negotiations about the project – created ties to Washington and maintained ties to London, Washington's most loyal ally.

Jackson understood the larger, global picture that made Nkrumah's political gamble worthwhile. Remember, Asante says, that in the end Jackson created a project that met the strict financial criteria of the World Bank at the same time that it actually served the ends selected by Nkrumah, the country's elected leader and the most popular figure on the continent, something that Lewis, his Ghanaian counterparts like Mensah, and other UN economists seemed to be unwilling to do. 'It was in desperation that Nkrumah turned to Jackson',[50] the Australian who, unlike the West Indian Pan-Africanist, seemed to Nkrumah be the real ally of the continent.

The value of the Volta Project in terms of stabilizing Ghana in the treacherous waters of cold war global politics was significant, if only temporary. By 1964, shortly after President Kennedy's assassination, US policy makers were planning for Nkrumah's overthrow and seeking the support of (in decreasing order of success) Britain's Conservative government, the World Bank, the US aluminium companies, and even Jackson, who remained staunchly loyal to Nkrumah's larger vision of Africa's future.[51]

[49] J. H. Mensah, interview with CNM, 21 Jan. 2005.
[50] K. B. Asante, interview with CNM, 21 Jan. 2005.
[51] See the declassified documents in Nina Davis Howland, ed., *Foreign Relations of the United States 1964–1968, Volume XXIV: Africa* (Washington, D.C.: US Government Printing Office, 1999), pp. 411–61. A secret telegram of 16 March 1964 to President Johnson from Averell Harriman reports his getting the private assessment from Jackson (identified as a UN Special Fund director and advisor to Nkrumah) of the country's economic future and of Harriman's effectiveness in pressuring Nkrumah to abandon any socialist policies, p. 458.

To a significant extent the Volta Project was about Africa's future. It was about demonstrating that Africans could succeed in something grand: a regional development scheme more massive than the TVA. Nkrumah's political gamble was really about the 'decolonization of the mind', about changing perceptions of what was possible on the continent, something that Jackson and Ward understood.

Finally, unlike Lewis, Jackson and Ward had personal qualities that endeared them to Nkrumah. They included a deep, sincere love of Africa and Jackson's unusual attentiveness to the harried leader, who was, indeed, someone he felt to be and treated as a dear friend. Mensah remembers one visit to the United Nations when a dog-tired Nkrumah was preparing to play his role as the spokesman for the continent. Jackson was running around, telling the hotel staff at what temperature to run Nkrumah's bath, straightening Nkrumah's tie. 'You could never get rid of him [Jackson]', Mensah, the Lewis partisan, says, grudgingly, but with a warm smile.[52]

Lewis, on the other hand, was not the type of man who fitted in easily in Ghana's empathetic, effusive, personal culture, and he was apt to say things that seemed more gallingly colonialist than anything that would ever come from the Australian's mouth. For example, in 1955, Lewis wrote:

> A low cultural level is one of the associates of poverty; much is made in nationalist circles of African art and music, but Africans are conscious that their music is not so great an artistic achievement as that of Beethoven, that they are without a literature, that their religions are on a rather low level, and their kinship and other social patterns, which are such a joy to the anthropologist, are too frail to withstand the ferments of the twentieth century.[53]

A little greater attention to international politics and a little less confidence in his own (self-acknowledged) limited understanding of culture were perhaps all that Lewis would have needed to be more effective.

The difference with regard to this dimension between Lewis and his contemporary EPTA colleague in Singapore, Albert Winsemius, is telling. Winsemius, the more successful advisor, had superior political and

---

[52] J. H. Mensah, interview with CNM, 21 Jan. 2005.
[53] From a 1955 paper, quoted in Frederick Cooper, 'Modernizing Bureaucrats, Backward Africans, and the Development Concept', in Frederick Cooper and Randall Packard, eds., *International Development and the Social Sciences: Essays on the History and Politics of Knowledge* (Berkeley: University of California Press, 1997), p. 83.

cultural instincts, even if his standing in the discipline of economics would never rise as high as Lewis's. Winsemius understood Singapore's basic cold war constraint: on independence it housed British bases, so had no opportunity for non-alignment and little scope, initially, for grandiose visions of its global role. This actually may have made things easier for Singapore, but it may not have looked that way at the time; Howe Yoon Chong, Singapore's former minister of health, reminds us that when Winsemius first came to the country his job was to determine 'how this godforsaken place could be fished out of this morass'. The Dutch economist, like Jackson and Ward, quickly came to cherish the country and people that the UN had asked him to advise. Howe says that all of Winsemius's subsequent visits were 'pilgrimages of love' to a country he considered his second home.[54] Ghanaians who knew Jackson say similar things about him. Ghanaians who knew Lewis, while convinced of his sincere commitment to the cause of Africans everywhere, remember little specific affection for their country.

Lewis's blind spots may even have affected his economics. The most telling early criticism of his theory of development came from a brilliant ethnographic economist, Polly Hill, based on her meticulous fieldwork among Ghana's cocoa farmers.[55] However, the lessons Lewis took from Ghana were primarily about the domestic politics of development, and they were lessons with which Hill agreed. Lewis took them to his immediate work with Hoffman and Lewis continued to introduce them into the UN development network until his death in 1991.

Lewis's starting point was the same as the final assessment of the Volta Project by one of the most renowned historians of Africa, Basil Davidson: 'The development of things, once again, came out as something quite different from the development of people.' One commentator elaborates that Davidson meant that the economic benefits initially supposed to have accrued to Ghana's people were 'sacrificed for the symbol of the Dam, which resonated internationally more than it intersected locally and spatially with people's lives'.[56] Like Davidson – an unwavering champion of African liberation – Lewis believed that Africans had an absolute right to rule themselves, to choose their own leaders, whether or not the decisions taken by those leaders turned out to be wise. Lewis would in no

---

[54] Quoted in Rachel Tan, 'Proven Wrong by a Fish', *The New Paper*, 20 March 1997, http://ourstory.asia1.com.sg/dream/lifeline/win1.html (accessed 26 July 2005).

[55] B. A. Gregory, 'Hill, Polly', in John Eatwell, Murray Milgate, and Peter Newman, eds., *The New Palgrave: Economics Development* (New York: W. W. Norton, 1989).

[56] Davidson, *Black Star*, p. 197; White, 'Kwame Nkrumah', 107.

way give comfort to the racists and apologists for colonialism who wanted to highlight foolish decisions made by black leaders. That is why he so strongly reaffirmed what was originally Wakefield's principle of publicizing development successes as the achievements of the governments of the developing countries, and not as those of external experts or the UN.

At the same time Lewis became adamant about injecting a commitment to political equality into the UN's development work. Africans certainly had the right to choose leaders who placed the production of internationally resonant symbols above their material needs, but they also had the right to remove those leaders. The straw that broke the camel's back, the act that triggered Lewis's ultimatum to Nkrumah, was not his October 1958 decision to go ahead with the dam, but his party's undermining of Ghana's democratic constitution that immediately followed. 'The fascist state', Lewis wrote in his letter of 11 December, 'is in full process of creation, and I find it hard to live in a country where I cannot protest against imprisonment without trial, or the new legislation prohibiting strikes and destroying trade union independence.'

Returning to Ghana two years after Nkrumah's overthrow, Lewis told an audience of university students that the heroic leader's tragic flaw had been his uncritical adoption of an egalitarian politics developed for the England of the Industrial Revolution – developed for Manchester – for an agrarian nation dominated by Accra:

> In Europe socialist parties were built by a coalition of trade unions and middle-class intellectuals. In Africa both these groups are on the wrong side. The underdog is the farmer, and both the trade unions and the educated classes live by sucking the farmer's blood. A truly socialist or egalitarian movement would presumably have to start in the countryside, but of all Africa's so-called socialist writers, the only leader who sees this very clearly is Mr Nyerere of Tanzania.[57]

Not coincidentally, Tanzania was, in the same year, the country pursuing one of the most aggressive of the UNDP-funded experimental world literacy programmes.

Five years later, when I studied in Ghana, unions of cocoa farmers and farm labourers were still illegal. Many of the restrictions on democratic participation that had begun in 1958 remained for another generation,

---

[57] W. Arthur Lewis, *Some Aspects of Economic Development* (London: George Allen & Unwin, 1969), pp. 76–7.

until the culmination of a long process of democratization, facilitated by UNDP, in the 1990s (see chapter 12). The fact that UNDP eventually played that role is, in part, Lewis's legacy.

The Special Fund and after

Lewis left Ghana to spend the Special Fund's formative year in New York. Philomena Guillebaud, one of the Special Fund's first dozen staff members describes him chairing staff meetings, 'with all the professionals present round the table. Lewis was incisive, outspoken and frequently brilliant, and the guidelines he produced . . . gave the Special Fund the focus which Hoffman had hoped for'.[58] Then it was off to the West Indies, where he presided over the transformation of the University College into a unique, multinational, multicampus university with a world-class engineering school, courtesy of 'a United Nations Special Fund allocation'.[59] In 1963, Lewis joined the Princeton economics department, where he remained the rest of his career, a short train ride from UN headquarters.

In the meantime, Jackson did end up as one of those overseeing the monumental Volta Project and working with the Special Fund. (His sculptured image welcomes visitors to MIT System's Engineering Division, in honour of his signal contributions to 'Macro-Engineering'.) After 1962, Jackson continued to troubleshoot for the UN development network. His marriage failed, but he and Barbara Ward ended up at the centre of two of the major, interconnected evaluations of the global development system completed in 1969 (one of the subjects of the next chapter). The first of these, the UN 'Capacity Study', commissioned by Hoffman, came from the collaboration of Jackson with Margaret Joan Anstee, perhaps the most accomplished of the UNDP's field officers. They and their small team produced what is widely considered to be the most remarkable report in the UN's history – comprehensive, visionary, practical, and even well written. Ward both initiated and helped pen the related, World Bank-sponsored, Pearson Commission Report, for which Lewis, a Commission member, was the chief economist and drafter.

Lewis's work then intersected again with Jackson's when Hoffman asked the economist to chair an independent panel of experts working

[58] Philomena Guillebaud, 'Special Fund Memoir', unpublished ms., 7 Nov. 2005.
[59] Faculty of Engineering, University of the West Indies at St Augustine, Trinidad, 'An Historical Note', http://www.eng.uwi.tt/engdocs/historical.htm (accessed 28 July 2005).

with UNDP's Governing Council to come up with a consensus on reforms in the light of Jackson and Anstee's conclusions, with which Lewis strongly agreed. Lewis was too busy to chair,[60] but he helped the shapers of the consensus to move the locus of power in UNDP in the direction recommended by Jackson and Anstee, from the New York office and the headquarters of the specialized agencies that had provided experts and scholarships, to the field, and especially to the governments of the developing countries themselves.

A few simple themes marked Lewis's later interactions with the UN system. He was always willing to go to New York if the agenda involved expanding policy and analysis to include more – usually previously overlooked – groups, as in 1972, when he chaired the crucial UN expert group on women and development (see chapter 8). He continued to push for the rationalization of the UN's development work, responding to one set of proposals for revamping the system of cooperation among the specialized agencies with the suggestion that their abolition might be better.[61] He remained disgusted by the irrationality of international politics. After one global conference he and Barbara Ward exchanged exasperated letters about the way in which cold war ideologies and politics impeded human development, Ward writing how wonderful it would be just to focus on getting 'clean water for everyone by – say – 1990. If we could do that we'd do more for human happiness than all the Maos & Castros & Fords & Doles (ugh) in creation.'[62] By 1980 Lewis had endured 100 meetings of the Commission on Transnational Corporations as it tried to come up with a code of conduct for powerful investors, like the aluminium companies that gained so much from their Volta concessions.[63] Then, in 1984, he was back in New York encouraging the involvement of non-governmental organizations in 'building a just world' (the photograph reproduced in this chapter is from that conference).

Both Yoichi Mine and the directors of the recent, massive United Nations Intellectual History Project (UNIHP) argue that the theme connecting all of Lewis's interactions with the UN development network is an unwavering egalitarian commitment, political as well as economic.

---

[60] Letters from Hoffman to Lewis, 27 May 1970, and Lewis to Hoffman, 8 June 1970, Lewis Papers, Box 6.   [61] Ibid., letter from Lewis to Martin Hill, 12 Feb. 1974.

[62] Ibid., letter from Ward to Lewis, 20 Aug. 1976.

[63] Ibid., letter from Lewis to Johan Kaufmann, 11 March 1980. Kaufmann was the Dutch ambassador at the centre of the SUNFED debate, a participant observer who wrote a pathbreaking book on UN decision making based on the events. Kaufmann was revising the book, and Lewis suggested that the corporate code negotiations could form the basis of an appendix on 'How Decisions are not Made'.

The UNIHP directors note that his first sentence in the Pearson Commission Report reiterates the main point of the first report he wrote for Owen: global economic inequality 'is the central problem of our time'.[64] Mine sees Lewis as a passionate, practical democratic theorist. His greatest contribution to the development theory actually used by international institutions today, Mine argues, is his critique of single-party government, *Politics in West Africa*, the most comprehensive statement of the lessons he drew from Ghana.[65]

Lewis's directions about 'how to spend' the Special Fund monies raised by Hoffman continued the EPTA commitment to the proposition that the people of the developing world know what is best for their own development. In addition, the Special Fund pre-investment studies of the 1960s reflected ideals that did not influence the studies for the grand projects of the 1950s – such as the dams at Peligre in Haiti, Aswan in Egypt, and Akosombo in Ghana. The Fund required deeper consideration of the impact on, and the views of, the people who would be affected.

Sartaj Aziz, a distinguished Pakistani planner who worked closely with Lewis on the Pearson Commission Report, recalls how the two of them pushed their views about the importance of egalitarian politics and sensible national economic policies to the fore. Aziz had written a chapter designed to put foreign assistance in what he considered its proper, far from primary, place as a factor in development. Lewis said that the chapter resonated with 'germs of what I've been thinking about. Could the report as a whole come in that mould?' Eventually, after overcoming the reluctance of some commissioners, the germs became one of the report's central themes, bringing questions of good governance, accountability, and the political sources of growing economic inequality to the centre of the global debate on development.[66]

Kwame Pianim, one of Ghana's most respected economists and a close collaborator with UNDP over many years, sees Lewis as preparing the intellectual space for the transformations of the Programme that came in the 1980s. That was when UNDP Administrator Bill Draper embraced 'advocacy' – promoting the status of women, the non-governmental organizations that make up civil society, and the kind of responsible private sector that Pianim championed through his most recent connection to UNDP, membership on the 2003 Commission on

[64] Louis Emmerij, Richard Jolly, and Thomas G. Weiss, *Ahead of the Curve? UN Ideas and Global Challenges* (Bloomington, Ind.: Indiana University Press, 2001), p. 175.

[65] W. A. Lewis, *Politics in West Africa (The Whidden Lectures for 1965)* (Westport, Conn.: Greenwood Press Reprint, 1982).   [66] Sartaj Aziz, interview with CNM, 10 Dec. 2004.

the Private Sector and Development. Most important, and the most connected to the lessons Lewis took from Ghana, has been the Programme's recent focus on promoting democratic governance.[67]

So, at the end of this particular story, we have a UNDP that has taken on tasks that may seem even larger than just trying to transform a nation and prove the capacity of a continent and its people through a marriage of macro-engineering and diplomacy. Unquestionably Lewis's preference for working 'upstream' in the flow of development policy – supporting democratic governance – seems much grander than the simple programmes of technical assistance that David Owen so loved ('you send in an expert, they are provided with a counterpart, and the counterpart learns'). Yet, as Pianim insists, the scrabble for hundreds of little aid projects, let alone the battles for things as large as the Akosombo Dam, can distract even the most well-meaning of governments from essential attention to economic strategy. Pianim says that he is 'One of UNDP's biggest advocates' because the Programme has learned, over a long time, how to help governments get that balance between attention to grand strategy ('upstream' work) and the focus on particular projects 'downstream' just about right.[68]

In the end the story of Ghana at the time of decolonization is not one about 'bad advice' – but, then, perhaps Singapore's contemporary story is not really about 'good' advice. Both stories illustrate that development is much more than projects, whether grand or small. Both Singapore and Ghana were experiments, experiments that no one at the time – not even brilliant people like Jackson, Lewis, Nkrumah, or Ward – could be sure would succeed or fail. Lewis had plausible reasons, in purely economic terms, for criticizing the Volta Project, and history may judge him to have been correct. Yet the project's goals were never purely economic, and in 1958 Lewis offered no plans to serve to those larger goals, even though his failure in Ghana led him to see, increasingly, that development required political equality. Sartaj Aziz is proud of the way in which the Pearson Commission Report both 'dethroned [development as] growth' at the same time that it put the giant, command-economy-like, foreign-assisted development project (the quintessence of 'development as efficiency') in its place. Nevertheless, it would be decades before there was an intellectual and practical convergence on 'development as freedom', a convergence that UNDP would foster.

[67] Kwame Pianim, interview with CNM, 21 Jan. 2005.   [68] Ibid.

6

Capacity, consensus, crisis, and consequences

More than twenty years separate Arthur Lewis's first public discussion of
the lessons he drew from Nkrumah's Ghana (in the mid-1960s) and
UNDP's embrace of 'development as freedom' in the 1990s. In the first
part of that interval, the subject of this chapter, UNDP followed an unexpected path. The 1960s ended and the 1970s began with expectations that
international support for economic development, and UNDP's role
therein, would grow dramatically in the decades that followed, and a long
period of self-assessment – based on that assumption – ended with the
agreement among UN members that has governed the Programme since.

'The Consensus' – which is how UN officials refer to this agreement,
capitalized and with the definite article – marked a high point of cooperation between the wealthy industrialized countries of the global 'North'
and the increasingly assertive global 'South'. The North–South conflict,
which became acute in the early 1970s, undermined the assumptions on
which UNDP's high expectations in the late 1960s rested. Instead of
robust growth, the international development business – especially
UNDP – faced financial stagnation. Instead of a global consensus on the
means and ends of development, ideological fragmentation and adherence to rigid positions became the norm.

Yet, even in this unexpected context, UNDP proved surprisingly
resilient. The Consensus and a set of subsequent reforms moved influence within the Programme away from the Specialized Agencies and their
headquarters and towards the field offices, which were often both more
practical and more creative than the organization's headquarters in New
York. A supportive new leadership at headquarters ensured that many of
the Programme's innovations that had been required by cost cutting also
strengthened the position of southern governments and staff from the
developing world; it was in the 1970s that UNDP became known as
'the development programme of the developing countries'. Moreover,
throughout the decade, UNDP's leadership found ways to maintain and
expand the UN development network by facilitating the establishment of

new agencies and nurturing them with the Programme's experience and resources. Consequently, by the mid-1980s, the UN network was, by many measures, both stronger and more effective than it had been when the major self-assessment began.

The Grand Assize and the Capacity Study

Forty years on, it is hard to recapture the sense of promise in the development community of the 1960s. John F. Kennedy had a commitment to international development that matched Roosevelt's and mirrored that of Paul Hoffman and the entire first generation of the UN's leadership. The material side of Kennedy's commitment (which continued under Lyndon Johnson) meant that UNDP's programme grew rapidly; expenditures in 1966 were 58 per cent higher than in 1964 and 30 per cent higher than in 1965.[1] Paul Hoffman initially understood his job as getting other Northern governments to raise their commitments in order to exploit the United States' pledge to provide 40 per cent of total funding.

This job was not that difficult; prosperity reinforces generosity, and the 1960s witnessed the fastest growth the industrial economies ever recorded. Moreover, international agreement on the principles of the global economic system was as strong, in the mid-1960s, as it had been in Franklin Roosevelt's day. After its first decade and a half of reluctance, the World Bank had become the major multilateral provider of investment assistance, cooperating closely with UNDP and quite comfortable with the Programme's agenda-setting, pre-investment role.

In 1967, UNDP and the World Bank began a series of coordinated assessments to determine how they could best face the expected problem of 'operations growing at an accelerating pace; projects moving faster into operation; and requests coming in at an accelerating pace'.[2] The problem was especially critical for UNDP. Since 1959, its share of total development assistance had been only 2 per cent, but UNDP's funds had grown at an average of 20 per cent each year, while the aid pool as a whole grew at a much more modest 4.5 per cent.[3] Hoffman asked his two most trusted lieutenants, Myer Cohen and Paul-Marc Henry (the heads of

---

[1] Estimates from Hans W. Singer, Draft of the SPIN Study, 16 August 1967, David Owen Papers, Box 25, Columbia University Library, New York.   [2] Ibid.

[3] Adriano Garcia, *International Cooperation and Development: The United Nations Development Programme Resident Representative System* (Quezon City: University of Philippines Law Center, 1982), p. 171.

UNDP operations and programming), to work with Hans Singer and Robert Jackson to produce a comprehensive 'Study of PreInvestment Needs' – the SPIN Study. The Bank's fourth president, George Woods, went further. He wanted a 'Grand Assize', an authoritative assessment of the whole international development system. In a speech written by Barbara Ward, Woods argued that the need for international solidarity was even greater in 1967 than at the time of the Marshall Plan. While industrial economies might be booming, much of the world still faced the prospect of famine, massive unemployment, and a fundamental crisis of hope.[4]

The first session of the 'Assize' was a small, closed conference held in May 1968 at a coastal inn close to Washington, D.C. In attendance were Barbara Ward, the heads of the US and Dutch development agencies, the coordinator of the Development Assistance Committee (the six-year-old club of bilateral aid providers), the World Bank's brand-new, fifth president, Robert S. McNamara (on the job less than three weeks), and Paul Hoffman and Robert Jackson, representing UNDP.

A month earlier, Lyndon Johnson, stung by his defeat in a major primary vote, had announced that he would not run for reelection. Six days later, Martin Luther King was assassinated. Warsaw Pact leaders had just met to discuss the mounting threat of Czechoslovakia's non-violent, democratic revolution, the Prague Spring. The United States finally made sufficient concessions to the North Vietnamese to get them to agree to peace talks on the night the conferees arrived. While the Assize sat, protesting students closed down Columbia University and Paris erupted.

At Columbia, the students chanted, 'The whole world is watching! The whole world is watching!', but few of the high-level assessors noted the events that were shattering the world that many of them had helped create. The head of USAID (the US Agency for International Development) did note that *public* interest in international assistance was weak in his country due to the pressing domestic issues of civil rights and Vietnam, which contributed to "ignorance about aid and development." Therefore Barbara Ward called for 'more success stories to build public support', but Paul Hoffman argued that the most persuasive justifications for aid remained the moral argument about solidarity, the recognition that 'development is good business', and the lesson of the world wars,

[4] Devesh Kapur, John B. Lewis, and Richard Webb, *The World Bank: Its First Half-Century* (Washington, D.C.: Brookings Institution Press, 1997), p. 184.

recently reiterated by Pope Paul VI: the material commitment of every society to less fortunate people around the world contributes to peace.[5]

McNamara announced that the Bank's major contribution to the Assize would be the report of the commission that was eventually headed by the former Canadian prime minister, Lester B. Pearson and led, intellectually, by Arthur Lewis. Hoffman reported that he was appointing Jackson as a special commissioner for an assessment of the 'UN jungle of proliferating agencies', producing a report which came to be known as the 'Capacity Study'. One consequence of the Byzantine structure, Hoffman argued, was the incredibly slow, and decreasing, rate at which projects were being implemented. (As Jackson would report, planned expenditures were always much higher than actual. In fact, 'the Programme as a whole is approximately one year behind schedule in its delivery'.[6]) The UN system, Hoffman argued, had to be able to find the capacity to use the sorely needed resources that would come with the expected increases in aid.

Hoffman's remarks, with their scepticism about the Specialized Agencies, anticipated some of the main conclusions of the Capacity Study. So did Jackson's. Both men saw a need to strengthen the role of UNDP's Resident Representatives. Jackson emphasized having a continuous presence of international development coordinators in the field rather than relying on what he called IMF (International Monetary Fund) and World Bank 'bombings' – short-term missions of economists who had no contextual knowledge of the countries whose fate they were expected to judge.[7]

That the Capacity Study would end up emphasizing the centrality of the field office and the Resident Representatives was not surprising for two further reasons.

First, for many UNDP staff members the country offices represented the Programme's 'essence'. Organization theorists note that a bureaucratic culture often singles out one role or a cluster of roles as being what the organization really is.[8] Thus, for example, despite the strategically central role of submarine-launched nuclear missiles throughout the cold

---

[5] Notes of Overseas Development Institute Tidewater Conference, 4–5 May 1968, Tidewater Inn, Easton, Md., Owen Papers, Box 26.

[6] Robert G. A. Jackson, *A Study of the Capacity of the United Nations Development System*, vol. 2 (Geneva: United Nations, 1969), p. 45.

[7] Notes of the Tidewater Conference, Owen Papers, Box 26.

[8] Edward H. Schein, *Organizational Culture and Leadership*, 2nd edn (San Francisco: Jossey-Bass, 1992), p. 12.

war, the 'essence' of the Soviet and US navies – the thing that most sailors and officers understood to be the core activity of their organizations – remained the work of conventional warships. In organizations with shorter histories, like UNDP in the 1960s, the self-image contained within the organizational culture often bears more relation to what is, in fact, strategically important about the institution. The country offices and the Res Reps were the essence of UNDP not only to its staff members, but also to most people working on development in the 1960s, and to the developing countries themselves.

Second, and moreover, Jackson reinforced this understanding of UNDP's essence by the particular way in which he approached the study. He only agreed to take the project on if Margaret Joan Anstee agreed to be his chief of staff.[9] The two had got to know each other at a 1966 global conference of Resident Representatives and Jackson quickly came to share the general opinion that Anstee was among the Programme's most impressive field officers.

For her part, Anstee immediately recognized the personal qualities that had made Jackson effective in so many situations. She moved into a villa outside Geneva to write the report, which acknowledges the cat, Thomas, 'the Capacity Cat', who shared the hardworking house that became a focus for the small staff that Jackson assembled. Richard Symonds, who moved into the villa immediately afterward, recalls inheriting the sociable Thomas as well as a cache of recyclables that told of the group's long hours.[10] The report's final text (which everyone attributes to Anstee) with its elegant style and gentle humour, equally attests to the warm atmosphere in which it was written.

For all its style, the 1969 Study was, of course, profoundly serious and often deeply critical of the haphazard way in which the UN's development network had been created. If a single paragraph had to serve as the report's summary, it might be this one:

> One can feel admiration and sympathy for the successive administrators and the successive programmes of the EPTA [Expanded Programme of Technical Assistance], the Special Fund, and UNDP, in their efforts to surmount the endless administrative and procedural hurdles presented by the UN development system. But none of this should mask the basic, sobering truth: that, in the final analysis, the principal losers were the developing

---

[9] Margaret Joan Anstee, *Never Learn to Type: A Woman at the United Nations* (Chichester: John Wiley & Sons, 2003), pp. 241–2.

[10] Richard Symonds, interview with the author (CNM) 7 July 2005.

countries, because the cumbersome machinery devised over the years could only be maintained at the expense of the operational efficiency of the pro-grammes of co-operation carried out on their behalf.[11]

The report took the position that development was a multifaceted problem involving politics, culture, and society as well as the economy. Among these factors, 'linkages and strength vary from one country to another'.[12] Thus, in reforming the UN's 'cumbersome machinery', the focus needed to be on empowering the unique combination of forces within each specific country.

To do that meant programming UNDP's entire set of activities within each country over a significant period of time and as a part of that country's own national (usually five-year) plan, a proposal that hear-kened back to Arthur Lewis's and Raúl Prebisch's original arguments about planning. Specific projects would be formulated by governments with the cooperation of the Res Rep, who would be given full authority to approve smaller projects. Larger projects would still involve cooperation with one of the executing Agencies, but it would be the government's plan, not the menu of services the Agencies wanted to provide, that would determine what UNDP would fund. Moreover, the Administrator – not a board representing all the Agencies (as had been the case with EPTA) and not UNDP's often cumbersome Governing Council (repre-senting donor and recipient countries) – would be responsible for approving larger projects. The Administrator and the country offices would be responsible for much more systematic evaluation and follow-up, which would not only help governments best use their resources, but also provide a record of 'lessons learned' that would aid UNDP's Governing Council in its *real* task of setting broad policy.

Making the UNDP Res Rep the UN Country Coordinator of all the work of the Specialized Agencies would reinforce the shift of responsibility to the field. The Coordinators would report to new regional bureaux for conti-nental regions corresponding to the UN's economic commissions, such as the intellectually vibrant ECLA (Economic Commission for Latin Ameri-ca), which had been led by Prebisch throughout its formative years.

Headquarters would have responsibilities for coordinating pledges and programming budgeting, creating a new common accounting system and an information system linking all the Agencies, and managing an autonomous, merit-based, and uniform personnel system, supported by a UN staff college.

---

[11] Jackson, *Study of the Capacity*, p. 23.   [12] Ibid., p. 18.

The personnel changes suggested in the Capacity Study would alleviate a host of problems:

> the short supply of many specialists; the non-competitive emoluments compared to those obtainable in many individual countries; inadequate job description; out-of-date rosters; shortage of recruiting personnel; the cancellation of posts; lengthy clearance delays on the part of recipient governments; and the varying performance of the National Committees who assist in the recruitment process.[13]

The promise of professionalization and the distancing from the cosy relationships with the Agencies (based in Europe and North America) and the National Committees (again, primarily west European sources of expertise) were particularly welcome to well-qualified junior officers from the developing world.

Trevor Gordon-Somers, who had moved from Jamaica's UN mission to EPTA's New York office in 1965, recalls that the Capacity Study 'provided a significant degree of hope that we were now beginning to build a more coherent organization and that we recognized that our service to the countries was the most important asset that we had'. He recognized that, nevertheless, the Study was 'controversial at some levels'.[14]

This was especially true at the top of the organization. David Owen, already leaving UNDP when the Study was published, was disappointed by its lack of acknowledgement of what had been accomplished by the ever growing network of technical assistance, and he worried about the grand ambitions that the Capacity Study appeared to endorse.[15] The men Hoffman had come to rely on the most after Arthur Lewis's return to the West Indies, Myer Cohen and Paul-Marc Henry, saw the report as an ill-founded attack on the centralized system of approving large-scale projects that they had brought to UNDP from the Special Fund.[16] The heads of the Specialized Agencies saw the Study as sounding the death-knell for

---

[13] Ibid., p. 51.

[14] Trevor Gordon-Somers, interview with Elizabeth Mandeville (EM), 12 April 2005.

[15] Roger Owen, interview with CNM, 7 Sept. 2004.

[16] This point was made by several informants including Alexander H. Rotival (interview with CNM, 14 Sept. 2004) and Bruce Stedman (interview with CNM, 3 Feb. 2005). However, they agree with Marge Fonyi (interview with CNM, 22 Sept. 2004), that Cohen, especially, tended to keep records in a way that would be difficult to continue if the Programme were to expand rapidly. He kept the facts of each country's allocation and the range of projects currently undertaken 'in his head' or written on any piece of paper that came to hand. He was always able to recall the facts quickly and with precision, but his skill was not something that a growing Programme could rely on forever.

their snug relationships that had become bureaucratic imperatives. And, finally, Hoffman, after initially embracing the Study and praising Jackson for it, abruptly changed his mind.

Almost everyone who remembers Hoffman's reversal – which took place over the first weekend that he had the time to read the Study's two volumes with care – points to a single offending paragraph:

> For many years, I have looked for the 'brain', which guides the policies and operations of the UN development system. The search has been in vain . . . [T]here is no group (or 'Brain Trust'), which is constantly monitoring the present operation, learning from experience, grasping at all that science and technology has to offer, launching new ideas and methods, challenging established practices, and provoking thought inside and outside the system. Deprived of such a vital stimulus, it is obvious that the best use cannot be made of the sources available to the operation . . . [T]he UN development system has tried to wage a war on want for many years with very little organized 'brain' to guide it. Its absence may well be the greatest constraint of all on capacity. Without it, the future evolution of the UN development system could easily repeat the history of the dinosaur.[17]

There is a remarkably lively debate among UN old-timers about this paragraph, about who really wrote it, what was intended, and how Hoffman understood it. Richard Symonds argues that Jackson was often a bit too blunt and Anstee, despite her unsurpassed field experience, not yet familiar enough with the extreme diplomacy required at UN headquarters:

> Most of us in this UN business start by writing a very good report and then we show it in drafts to one or two real friends who tell us, 'You know, this is absolutely splendid, . . . you've outdone yourself, but now, what do you want to get *done*?' And then you have to throw all the coarse bits out, which is terribly sad. But Jacko wasn't like that.[18]

Jean-Jacques Graisse, one of the very few people in daily contact with Hoffman, remembers asking Jackson what the merit was

> of using these words which were obviously going to create a major crisis with PGH [Paul Hoffman] but also frankly with most of the managers. I believe it was Jackson although I now cannot remember exactly [which of the authors], who told me that, with the Pearson Report also on the table, the text of the capacity study needed a few exciting pearls if the media was to show an interest.[19]

---

[17] Jackson, *Study of the Capacity*, pp. 12–13.
[18] Richard Symonds, interview with CNM, 7 July 2005.
[19] Jean-Jacques Graisse, electronic mail to CNM, 16 Oct. 2005.

The most senior of the observers, and perhaps the person who knew Hoffman the best, Sir Brian Urquhart, sees it this way:

> Jacko made a terrible mistake. I was devoted to him, but Jackson really was rather like Theodore Roosevelt. He was about 10 years old in some ways, and he made a joke – well, he thought it was a joke . . . saying, as far as I remember, that there were a number of dinosaurs and cavemen in the system. And Paul Hoffman, who was the head of the Development Programme, among others, took violent umbrage at this, and rallied all of his fellow Directors-General and others. It was ridiculous, because the Capacity Study was a perfectly sensible study, but, as so often happens, it was ruined by one sentence.[20]

With all deference to Sir Brian, the actual paragraph, in its context, says something different. Jackson (or Anstee) was just making the perfectly sensible point that the dispersed system of UNDP and the Specialized Agencies, with no real centre of evaluation, could not learn from its vast experience, a point often made by others, including Hoffman himself.[21] Jackson and Anstee simply added the prescient observation that unless the UN network developed that capacity, it was likely to stagnate and eventually become irrelevant.

Unfortunately, this has become a case of, 'This is the UN, sir. When the legend becomes fact, print the legend.'[22] Certainly, Hoffman may have *understood* the Study in the way Urquhart suggests. Hoffman had turned 79 when the Study was published, at the end of a year whose rush of events made many a younger man feel like a dinosaur. Trevor Gordon-Somers remembers the UN rumour mill being rife with the claim that Jackson, twenty years Hoffman's junior, was angling to replace him.[23] In any event, while Hoffman need not have chosen to see Jackson and Anstee's report as critical of him, he definitely did choose to read it that way.

Perhaps the Administrator found some solace in the fact that the World Bank's major contribution to the Assize, the Pearson Commission Report, *Partners in Development*,[24] also disappointed its sponsor. Arthur Lewis and Sartaj Aziz complicated what the World Bank president had

---

[20] Brian Urquhart, interview with Thomas G. Weiss (TGW), UN Intellectual History Project, 6 Jan. 2000.   [21] See p. 112, above.

[22] A slightly amended version of the tag line in John Ford's 1962 classic film, *The Man Who Shot Liberty Valance*.   [23] Trevor Gordon-Sommers, interview with EM, 12 April 2005.

[24] Commission on International Development, *Partners in Development* (New York: Praeger, 1969).

expected to be a simple call for greater international solidarity. The report's focus on the nature of national policies and the degree to which they were politically legitimate opened up issues that the Bank had previously ignored.

Hoffman had expected a practical statement of how, with a few changes, the UN system could quickly develop the capacity to use the rapidly growing financial resources that the SPIN Study anticipated. Yet, given that overall development assistance – and contributions to UNDP, in particular – failed to grow, both UNDP and the Bank were lucky that the experts they had commissioned went beyond their mandates to say sensible things that did not depend on their sponsors' expectations about development finance.

The consensus, new dimensions, and identification with the developing world

Even though the Capacity Study lacked the active endorsement of UNDP's chief, it found wide support among Southern governments, from Castro's Cuba – which produced a critical analysis that is almost as well written as the Study itself[25] – to the Shah's Iran.[26] Equally important were a group of major aid givers, including the United States and the Nordic countries.[27]

Within the Governing Council, a young Indian diplomat, Muchkund Dubey, led the effort to take 'some element of the Capacity Study' while trying to settle 'contentious issues in favour of the developing countries'.[28] The result was the (aforementioned) Governing Council Consensus of June 1970, supplemented by a set of agreements reached at the beginning of 1971.[29]

Given the influence of the Specialized Agencies within important ministries in many developing countries, it was perhaps inevitable that their roles would not be as curtailed as Jackson and Anstee had wished. Dubey also 'personally felt the agencies were quite important' because they were

---

[25] *A Study of the Capacity of the United Nations Development System: Cuba's View* (Geneva: UNDP, 1970).

[26] United Nations Archives, Series 290, Box 70, folder 35, Position of the Iranian Government on the Jackson Report, 13 June 1970.

[27] Muchkund Dubey, interview with CNM, 11 Dec. 2004.   [28] Ibid.

[29] See UNDP, *Report of the Governing Council: Tenth Session (9–30 June 1970)*, 70/34 and *Eleventh Session (14 January–2 February 1971)*, 71/14.

where the UN's expertise resided, perhaps not in a single brain, but in a collective brain that seemed to be the only thing that could balance all the expertise that was being built within McNamara's World Bank, an organization that many Southern governments considered to be biased against them.[30]

The Governing Council gave the Res Reps much greater control over UNDP funds, but abandoned the Capacity Study's plan to make them the true leaders of unified UN country offices. The Res Reps got a new title, 'Resident Director' (which was unpopular and quickly abandoned[31]), but no new sources of influence over the country representatives of the Agencies.

The Consensus also jettisoned Jackson and Anstee's recommendation that UNDP tie its aid to the specific planning cycles of each country. In part, this was a concession to the large number of developing nations that still did not have a real planning capacity. It was also a concession to Northern governments that did not want to be held to long-term pledges of aid. Because the five-year plans of different countries begin in different years, the Capacity Study recommendations would have required donors to give regularly updated indications of the aid they planned to give as much as nine years into the future. As a compromise, the Consensus created five-year cycles of UNDP funding that applied to all developing countries at once. At the beginning of each cycle, each country with a UNDP programme would be given an Indicative Planning Figure (IPF) suggesting the level of funding the country could expect in each year of the cycle. Donor governments would only be required to give their (non-binding) indications of the contributions they would make to the Programme every fifth year, and would only have to look forward five years.

From Dubey's point of view, other key parts of the Consensus included the creation of four Regional Bureaux: Africa, Asia, Latin America, and Europe, the Mediterranean, and the Middle East (BEMME). An unwritten part of that agreement, which has been maintained ever since,

---

[30] Muchkund Dubey, interview with CNM, 11 Dec. 2004.

[31] Garth ap Rees (electronic mail to CNM, 27 Sept. 2005), who spent eighteen years as a Res Rep, recalls the 1971 meeting where the Resident Representatives gave their input into the reforms, 'They only really opposed one recommendation which was that we should be called Resident Directors. Hernan Santa Cruz, then President of the Governing Council, drew the loudest round of applause of the whole meeting when he told us that he would ensure that we would continue to be called Res Reps!' Santa Cruz had represented Chile at the UN in various capacities since the beginning, including as part of the drafting committee for the Universal Declaration of Human Rights.

was that a national of the region would head each Bureau, located at
headquarters, while nationals of major donor countries would head the
various cross-regional administrative bureaux concerned with finance,
personnel, and the like.

This decision fundamentally changed the make-up of the group of
senior officers reporting directly to the Administrator. In 1968, the group
included Owen from the United Kingdom, Paul-Marc Henry from
France, two Americans (Myer Cohen and Bruce Stedman), three eastern
Europeans, and Rajendra Coomaraswamy, whom Owen had recruited
from Ceylon (now Sri Lanka).[32] After the Consensus, Hoffman's effective
cabinet no longer included the departed Owen or Henry – the latter of
whom left largely in protest over the changes initiated by the Capacity
Study. Coomaraswamy became head of the Asia Bureau. Serjige Makiedo,
from Yugoslavia, who had been in charge of Research and Training,
became head of BMME. Michel Doo Kingué, of Cameroon, led the Africa
Bureau, and Gabriel Valdés, former Foreign Minister of Chile, took over
programmes in Latin America.

Equally significant in its effect of shifting power towards the developing countries were proposals to move decision making about particular
projects away from the Governing Council and New York. Dubey had
preferred the wording, 'By the very inclusion of a project in a country
programme, it should be deemed to have been approved.' That was not
accepted, but, by empowering the Res Reps and the Administrator, who
would probably delegate this power to sympathetic Bureau heads,
Dubey's goal was largely achieved.[33]

Finally, the Consensus gave a nod towards the Capacity Study goal of
coherent evaluation, but prescribed that evaluation would only be undertaken with the agreement of the government concerned and would be
carried out by the government and UNDP along with the executing
agency.

In the end, those who shared the goals of the Capacity Study had
reason to be disappointed. The Consensus provisions on evaluation and
the preservation of the central role of the Specialized Agencies undercut
attempts to create a single organizational 'brain'. Implementation of
other parts of the Consensus may have made the problem worse. Chuck
Lankester, a young Canadian recruited to UNDP in 1969 for his forestry
expertise, recalls how, before the Consensus, he had had 'absolute

[32] Staff of the United Nations Development Programme, 19 January 1968, Owen Papers, Box 23.
[33] Muchkund Dubey, interview with CNM, 11 Dec. 2004.

control' over twenty or thirty projects in different parts of the world, effective projects from which a great deal of relevant scientific knowledge was being accumulated. After the Consensus, he – and everyone else in similar positions – was called in and asked whether they wished to be a technical specialist or a line officer in one of the new bureaux; to do both would now be impossible. 'Brilliant minds, put into this structure, were [thus] marginalized.'[34]

Lankaster's contemporary, Robert England, adds that a final, unwritten part of the Consensus

> formalised a level of hypocrisy with regard to UNDP's core resources: for several [five-year IPF] cycles, there was a politically determined commitment to an 8 per cent annual growth in resources, which in the 1970s and 1980s proved in practice to be nearer 4 per cent. This gave rise to a 'concertina style' of resource management, with overblown country programme resource frameworks, which were subsequently cut back . . . This in turn tended to undermine governments' confidence.[35]

That UNDP did not, as a result of such brainless policies, die like the dinosaurs was largely a consequence of the last of a set of significant changes in top personnel that took place in the early 1970s. Hoffman finally retired in 1971 and, deferring to a nomination made by US President Richard M. Nixon, UNDP's various governing bodies confirmed Rudolf Peterson, a prominent US banker, as the second Administrator. Peterson arrived with a US pledge to double its contribution to the Programme very rapidly.[36] Despite this promising start, the new Administrator, who divided his time between UNDP and the California-based Bank of America where he still served as director, spent more than a year struggling to set up an effective administration, first relying on C. V. Narasimhan (who also continued to work as chief of staff for UN Secretary-General U Thant) and then Myer Cohen as his deputy. After Cohen's retirement, in 1972, Peterson created two posts of deputy, one for Bert Lindstrom of Sweden (an increasingly important donor), the other for I. G. Patel, an eminent Indian economist who later served as Director of the London School of Economics. Like W. Arthur Lewis before him, Patel managed to have a profound impact on the future of the UN development network during a short tenure as its number two.

---

[34] Chuck Lankester, interview with Neysan Rassekh (NR), 9 Nov. 2004.
[35] J. K. Robert England, electronic mail to CNM, 21 Sept. 2005.
[36] Charles Perry, interview with NR, 28 March 2005.

Also, like Lewis, Patel found much of the culture of the UN development network to be distasteful: wastefully long Governing Council meetings, extraordinarily complex bureaucratic mechanisms 'created for dealing with what was not that much to deal with', and a 'reactionary and conservative' staff that constantly criticized the Bretton Woods agencies, even though they were, in many ways, much more progressive than UNDP:

> At the Bank and the [International Monetary] Fund there was no difficulty by then in using . . . money to buy goods in India. In the UNDP you simply could not: 'Oh, no, this is for aid. How can you use aid money to buy something local?' You could not send an Indian scholar studying in California to India [as a UNDP expert].[37]

Patel's assistant, Muchkund Dubey, the diplomat involved with the Consensus (recruited to the UNDP staff from India's UN mission) recalls that two or three months after Patel arrived, he mentioned that 'his best ideas came when he can't sleep and so starts writing'. He then handed Dubey four or five pages, listing the things that were easy for the World Bank to do, plus the notion of being flexible about buying equipment (so that the likes of Richard Symonds would not have to be borrowing the Rwandan presidential Volkswagen), and the even more radical notions that UNDP should be able to fund capital projects ('We may bring in medical experts, bring in medicines, etc. – but we can't build a hospital!?') and that governments of developing countries, themselves, could execute projects. 'Why', Patel asked Dubey, 'can't these things be done?'[38]

Even though Patel thought that the Consensus was 'overblown and overdone' and that 'the real issues had not been addressed', he came to rely on Dubey to help develop what they called 'New Dimensions in Technical Cooperation' and then 'formed a new [Governing Council] Consensus around that'.[39] They proposed a fundamentally new understanding of UNDP's technical assistance and pre-investment roles. The Programme's aim would be to promote the self-reliance of developing countries by building up their managerial, technical, administrative, and research capabilities. Under that formulation, the valence of many things UNDP had long considered 'bad' suddenly reversed: it would be *good* for developing countries to build their capacity by executing their own projects, using national experts, buying goods from local companies, and

---

[37] I. G. Patel, interview with Yves Berthelot, UN Intellectual History Project, 9 March 2001.
[38] Muchkund Dubey, interview with CNM, 11 Dec. 2004. The quotation on medical experts is from I. G. Patel, interview with EM, 23 May 2005.
[39] I.G. Patel, interview with EM, 23 May 2005.

making sure that capital investments kept up with increasing technical abilities (that is, seeing that a country had the bricks and boards needed to make the best use of its brains and books).[40]

As Patel expected, developing countries strongly endorsed his proposals from the beginning. The Scandinavians and the Dutch were 'taken by it', the British indifferent but persuadable. Of the important donors, only the Americans were opposed, but the Governing Council endorsed the formulation in its summer 1975 session.[41]

Some of the staff members that Patel considered 'reactionary and conservative' saw some of his 'New Dimensions' as a giant step backwards. Margaret Joan Anstee recalls,

> I. G. thought I was a dyed-in-the-wool imperialist. I said, 'It's not that. What added value are you giving when you fund national experts? . . . [W]hat we are giving is know-how that doesn't exist in the country. In a poor country it can be very basic know-how. In more developed countries, it can be something extremely sophisticated and done in different ways. But once you start funding national experts, what you are really doing is providing budget support, i.e., simply money.' Therefore, the whole technical assistance *raison d'être* of the UNDP, which differentiates it from the Bank and other purely financial agencies, goes by the wayside.[42]

In the end, though, it was more the 'Indian scholar studying in California' who became the norm of the UNDP national expert, that is to say, people who clearly were bringing new capacities to the agencies to which they were assigned.

Moreover, the learning theory underlying Patel's 'New Dimensions' differs from the one underlying Anstee's critique. Patel's ideas came from closer to the 'join', 'development as freedom' pole than to the 'tell', 'development as efficiency' pole where the UN network had begun. Recall Arthur Lewis's early comment, 'Men learn administration by participating in it.'[43] Organization theorist Paul Carlile writes about how simple knowledge 'transfer' regularly fails because relevant knowledge is always localized, embedded, and invested in particular practices.[44] Effective

---

[40] Garcia, *International Cooperation and Development*, p. 283.
[41] UNDP, *Report of the Governing Council Twentieth Session (11–30 June 1975)*, 75/34.
[42] Margaret Joan Anstee, interview with TGW, UN Intellectual History Project, 14 Dec. 2004.
[43] Page 49, above.
[44] Paul R. Carlile, 'Transferring, Translating, and Transforming: An Integrative Framework for Managing Knowledge across Boundaries', *Organization Science*, 15, 5 (2004): 555–68. Carlile builds on a standard argument about tacit knowledge from Michael Polanyi, *The Tacit Dimension* (Garden City, NY: Doubleday, 1966).

technical assistance must involve, at the very least, the translation of knowledge into its new context – something that should make an organization like UNDP welcome experts who are equally comfortable in the culture that originated the knowledge and the culture that is receiving it, people who, in Carlile's terms, can 'translate' effectively, some of whom are bound to be nationals. The 'national counterparts' of David Owen's day could play that role, but so could national experts. Ultimately, though, real learning through participation and real empowerment involves the recipients' ability to 'transform' knowledge in ways that serve their own purposes and even contribute to the society from which the original knowledge came. Patel's 'New Dimensions' even pointed in that direction.

Perhaps more prosaically, the New Dimensions' provision for government execution broke the monopoly of the Specialized Agencies, one of the Capacity Study's goals. Moreover, the other notable accomplishment of Peterson's administration (although actually planned and developed under Hoffman) was the establishment of an 'Office of Project Execution' (OPE) to implement projects rapidly, often by subcontracting to private firms, one of the Capacity Study's recommendations. OPE's speed, efficiency, and convenience quickly made it a favourite of UNDP project officers and the governments of many developing countries. In 1977, the alternative mechanisms for execution allowed the Programme to make the first fundamental revisions of its agreements with the Specialized Agencies. They became subcontracting relationships that focused on objective measures of results, rather than simply means for UNDP to pass funds to the Agencies that were then empowered to decide whether they were 'satisfied' with a project's results.[45] With 'New Dimensions' and with UNDP taking a more direct role in project execution, the Programme began to secure its reputation as the development agency (and not just the funding source) that was the most responsive to the developing countries.

Running the gauntlet for US funds

UNDP's closer identification with the South may have come at a cost: the alienation of the country that had been the major sponsor of the UN

---

[45] John Olver, interview with CNM, 27 Sept. 2004. Memo from I. G. Patel to Gabriel Valdés, re: UNDP/Agencies' Basic Agreement, From the F. Bradford Morse Papers, in The Howard Gottlieb Archival Research Center, Boston University, Box 247.

development network from the beginning – the United States. Recall that in the 1950s, the United States provided more than half of EPTA and Special Fund resources. In the 1960s Hoffman could still rely on a US pledge to provide 40 per cent of UNDP funds. This proportion was much higher than the US share of total, non-voluntary, assessments for the regular budget of the United Nations; until 1974, the dues paid by the United States covered 33 per cent of the UN's costs. In 1972, the United States demanded (successfully) that its share of the regular budget be reduced to 25 per cent. At the same time, the United States joined a group of countries (including France, Italy, and Japan) whose 'shares in total UNDP contributions were materially lower than their UN shares'. In contrast, the Scandinavian countries and the Netherlands, 'contributed to UNDP (in 1976) approximately ten times the share indicated by the UN scale of assessments', while 'Belgium, Canada, Finland, India, Iran, Saudi Arabia, and the UK' contributed 'close to double their respective UN shares'.[46]

The relative decline in US support for UNDP reflected the escalating North–South conflict. In late summer 1971, the US government, which had been borrowing money rather than raising taxes to pay for its unpopular war in Vietnam, abandoned many of the commitments it had made in support of the Bretton Woods monetary system because they would have eventually restricted US borrowing. The new US policy gave President Nixon the ability to increase government spending and boost the national economy before he faced reelection in 1972, but an unanticipated consequence of Nixon's decision was the coalescence of an African, Asian, and Latin American alliance that demanded the reform of international economic institutions, a 'New International Economic Order' (NIEO) to replace the institutions that no longer worked as they once did.

For more than a year, the NIEO demands seemed purely rhetorical, but then, in October 1973, Arab members of OPEC (the Organization of the Petroleum Exporting Countries), led by Saudi Arabia, supported Egypt's war against Israel with 'the oil weapon', temporarily cutting off sales to the United States and the Netherlands. Prices soared and, in the United States especially, a critical petroleum shortage ensued, with long queues at service stations and some people unable to afford heat throughout the cold winter of 1973–4. Seven years of 'stagflation' – rising prices without

---

[46] UNDP interoffice memorandum from David E. Feldman, Deputy Director, PPD, to Timothy Rothermel, Executive Assistant to the Administrator, Re: A View on UNDP Resources, 6 Dec. 1977, p. 4. Used courtesy of Bruce Hillis.

growth – followed, seven years marked by an increasingly assertive Southern alliance in the General Assembly that passed a series of resolutions that were anathema to the Assembly's host country and, even more, to its host city, with the largest Jewish population of any urban area in the world. For many in the United States, the most notorious of the resolutions, in 1975, declared that 'Zionism is a form of racism and racial discrimination'.[47]

While the North–South conflict seems to provide sufficient explanation for the stagnation in US financial support for UNDP at a time when the Programme had planned for US support to grow, a more detailed look at the process of US funding in the early 1970s gives better insight into the problems the Programme would continue to face.

Like Muchkund Dubey, Roy Morey was a young rising star in his country's foreign service who would move from interacting with the UN network in a key role within his national government to a distinguished career in UNDP. In 1973 Morey began serving as the Deputy Assistant Secretary in charge of economic and social issues within the International Organization Bureau of the US State Department. In that job he was in charge of securing US commitments to all the voluntarily funded UN economic agencies, including UNDP. Morey's description of the stops he needed to make along the way in order to gain authorization to fund US pledges gives a clear picture of the obstacles.[48]

First, there was an issue of broad policy. The US decision to reduce its portion of regular UN funding to 25 per cent meant that the Nixon administration treated it as given that the US portion of overall voluntary contributions would be no higher. Once that was made clear to other donor countries, Morey still needed to square proposed contributions with two groups within the executive branch. First was the Office of Management and Budget (OMB), with its desire to curb any unnecessary spending after almost a decade of deficit-financed war. An even more significant obstacle was USAID, which had its own bureaucratic interest in shifting the balance of US development funding to bilateral programmes. Charles ('Pete') Perry, who worked as UNDP's Washington liaison under Hoffman and the three subsequent Administrators, says that AID officials 'spread poison

---

[47] UN General Assembly Resolution 3379, 10 November 1975. A summary of the period can be found in Craig N. Murphy, 'What the Third World Wanted: The Meaning of the NIEO', a chapter of Global Institutions, Marginalization, and Development (London: Routledge, 2005), pp. 103–17. Perhaps the best analysis of the politics of the oil weapon is Mohamed Heikal, Road to Ramadan (New York: Ballantine Books, 1976).

[48] Roy Morey, interview with CNM, 24 March 2005.

about UNDP in the halls of Congress', using the Capacity Study to say that the United Nations was 'like a dinosaur without a brain'.[49]

USAID's bureaucratic interest was supported by the theory of international relations embraced by the leading foreign policy figure in the Nixon and Ford administrations, Henry Kissinger. Kissinger had no sympathy for the original justification for the UN development network – that a better international system was one where all states accepted material responsibilities towards less fortunate societies. He saw foreign assistance only as a tool to serve the more specific interests of a donor. Therefore he preferred bilateral to multilateral aid. When it came to multilateral agencies, Kissinger preferred those that could be most easily directed towards US political aims, for example, the World Bank, which supported Kissinger's policy of destabilizing Allende's government in Chile.

Pete Perry believes that USAID succeeded in stopping the quick doubling of US funds to UNDP that the SPIN Study anticipated. Roy Morey's description of the difficulties in Congress gives a clear picture of why the agency could be successful. To get an appropriation for UNDP meant getting past the relevant committee chair, Otto Passman, a 'rough-hewn, race-baiting' Democrat from Louisiana. 'Passman', Morey says, 'had as much regard for the UN as he did for the Soviet Union.' In one session, the representative demanded to see some results produced by the Programme: 'I never see any projects', Passman fumed. Morey called for support from New York, where the (perhaps dinosaur-brained) UNDP public affairs office filled a U-Haul trailer with boxes of unedited project documents. The boxes were impressive for their volume, but their mere presence hardly provided the information that the committee chair had requested.

The growing US hostility towards the United Nations gave Passman and other isolationists an unusually strong group of allies. The original issues of the North–South conflict were not the only problem. In 1973 an internationalist Republican congressman from Massachusetts, F. Bradford Morse, explained to the United Nations Association of Minnesota that his more conservative colleagues blamed the United Nations for harming US businesses by imposing sanctions on chromium exports from white-ruled Rhodesia and by proposing ever-stronger international labour standards that would affect foreign manufacturers operating across the global South. Many in Congress also faulted the United Nations for admitting the People's Republic of China (even though President Nixon was the one who had been leading the effort to

---

[49] Charles Perry, interview with NR, 25 March 2005.

bring China into the global fold), and for 'failure to act on terrorism' (meaning, at that time, the hijacking of commercial airliners, an issue that primarily affected relations between the United States and Cuba).[50]

In sum, the North–South conflict only provided the background for the change in US policy towards UNDP. The conflict strengthened the arguments of isolationists in Congress – largely Democrats from the South and Republicans from the Midwest and West – heirs of those who had blocked US entry into the League of Nations at the end of the First World War and forced the UN Relief and Rehabilitation Administration to disband at the end of the Second. UNDP also ran foul of the bureaucratic interests of the thriving, bilateral development agency that Kennedy had built up to demonstrate the US commitment to a world without want. At the same time, the most powerful US foreign policy makers abandoned the worldview underlying both that commitment and UNDP. Support of multilateral aid programmes over which the United States had limited influence became somewhat superfluous, a matter, perhaps, of good public relations, but something that could be given up if funds were needed elsewhere.

The financial crisis, Brad Morse, and Arthur Brown

While Washington's attitude towards UNDP began to change, at the latest, in 1971, it took four years for the impact of the increasingly negative US view to be recognized in New York. When it did, the Programme faced a major financial crisis.

The Division of Finance had forecast the United States' contributions for fiscal years 1974 and 1975 as more than 20 per cent higher than its pledges turned out to be.[51] In the meantime, *actual* funding from the United States was even lower, more like half what had been anticipated, according to Patel. The United States, and some other donors, had adopted a practice of cutting off funds to particular projects as a way of pressuring UNDP and the executing agencies to speed up their still abysmally slow rates of delivery.[52] To try to deal with the same perception

---

[50] F. Bradford Morse, Speech to the UN Association of Minnesota, 1 May 1973. Morse Papers, Box 247.

[51] UNDP Division of Finance, 'Chronology of Events of Financial Liquidity Crisis – 1975', 28 Nov. 1975, p. 1.

[52] I. G. Patel, interview with EM, 23 May 2005. Ryo Oshiba, 'Budgetmaking in the United Nations Development Program: An Analysis of Expenditures for Technical Assistance', *International Studies Quarterly*, 29, 3 (1985): 313–26.

that UNDP was not using the funds entrusted to it in a timely manner, Peterson had instituted a practice of 'over-execution', giving the Agencies funds for a vast stream of projects long before the Agencies had begun to carry them out. Therefore, when New York began to see a huge cash-flow problem, many of the Agencies were holding millions of dollars of unused UNDP funds; yet they also anticipated huge new transfers.[53]

Some additional perverse aspects of UNDP financial planning contributed to the crisis. Inflation – especially the unprecedented burst of general inflation after the first oil crisis – more than doubled the cost of UNDP experts, something the Programme failed to take into account. Moreover, in some situations, the Programme accounting had treated non-convertible currencies as if they were reliable assets.[54] Finally, the shift to allocating the pool of UNDP funds to countries through fixed IPFs caused significant problems. New York initially allowed annual programming – commitments of funds to a particular country – up to the full IPF, even if donors had not actually provided the funds. Moreover, the first cycle of commitments did not anticipate a host of newly independent countries (largely the result of the break-up of the Portuguese empire after the military coup that spurred Portugal's democratic revolution in1974), which required the awarding of additional IPFs. An independent analysis later concluded that the shift to country programming, by itself, created budget deficits of at least 10 per cent a year in the early 1970s.[55] Margaret Joan Anstee stresses this last set of problems; it 'was really a cash-flow crisis largely due to the fact that the Governing Council had not accepted the system of rolling IPFs, which were a central pillar of the Capacity Study's country programming system'.[56]

It would be hard to say that the Programme responded with alacrity or courage to the first signs of the cash-flow problem. Anthony Gilpin, an officer returning from a mission to assess the needs of the former Portuguese colonies, wrote in his journal,

---

[53] Charles Perry, interview with NR, 25 March 2005. Bruce Hillis, interview with EM, 19 April 2005.

[54] Trevor Gordon-Somers, interview with EM, 12 April 2005. UNDP Division of Finance, 'Trend Analysis of 1972–1978: Relations Between Project Budgets and Expenditures', 15 Sept. 1978, p. 2.

[55] Oshiba, 'Budgetmaking in the United Nations Development Program', p. 319. George Arthur Brown's similar view of the sources of the crisis is summarized in Pranay Gupte, *The Silent Crisis: Despair, Development, and Hope in a World Without Borders* (New Delhi: Vikas Publishing House, 1990), pp. 145–6.

[56] Margaret Joan Anstee, interview with TGW, 14 Dec. 2000.

> I learnt, indirectly, of UNDP's 'liquidity crisis', the implications of which
> seemed to call in question one of the main purposes of my travels . . . On my
> return to New York, I was shocked to find that the sums allocated to the
> former Portuguese territories, far from being increased, had actually all
> been somewhat reduced. I had been left in the dark by headquarters and
> now felt that my efforts had been largely wasted. I was in for another shock
> when I reported at the UNDP office which I found was now housed in a
> brand-new skyscraper facing the main UN building across First Avenue . . .
> After a couple of days, I was offered a small inside office, which was a glori-
> fied store-cupboard without even a telephone.

Not surprisingly, morale suffered. 'There were', Gilpin continues,
'other disgruntled people besides myself, and one of these took more
drastic action. The new building suffered several mysterious small fires
which caused the whole place to be evacuated.'[57]

Unfortunately, UNDP was not in a position to outfit its new offices.
Bruce Hillis (one of the financial crisis whistle-blowers), only barely convinced the landlord that they could make the rent. Hillis, then a very
junior financial officer, also ended up with the task of calling the executing Agencies to tell them that UNDP would not be giving them any funds.
A cable addressed to the Directors General sat around for days, but was
never sent because no one would accept the responsibility for signing it.
When Hillis, on his own initiative, called the Agencies, 'They were
stunned – they were looking to *receive* money from UNDP!'[58]

The unexpended funds held by the Agencies became part of UNDP's
salvation. The Programme 'borrowed' some of them back, and convinced
some donors to pay pledges early. Nevertheless, the Programme's real
deliverance only came with the arrival, in 1976, of Brad Morse, UNDP's
third Administrator. Morse, Hillis says, 'Came in and just recognized that
his primary function was to get us money. He became our bagman.'[59]

He became more than that, but initially, Morse's great contribution to
the Programme did come from his skill at playing that role. Morse was a
natural politician, a successful US congressman from an industrial district north of Boston, a Republican in a Democratic Party state. In 1968
Morse had been one of the few liberals to support Richard Nixon's bid for
his party's nomination – 'Because he was going to win it anyway'.[60]

---

[57] Anthony Gilpin, Personal Journal, September 1974–April 1976, undated entry, Oxford,
Bodleian Library, MS Eng. c. 4675, p. 20, folio p. 284.
[58] Bruce Hillis, interview with EM, 19 April 2005.   [59] Ibid.
[60] Morse's explanation as reported by Timothy S. Rothermel, interview with CNM, 28
April 2005.

President Nixon repaid the favour by supporting Morse's bid to replace Ralph Bunche as the highest-ranking American in the UN Secretariat proper when the Under-Secretary-General retired in 1972. Morse proved very successful in that role and Nixon then nominated him to replace Rudolf Peterson at the end of his unfortunate term.

Morse immediately improved morale and rapidly worked to improve the Programme's financial condition. Perhaps his greatest early contribution was his recruitment, in 1978, of George Arthur Brown to replace both the man who had become Morse's friend, I. G. Patel, and Bert Lindstrom, Peterson's other deputy. Brown became UNDP's single deputy, with the title Associate Administrator.

Brown may well be the most universally respected figure in the history of the Programme. He continued as Associate Administrator under Bill Draper, who recalls, 'I immediately was drawn to George Arthur Brown, who was stellar. I've often referred to him as the finest, most capable person I ever worked with, and I've worked with a lot.'[61] Elena Martínez, chief of staff of the next Administrator, Gus Speth, says, 'The Morse–Arthur Brown team is the best team this organization has had in its history. Morse did external relations, mobilized resources, worked with the US Congress, etc. Arthur was the brains behind the organization – [a] superb manager, superb intellect.'[62]

Brown, 'a cautious, guarded man, one not easily taken in by appearances', a former director of the Jamaican Central Bank who had 'always run his own shop' was initially reluctant to work with the ebullient American who seemed to more than fill every room he entered, 'smiling a good deal, vigorously pumping his visitors' hands, and talking in a booming voice'. Morse assured Brown that there would be no 'boss relationship' between them. [63]

Remarkably, none developed; Draper's second Associate Administrator, Luis Maria Gomez, calls Morse and Brown 'the Dynamic Duo',[64] but Brown was no Robin to Morse's Batman. They divided their tasks. While 'the administrator lived ceaselessly in his own high-flying world of meeting with heads-of-government and putting in 20-hour days in Godforsaken places', Brown worked with staff to design programmes responding to fundamental development needs while ensuring that the

---

[61] William H. Draper III, interview with CNM, 28 Sept. 2004.
[62] Elena Martínez, interview with CNM, 3 June 2004.
[63] Gupte, *Silent Crisis*, p. 147, from his interviews with Brown.
[64] Luis Maria Gomez, interview with NR, 12 Dec. 2004.

Programme would avoid further demoralizing financial crises for the next twenty years.[65]

Expanding activities and elaborating the UN network

Brown and Morse had two characteristics essential to the task of expanding the UN's development activities in the late 1970s: they accepted the argument behind the UN majority's NIEO and they were realists; they were willing to make virtues out of necessities.

In 1974, when he was Under-Secretary-General, Morse made an eloquent defence of the NIEO:

> The inequity in the distribution of the wealth generated by the world's natural resources should be reason for even deeper concern. The present economic order has permitted the developed world to receive vastly more than its fair share from the exploitation of the world's natural resources. It has, in effect, shortchanged the developing world by augmenting its own wealth and power to the comparative disadvantage of those nations whose resources it depleted . . . A strong case can be made that there is a moral obligation on the part of the developed world to initiate changes in international economic relationships . . . It bears, in my view, the primary responsibility . . . for the creation of new international economic relationships which will conform to ideals of justice, equality, and social progress to which we have all subscribed.[66]

Morse's bona fides as an ally of the United Nations' Southern majority were never in question. Neither were Brown's; he came to UNDP from the International Bauxite Association, one of the many OPEC-like commodity producer alliances that many, in the 1970s, believed would reverse the 'inequity in the distribution of the wealth generated by the world's natural resources'.

Morse and Brown sometimes used their reputations in the South to gain majority support for new UN development programmes or funds that were the hobbyhorses of a very few wealthy states. This was the one way in which the UN network could grow substantially in a period of great conflict about development. In fact, it is conflict over how development can be achieved that explains one of the first things noticed by students of international organizations: the profusion of development

---

[65] Gupte, *Silent Crisis*, pp. 148–9.
[66] F. Bradford Morse, Remarks to the Stanley Foundation Strategy for Peace Conference, Warrenton, VA, 19 October 1974, pp. 4–5, Morse Papers, Box 247.

agencies, in stark contrast to other fields where there is usually only one global organization. There is *one* Universal Postal Union and *one* International Labour Organisation, but, at the global level alone, there is the World Bank (made up of five organizations), UNDP, UNICEF, the World Food Programme, and many more.

It is in the nature of multinational institutions that, in the end, they must serve the interests of all their member states. Nevertheless, when the initial idea of an organization is mooted, it is rarely possible to convince all states that the proposed organization deserves their support. This is where benefactors come in: individuals, states, or other organizations are needed to underwrite the initial cooperation until its benefit is proved to all potential members, in the way, for example, in which the United States acted as the benefactor of EPTA, the Special Fund, and UNDP in the 1950s and 1960s.[67]

That many potential benefactors can be found for new development organizations is a result of the fundamental problem that 'development' is meant to solve: the steepness of the income gradient between North and South means that there can be many combinations of wealthy states able to sustain any one part of the vast array of international development agencies.

Paul Hoffman had used this fact to good effect throughout his tenure, especially in the foundation of the UN Fund for Population Activities (UNFPA) and UN Volunteers (UNV).

UNFPA began as an offshoot of UNDP and it remains under the same executive body. One impetus for the Population Fund was a growing awareness in the 1960s among some global elites that rapid population growth in the developing world could wipe out the effects of even very positive economic growth. The view that population growth was a 'problem' was widely shared among many of the leading figures within UNDP, including Richard Symonds (who was hired by Secretary-General U Thant to write a report on the UN's past and future population roles) and David Owen (who moved from UNDP to head the International Planned Parenthood Federation). The strongest support, internationally, came from the US Congress and the Lyndon Johnson administration, including US Defence Secretary Robert McNamara, who then moved to head the World Bank.[68]

---

[67] For the larger historical pattern see Craig N. Murphy, *International Organization and Industrial Change: Global Governance since 1850* (Cambridge: Polity Press, 1994).

[68] Richard Symonds and Michael Carder, *The United Nations and the Population Question, 1945–1970* (New York: McGraw Hill for the Population Council, 1973), pp. 188–9.

Hoffman became convinced of the need for a separate UN fund at a meeting of UNDP's Governing Council in Manila, where he met and befriended Rafael Salas, a skilled and honourable man serving under the Philippines' increasingly corrupt president, Ferdinand Marcos. In 1968, responding to an open invitation from Hoffman, Salas fled the Philippines to serve as UNDP's population consultant. Based on Salas's preliminary work on funding and staffing, and on Symonds's report, the General Assembly approved the creation of UNFPA, and Salas became its head, in 1969. The outcome was an organization that could actively pursue the population side of development at a time when many African, Asian, and Latin American governments considered the issue to be a diversion from the quest for the NIEO. The separate voluntary fund provided a place for interested donors to contribute. Salas, who was Roman Catholic, and his close collaborator and successor, Nafis Sadik, a physician from Pakistan, both gave the new institution legitimacy to the UN majority and quickly gained much more universal support for its aims.

UNDP's Governing Council created UNV in 1971 as a global equivalent of the US Peace Corps and the other national programmes for young development volunteers that began in the 1960s, including Iran's Universal Welfare Legion.[69] UNV differs from the Peace Corps and the many similar programmes of wealthy nations in two ways: the vast majority of UN volunteers come from the developing world and most are highly skilled professionals, not young people who have yet to develop professional competencies.

Iran served as the new programme's major sponsor and initial benefactor. UNV's first coordinator, Assad K. Sadr of Iran, was only able to place about 150 volunteers in the field at any time. Excellent volunteers from the developing world were plentiful, but Sadr's funds were not. Initially, many industrialized countries refused to cooperate with UNV, seeing it as a threat to their own programmes. In 1974, a new coordinator, John Gordon, a Canadian, worked closely with key UNDP figures, including Hoffman's budget chief, Bruce Stedman – 'who taught me about lobbying delegations and who helped draft several of the Governing Council resolutions' – to form a larger group of supporters, including the development volunteer programmes of Ireland, Japan, and the Netherlands.[70] When Morse arrived in 1976, he ramped up appeals

---

[69] William Adriansolo, interview with NR, 15 Dec. 2004.
[70] John Gordon, 'Taking on Early Challenges', *UNV News*, 91 (June 2001), http://www.unv. org/infobase/unv_news/2001/91/01_03_91_jgordon.htm (accessed 15 Aug. 2005).

for voluntary contributions to UNV, concentrating on the wealthy countries that had built the strongest cooperative relations with the new UN programme.[71]

Similarly, in the early 1970s, the General Assembly gave UNDP responsibility for the UN Capital Development Fund (CDF), a programme with 'high intentions and low resources'[72] whose origins went back to the early debates over setting up a multilateral development financing facility that would not be a foreign policy tool of the donor countries. The General Assembly gave CDF an operational mandate in 1966, as part of the negotiations that led to UNDP, but, in its early years, CDF had few resources other than non-convertible currencies contributed by some developing countries. In 1973 the UNDP Governing Council narrowed the focus of the CDF: it would concentrate on capital projects in the least developed developing countries. Based on that mandate, Morse was finally able to secure significant contributions from the Netherlands and the Nordic countries.

When Morse arrived, UNDP also had responsibility for a relatively new, 'UN Revolving Fund for Natural Resources Exploration', designed, in part, to attract money from the newly rich petroleum exporting countries, and a Special Unit on Technical Cooperation among Developing Countries (TCDC), one of I. G. Patel's great interests. Both programmes initially suffered from the high intentions/low resources dilemma, but Morse was able to find funding for a set of activities matching technological needs and capacities in different regions of the developing world, especially Latin America and the Caribbean, beginning in 1983. In part, the regional success reflected a particular interest of Latin American states with independent scientific and engineering capabilities, such as Argentina, which had sponsored the key intergovernmental conference on TCDC in 1978.[73]

Perhaps Morse's most successful UNDP spin-off was an agency he brought to the Programme from the UN Secretariat proper. The early 1970s witnessed a devastating drought and famine over much of West Africa's Sahelian region. Records from the centuries of Portuguese colonialism suggest that shortages of rain may have caused periodic widespread crises for at least 400 years. The last had taken place immediately

[71] Bruce Stedman, interview with CNM, 2 March 2005.
[72] The description offered by J. K. Robert England, interview with CNM, 20 May 2004.
[73] Garcia, *International Cooperation and Development*, p. 199; UNDP Special Unit for TCDC, *20 Years of South–South Partnership Building, 1978–1998: An Assessment of Technical Cooperation among Developing Countries* (New York: UNDP, 1999), pp. 20–2.

after the Second World War.[74] However, the food crisis of the early 1970s was the first in the context of an international system of states committed to aiding those who were less advantaged.

The disaster took place in a largely Islamic part of the world, albeit with significant Christian communities along the devastated parts of the West African coast and in the drought-stricken islands. Observing the horror, Barbara Ward wrote:

> If the human race cannot agree on food, on what can they agree? If the self-proclaimed 'Christian' countries of the West who pray, 'Give us this day our daily bread', are not prepared to give it to anyone else, they deserve the mockery and collapse that follow upon too wide a breach between principle and practice. If those who worship Allah, the all-Merciful, the all Compassionate, do not spontaneously help those who their new wealth most depresses, they, too, weaken the ultimate moral cement of their own societies. 'The Peoples of the Book' who have monopoly control of what the world most needs – bread and energy – are directly challenged to go beyond the 'idols of the market' and to create instead a moral community for all mankind.[75]

Acting in the name of all humanity, the UN eventually did respond. UN Secretary-General Kurt Waldheim (who had succeeded U Thant in 1972) established a Special Sahelian Office and gave Morse oversight. Morse quickly hired Galal Magdi, an Egyptian who worked with the Canadian International Development Agency, to raise funds and build up the programme.

Magdi helped Morse secure unprecedented support from many of the Arab oil producers, especially Saudi Arabia. In fact, Morse probably raised more new aid from the increasingly prosperous oil producers than did any of the scores of other aid entrepreneurs who tried throughout the 1970s. Burkina Faso's Bernard Lédéa Ouedraogo, the West African who has been the most widely honoured for policy innovations that have successfully combated hunger, says that UNDP's work was an essential element of the international strategy that both contained the famine and quickly rebuilt herds and farms.[76] Nevertheless, Magdi notes, with a sense

[74] António Carreira, *Demografia caboverdeana, subsídios para o seu estudo (1807/1983)* (Praia: Instituto Caboverdeano do Livro, 1985); António Carreira, *Cabo Verde, formação e extinção de uma sociedade escravocrata (1460–1878)*, 2nd edn (Praia: Instituto Caboverdeano do Livro, 1983).

[75] Barbara Ward, 'Foreword', in Sartaj Aziz, *Hunger, Politics and Markets: the Real Issues in the Food Crisis* (New York: New York University Press, 1975), p. xv.

[76] Bernard Lédéa Ouedraogo, interview with CNM, 15 Jan. 2005.

of grievance, that when he first tried to marshal the UNDP Res Reps in West Africa behind the Secretariat programme, he was sometimes met with a lack of interest or outright hostility. That attitude changed both with the continued success of the larger office, UNSO (the UN Drylands Development Centre) that grew out of the Sahelian Office, and with the shift of the programme to UNDP when Morse himself moved across the street from the Secretariat proper to UNDP's new 'skyscraper'.[77]

Brad Morse's realism extended beyond elaborating the UN development network in order to build different coalitions of benefactors to support various worthy ends. Both he and Arthur Brown embraced programme innovations that reduced cost and improved the delivery of UNDP services. For example, as Trevor Gordon-Somers (who eventually rose to be in charge of much of the UN's development work in Africa) argues, one of the most positive consequences of the financial crisis was UNDP's durable new conviction that scarce resources should go to those who most needed them.[78]

Many of the innovations that Brown and Morse embraced reinforced the trend, which both so strongly supported, of shifting power within UNDP towards the developing world. One way to cut costs, for example, was to increase the responsibilities undertaken by the 'national' staff within the country offices. (National staff members are paid at prevailing wages in the local market and do not incur international travel costs for relocation and home leave.) Opening most of the upper-level jobs in country offices not only increased local ownership of UNDP programmes, it also created a much more global pool of potential applicants for international staff and for positions at headquarters; staff members who proved their excellence in their own country often found opportunities, both short-term and long-term, in other UN offices.

Similarly, in Brown and Morse's day, UNDP found a way to embrace the idea of using national experts that proved particularly successful, the TOKTEN programme. TOKTEN stands for 'Transfer of Knowledge Through Expatriate Nationals', something that proved to be much more significant than Patel's original thought about sending an 'Indian scholar studying in California to India'. It was, instead, a Turkish mechanical engineer, working in California, who piloted the project, which was invented by Nessim Shallon, the Res Rep in Ankara. The engineer had been recruited to help establish a department in one of the

[77] Galal Magdi, interview with CNM, 22 April 2005.
[78] Trevor Gordon-Somers, interview with EM, 12 April 2005.

UNDP-supported successors of the Middle Eastern Technical University, Karadeniz Technical University.

In most cases, the people UNDP brought back for short-term consultancies were global leaders in their fields – from applied mathematics, to medicine, and water resource management – the kind of people whose careers in Europe and North America lead to so much hand-wringing about the 'brain drain' from the South to the North. They were also people with deep cultural understanding and deep commitment, for whom the 'translation' or 'transformation' of knowledge (rather than its mere 'transfer') was second nature.

In 1987, ten years after the TOKTEN programme began, it was operating in twenty-five countries. While I researched this book, I visited five of them (China, Egypt, Haiti, India, and Pakistan) and spoke at length with government officials and development analysts from three others (Cape Verde, Trinidad and Tobago, and Turkey). Each of these countries has a significant diaspora of scientists and engineers, in Canada, France, Germany, the United Kingdom, or the United States (the major sources of TOKTEN experts).

When I asked, 'What have been UNDP's two or three greatest contributions to the development of your country?', TOKTEN was almost always part of the response. The views of Rehanna Hyder, a national officer from Pakistan whose career took off in the Morse years, are typical, 'mineral self-sufficiency, civil aviation, and TOKTEN', but 'TOKTEN is part of the explanation of the other two', and, she adds, of UNDP's contribution to Pakistan's power sector and its leadership in civil engineering and materials science.[79]

M. A. Cheema, a former Director General in Pakistan's Ministry of Labour and long-time national coordinator for TOKTEN, cites three recent cases of which he is particularly proud. There is the shift of many of Pakistan's automobiles from petrol to cheaper, less polluting, compressed natural gas (CNG) – a technological field in which Pakistan is now one of the world's leaders – the result of a TOKTEN visit by an expat from New Zealand. And there are two health institutions, the world-class cancer hospital in Lahore (founded by the famous cricketer, Imran Khan) and the country's first major AIDS centre, both spearheaded by TOKTEN volunteers who returned many times.[80]

[79] Rehanna Hyder, interview with CNM, 7 Dec. 2004.
[80] M. A. Cheema, interview with CNM, 7 Dec. 2004.

Rehanna Hyder thinks a bit more. There is also something about having national officers in responsible positions at the same time: it could be 'very exciting' because, as a national, you could coordinate well, 'with the government side . . . and also with the experts themselves'. There was 'less duplication and more communication. You could facilitate so much. It's a good feeling.' She recalls the bad old days of grandiose aspirations and New York's dominance when she was first recruited, '[We had] a huge telex, from this end [of the table] to that end, and the purpose of the telex was the "Committee to Reduce Paperwork". Classic! It was simply awful.'[81] The new UNDP, the development programme *of* the developing countries, may have been as much the consequence of bad planning and external constraints as it was the result of all the careful studies at the end of the 1960s, but it was, nonetheless, more effective, less wasteful, and more widely respected than the original UN programmes out of which it grew.

[81] Rehanna Hyder, interview with CNM, 7 Dec. 2004.

7

Engaging liberation movements and revolutionary states

Indeed, much was positive about becoming the development programme of the developing world, even if not all the factors that moved UNDP in that direction had been anticipated or welcomed by its first generation of leaders. The downside was that the Programme risked becoming irrelevant, at best, to UNDP's early champion and major supporter, the United States government, an important critic of the new assertiveness of the Third World.

By the mid-1970s, the anti-Third World coalition within the US government had two factions, each with its own argument against a UNDP that had become identified with the developing nations. Traditional US conservatives – some of them isolationists, more of them advocates of a 'Free World' alliance against 'global communism' – believed that UNDP's universalism reinforced Third World tyrants including those who, in this view, had created the oil crises of 1973–4 (following the October War against Israel) and 1979 (after Iran's Islamic Revolution). In contrast, there were the self-described political 'realists' – including Richard Nixon and Henry Kissinger – who were willing to live with tyrants and communists as long as they respected the global status quo.

Brad Morse had UNDP take on new activities that responded to the realists' criticism of UN development assistance and helped quiet that group's larger fears. Ironically, perhaps, Morse did so by having the Programme reach out to, and to work with and cultivate, those developing states and nationalist movements that were most often lambasted by US conservatives as their country's greatest enemies: 'Red' China, Vietnam, revolutionary Iran, the Palestinians, and nationalists on the left throughout southern Africa.

This legacy of Morse is doubly ironic because even his strongest advocates rarely credit him with a unified vision, a particular direction in which he wanted to take UNDP. Recall Elena Martínez's conclusion that Arthur Brown acted as 'the brains of the organization', while Morse

7.1 F. Bradford Morse

mobilized resources.[1] John Olver, the 'Mohican' to whom Morse turned
to run his programme in Palestine, notes that Morse was never one to 'get
bogged down in the efforts to convince the world that UNDP's work had
a coherent intellectual orientation'. Morse was open to 'politicians and
operators', ever ready to start up new programmes,

> that some people might consider marginal, but that he saw as a chance to
> change the minds of some of the people who brought over the money and
> the donor countries. So he went along with a lot of things that I guess
> proved to be politically advantageous at the time, but that became barnacles
> on the side of the ship.[2]

Nevertheless, when it came to understanding the complexity of US
dissatisfaction with the United Nations and the Third World, Morse
knew much more than anyone else in the Programme as a former US congressman and President Nixon's nominee to UNDP. Even if his agenda
developed incrementally out of a sequence of timely interactions with
different 'politicians and operators', it reflected the complex understanding of international relations that Morse had developed long before he
entered the United Nations.

When realists of Nixon's or Kissinger's stripe considered China,
Vietnam, revolutionary Iran, the Palestinian Liberation Organization

[1] Elena Martínez, interview with the author (CNM), 3 June 2004.
[2] John Olver, interview with CNM, 3 Aug. 2004.

(PLO), the African National Congress (ANC) or the South West Africa People's Organization (SWAPO, the nationalist movement in what is now Namibia), their primary worry was that these states and movements had no commitment to the international status quo. They were, in that sense, 'revolutionary' – willing to upset the international order that the United States had helped to create and from which it benefited. In theory, such 'revolutionaries' might be socialized to international norms and thus made less threatening.[3] However, due to strong domestic opposition, this was a difficult policy for the United States to pursue. The US movement hostile to the Chinese Communist régime had been powerful since the 1940s. Many US citizens remained traumatized by the defeat in Vietnam. US supporters of Israel and those outraged by the petroleum price increases of the 1970s considered the Palestinian nationalist movements, many Arab governments, and Iran's revolutionary régime to be enemies. And US mining interests and many staunch anti-communists embraced the white-minority governments in southern Africa.

What was complex for the United States was straightforward for the United Nations. In fact, UNDP's universalism and the assertive Third World's demand that some movements be treated as the legitimate governments of particular territories mandated that UNDP engage many of those whom US conservatives considered to be 'enemies'. Similarly, most of UNDP's important donors other than the United States – the Nordic countries and the Netherlands especially – enthusiastically supported UNDP's engagement with many liberation movements and with some 'enemies' of the United States, including Vietnam. That engagement helped transform 'revolutionary' movements and states into more 'status quo-oriented' powers.

Beginnings in Romania and southern Africa

Some argue that an early UNDP foray into socialization of this sort (helping to transform revolutionary states into status-quo-oriented powers) came with the opening of its first office in a Warsaw Pact country. Yet, when the Programme set up shop in Romania in 1971, it was more a matter of helping a status quo power become less aligned to the weaker of

---

[3] G. John Ikenberry and Charles A. Kupchan, 'Socialization and Hegemonic Power', *International Organization*, 44, 3 (summer 1990): 283–315. Henry Kissinger, *A World Restored: Metternich, Castlereagh and the Problems of Peace, 1812–22* (Boston, MA: Houghton Mifflin, 1957), p. 2, presents one version of the problem caused by revolutionary states.

the bipolar giants. The office took over responsibility for the administration of a programme that, earlier, had been run out of the UNDP office in Geneva, which also oversaw cold war-era programmes in Albania, Bulgaria, Czechoslovakia, Hungary, and Poland. UNDP and its predecessors had long had offices in non-aligned Yugoslavia and in Havana, the capital of the Soviet Union's developing country ally, Cuba, but the Programme would open no other offices in eastern Europe until the end of the cold war.

For Romania, UNDP was a window to the West. In the 1970s and 1980s, the Programme provided various government agencies with information technology and training in modern management, as well as access to non-Soviet agricultural and industrial technology. The Romanian government saw the assistance as essential to its goal of achieving greater autonomy from the Soviet Union. Romania's relative success in this endeavour, and UNDP's demonstrated political neutrality, laid the groundwork for the Programme's decisive role in eastern Europe after the cold war.[4]

The Nixon administration quietly supported Romania's move towards greater independence and, as UNDP Administrator, Brad Morse paid attention to the Romanian office, but this was not the inspiration for what became his signature policy. That came, instead, from Africa, the region that had become Morse's passion when he worked in the Secretariat proper. In 1974, at the height of the New International Economic Order (NIEO) debate, the UNDP Governing Council had instructed Morse's predecessor to treat 'the National Liberation Movements recognized by the Organization of African Unity [OAU]' as partners in 'matters pertaining to the people of their respective territories'.[5] In 1977, Morse opened a UNDP Liaison Office with the OAU (linking it to UNDP's liaison with the UN Economic Commission for Africa) in Ethiopia's capital, Addis Ababa, an office through which UNDP relations with the liberation movements could be maintained.[6] Other critical connections were made in Lusaka, Zambia, the headquarters of many of the movements, and, after majority

---

[4] Alexander H. Rotival (UNDP's first Res Rep in Romania), interview with CNM, 14 Sept. 2004. Ion C. Popescu, 'A Dynamic and Effective Partnership for Development: Romania – United Nations Development Programme', *Romanian Journal of International Affairs*, 3, 1 (winter 1997): 138–58.

[5] UNDP, *Report of the Governing Council: Eighteenth Session (5–24 June 1974)*, 74/26.

[6] Ngila Mwase, 'The UNDP Representation to the African Union and Liaison Office with the Economic Commission for Africa (RAULOE): Achievements during the Period 1977–2004', unpublished paper, UNDP Maputo, March 2005.

rule came to Zimbabwe in 1979, in that country's capital, Harare, as well as in Tanzania, where UNDP supported the secondary schools and the development centre set up by the ANC.[7]

UNDP assigned some of its most skilled officers to this work, including Trevor Gordon-Somers (who later occupied the top positions in the Regional Bureau for Africa), Ahmad Tejan Kabbah (Sierra Leone's current president), and Shekou Sesay (who heads Kabbah's cabinet).

Sesay remembers the help provided to the leaders of the Zimbabwean, Namibian, and South African movements resident in Zambia:

> We gave them a lot of technical assistance, gave them a lot of training pro-grammes, fellowships, placing their students in other African countries, trips to New York . . . to touch base with the General Assembly. This was the great period of the UN being involved with the liberation movements. Of course, when you look at my background, coming from a country which had recently gotten its independence . . . I felt quite good . . . [We in UNDP] were the people who translated all those great [General Assembly] decolo-nization resolutions into practical terms.[8]

One of the most important Lusaka-based projects, the United Nations Institute for Namibia (UNIN), operated with significant UNDP support from 1976 to 1990, when Namibia became independent. The Institute provided training, research, and foreign work experience that prepared liberation movement cadres for the job of governing:

> At independence, the Institute's Director, Hage Geingob, became Prime Minister. Three senior staff members became Speaker of the Parliament and Ministers for Education and for Information and Broadcasting. Other func-tionaries who related very much with the Institute also joined the Cabinet, as did a few of the graduates.[9]

UNIN conducted significant research projects that informed the struc-ture of the new country's government and many of its basic laws and public policies. Today, Namibia has a competent government, excellent relations with the rest of the world, and 'what is considered Africa's most democratic constitution',[10] thanks, in large part, to this work.

---

[7] Petu Serote, 'Solomon Mahlangu Freedom College: A Unique South African Educational Experience in Tanzania', *Transformation*, 20 (1992): 47–60.

[8] Shekou Sesay, interview with CNM, 10 Jan. 2005.

[9] Ngila Mwase, 'UNDP and the United Nations Institute for Namibia, 1976–90', unpub-lished paper, UNDP Maputo, March 2005, p. 1.

[10] Robert J. Griffiths, 'Democratisation and Civil–Military Relations in Namibia, South Africa, and Mozambique', *Third World Quarterly*, 17, 3 (1996): 473.

This outcome was completely unexpected by those who controlled US policy in Brad Morse's day. Many considered the men and women trained by the Institute and other UNDP projects to be incapable of embracing constitutional government and the rule of law. SWAPO was an enemy plotting a 'Marxist takeover' of Namibia, in the opinion of the US Justice Department lawyer who looked into the matter.[11] Because of such views, Gordon-Somers notes, the 'political impediments' to UNDP's support of the Namibian liberation movements were very great, but, under Morse, the Programme 'was not shy in taking on these responsibilities' and it 'certainly paid off'.[12]

Given those impediments, why did Morse, the 'bagman', the chief fundraiser, risk alienating UNDP's largest donor? It was not just a way of pursuing US goals by other means. Morse was *not* simply trying to tame the radical African movements with a more effective realist policy than the so-called 'tar-baby option' (of sticking with the white minority régimes)[13] preferred by Henry Kissinger. Had that been Morse's goal, UNDP would have been satisfied to leave Namibia with a weak and ineffective government. However, despite the predictions of some perceptive critics of both the UN's role and of other international efforts to aid democratization in Africa, the United Nations did not train SWAPO leaders to become aid-dependent crony capitalists indebted to the global status quo.[14] Ngila Mwase, UNIN's research director recalls,

> One of my worries . . . was that the UN (UNDP and UNIN) was spoon-feeding the cadres and that they would be very donor dependent. This has not happened – the government has been the least dependent [in Africa], wanting to do things on their own. (Of course, they have minerals, but they still could have lost initiative.) I am happy I was wrong.

He contrasts this outcome to Zimbabwe, where similar 'pre-independence' work had to be done 'at the last minute', in the short

---

[11] Neil A. Lewis, 'Old Memo from Roberts the Young Lawyer Shows a Caustic Side', *New York Times*, 4 Sept. 2005, http://www.nytimes.com/2005/09/04/politics/politicsspecial1/04roberts.html?ex=1126756800&en=a128c06b58cf5316&ei=5070&pagewanted=print (accessed 13 Sept. 2005).

[12] Trevor Gordon-Somers, interview with Elizabeth Mandeville (EM), 12 April 2005.

[13] The classic analysis of this failed policy was done by Anthony Lake, later President Clinton's National Security Advisor, *The 'Tar Baby' Option: American Policy Toward Southern Rhodesia* (New York: Columbia University Press, 1976).

[14] Henning Melber, ed., *Reexamining Liberation in Namibia: Political Culture since Independence* (Uppsala: Nordic Africa Institute, 2004), Rita Abrahamsen, *Disciplining Democracy: Development Discourse and Good Governance in Africa* (London: Zed Books, 2001).

window between 1976 and 1979.[15] Yet, even in Zimbabwe, UNDP's failure was not one of fostering dependency. UNDP simply did not build the liberation movements' capacity to govern as well as the United Nations would in Namibia, where majority rule came ten years later.

Shekou Sesay tells a story that better explains Morse's motivation: his love of Africa and the very personal level of his concern about development. In 1976, Sesay was called to headquarters to work with Margaret Joan Anstee on Morse's task force that restructured the Programme in the wake of the financial crisis. While Sesay was in New York, Morse received a letter from a farmer in Sierra Leone requesting UNDP's help. Morse was touched. He gave the letter to Anstee, who asked Sesay to travel through Sierra Leone on his way back to his permanent assignment. The Res Rep in Freetown assigned Sesay a car and driver. They drove for hours to the end of a tiny road; Sesay hitched up his robe and walked the last four kilometres down the track that led to the farmer's house:

> 'Excuse me', I said, 'you wrote a letter to the Administrator in New York about your farm?'
> He said, 'Yes'.
> I said, 'I have been sent to come and meet you.'
> He said, 'Really?'
> I said, 'Yes'.
> He said, 'but you are not white?'
> I said, 'No, I am not'. . . I was speaking Krio . . . We discussed. I thought he was a bit incredulous, so I said, 'Let's sit down and tell me exactly what you want'. So we sat down, wrote it up, brought it to Harper [the Res Rep]. We developed a programme for this farmer . . . Whether he prospered or did not prosper I really do not know . . . but, for me, this speaks a lot about UNDP.[16]

It also says a lot about its Administrator at the time. When Morse died, in 1994, he was eulogized in Congress by a colleague who said, 'Millions of Africans are alive today because of his selfless dedication and hard work, but not one of them knows his name.'[17] However, this was only a few months after South Africa's first democratic elections, and certainly

[15] Mwase, 'UNDP and the United Nations Institute', pp. 4–5. Garth ap Rees notes that UNDP's predecessors had programmes in Rhodesia from 1962 to 1965, but left after the unilateral declaration of independence by the white minority government, electronic mail to CNM, 21 Dec. 2005.   [16] Shekou Sesay, interview with CNM, 10 Jan. 2005.
[17] Benjamin G. Gilman, in the House of Representatives, 1 Feb. 1995. *Congressional Record* (Washington, D.C.: US Government Printing Office, 1995), p. E243.

many of the ANC leaders who had been supported by UNDP in Tanzania and Zambia and who had followed Nelson Mandela into power knew *precisely* who Morse was. Victor Gbeho, Ghana's long-serving UN ambassador and, for many years, the leader of the group championing the African liberation movements within the General Assembly, says, 'Remember, Morse was a legend, larger than life yet available to *everyone*, completely open on the issues, and willing to do what was right.'[18]

China

Morse's doing 'what was right' was less of a problem for his friends in Washington when it came to another UNDP foray into the socialization of revolutionary governments. In 1978, Long Yongtu was serving in the Chinese mission to the UN in New York when Brad Morse and Andrew Joseph, the Sri Lankan head of UNDP's Asia Bureau, made a courtesy call and asked a visiting vice-minister if China were interested in receiving UNDP assistance. The answer was so unexpected that Joseph turned to Long to check if there had been a mistranslation. 'No, the translation is correct.' As part of Deng Xiaoping's new economic policy, China had decided to call on one development organization – the one they considered the most trustworthy and politically independent – to help with a long-term plan to engage with the global economy at large.[19]

Thus began China's (and Long's) more than twenty-five-year relationship with UNDP. (As part of the developing relationship, Long served for several years as a staff member of the Asia bureau; later, he led China's successful negotiations to join the World Trade Organization (WTO)). In the early years, Long recalls, China's primary requests were for technology, to give Chinese enterprises access to decades of foreign inventions. It was particularly important, Long argues, that under the 'New Dimensions' policies instituted in the 1970s, UNDP could provide equipment. 'Originally, we thought genuine assistance meant something you could touch', even if the primary reason for bringing UNDP to China was to provide reform-minded officials with access to a broad range of international experience. 'There is', Khalid Malik, the most recent Res Rep in Beijing, says, 'a Chinese proverb, "Only cross a river when you can see the stones". China wanted UNDP to provide models of the changes that would be needed to create a modern state, to provide the stones to cross the river.'[20]

[18] Victor Gbeho, interview with CNM, 19 Jan. 2005.
[19] Long Yongtu, interview with CNM, 1 Dec. 2004.
[20] Khalid Malik, interview with CNM, 10 Jan. 2006.

By the mid-1980s, when Long was put in charge of the Chinese side of the relationship, 'We had realized that "software" projects were even more in the nature of UNDP.'[21] That lesson had been learned, for example, in 1981, when UNDP had arranged for Jiang Zemin, then Vice-Minister for Foreign Trade, and other junior ministers to visit export-processing zones on four continents. They returned committed to a new phase of trade liberalization. Twenty years later, Jiang, then China's president and head of the Communist Party, told Mark Malloch Brown that only UNDP could have organized that trip. Bilateral donors would have shown the Chinese only their own export processing zones, and the World Bank would have considered the whole thing too politically fraught.[22]

Experiences like Jiang's created space for Long and one of his major partners, Roy Morey, to offer UNDP's services in support of even more significant reforms. Morey, recall, had been Nixon's Deputy Assistant Secretary of State. He joined Morse's UNDP in 1978 and was made Res Rep in Beijing in 1988. Morey's job was far from easy. 'The Chinese', he remembers, 'would not *say* that they wanted a market economy. Those were words you could never use.'[23] Yet, compared with a few years later, this was a time of relatively open conversations about politics and economics, a time when many new ideas could enter the country. Long recollects how radical one of the new concepts adopted from UNDP originally seemed, the notion of 'civil servants', something that did not quite fit with the image many revolutionary cadres had of themselves.[24]

Much of the openness ended with the June 1989 crackdown on the pro-democracy protests in Tiananmen Square. While Chinese colleagues privately told Morey that they were glad UNDP had a 'hidden agenda' of support for an open society and human rights,[25] the 'upstream' reforms to which UNDP contributed in the 1990s were primarily in the economic field. They included a package of twenty-two economic laws that explicitly laid the foundation for a market economy, as well as the introduction of the second fundamentally new concept of government about which UNDP's Chinese partners remark: the idea of 'social security'. This was even more problematic to many older revolutionaries than the idea

---

[21] Long Yongtu, interview with CNM, 1 Dec. 2004.
[22] Memorandum report re: UNDP 1999–2005, Accomplishments and Remaining Challenges from Mark Malloch Brown to Kemal Dervis, August 2005, p. 4. Roy Morey, interview with EM, 4 April 2005.   [23] Roy Morey, interview with EM, 4 April 2005.
[24] Long Yongtu, interview with CNM, 1 Dec. 2004.
[25] Roy Morey, interview with EM, 4 April 2005.

of a 'civil service'. Under China's old command economy, work units were responsible for minimal levels of food, shelter, and clothing. In a market economy that encourages people to move from job to job and place to place, the collective responsibility for welfare has become more complex.[26]

Despite the continuing repression of political dissent, UNDP eventually became involved with issues the Chinese government has found controversial, issues that come from the Programme's own agenda, including the empowerment of women and the protection of the environment, the signature goals of Administrators Bill Draper and Gus Speth respectively. Goa Hongbin of the Meeting Group for Poverty Reduction in the [Chinese] State explains that, since 1986, UNDP has been an important source of policy innovation and capacity building for those charged with responding to the inequality created by China's new economic policy. UNDP also facilitated rapprochement between China and the major funders concerned with poverty reduction, especially the World Bank.[27] More recently, since 1996, the Programme has been a major partner in China's experiments with grass-roots democracy, producing training materials for civil servants in Beijing (many of whom are suspicious of the initiative) and for aspiring village leaders and rural citizens who are learning to vote, organize meetings, and prevent village-level corruption for the first time.

One of the young policy makers involved in what may prove to be China's most lasting move towards liberal democracy, Zhan Chengfu, explains that some of UNDP's assistance has been supportive in surprising ways. During a UNDP study tour of local institutions in France, Germany, the Netherlands, and Switzerland, he and other policy-makers were surprised how few European mayors were elected directly. The Chinese officials believe that, in this respect, their new rural democracy is a model for the world, something that, they say, has reinforced their commitment to a much larger process. Zhan is optimistic about the future. 'Now we are faced with a lot of pressure. Some people question why if farmers can impact at the local level, why not at a higher level?' Inevitably, county and provincial elections 'will have to become more transparent' and, eventually, the People's Congress strengthened and made more democratic.[28]

---

[26] Wang Yue, current head of UNDP's main partner in China, the China International Centre for Economic and Technical Exchanges, interview with CNM, 1 Dec. 2004.
[27] Gao Hongbin, interview with CNM, 2 Dec. 2004.
[28] Zhan Chengfu, interview with CNM, 2 Dec. 2004.

Some China watchers argue that its conservative leaders' greatest fear is not majority rule, but the break-up of the country that might follow from the extension of the civil rights needed to maintain a liberal democracy. Therefore I was not surprised that, as I planned my 2004 research trip, my government hosts found many reasons why it would be inconvenient or unproductive for me to visit UNDP projects concerned with poverty reduction and cultural empowerment of Tibetans and of the Muslim communities of western China. Yet even the existence of those projects is remarkable, a sign of the trust that has developed between UNDP and the Chinese authorities.

I did visit Shanghai, a place where the impact of UNDP's work could seem even more ominous to traditionalist cadres in Beijing than the Programme's empowerment of distant minorities. Shanghai is becoming much more embedded in the larger world than is China as a whole. My host was Dong Hui ('Call me "Bob"'), soon to move to the US office of the Shanghai government's holding company ('Shanghai's mission in New York'.) Dong has long worked with the Shanghai municipality and UNDP on information technology initiatives that linked business and government and helped the city and region become a global financial and manufacturing hub.

He is especially proud of a series of five UNDP-supported 'High Level Forums on City Informatization in the Asia–Pacific Region'.[29] The Forums bring together senior government officials and corporate leaders throughout the region to focus on the use of information technology to improve governance and the delivery of urban services and to create the infrastructure necessary for effective participation in the global economy. By the third Forum, the Shanghai meetings had become global events, with discussions on e-government problems and solutions from cities in Argentina, Canada, Jamaica, and Sudan, and with representatives from countries in all parts of the world. UNDP has borne very little of the Forums' costs, but, Dong points out, the reputation of UNDP's on-the-ground work throughout Asia and the rest of the world was what convinced many governments and companies to attend.

To be sure, the purpose of the Forums is two-fold. It is, in the first instance, for developing municipalities around the world to exchange information and best practices. In that way, it is part of China's attempt 'to pay UNDP back' for all its help – to extend China's assistance, through UNDP, to other countries in the same way that UNDP had provided the

[29] Bob Dong, interview with CNM, 4 Dec. 2004.

means for others to aid China at a time when its leadership trusted only the UN Programme. In that sense, it is highly appropriate that Shanghai, the city where Jiang Zemin got his political start, would be the host. Nonetheless, the Forums are also trade fairs for Shanghai, events that help position the city at the centre of the global Information Age economy. The summary assessment of UNDP's role in China in the government's official history reads, 'UNDP has facilitated the achievement of the great mission "let the world know China and China know the world".'[30] Dong uses almost the same words: 'UNDP lets *Shanghai* know the world's other cities, and them know us', which contributes to the city's economic dynamism, its political autonomy, and its embeddedness in world society, something that may contribute to global peace, even if it weakens the bonds that hold the parts of China to its centre.

Palestine

If Morse were still alive, it is probably not the China programme that would give him his greatest sense of accomplishment. Rather, it is UNDP's Programme of Assistance to the Palestinian People (PAPP). Basem Khader, who began his UN career in the days of Libya's decolonization, remembers Morse's attachment to Khader's own country, 'He had a sign in his office which said "Welcome" in Arabic. And he never failed to remind me that of the twenty-one Res Reps he appointed to the Arab region, five were Palestinian!'[31] Morse put his closest associates in charge of PAPP. When I visited the office in 2005, more than twenty-five years after the programme started, one of them, Tim Rothermel, who was with Morse in his congressional office, remained the boss.

PAPP's origins go back to the Camp David accords of September 1978. The first chapter of the agreement between Israel and Egypt envisioned the rapid transfer of authority to a democratic transitional government in Gaza and the West Bank. In order for that to happen, conditions in those Palestinian territories – whose infrastructure and economy had been neglected throughout twelve years of occupation – would have to improve rapidly. To do that would require the help of an organization that could cooperate both with Israel and with the political authority accepted by the vast majority of Palestinians, the Palestine

---

[30] China International Centre for Economic and Technical Exchanges, *An Overview of UNDP-China Cooperation, 1979–2001* (Beijing: CICETE, 2002), p. 11.
[31] Basem Khader, letter to CNM, 20 Sept. 2005.

Liberation Organization (PLO), which the Israelis still considered a terrorist band. Even though President Jimmy Carter had mediated Camp David, the United States could not play this role because Carter had promised Israel that his government would have no dealings with the PLO. (In 1979, his UN ambassador and close friend, Andrew Young, was forced to resign after a routine interaction with the PLO's UN delegate that took place when the Israeli prime minister was hospitalized and, therefore, unavailable to quell the storm when US lobbyists supporting Israel learned of the encounter.[32]) Israel had long distrusted the main UN organization operating in the region, the UN Relief and Works Agency for Palestinian Refugees in the Near East (UNRWA), set up in 1950, but it had a cordial relationship with UNDP. After having good relations with UNDP's predecessors, Israel had agreed not to take UNDP core funding in order to avoid political battles in the Governing Council, and the Programme, and its predecessors, had placed Israeli experts all over the world.

After preliminary discussions with Israel and the United States, Morse asked John Olver, who had recently retired, to return to UNDP and set up something fundamentally new. PAPP's job involved 'bricks and boards' as much as 'brains and books'. It built classrooms and schools, expanded hospitals, trained doctors, set up fish markets and chicken farms, built up cultural institutions, hired a world-class soccer coach, and set up three large offices and acquired a fleet of vehicles to administer the whole.[33] Much of what was needed was well outside UNDP's experience, standard operating procedures, or a narrow interpretation of its mandate, but, Olver says, the 'gifted', 'relentlessly hardworking', Arthur Brown quickly found ways to do everything the field office required.[34]

By the time Israel finally left Gaza to a Palestinian civil administration in 2005 (more than twenty years later than had been anticipated at Camp David) UNDP was ubiquitous and respected throughout the territories. When I visited, four months before the withdrawal, senior Palestinian leaders, including Hannan Ashwari and Haidar Abdel Shafi, went out of their way to document PAPP's role in the emergence of a democratic Palestinian state. Ashwari was poetic, talking about UNDP as the

---

[32] Andrew Young in an 'Eyewitness' edition of Robert Scheer, 'National Column', *Los Angeles Times*, 12 Sept. 1993.

[33] All examples from UNDP PAPP, *Twenty Years of Partnership in the West Bank and the Gaza Strip* (Jerusalem: UNDP/PAPP, 1999), and John Olver, *Roadblocks and Mindblocks: Partnering with the PLO and Israel* (Rye, NY: self-published, 2002).

[34] Olver, *Roadblocks and Mindblocks*, pp. 12–13.

Palestinian's 'first partner', like your oldest lifelong friend.[35] Abdel Shafi, the leading secular nationalist leader in the Gaza Strip (a man as deeply and widely respected among Palestinians as was the late Yasser Arafat), detailed the involvement of UNDP in every stage of Palestine's political development from the 1991 Madrid Conference onwards, but noted that the story actually began 'much earlier'.[36]

Jawdat Khoudary, a contractor, one of Gaza's most successful businessmen, explains that, ever since 1980, UNDP has been building the capacity of Palestinian managers, professionals, craftspeople, and workers simply because it always placed Palestinians at the centre of its projects that created infrastructure and new industries. 'I belong to UNDP. My company belongs to UNDP.' The Programme's projects trained a generation of civil engineers, planners, and managers, and allowed them to move up within Palestinian enterprises in a way that was not possible within Israeli companies.[37] Moreover, like the Expanded Programme of Technical Assistance (EPTA) and UNDP in the colonial world of the 1960s, PAPP has always understood that a country needs more than just lively enterprises and good government. Perhaps Khoudary's greatest love is his jasmine-scented, dove-filled garden lined with 'relics of the civilizations that have influenced Gaza, artifacts unearthed by construction workers or winter rains or rolled ashore by rough seas . . . Roman, Greek, Byzantine and Mameluke'.[38] The collection will be the centrepiece of an outstanding public museum, something that will have begun, like Khoudary's own business, as an unintended consequence of early PAPP involvement.

Today PAPP's support of Palestinian culture is much more direct. On the beach, at the end of the surprisingly attractive mishmash of vernacular architecture that makes up one of Gaza's overcrowded refugee camps, Jean-Baptiste Humbert, Director of the Archaeological Division at the École Biblique et Archéologique Française in Jerusalem, watches a Palestinian team uncovering a huge Roman mosaic. It is the floor of one of the villas that have lined this magnificent coast for more than 2,000 years. Humbert praises UNDP for its support of this and dozens of other projects. He assures me that, while the world may not yet know it, *Palestinians* now understand the astonishing historical richness of every

---

[35] Hannan Ashrawi, interview with CNM, 30 April 2005.
[36] Hairdar Abdel Shafi, interview with CNM, 30 April 2005.
[37] Jawdat Khoudary, interview with CNM, 1 May 2005.
[38] James Bennett, 'With Israeli Departure, Gaza's Dreamers Emerge', *New York Times*, 15 Aug. 2005.

7.2 Soccer game at the Shati Refugee Camp Youth Centre, rebuilt by UNDP

part of their land. Like so many others, this site could be expanded over many acres, but it is beginning to encroach on a local soccer field. 'Of course', Humbert says, 'the people of the camp need football, too.' And, just in case I hadn't yet heard the story, he began to tell me how UNDP had built soccer fields in Gaza and Jericho, recruited the Argentine coach who helped set up a league structure and win FIFA (Fédération Internationale de Football Association) recognition. 'And Ronaldo (the Brazilian soccer star and UNDP Goodwill Ambassador) will be in Ramallah soon.'[39] He was there and, of course, in Tel Aviv, in May 2005, making the same argument for peace.

Most of PAPP's contributions to peace have been more direct. It provided training and support for the first Palestinian negotiators, such as Abdel Shafi and Ashwari, with whom Israel was willing to deal directly and publicly. After the 1993 Oslo Accords, which ushered in the present era of limited local control under the Palestinian Authority, PAPP supported the institutions that have helped to build a modern and effective state, such as the Institute of Law at Birzeit University,[40] and backed every stage in the development of the territories' electoral system. Tim

[39] Jean-Baptiste Humbert, interview with CNM, 1 May 2005.
[40] Camille Mansur, interview with CNM, 29 April 2005.

Rothermel argues that the Territories' free elections would not have become commonplace without UNDP's 'less glamorous but essential work'. Immediately after the 2002 appointment of the Central Elections Commission (CEC),

> it was the UNDP that provided and furnished the CEC offices, contributed experts – international, and expatriate Palestinians and nationals – and provided for the employment and training of key CEC staff. Systems for registration, vote tabulation, and data entry were put into place as well as mechanisms for observer accreditation and voter education.

During the 2005 presidential elections, after the death of Yasser Arafat, UNDP also established and operated a liaison and support unit for international electoral observers.[41]

PAPP's impact on the government is even more direct. Nabil Sha'ath, Palestine's deputy prime minister, and the Authority's long-time minister for international cooperation, asks me to look at the cabinet appointed after Abbas's election. In 2005, four ministers – those with responsibility for agriculture, women's affairs, communications and technology, and with the non-governmental sector – were former PAPP employees. 'Many more have worked on PAPP projects', and the number of people with PAPP experience throughout the civil service is vast.[42]

PAPP has been able to play such a central role in Palestine's political development due to the trust it established and maintained with both Israel and the PLO. Until Arafat's return to Palestine in 1993, Rothermel and his predecessors made frequent trips to the PLO leadership in exile, coordinating each new aspect of the programme with them as well as with non-governmental Palestinian leaders within the territories themselves.[43]

Lana Abu Hijleh explains why those in the Territories came to trust UNDP. In the dark years of the 1980s, after the Israeli invasion of Lebanon and throughout the first intifada and the accompanying Israeli crackdown, PAPP, unlike most development agencies, 'did not run away'. This devotion was something that impressed Abu Hijleh's father, a physician, and her mother, a teacher and activist for women and the environment.[44]

---

[41] Timothy S. Rothermel, 'Palestinian Elections: Chance for a Model Democracy', *Christian Science Monitor*, 27 Dec. 2004, http://www.csmonitor.com/2004/1227/p09s01-coop.html (accessed 27 Sept. 2005).   [42] Nabil Sha'ath, interview with CNM, 30 April 2005.

[43] Rothermel, interview with CNM, 1 May 2005, Olver, *Roadblocks and Mindblocks*, pp. 166–70 describes the first visit with Arafat in 1983.

[44] Lana Abu Hijleh, interview with CNM, 29 April 2005.

Abu Hijleh herself, after studying engineering in the United States, returned to Palestine shortly before the 1987 intifada, and proudly worked for UNDP for almost twenty years.

In addition to the trust PAPP developed within the region, the Programme has also relied on a great deal of external support, especially from Palestinians living abroad. PAPP operates one of UNDP's most effective TOKTEN (Transfer of Knowledge Through Expatriate Nationals) programmes. It has brought some 400 expatriate professionals – especially in the planning, information technology, agriculture, and health fields – to the territories since 1994, not only transferring skills, but also solidifying transnational support for a democratic state. Jehan Helou, a TOKTEN community education consultant, explains,

> You feel that you are using your life long expertise to support an emerging, struggling civil society, determined to fight for its liberation and development. You see people defying their difficult situation and accepting the process of learning and of change with great determination.[45]

Similarly, the trust PAPP had gained before the Oslo Accords has meant that, since then, the Programme has become a preferred vehicle for countries newly interested in contributing to peace in the region. Thus Japan has become, by far, the largest donor to PAPP, and Germany, the Islamic Development Bank, the Saudi Committee for Palestine Relief, and South Korea have all recently become major donors.[46]

Finally, as in many other places, UNDP in Palestine is often able to act as the key coordinator and fundraiser for stand-alone programmes that attract a great deal of global support. It did so for a massive infrastructure, restoration, and private-sector development project, 'Bethlehem 2000', that transformed the ancient city. The official organizers of the group included Pope John Paul II, the World Bank's James Wolfensohn, and Nelson Mandela, but it was UNDP that raised the money and helped the Palestinian Authority achieve its ambitious redevelopment goals.[47]

Yet PAPP's work is not only with Palestinians and international donors. The trust of Israel – the resource that gave Brad Morse his first opportunity to engage with the Palestinians more than twenty-five years ago –

[45] UNDP/PAPP, *TOKTEN: 10 Years of Brain Gain* (Jerusalem: UNDP/PAPP, 2004).

[46] Elisabeth Rehn and Jean Claude Aime, *UNDP in the Occupied Palestinian Territory: Programme Review 2005* (New York: UNDP, 2005), p. 31.

[47] Hind Khoury, interview with CNM, 28 April 2005; Palestine National Authority, *Bethlehem 2000 Chronicle: The Story of a National Palestine Development Project* (Bethlehem: Centre for Cultural Heritage Preservation, 2002).

continues to create new opportunities. UNDP supports a number of psychological and conflict resolution programmes to help people cope with the consequences of living in a place that remains so violent and insecure. In recent years one of the more important of these has been led by an Israeli, Gilead Ben-Nur, who engages Israeli settlers in Gaza and the West Bank in dialogue with each other, other Israelis, and with Palestinians about their shared future.[48] In addition, UNDP is able to support small, but telling gestures, like the recent decision of the Palestinian Authority in Jericho to use some of its limited funds for the restoration of the city's ancient synagogue. Not surprisingly, according to Rothermel, even though he and his predecessors have occasionally been vehemently criticized by partisans of Israel in the US media and in Washington, in most cases, the Israeli government has quietly asked its friends to desist.[49]

PAPP has not diminished the outrage Palestinians feel about an occupation that was supposed to end within five years after Morse began the Programme. Yet the manager of the TOKTEN programme, Mounir Kleibo – after hours of driving together, stopping at all the uncomfortable checkpoints, talking about the places that he hasn't been able to visit since he was a boy and those he is likely to be cut off from in the near future, about friends who have lost their lives, and a son whose interest in knowing and understanding his neighbours may be diminishing after the frustration of trying to maintain ties after special youth programmes end, comparing otherwise similar lives centred on family and friends – remarks softly that PAPP is really about putting the bitterness in its place. It has given Palestinians 'a beautiful future' on which to focus.

Months after leaving Palestine, I happened on a newspaper story about Lana Abu Hijleh's mother, who was killed by an Israeli soldier in 2002. Shaden Abu Hijleh was just sitting on her balcony in Nablus with her husband and her son, an 'accidental martyr' of the tense occupation.[50] Shaden Abu Hijleh's death is something that can never be far from her daughter's mind, yet when I spoke with Lana Abu Hijleh, her mother's death never came up. There was too much else to talk about: seventeen years of improving utilities and building schools, all the complex

---

[48] Gilead Ben-Nur, interview with CNM, 29 April 2005. Akiva Eldar, 'Searching for the Right – and Left – Words', *Haaretz*, 13 May 2005, http://www.haaretzdaily.com/hasen/pages/ShArt.jhtml?itemNo=575411 (accessed 27 Sept. 2005).

[49] Rothermel, interview with CNM, 1 May 2005.

[50] Nicole Gaouette, 'Attention Builds over a Slain Civilian: A Palestinian Grandmother's Death Tests Israel's Justice System', *Christian Science Monitor*, 10 Jan. 2003, http://www.csmonitor.com/2003/0110/p01s04-wome.htm (accessed 27 Sept. 2005).

preparations throughout the negotiations that brought in the Palestinian Authority, the hundreds of young men and women who had become skilled, self-confident, and hopeful. Protracted conflicts end only when our grievances come to occupy less and less space in our lives. In Palestine, UNDP has helped that process begin.

Vietnam

However, in terms of the extent to which Morse's engagement with Palestinian nationalists aimed to bridge the gap between them and the United States, PAPP has not been completely successful. In 2005, people like Haidar Abdel Shafi remained suspect in Washington because their commitment to a democratic Palestine led them to embrace the idea of bringing the militant Islamist Hamas and Islamic Jihad groups and left-wing Palestinian groups into the Palestinian government. All remain groups that the United States and Israel see as 'terrorists'.[51] On this dimension, therefore, the programme that Morse began in Vietnam has been much more successful, something that would have seemed extremely unlikely at the time both programmes began.

On 30 April 1975, the forces of the Hanoi-based government captured Saigon, ending the North's thirty-year war with South Vietnam and the United States. For many years afterwards the newly united country remained isolated from the rest of the world. Initially, only the Soviet Union, its satellites, and neutral Finland and Sweden maintained normal relations. In 1977, responding to overtures from the United Nations in New York, Vietnam entered the United Nations and UNDP set up shop in war-ravaged Hanoi.[52]

As in China, early UNDP support focused on the provision of capital equipment and the technology it embodied. This began to change in 1986 when the Communist Party adopted its *doi moi* (renovation) policy, embracing a 'socialist market-based system' at about the same time that Mikhail Gorbachev initiated economic *perestroika* (restructuring) in the Soviet Union.

The collapse of the Soviet Union in the early 1990s lent much greater urgency to this effort. Vietnam, which for thirty years had relied on significant Soviet aid, faced a devastating economic crisis. People were starving. To the north, China's new economic policy had proven much

---

[51] Haidar Abdel Shafi, interview with CNM, 30 April 2005.
[52] The Government of the Socialist Republic of Viet Nam and UNDP, *UNDP–Viet Nam: The Story of a 25-Year Partnership* (Hanoi: UNDP, 2003), p. 3.

more successful. In 1991, Vo Van Kiet, Vietnam's prime minister, somewhat in desperation asked Singapore's veteran leader Lee Kuan Yew to become Vietnam's 'economic adviser'. Lee agreed to visit, 'not as an adviser, but to brainstorm ideas on their change to a free-market economy'.[53] At a Hanoi seminar at the end of his April 1992 visit, Lee began his remarks with, 'I am so glad UNDP is helping you here in Vietnam, because . . . UNDP played a very important role in establishing Singapore.'[54]

The man to whom Vo Van Kiet turned to fulfil Lee's implicit promise was Roy Morey, just reassigned from China to be Res Rep in Hanoi. Morey remembers being greeted by the Italian ambassador, who outlined a set of organizational and personal assets that would leave Morey with a tremendous obligation: as the representative of UNDP, the Italian said, Morey would 'have better access to the senior leadership' than anyone else in the diplomatic corps. The government saw UNDP as interested only in helping the country, unlike the bilateral donors and the development banks, and as a friend who had been with them during the 'bloody, traumatic' days after the war 'when nobody really liked Vietnam'. Moreover,

> you have served for four years in China . . . The Vietnamese would hate for anyone to ever think that they ape the Chinese, and they don't, but there's no country that they follow more closely. They'll be very interested in knowing what the programme was like and what will be applicable.[55]

In many respects, UNDP's activities in Vietnam did come to parallel its work in China. There were major projects on public administration reform and on creating a better regulatory environment for business. By 1997 UNDP was supporting Vietnamese experiments in grass-roots democracy and the kinds of projects for women and for the environment that Draper and Speth also promoted in China.[56] Moreover, as in China, UNDP facilitated the rapprochement between the Communist government and the World Bank, leaving the country with a close relationship between UNDP and the Bank that Mark Malloch Brown and James Wolfensohn considered to be 'a model for the world'.[57]

In other respects, UNDP's Vietnam programme was very different. The Vietnamese project that gives Morey the most satisfaction was a

[53] Lee Kuan Yew, *From Third World to First, the Singapore Story: 1965–2000* (New York: HarperCollins, 2000), pp. 312–13.
[54] Roy Morey, interview with EM, 4 April 2005.   [55] Ibid.
[56] *UNDP–Viet Nam*, pp. 7, 10, 13; Jan Mattsson, interview with CNM, 3 June 2004.
[57] Roy Morey, quoting Malloch Brown, interview with EM, 4 April 2005.

comprehensive land reform programme worked out in cooperation with the state of South Australia. The reform gave farmers land certification, which allowed them to sell their rights, pass them on to heirs, and borrow against their value. The result was the generation of a vast array of rural enterprises – small shops and new industries – which meant that Vietnam, under *its* new economic policy, would not experience a deepening of inequality as great as that which took place in China.[58]

In Vietnam Morey also worked more directly than he had in China to bring the country into the international diplomatic mainstream. UNDP pushed the long-dormant Mekong River project forward by helping mend Vietnam's long-strained relationship with Thailand, the United States' ally throughout the war. At the same time the Programme facilitated Vietnam's entry into the Association of South East Asian Nations (ASEAN) by organizing study tours and internships at ASEAN headquarters in Jakarta to familiarize Vietnamese officials with the organization's procedures and culture. And Morey made special efforts to find ways for Vietnamese to visit the United States, to the extent that after the two countries established full diplomatic relations in 1995 the new ambassador, Le Van Bang, introduced Morey as the man who 'did more than anyone else to help in the normalization of relations between his country and mine'.[59]

That introduction would have provided another moment of great satisfaction for Brad Morse, but it did not mark the end of UNDP's work in bridging differences between Vietnam and the rest of the world. Throughout the Asian financial crisis of 1997–9, UNDP worked with the government to find policies that allowed Vietnam to maintain high growth rates when many other economies in the region fell into deep recession. UNDP mobilized 'world class policy advisors such as Professor Joseph Stiglitz, the 2002 Nobel laureate in economics, and Professor Janos Kornai, a world renowned expert in transitional economics', whose advice proved unusually effective. More recently, UNDP has provided training and key 'impartial advice' in support of Vietnam's effort to enter the WTO by 2007.[60]

Iran

Thirty years on, the drama of UNDP in Vietnam has reached its denouement; the engagement with the revolutionary state contributed to a particular form of development, and that contributed to international

---

[58] Roy Morey, interview with EM, 4 April 2005; *UNDP–Viet Nam*, p. 12.
[59] Roy Morey, interview with EM, 4 April 2005.   [60] *UNDP–Viet Nam*, p. 15.

peace. The probable endings of the stories in Palestine, China, and throughout southern Africa are also clear. That is less true in Iran, the last UNDP special engagement of the Morse years to be considered here.

Of course, the story of UNDP in Iran is much longer and more complex than UNDP's relationship with any of the countries this chapter has discussed so far. In 1951 Tehran received one of the first Resident Representatives. The country was always one of the top five recipients of EPTA and Special Fund support. It was the second country to experiment with the TOKTEN programme and, by the 1970s, had become a major sponsor of UNDP innovations: the government and the Shah's family provided significant seed capital for both UN Volunteers and UNIFEM (the UN Development Fund for Women, a topic of the next chapter). In sum, the relationship between UNDP and the rulers of Iran was all too comfortable and close. Folke Schimanski, a young, Swedish Assistant Programme Officer assigned to Tehran in the mid-1960s remembers a UNDP staff 'living at a standard . . . far above the majority of the population', focused on the 'predominantly Anglo-American cocktail party society', and funding pointless surveys by disregarded foreign experts against the painful background of

> the gruesome activities of SAVAK, the secret police of the Shah . . . But there was of course not much we could do; when I happened to witness how the police clamped down on a student demonstration I was called to a most alarmed Res Rep for a discreet report whereafter he begged me not to mention anything about what I had seen.[61]

When the Shah was forced from the country in January 1979 and the Islamic Revolution consolidated, UNDP international staff and foreign experts evacuated (some local staff say 'fled'). The Revolutionary Guard confiscated the Programme's largest local fleet of vehicles, and the country office, like many of the embassies in Tehran, began to be boarded up.

That November, militants occupied the US embassy, where diplomats were then held hostage for more than a year. In response, the United States and its allies began to isolate the revolutionary régime, economically as well as politically. That isolation deepened when Iraq invaded in September 1980, the beginning of a devastating eight-year war.

The downward spiral in Iran's foreign relations would be hard to break. Revolutionaries with no experience in international diplomacy and little understanding of international relations took over the top jobs.

---

[61] Folke Schimanski, electronic mail to CNM, 13 March 2005.

They relied on equally young, and relatively inexperienced, civil servants. Yet, one of these, Hamid Nazari, knew of an untapped source of hard currency for the strapped régime, the unexpended core funding set aside for Iran by UNDP. The Programme could become a 'granter of last resort'. Characteristically, Brad Morse made it clear that the money, about US$11 million, was still available. He dispatched Denis Halliday, whose distinguished field career had begun in Tehran in 1964. Halliday found ways to paper over the expropriations of vehicles and equipment, negotiated projects with those ministries that could overcome their suspicion of the United Nations (especially the ministries concerned with agriculture and labour), and helped prepare a submission for the 1982 Governing Council, the first Country Programme for the Islamic Republic.[62]

Soudabeh Amiri, an education specialist and journalist, returned to her country in 1978 from graduate work in the United States, full of hope in those early days of the revolution. She became one of the first people to be hired by the new office. Her idealism remained with her and only became reinforced within UNDP, despite the harsh and illiberal turn taken by the war-besieged government. 'We had the dreams of the first UN', of UNDP's founders. If nothing else, UNDP, as the one international agency that remained in Tehran, became the intermediary between Iran and the rest of the UN system. Amiri remembers the pleasure and excitement as each new office opened, UNHCR (the High Commissioner for Refugees), ITU (the International Telecommunications Union), IAEA (the International Atomic Energy Agency), eventually forty or fifty if you include the regional organizations and bilateral development agencies that UNDP helped introduce to the régime.[63]

That process still goes on. When I visited Tehran in March 2005, UNDP operated from the central offices in the beautifully redecorated 'UN House', with every floor but one filled by other agencies. The top floor is set aside for the World Bank, whose return to the country had been a major project of the last Res Rep.[64]

In the early years, the new UNDP office did much more than serve as a go-between to other international actors. The Islamic Revolution immediately preceded the global revolution in information technology, but as late as 1984 a computer was almost impossible to find in any Iranian government office. UNDP's hard-currency grants brought in computers

---

[62] Hamid Nazari, interview with CNM, 3 March 2005.
[63] Soudabeh Amiri, interview with CNM, 3 March 2005.
[64] Frederick Lyons, interview with CNM, 3 March 2005.

and provided the necessary training.[65] The reestablishment of the TOKTEN programme, from which the Shah's Iran had been a major beneficiary, helped post-war Iran reestablish its oil industry and greatly increase the amount that could be extracted from its reserves. And 'many of the things you can see in the reform agenda', the moves towards political openness and towards a climate more conducive to private business that marked the first half of the present decade, 'came from the experience Iranians gained abroad from programmes supported by UNDP'.[66]

Sitting in a state-of-the-art management classroom in Sharif University of Technology, two of the country's leading economic planners, Masoud Nili and Ali Naghi Mashaiekhi treat me to a personal seminar on the Islamic Republic's changing economic policy that reinforces the point. Immediately after the Revolution, when Mashaiekhi had just returned from MIT's Sloan School and Nili was a radical student, economic sanctions, the demands of the war, and the egalitarian goals of the Revolution all contributed to a command economy that served an important purpose but was very inflexible and, ultimately, stagnant. Those few in the new government who had studied economics had learned a simplistic version of the leftist theories of the 1950s, a bit of Soviet planning plus a few lines from Hans Singer and Raúl Prebisch, largely taken out of context. Since the end of the war, the failure of the earlier policy has been widely accepted, but it has taken time for elected officials, clerical leaders, and Iranian planners to envision something different. Visits by well-known Iranian economist from abroad and training sessions with a variety of international experts working on particular problems – such as joining the WTO or bringing Iran's exchange system in line with International Monetary Fund guidelines – have been invaluable and, certainly, only UNDP was initially considered neutral enough to link the country to non-partisan advice.[67]

However, in Tehran, the perception of UNDP as non-partisan is far from universal. This is still a city of foreign spies and deep secrets. People find ways to tell visitors that part of the national staff of most international agencies are suspected to be agents placed there because elements in the government suspect the agencies of undermining the Revolution.

Nevertheless, in Iran, UNDP does not shy away from the advocacy work that it has embraced for almost twenty years. It supports the country's major NGO (non-governmental organization) Resource

---

[65] Hamid Nazari, interview with CNM, 3 March 2005.
[66] Soudabeh Amiri, interview with CNM, 3 March 2005.
[67] Masoud Nili and Ali Naghi Mashaiekhi, interview with CNM, 6 March 2005.

Centre[68] and Nasrin Mosaffa's world-renowned Centre for Human Rights Studies at the University of Tehran, which, with UNDP funding, has produced a library of translations of the world's most significant philosophical and legal writings on individual and collective rights.[69] Certainly, there may be powerful people in the Iranian government who consider the resulting wide distribution of Amartya Sen's *Development as Freedom* as something deeply subversive. Yet the focus of Mossafa's scholarship is on the Qur'anic version of universal rights and the quotation that most often appears in the Centre's work is from Imam Ali: 'Do not be subject to others, for your God has created you free.'

Still, it is also true that when Mark Malloch Brown hosted the major address at the United Nations in 2004 by the Nobel peace laureate Shirin Ebadi, he was honouring someone considered by her government to be a thorn in its side, and, outside economic planning circles, every Iranian government official I have met has worried about UNDP's advocacy of 'democratic governance'.

Bagher Asadi, Iran's cosmopolitan former UN ambassador and former head of the Third World alliance, the Group of 77, is typical. 'Of course, real, genuine democracy is essential', but UNDP struck a 'better balance, pre-1990, before the end of the cold war', when 'the right to development', not 'democratic governance', was at the centre of UNDP's mission. (Morse's advocacy of the NIEO comes to mind.) Asadi worries that Malloch Brown has stuck 'too close to the American line'. Nevertheless, no critique of undemocratic governance 'could be taken care of by other parts of the UN', no other organization's criticism would be accepted in many parts of the world.[70]

However, in Iran, where so many conversations about the future include the comment, 'if we avoid war with the United States', it is unclear whether the increasing engagement with UNDP both feared and desired by the revolutionary government will have the same impact as similar previous engagements in other places.

Caveat

It is important to be clear about the changing context of Morse's policy, about the limits to what UNDP can accomplish in engaging

---

[68] Bagher Namazi, interview with CNM, 7 March 2005.
[69] Nasrin Mosaffa, interview with CNM, 6 March 2005. She specifically highlighted both individual and group rights, a particular interest of the centre.
[70] Bagher Asadi, interview with CNM, 3 March 2005.

revolutionary movements and states, and about what UNDP may have given up at the same time that it adopted this new strategy.

Iranians who welcome UNDP advocacy of human rights yet who worry that the Programme has been too influenced by the United States fear that, when it comes to militarily weaker states, the United States, ultimately, will brook no alternative to its hegemonic aspirations. Iran can become increasingly democratic and its economy increasingly productive, but, many Iranians believe, it will still be impossible for many US leaders to see the Islamic Republic as anything more than one pole of the 'Axis of Evil'. Others make the more general point that the greatest of today's status quo powers is apt to see any government that does not accept its economic supremacy as 'revolutionary'.

In 1997, Erskine Childers, UNDP's former information chief who, with Brian Urquhart, co-authored the most thorough plan for the reformation of the United Nations written in the 1990s, complained bitterly about the new goal articulated by the US government and many within his old organization,

> If I may ask in an Irish way, what in the name of God is 'market democracy'? Thirty years ago the phrase would have been strongly challenged as the intellectual rubbish that it is – or the insidiously undemocratic trickery that it also is.[71]

The phrase was 'insidiously undemocratic', Childers believed, because the hegemonic idea for the United States was the 'market', creating a profitable openness to multinational enterprises, something to which 'democracy' could easily be sacrificed.

There is a complex scholarly literature that provides some support for Childers's acid remark. William I. Robinson persuasively demonstrates a shift in US foreign policy that took place in the mid-1980s, in the middle of the Reagan administration. Prior to that, the cold war-era United States was willing to use covert military force against, and considered authoritarian régimes preferable to, many Third World democratic movements on the left, despite US rhetoric about promoting democracy. Reagan, George H.W. Bush, and Bill Clinton brought US policy closer to the long-standing rhetoric, actively supporting the rise of liberal democracy, on the condition that the new democratic state be limited, that it *not*

---

[71] Erskine Childers, 'The United Nations and Global Institutions: Discourse and Reality', *Global Governance*, 3, 3 (1997): 272.

be used to challenge the economic status quo.[72] Reversing Nixon's 'tar baby option' policy, a Republican president welcomed the release of Nelson Mandela, as long as he left his radical economic ideas back on Robben Island. As a result, even though the large state sector created by the mid-twentieth-century apartheid state made it possible for Afrikaners to rise to equality with South Africa's anglophone ruling class, the new, downsized South African democratic state of this century cannot do the same for its black majority.[73] The change in US policy changed the context of Morse's innovation, making some engagements with revolutionary movements (e.g. SWAPO and the ANC) more likely to be successful.

Southern Africa, critics argue, has gained democracy without economic transformation. Other societies with which UNDP has worked closely have gained economic transformation, without democracy. In Tibet, for example, UNDP has undoubtedly helped ethnic Tibetans to reduce their economic reliance on the central government. The Programme is even sponsoring a potentially far-reaching series of conferences on prospects for the greater economic integration of Tibet with its near South Asian neighbours,[74] something that could create a counterbalance to the power centre in Beijing. However, the Programme certainly has not broached the subject of allowing regional autonomy under a democratic régime. As a report on the larger pattern explains, in China UNDP has been concerned with

> minority recognition, minority inclusion, participation, poverty, cultural and education rights, but not directly dealing with conflict issues. Our strategy has been to focus . . . on comprehensive human development in term[s] of self-capacity building. If this objective [is] achieved, then many development rights could be protected and social and political conflicts would then be avoid[ed].[75]

Critical international relations scholars would argue that UNDP's engagements with revolutionary states and parties can be understood as

---

[72] William I. Robinson, *Promoting Polyarchy: Globalization, US Intervention, and Hegemony* (Cambridge: Cambridge University Press, 1996).

[73] Janis van der Westhuizen, *Adapting to Globalization: Malaysia, South Africa, and the Challenge of Ethnic Redistribution with Growth* (New York: Praeger, 2002).

[74] 'Summary Note, Tibet International Seminar on Trade and Development', unpublished report, UNDP Beijing, October 2005.

[75] Daniel Wang, 'A Boundary Terrain or One of Our Central Development Targets? A Report on UNDP China's Practices for the Development of Minorities', unpublished report, UNDP China, 1 July 2003.

part of a larger 'hegemonic project', not a project for the narrow hegemony of the United States, but something quite different, the hegemony of a single global market economy.

Recall that, since its beginning, the industrial system has had a logic of market expansion and innovation, what we now call 'globalization'. England provided a sufficient market area for the Industrial Revolution of the cotton mills. A century ago the new lead industries of the Second Industrial Revolution (chemical, electrical, and branded consumer products) grew within the larger market areas of extended nation-states, the British Empire of the 'new' imperialism, the 'German' market area of continental Europe, and the Pan-American market area centred on the United States. The industries of the automobile and jet age grew, organically, in the 'free world' market area that linked western Europe, North America, and Japan to their economic dependencies in Africa, Asia, and Latin America.

The current era sees a push towards a single, global market engineered by what the authors of the major study of contemporary business regulation call 'the global lawmakers . . . the men [sic] who run the largest corporations, the US and the EC'.[76] Their interests are not the same as the interests of the lawmakers of any one country. They are, instead, part of what Robinson calls an emerging 'global capitalist historic bloc'.[77] Within this bloc, UNDP, and Morse's innovation (whatever his original intentions), could be thought of as something that served to circumvent the resistance of traditional conservatives to policies that would let 'revolutionaries' – from China to Iran, from SWAPO to Hamas – come to see their own *interest* in participating in a stable global market economy.

However, to the extent that UNDP becomes part of such a movement, it may give up some of the roles it played in the past. Ambassador Asadi worries about one of these: acting as an advocate of every society's 'right to develop', and thus as a critic of those elements of the international status quo conspiring to deny that right. For example, Morse and all the leaders of the UN development network before him regularly reproved the developed nations for failing to create an international institutional environment conducive to most states' development. To the extent that UNDP leaders after Morse have ignored this theme, Asadi may be correct. I am not sure that they have. It may just be that, today, the locus of

---

[76] John Braithwaite and Peter Drahos, *Global Business Regulation* (Cambridge: Cambridge University Press, 2000), p. 642.

[77] William I. Robinson, *A Theory of Global Capitalism: Production, Class, and the State in a Transnational World* (Baltimore: Johns Hopkins University Press, 2004).

UNDP's criticism of the rich nations has shifted from the speeches of Administrators – heard only by ambassadors like Asadi – to the *Human Development Reports*, whose audience is much larger.

A more significant change may have to do with what UNDP tells the poor nations to do. UNDP (and EPTA before it) originally embraced multiple strategies of development as a matter of principle. Frederick Lyons, who was Res Rep in Tehran when Asadi served in New York and Geneva, served in Brad Morse's day in another 'revolutionary state', Cuba, a country whose continuous relationship with UNDP is almost as long and cooperative as the interrupted relationship with Iran. Lyons wishes that the Cubans would be more effusive about the role UNDP has played in the country, even though it is commonplace for Cuban leaders, including Castro, to credit UNDP for helping develop sectors such as biotechnology.[78] Given Cuba's isolation by the United States, Castro's goal of being at the forefront of the life sciences and maintaining one of the world's most effective medical systems required the partnership of an organization that could make links to the world's best scientists and provide access to all the world's technology. That was UNDP's role. The result was a poor country whose health and education profile looks like that of the very richest countries. Lyons emphasizes that UNDP has been in constant dialogue with the Cubans about the opportunity costs of the huge investments they have made in science and medicine, but those costs have been weighed consciously by a government that has chosen something other than what seems to be becoming a standard global model.

I suspect that if UNDP's well-timed embrace of 'market democracy', one of the secrets of the success of Morse's policy of engagement, had been biased towards 'democracy' rather than the market, I would have no qualms about being the policy's uncritical champion. Yet, despite the valid qualms that many have about this new direction that UNDP's work took in the late 1970s, its potential contribution to peace remains.

[78] Frederick Lyons, interview with CNM, 3 March 2005; on Castro, Margaret Joan Anstee, electronic mail to CNM, 3 Dec. 2005.

8

A learning organization: women, Latin America, and Africa

Morse's UNDP did begin to challenge a nation's 'right to develop', not by ignoring it, but by laying the foundations for the assertion of an *individual's* development rights and of the need for a democratic, capable, and autonomous state to assure them.[1] Three Programme innovations of the 1980s laid the foundations on which Sustainable Human Development and the Millennium Development Goals (MDGs) – the eventual guides for UNDP's work – would be built. UNDP's engagement with the Women in Development movement, and the embedding of the UN Development Fund for Women (UNIFEM) within UNDP, helped shift the locus of the Programme's attention from countries to individuals. The particular focus of the Latin American Bureau on democratization anticipated a similar change in the focus of the Programme as a whole. At the same time, the Bureau piloted new kinds of partnerships with government that would make UNDP's promotion of democratic governance effective. Finally, in Africa, in response to the economic crises of the 1980s and the attempts to impose a single, formulaic response (the so-called 'Washington Consensus'), UNDP helped to build regional and national capacities to devise alternative strategies that could more effectively protect vulnerable persons.

The stories of the setting of each of these three cornerstones have to be told somewhat separately, because that is how they began: as the innovations of one or another relatively autonomous part of UNDP. The Bureaux that are important to the Latin American and African stories are the consequence of the early 1970s Consensus and the power of the developing countries that had been reinforced by the post-financial-crisis reforms. At the centre of UNDP's engagement with women is one of the semi-autonomous agencies, the 'barnacles on the side of the ship' that Brad

[1] Asuncion Lera St Clair of the University of Bergen's Centre for International Poverty Research calls this the UNDP's shift 'from poor countries to poor people', in her 'The Role of Ideas in the United Nations Development Programme', in Morten Bøås and Desmond McNeill, eds., *Global Institutions: Framing the World?* (London: Routledge, 2003), pp. 178–92.

Morse allowed to form as a way of expanding the United Nations' resources for development. These power centres – the Bureaux and new, associated programmes and funds – unintentionally gave UNDP some of the characteristics of a 'learning organization', one in which new ways of achieving collective goals can be discovered and tried and where the overall mission and role in the world can be rethought, collectively and regularly.[2]

Ernst B. Haas, one of the most thoughtful students of international institutions, argues that very few intergovernmental organizations ever had the capacity to change in anything other than an ad hoc, adaptive way. Few have been able to generate reflective knowledge, create new practices based on that knowledge, and maintain the organization's legitimacy in the eyes of an overwhelmingly powerful group of their member countries.[3] Despite the Capacity Study's predictions, the United Nations' development network has been able to do that. It would take more than just the innovations described here. Jan Mattsson, who was on the 1993 transition team for the new Administrator, Gus Speth, recalls that team members used to tell each other, 'There is a lot of knowledge in UNDP, but UNDP doesn't know what it knows.' More recently invented mechanisms for knowledge sharing helped to solve that problem.[4] In Morse's day, the question was whether UNDP would be able to generate organizationally significant knowledge in the first place.

Before the reorganization at the beginning of Morse's term, innovation within UNDP was largely either a matter of the Administrator's directive (usually, telling staff to pay heed to his creative number two), or else a fortuitous response to opportunities in the field. After the reorganization, the Regional Bureaux and the affiliates provided the Programme with the specific foci, organizational memory, and greater ability to experiment that are needed for regular innovation. This would keep UNDP 'ahead of the curve' long after the advantage of being the first major multilateral development institution had waned.

Women and the focus of development

In September 2000 the 189 member countries of the United Nations, most of them represented by their head of government, agreed to focus

---

[2] Peter Senge, *The Fifth Discipline: The Art and Practice of The Learning Organization* (New York: Doubleday, 1990), p. 3.

[3] Ernst B. Haas, *When Knowledge Is Power: Three Models of Change in International Organization* (Berkeley: University of California Press, 1991).

[4] Jan Mattsson, electronic mail to the author (CNM), 29 Dec. 2005.

on a limited set of global development goals. The goals include eliminating gender disparity in education at all levels, achieving universal primary education (which will require massive efforts to educate girls), reducing maternal mortality, and going a long way to eradicating extreme poverty and hunger (whose victims are overwhelmingly women and children), all by 2015.[5] In 1985, fifteen years before the 'Millennium Declaration', these issues appeared on no authoritative lists of the most pressing development problems, except those compiled by scholars and policy makers associated with the Women in Development movement and reflected in the resolutions of the 1985 Nairobi conference that marked the end of the first UN Decade for Women.

UNDP and especially UNDP's affiliate, UNIFEM, played a role in this significant conceptual change. To understand that role, we need to go back fifteen years further, to the late 1960s and early 1970s, when the United Nations as a whole began to be aware of the centrality of women to development. Of course, from its beginning, there was an official place for consideration of a women's agenda in the Commission on the Status of Women, many Expanded Programme of Technical Assistance (EPTA) and UNDP projects paid attention to women without specifically working to empower them, and the UN Children's Fund (UNICEF) had to focus on mothers and by the early 1960s was supporting anti-colonial and development-oriented women's clubs, such as Kenya's Maendeleo ya Wanawake, under the assumption that community development and women's empowerment aided children.[6] And because the World Food Programme both serves the world's most desperately poor and often employs agricultural labourers in food-for-work programmes, it became, early on, 'the largest supporter of development projects involving and benefiting poor women'.[7] Nevertheless, it is back in Africa, and with the Economic Commission for Africa (ECA) that the larger UN story begins.

It is difficult for anyone with direct experience south of the Sahara to ignore the role of women in development. In most parts of the continent, women do the vast majority of farming for local consumption, and, in many regions, they dominate trade. (When I was a student in Ghana,

---

[5] UN General Assembly, Resolution 55/2, 'United Nations Millennium Declaration', 18 Sept. 2000.
[6] Maggie Black, *The Children and the Nations: The Story of UNICEF* (New York: UNICEF, 1986), p. 183.
[7] D. John Shaw, *The UN World Food Programme and the Development of Food Aid* (Houndmills: Palgrave, 2001), p. 4.

I remember being told by one male chief about the 'fairness' of this division of labour: women are in charge of raising food and running the local market, while men raise the cash crops and 'make the decisions'(!).) When R. K. A. Gardiner, a Ghanaian economic planner (a colleague of both Arthur Lewis and Robert Jackson), headed the ECA, he commissioned a set of important studies exploring the implications of women's centrality to the real work of development.[8] In his annual report in 1966, the year of Nkrumah's ouster, Gardiner reflected on the failure of capital-intensive industrialization in many countries, not just his own. He began to call for 'multiple small-scale investments . . . of a labour-intensive type . . . small- or medium-scale industries geared to national consumption patterns, and transportation and communications links between farmer and the consumer', investments that, in a country like Ghana, would inevitably centre on women.[9]

Meanwhile, after extensive fieldwork in Senegal, the Danish economist and development advisor to U Thant, Ester Boserup, wrote her paradigmatic *Women's Role in Economic Development*, which was published in 1970.[10] Boserup had already made a name for herself for studies that complicated the picture of peasant agriculture that Arthur Lewis had presented in his early theory of development, and she had begun to challenge simplistic arguments about rapid population growth always being a 'problem'. A Secretariat report based on Boserup's book and the ECA's five-year plan for women and development became the main working documents for a 1972 UN Expert Group Meeting to 'advise on broad policy measures regarding women's role in economic and social development'. The Secretariat called in W. Arthur Lewis to chair the group that included Leticia Shahani of the Philippines, who would head the 1985 women's conference in Nairobi, and Margaret Snyder (representing Gardiner's ECA), who would become UNIFEM's first Executive Director. Snyder calls the 1972 UN gathering 'The first global meeting on women and development'.[11]

That meeting, and lobbying from a resurgent women's movement in western Europe and the United States, led to the United Nations' declaration of 1975 as 'International Women's Year', with the UN Women's Conference in Mexico City as its highlight. The conference declared a 'UN Decade for Women' and established a small 'Voluntary Fund for the

---

[8] Margaret Snyder, *Transforming Development: Women, Poverty and Politics* (London: Intermediate Technology Publications, 1995), pp. 18–23.
[9] Quoted in Snyder, *Transforming Development*, p. 13.   [10] London: Allen & Unwin.
[11] Quoted in Snyder, *Transforming Development*, p. 17.

UN Decade for Women', financed by the United Kingdom and Iran's Princess Ashraf. In 1978 a group of American feminists convinced the administration of President Gerald Ford to match the existing contributions, and what would become UNIFEM became operational, with Peg Snyder as its director.[12]

Snyder's UNIFEM saw its role as piloting the kinds of projects Gardiner had discussed in the 1960s. The Fund's current Executive Director, Noeleen Heyzer, explains that Snyder set up

> revolving funds to establish small income-generating work for women like the tailor shops, and cottage industries . . . [Snyder] argued, 'Until you change where the larger development money goes, you need to quickly put money directly in the hands of women at the community level.'[13]

Even with very limited funds, UNIFEM quickly demonstrated some very successful new ideas, including micro-credit schemes run by women, which Snyder piloted around the world shortly after Muhammad Yunus began his action research that would result in the celebrated Grameen Bank.[14]

In UNIFEM's first years, the accepted understanding of the role of women in development began to shift. At the Mexico City conference, the emphasis had been more on development's impact on women than on women's impact on development. Yet Ester Boserup had been at pains to demonstrate that in terms of any coherent, empirical understanding of 'development', women were at its centre, not only doing most of the reproductive labour of society, but also accounting for the majority of time worked in all sectors.

Still, it was difficult to give up older theories of development that, at best, put women in a supporting role. I recall one celebrated academic colleague telling me in 1979 about the pain she felt when she realized that she was no longer interested in 'the woman problem in Marxist theory', but, rather, 'the proletariat problem in feminist theory'.[15] The transition was equally hard for Fabians, liberals, and economists of every other stripe.

---

[12] Margaret Snyder, 'Women, Poverty and Politics: Highlights of American Women's Work with UNIFEM 1975–1990, and Challenges Today', annual meeting of UNIFEM/USA, Sarasota, Florida, 3 June 2001.

[13] Noeleen Heyzer, interview with Thomas G. Weiss, UN Intellectual History Project, 21 Feb. 2002.

[14] Margaret Snyder, interview with CNM, 22 Sept. 2004.

[15] This was Nancy Hartsock, the philosopher known for her work on feminist epistemology, e.g., *The Feminist Standpoint Revisited and Other Essays* (Boulder, Colo.: Westview Press, 1998), as well as the implications of the interconnections between women and global poverty.

Rather than embracing feminist theory as the core to understanding development, most analysts took the easier path of adopting a non-paradigmatic approach that asked whether the conditions of women within society had an impact on a variety of development indicators including income per capita, technological innovation, and sustainable levels of population growth. This was the strategy promoted by two, linked international conferences in 1976 attended by many of the women at the centre of the UNIFEM and UNDP stories, including Boserup, Snyder (representing ECA), and Joan Dunlop, who would later become Mark Malloch Brown's headhunter, the person in charge of bringing new expertise to the highest levels of the Programme.[16]

Boserup's example, and the research agendas set in the mid-1970s, led investigators to erase the border between the 'public' realm of the 'national' economy and the 'private' – and so perceived as economically less important – world of the household, the women's domain. Studies soon proved the centrality of women's empowerment to rational population outcomes, which helped to secure this as the focus of the work of the UN Fund for Population Activities (UNFPA). Research also demonstrated the centrality of women's employment and empowerment to poverty reduction and the critical role of women's education and political equality in the maintenance of an innovative society and growing economy. By 1985, at the Nairobi conference marking the end of what would be the first Decade for Women, Brad Morse could remark that development programmes that failed to take into account the centrality of women's productive roles were 'not only morally indefensible, but economically absurd'.[17] Moreover, the experience of UNDP projects designed to aid women proved that those that had been designed by the

[16] The first, attended by over 500 women from more than fifty countries although dominated by scholars from the United States, took place at Wellesley College. It was followed immediately by a smaller meeting, under the leadership of scholars from the South. The reports of the two conferences are Wellesley Editorial Committee, *Women and National Development: The Complexities of Change* (Chicago: University of Chicago Press, 1977) and *Report of a Wingspread Workshop: Women and Development* (Racine, Wi.: Johnson Foundation, 1976). The participant lists for both conferences are in the Wellesley College Archives, unprocessed materials, A82-025, Box 7.

[17] Quoted in Snyder, *Transforming Development*, p. xv. Janet Hunt (among others) sees the change as one from a focus on 'Women *in* Development' to 'Women *and* Development'. See her 'Gender and Development', in Damien Kingsbury, Joe Remenyi, John McKay, and Janet Hunt, *Key Issues in Development* (Houndmills: Palgrave Macmillan, 2004), pp. 243–65.

women they were meant to serve, and that gave them new skills or income, were the most effective.[18]

Shortly afterwards, in 1986, Morse's successor, Bill Draper, put attention to women and advocacy for women at the centre of the Programme's work. He created the Women in Development Division and hired Ingrid Eide, a Norwegian who had already distinguished herself in government and as one of the world's leading scholars on gender and peace. For Draper, it was simple:

> Half the people are women, most of the work is done by women . . . those countries that were open to human rights and women's advancement and respect seemed to be doing a lot better and that was pretty evident and those that were holding back seem to be doing worse.[19]

Haleem Ul Hussain, who directed a number of UNDP-funded livestock projects for the Pakistani government, recalls one particularly important case where research of this sort shifted the views of a prominent development thinker. Ul Hussain remembers a conversation with Mahbub ul Haq, who returned from the World Bank to be Pakistan's Planning and Finance Minister from 1982 to 1988. Studies demonstrated that the country's rural population, including the land-poor and landless, had tremendous wealth invested in livestock. A typical family might have a buffalo (for milk), four or five sheep or goats (readily convertible into cash), and many indigenous chickens, 'all in the exclusive domain of women'. Taken together,

> *This livestock was more valuable than all major crops in the country* . . . When I said this to Mahbub, he said, 'I don't believe it.' He said, 'No, this can't be true.'

If it were true, intelligent economic planning would have to place much more emphasis on this crucial rural 'household' sector, and on the conditions of the women who maintained it. For all ul Haq's scepticism the evidence was overwhelming, and he, like Gardiner and Lewis before him, was convinced.[20]

---

[18] Devaki Jain, *Women, Development, and the UN: A Sixty Year Quest for Equality and Justice* (Bloomington, Ind.: Indiana University Press, 2005), p. 57. Nüket Kardam, 'The Tripartite System of the United Nations Development Programme', *Bringing Women In: Women's Issues in International Development Programs* (Boulder, Colo.: Lynne Rienner Publishers, 1991), p. 24.

[19] William H. Draper III, interview with CNM, 28 Sept. 2004.

[20] Haleem Ul Hussain, interview with CNM, 8 Dec. 2004.

The research that firmly established the central role of women in development, and the women's organizing that promoted these findings, built the bridge between 'development' and 'human rights' that would eventually contribute to UNDP's understanding of 'human development' and some of the *Human Development Reports* that ul Haq initiated. Noeleen Heyzer puts it, succinctly, 'Women changed the *human rights* agenda',[21] especially among those who had concentrated their attention on political liberties. Economic issues and the social exclusion within the 'private' household came to the fore. Eventually, the shattering of the boundary between the public and the private would create a global concern about the violence that goes on in the home. However, even the earliest studies that proved the centrality of women's work and the importance of their empowerment to society-level development indicators decisively shifted 'development' from being more than an issue of the empowerment and equality of nations. It also became an issue of the empowerment and equality of individuals.[22]

In 1985, after the Nairobi conference, Morse brought UNIFEM, the institutionalized continuation of the Voluntary Fund for the UN Decade for Women, into UNDP as an autonomous affiliate. Contributions to the Fund then finally started to take off, and a sometimes uneasy, but always highly productive, partnership began.

In the early years, UNDP field offices frequently built on the empowerment projects that Snyder began. One of Snyder's fondest memories is giving Wangari Maathai, the Kenyan environment, democracy, and women's rights activist, her first grant. Maathai's new connection to the United Nations then 'began to open doors' for her movement and helped it to become the effective instrument that brought Maathai global recognition, including the 2004 Nobel Peace Prize. 'UNDP', Snyder argues, 'initially wouldn't have supported them.' Maathai ran a non-governmental organization (NGO), and the Programme was usually constrained to work only with the government (even after Draper instituted a series of innovative small grants programmes for NGOs).[23] Yet, after UNIFEM's initial grant, UNDP's Chuck Lankester 'slipped her [Maathai] 10,000 dollars since

---

[21] Noeleen Heyzer, interview with TGW, 21 Feb. 2002.
[22] Joanna Kerr traces this change as beginning with a second Wingspread conference in 1982, 'From "WID" to "GAD" to Women's Rights: The First Twenty Years of AWID', Association for Women's Rights in Development Occasional Paper No. 9, October 2002. See also Nüket Kardam, 'Women and Development', in Peter R. Beckman and Francine D'Amico, eds., *Women, Gender, and World Politics* (Westport, Conn.: Bergin & Garvey, 1994), pp. 141–53.
[23] Margaret Snyder, interview with CNM, 22 Sept. 2004.

the Kenyan government was corrupt and couldn't get anything done'. He got into 'terrible trouble' in Nairobi, but he had the support of New York against any pressure Kenya might try to exert on the Governing Council.[24]

Suraj Kumar, a Programme officer in UNDP's Delhi Human Development Resource Centre, says that, at its best, UNDP is a great 'venture socialist', an organization that finds and supports social ventures like Maathai's in their very earliest stages, helping them get off the ground and making the bet that, with the help of that small investment, they will thrive. Like a venture capitalist, UNDP has to be able both to identify and to trust supremely creative individuals, who often come from the NGO world of 'free spirits'. Unfortunately, UNDP is constrained to act with governments, so that investments that are going to NGOs usually must be indirect.[25] Given those constraints, UNIFEM's demonstrated success in piloting such activities provided an important lesson, a reason for the Programme to find ways to overcome some of its own bureaucratic impediments in order to achieve this 'venture socialist' goal.

Not surprisingly, in Palestine, where UNDP has no sovereign government partner and where the Programme has significant resources and great autonomy, its impact on the lives of women has been profound. UNDP studies set much of the current national agenda for women's rights and empowerment within the territories and a women's rights activist, Zahira Kamal, who for many years worked for UNDP, became the Palestinian Authority's Minister of Women's Affairs in 2005.[26] Similarly, in China, Roy Morey began to build links with the All-China Women's Federation, which he considered to be the very best of the NGO sector, but still, of course, a semi-official organization, and thus a group to which UNDP could be linked.[27] The Federation's projects – retraining women displaced by the changing economy, establishing micro-credit schemes that can be sustained without frequent injections of government cash and control (which had been the usual practice in China[28]), and

---

[24] Chuck Lankester, interview with Neysan Rassekh (NR), 9 Nov. 2004.

[25] Suraj Kumar, interview with CNM, 13 Dec. 2004. The idea of NGO 'free spirits' is from Antonio Donini, 'The Bureaucracy and the Free Spirits: Stagnation and Innovation in the Relation between the UN and NGOs', *Third World Quarterly*, 16, 3 (1995): 421–40.

[26] 'Toward Gender Equality', *Focus* (A Magazine of the Communication Office of UNDP/PAPP), 1 (2005): 12–13.

[27] Roy Morey, interview with Elizabeth Mandeville (EM), 4 April 2005.

[28] Long-time UNDP partner, Dai Genyou, Director General of the People's Bank of China, insisted to me that self-sustaining, self-financed micro-lending schemes were impossible, given the level of skills and reliability of the poor (interview with CNM, 1 Dec. 2005). He was unaware of the work done by the All China Women's Federation.

creating hundreds of new businesses, including low-cost private enterprises to care for an aging population – are some of the most successful 'venture socialist' endeavours in this massive society that is moving from economically stagnant communism to inegalitarian capitalism.

Zhang Jing, the Federation's Director General in charge of international cooperation, says that the greatest, and largely unexpected, benefit of the UNDP partnership has been capacity building within the Federation, especially at a local level. Her words sound like Arthur Lewis's: 'Women who do implementation, learn leadership.' She laughs and says that even she has benefited. A dozen years before, even she would have been afraid to talk to someone from New York as she is now, without a script and in a foreign language.[29]

UNDP's experience with the Federation, and the trust developed with the Chinese government, proved particularly important in 1995, during the negotiations that led up to the successful Fourth World Conference on Women, in Beijing. The Chinese authorities were very anxious about the meeting. Sarah Burd-Sharps, the only person in the United Nations' Beijing office who worked full-time on the conference, remembers being followed and her rooms being bugged, perhaps by officials under the illusion that somehow she was running the whole affair.[30]

Just a few months before the conference, the Chinese government decided to move the critical meeting of independent women's groups, the NGO Forum, to Huairou, a city 45 kilometres from the capital. The government assured organizers that, if they accepted this more distant site, the Forum would remain open and all participants would be granted visas. Arthur Holcombe, Morey's successor as Res Rep, is proud of the role UNDP played in assuring that this promise was largely kept. In the end, representatives of groups like the Free Tibet Movement, women's organizations in Taiwan, and others pushing for Chinese democracy were able to participate.[31] Feminists regularly cite the Forum as a world historical event, one of the most important moments in the evolution of the global women's movement, and of global governance as a whole.[32]

Yet despite UNDP's critical role in 1995 the Programme's support of gender equality over the last decade has been spotty. One of Holcombe's successors, Khalid Malik, argues that, since the Beijing Conference,

[29] Zhang Jing, interview with CNM, 1 Dec. 2004.
[30] Sarah Burd-Sharps, interview with CNM, 4 June 2004.
[31] Arthur Holcombe, interview with CNM, 21 April 2004.
[32] For example, in Alison Jolly, *Lucy's Legacy: Sex and Intelligence in Human Evolution* (Cambridge, Mass.: Harvard University Press, 1999), pp. 405–34.

UNDP's central actors (the Res Reps and the leadership of the Bureaux) are no longer 'at the table' on gender equality. He sees this as an unintended consequence of Mark Malloch Brown's admirable policy of deferring to the autonomous affiliate, UNIFEM, which has the expertise and historical leadership on gender issues. However, Malik argues, 'UNIFEM was never meant to hold up the *advocacy* role.' It does not have UNDP's material resources and it does not have UNDP's access to the centres of government power.[33] But, of course, there is nothing to stop a Res Rep from working closely with UNIFEM and advocating the UNIFEM agenda.

Malloch Brown sees things differently, citing the many UNDP country offices that sponsor dialogues between women's groups and governments as they develop their Poverty Reduction Strategy Papers (PRSPs, the indicative plans required by the World Bank and the International Monetary Fund since 1999). UNDP has helped to make some PRSPs 'comprehensively gender-sensitive', aided by precisely the kind of access and resources that Malik says UNDP should be using.

The PRSP dialogues reflect Malloch Brown's larger belief in the effectiveness of data-driven politics: providing clear goals, like the MDGs, for which governments and international organizations can be held accountable, and giving UNDP's support to the groups interested in ensuring that that is done.[34]

Of course, that kind of politics is only as good as the goals for which the authorities are held accountable. The eminent feminist historian, Jane Parpart, questions whether achieving the MDGs would really empower women. She recognizes their origin in the debates about women and development a generation ago, 'But we know much more now; we have moved on. UNDP has not.' She sees the Programme's satisfaction with the MDGs as being of a piece with the 'stonewalling' her South African students have experienced when trying to study UNDP's programmes for women in their own country. She suspects that her students have received so little cooperation from UNDP's Johannesburg and Pretoria offices because, despite the Programme's rhetoric on women, 'There is little there.'[35]

Kalyani Menon Sen, who spearheaded much of UNDP's recent gender work in India, agrees. Actually empowering women is quite radical, but

[33] Khalid Malik, interview with CNM, 2 Dec. 2004.
[34] Memorandum report re: UNDP 1999–2005, Accomplishments and Remaining Challenges from Mark Malloch Brown to Kemal Dervis, August 2005, pp. 19–20.
[35] Jane Parpart, interview with CNM, 20 Oct. 2005.

'UNDP lives in terror of saying or doing something that will annoy the government.' So you have to 'dumb down the language', grossly simplifying what feminist research has proven, 'at the start'.

> The extent to which I think UNDP has capitalized on this conceptual space for working on women's rights is actually limited . . . [We always] plan with a much bigger canvas, with a much more radical objective, than what is finally delivered. For example, you might have a programme geared towards improved access to rights for women. Because UNDP is big on micro-credit, the programme has to have a micro-credit bent. Then when UNDP implements, it's just down to micro-credit. Even if that space is there, it's bounded by UNDP's limitations in terms of being here to support government policies or programmes. Radical work on gender is not possible. Sad, but it was also an education for me to realize the limitations of an institution like this. From the outside, it's quite impressive and overwhelming. It's only when working inside that you recognize the constraints.

However, even Sen ends on a note that sounds like Malloch Brown's: looked at properly, the glass is half-full. UNDP, Sen notes, has 'a subversive way of supporting radical organizations' that makes them

> visible on national stages because UNDP partners get invited to stuff, policy dialogues, included in various meetings, and so on. Basically, they're women's organizations doing good, solid work. Some innocuous part of their work is picked up and supported by UNDP. Once they're through the policy dialogue door, they can develop on their own and be respected and radical, bring up the critique, the questions, etc.[36]

UNIFEM and UNDP played this same role when they first supported Wangari Maathai a generation ago.

Political theorists would say that UNDP and UNIFEM have regularly helped to 'open the political space', both globally and within many countries, for discussion of more radical ideas about the empowerment of women.[37] Political space is an essential ingredient in policy learning, and the MDGs of 2000, for all their inadequacy, reflect a great deal of learning over one generation. By adopting them, many powerful institutions – both governmental and intergovernmental – have come to embrace an

---

[36] Kalyani Menon Sen, interview with CNM, 14 Dec. 2004.
[37] Many sources could be cited for the concept. Perhaps the most directly relevant is Hannah Arendt, *The Human Condition* (Chicago: University of Chicago Press, 1958), but Arendt is deeply indebted to classical authors and the European and Islamic scholars who maintained their tradition. See J. Peter Euben, 'Arendt's Hellenism', in Dana Villa, ed., *The Cambridge Companion to Hannah Arendt* (Cambridge: Cambridge University Press, 2000).

egalitarian, human-centred view of development that was not common-place in the 1970s. Moreover, those institutions have accepted the central role of women, and of their empowerment, in any attempt to achieve the society-wide development goals (e.g., economic growth and the equality of nations) that, earlier, were the only centre of attention.

Latin America, 'local resources', and support for democratization

I first learned of the concept of 'political space' in 1974 in a graduate school introduction to comparative politics at the University of North Carolina. One of our professors was Ricardo Lagos Escobar, an economist on the left who had been appointed Chile's ambassador to Moscow by Salvador Allende, but never took up the post; General Pinochet's coup replaced Allende in 1973, before the Chilean legislature confirmed Lagos's appointment. For the professor, Carolina was the first of many stops on the way back to the centre of Chilean political life. The next was a UNDP consultancy in Buenos Aires and then six years in the UN-sponsored regional employment programme, which brought Lagos back to Chile in 1978. In the 1980s he led Chile's Democratic Alliance, in the 1990s he held various positions in the governments that returned the country to democracy, and, in 2000, he was elected his country's president.

Lagos is one of the most prominent of the democratic leaders whose 'recycling' was an innovation in the era (1971–81) when Gabriel Valdés, Chile's former Foreign Minister, was the first director of what is now UNDP's Regional Bureau for Latin America and the Caribbean (RBLAC).[38] While sustaining those democratic leaders may have been UNDP's greatest contribution to the early stages of the global democratic wave that began in the 1980s,[39] it was the Bureau's development of '100 per cent cost sharing' that both helped sustain that wave and had the greatest impact on the further evolution of the Programme as a whole. '100 per cent cost sharing' means that UNDP administers a project, even though all of its costs are paid by the developing country's government.

---

[38] Recall chapter 1, pp. 10–11.

[39] Perhaps the most widely cited book on the phenomenon is Samuel P. Huntington, *The Third Wave: Democratization in the Late Twentieth Century* (Norman, Okla.: University of Oklahoma Press, 1993); the most thorough empirical analysis, which calls some of Huntington's conclusions into question, is probably John O'Loughlin, Michael D. Ward, Corey L. Lofdahl, Jordin S. Cohen, David S. Brown, David Reilly, Kristian S. Gleditsch, and Michael Shin, 'The Diffusion of Democracy, 1946–1994', *Annals, Association of American Geographers*, 88, 4 (1998): 545–74.

Three figures that regularly appear in UNDP's annual reports illustrate that impact within the Programme.[40] The graph in figure 8.1 shows UNDP's income, now some US$4 billion a year (about one fifth of what the World Bank disburses in loans and one fifth of the total aid provided by the largest bilateral donor, the United States).[41] UNDP's regular resources, the contributions of members, and contributions to funds such as UNIFEM have all been relatively stagnant (and, in real terms, declining) for some time, a pattern that goes back to the end of the Morse era. Yet the Programme's overall income has increased as a result of 'local resources' and 'other donor resources'.

'Local resources' – funds from developing country governments – are primarily from Latin America, and the largest local contributions have come to dwarf UNDP's income from all but the largest of the traditional donors. The story revealed in these figures (see figure 8.2 and table 8.1), and its connection to the more significant story of UNDP's contribution to sustaining democracies, is a bit complicated and its explication requires the introduction of one additional bit of UNDP jargon and the history of the policy to which it refers: 'national execution' (NEX).

Throughout the first generation of UN technical assistance, the Specialized Agencies 'executed' projects. They hired the experts, supervised their work, and carried out any detailed project evaluation. In contrast, by the early 1990s the vast majority of UNDP projects were carried out by recipient governments themselves, and a 1992 General Assembly resolution set such 'national' execution as the norm.

Most accounts of NEX treat it as part of Patel's 'New Dimensions' (see chapter 6), and trace its origin to a 1976 Governing Council decision.[42] Nevertheless, as with many of the Programme's most important innovations, NEX existed before it received the Council's sanction. In 1970 Arthur Lewis, who had already used UNDP support to start the University of the West Indies engineering school, returned to his

---

[40] Those in this chapter come from *United Nations Development Programme Annual Report 2005* (New York: UNDP, 2005), pp. 40–1.

[41] World Bank, 'Operational Summary, Fiscal 2005', http://web.worldbank.org/WBSITE/EXTERNAL/EXTABOUTUS/EXTANNREP/EXTANNREP2K5/0,,contentMDK:20635316~menuPK:1512365~pagePK:64168445~piPK:64168309~theSitePK:1397343,00.html; Organisation for Economic Cooperation and Development, 'Preliminary Official Development Assistance (ODA) by donor in 2004', http://www.oecd.org/document/7/0,2340,en_2649_34447_35397703_1_1_1_1,00.html (accessed 1 Nov. 2005).

[42] See ch. 2, 'National Execution Background', of Fuat Andic, Richard Huntington, and Ralf Maurer, *National Execution: Promises and Challenges* (New York: UNDP Office of Evaluation and Strategic Planning, 1995).

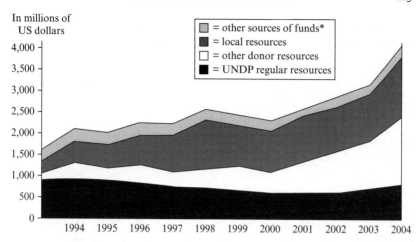

*Includes income of administered funds (UNCDF, UNIFEM and UNV), extra-budgetary resources, miscellaneous income and management service agreements.

8.1 UNDP's resources, 1994–2004

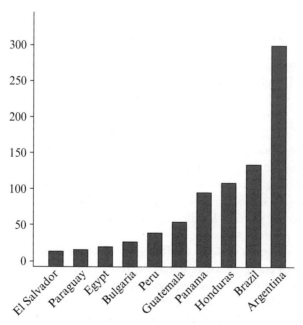

8.2 Local resources, 2004 (top ten Programme countries, expressed in US$ million)

Table 8.1. *UNDP income received, 2004 (top fifteen donor countries).*

	US$ million	
Donor	Regular resources	Other resources
United States	99	145
Norway	98	74
Netherlands	94	83
Japan	87	93
Sweden	85	65
United Kingdom	72	161
Denmark	60	27
Canada	48	50
Switzerland	41	16
Germany	33	23
France	20	9
Italy	18	52
Finland	17	12
Belgium	16	21
Ireland	16	10

colleagues to ask for support for a second, region-wide institution, the Caribbean Development Bank (CDB). UNDP funded the expert study that designed the CDB as well as most of its planning work in its first three years, when Lewis served as its president. The World Bank briefly played a role as the executing agency of the first project, but that seemed to Lewis like adding an unnecessary level of bureaucracy. With Valdés's blessing, the project quickly became 'self-executing' – the responsibility of the member governments of the CDB – and 'the first "government executed" project anywhere'. The success of the Lewis-era CDB projects helped to secure support for the 'official' adoption of the new modality by UNDP as a whole.[43]

In Latin America and the Caribbean, where many governments had a great deal of competence, either as the result of more than a century of independence or else as a consequence of a long tradition of local recruitment of the colonial civil service (as in Lewis's St Lucia), the new modality took off quickly. When the Argentine military acceded to elections in

[43] Michael Gucovsky, electronic mail to CNM, 11 Oct. 2005. Lewis discussed UNDP's role in his 1971 and 1973 Statements to the CDB's Board of Governors, http://www.caribank.org/pres_statements.nsf/pages/LEWIS (accessed 1 Nov. 2005).

1983, RBLAC had a decade of experience with NEX on which the country's Resident Representative, Eduardo Gutierrez, could rely. As is so often the case for Res Reps in times of political and economic crisis, Gutierrez found himself at the centre of frantic discussions between all the democratic forces. He helped to connect the economic teams of both the leading political parties and he convinced both parties to include members of the other in the country's new democratic government, which facilitated a united effort to clean up or address 'the total disarray' that the military had left.[44]

Argentina needed talented people. It needed specific equipment, including the early IBM personal computers that were used to track and manage the military's morass of foreign debt. In addition the new government needed to gain the trust of the international financial institutions, so that its debts could be renegotiated and projects to stimulate the moribund economy and rebuild fractured state institutions could begin.

Standing in the way was Argentina's cumbersome bureaucratic system and obsolete legislation. Many government posts remained empty. Others were filled by military cronies bent on impeding reform. Complicated procurement procedures made the purchase of new equipment a nightmare, and Argentina's long-standing policy of developing national champions in new technological fields meant that imported computers, telecommunications equipment, and other goods were subject to high tariffs. Official salaries for many government positions were far from competitive, giving the many skilled Argentines who had fled abroad little incentive to return. Meanwhile the World Bank and many bilateral donors feared that an unaccountable civil service and a growing culture of corruption would doom any new projects. Even if new loans and grants were approved, it seemed unlikely that the government would be able to use the funds in a timely and efficient manner.

Gutierrez recognized that, with a slight tweaking, the NEX modality could solve all these problems at once. Key organs of the new government could transfer Argentine funds to UNDP (including funds borrowed from the World Bank). The government would administer 'UNDP projects' unhampered by the various impediments. Argentina could then hire talented people (often from the Argentine diaspora), paying UN internationally competitive consultancy rates rather than the miserable salaries written into national law, procure equipment rapidly and at the lowest price, and use UNDP's sophisticated systems of record keeping

---

[44] Eduardo Gutierrez, interview with CNM, 3 Aug. 2004.

and its transparent, competitive hiring and purchasing policies to satisfy other international donors.

UNDP also gained from '100 per cent cost sharing'. It provided a formal way for RBLAC to support some of the democratic forces with which it had been informally allied from the Bureau's beginning. In addition, the modality provided a small cushion of funding – a 3 per cent administrative fee that the Programme charged on each of the cost-sharing projects – that could help support additional experiments in promoting democracy. Finally, the Argentine-funded projects inflated UNDP's income, making it look like a bigger player in the international aid game at a time when donor resources were stagnating.[45] This win–win proposition meant that by the end of the 1980s 'light-blue balls', representing UNDP projects, covered much of the 'Christmas tree' of the Argentine government organization chart.[46]

The same modality quickly spread across Latin America's other new democratic régimes. In 1985 Brazil's new elected leaders faced the same problems that had confronted Argentina when the generals stepped down in 1983. Similarly, as the wars dividing Central America ended in the 1990s, the same modality proved useful to the new governments. El Salvador's case is illustrative: all parties to the peace accords of 1992 trusted UNDP enough to ask for its help in their implementation. The cost-sharing modality proved critical to the rebuilding of an effective government, and the success of that process has left UNDP in a position to facilitate recent dialogues between government and groups within civil society on far-reaching fiscal and social reforms.[47]

By the middle of the 1990s, back in Buenos Aires, the burden of hosting the stream of visitors interested in copying the Argentine model forced UNDP's partners to produce an official video in which they outlined their experience and answered the most frequently asked questions.[48] The video's message was an example of the significant lessons that UNDP has helped to transfer from one new democratic régime to the next. In addition to sharing the experience of other states, RBLAC has used the cushion provided by its administrative fees to fund research that increased the region's, and UNDP's, understanding of democracy and

[45] The last is a point made more generally, for all organizations that use this modality, by Flavia Galvani and Stephen Morse, 'Institutional Sustainability: At What Price? UNDP and the New Cost-Sharing Model in Brazil', *Development in Practice*, 14, 3 (2004): 311–27.
[46] Eduardo Perez, interview with CNM, 3 Aug. 2004.
[47] Jose Vicente Troya, interview with EM, 7 June 2005.
[48] Carlos Kulikowsky, interview with CNM, 4 Aug. 2004.

development. The Bureau supports the region's complex array of national, sub-national, and even municipal human development reports and its many creative ways of bringing the research embodied in those reports to a larger public, for example a version of the 2002 Argentine Human Development Report used in secondary schools throughout the country.[49] RBLAC Director Elena Martínez points out, 'We have eighty-eight social scientists working for us in different field offices within the National Human Development Report teams. That is the brain of this bureau and no other bureau has that.'[50]

Perhaps the Bureau's most significant social science contribution has come through a series of complex, empirical reports about the state of democratization in Latin America. The reports have been followed by high-level public symposia in many countries, in Europe and the United States as well as across the region.[51] Dante Caputo, who was Argentina's foreign minister and one of UNDP's main partners back in 1983, heads the project. He sees the symposia as essential contributions to further learning about how to strengthen democratic governments. So are the 'civic dialogues' that RBLAC has sponsored in countries facing potential economic and political crises, in El Salvador, Guatemala, and Jamaica, and 'to a lesser degree' in Bolivia, Panama, and Peru, and especially in Argentina, in the wake of the 2001 financial crisis. These are multi-stakeholder discussions in which NGOs, the Catholic Church, and many political parties work to reach agreement on broad policy directions.[52] In a sense, they are a more formal version of the kind of work that Eduardo Gutierrez did in Argentina throughout the political crisis of 1983.

Ideally, such forums secure broad consensus on the continuing value of democracy as well as on the next set of economic policies to be tried, recognizing that history offers complex lessons of what *has not* worked, but no certain lessons about what *will* work. In the face of such uncertainty, widespread agreement on the reasonableness of a government's economic plans can be crucial to social harmony. This is one of the major lessons that RBLAC (and through it, UNDP as a whole) has learned over the last two decades.

However, critics within Latin America argue that the starting point for this learning – the '100 per cent cost-sharing modality' – may now have

---

[49] *El Dessarrollo Humano en la Argentina del Siglo XXI* (Buenos Aires: UNDP, 2003).
[50] Elena Martínez, interview with CNM, 3 June 2004.
[51] The various reports and the calendar of symposia can be found at http://democracia.undp.org/Prensa/Default.asp?Menu=21&Idioma=2 (accessed 1 Nov. 2005).
[52] Elena Martínez, interview with CNM, 3 June 2004.

little to do with supporting democracy.[53] In countries that are still emerging from decades of political turmoil, the continued reliance on Eduardo Gutierrez's innovation makes some sense. Nevertheless, in large, administratively sophisticated, and relatively prosperous countries with twenty years of democratic experience – places like Argentina and Brazil – it seems perverse that key parts of the government would still be run as UNDP projects. The more logical alternative would be administrative and legislative reform: new laws that would raise the salaries of key civil servants to international levels, allow the rapid purchase of goods from the cheapest suppliers through systems of open, competitive bidding, and require administrative efficiency and transparency. Yet, as the most prominent critics of the continuation of 100 per cent cost sharing in Brazil acknowledge, 'these are not simple reforms because they involve profound alterations to structures of public life and there is seldom a consensus on what should be done'. That is why governments continue to turn to UNDP to help them administer their programmes.[54]

Some Latin Americanists argue that the greatest impediment to reform is the region's populist political culture. Writing about Brazil, journalist Franklin Foer exaggerates to make a point about this culture:

> Despite advances towards democracy . . . these unabashed crooks have no compunction about pocketing money devoted to school lunch programmes and steering massive contracts to their family businesses. But populists have mastered a few good tricks that make them popular: While they steal for themselves, they also know how to steal for their constituents, pushing money into ostentatious public works projects. It's a style that has been reduced to a common aphorism used to justify support for them, 'He steals, but he makes'.[55]

Patricio Navia of Chile's Universidad Diego Portales makes a similar argument, but with greater evidence and less flash: Latin America's most popular leaders rarely use their mandate to push for the constitutional, administrative, and legislative reforms needed to transform the political culture. In fact, of all the presidents since the beginning of the last democratic wave, only Ricardo Lagos has had both the popularity and the will to push through such alterations in the structures of public life.[56]

---

[53] This is Galvani and Morse's central argument.
[54] Galvani and Morse, 'Institutional Sustainability: At What Price?', 311.
[55] Franklin Foer, *How Soccer Explains the World* (New York: HarperCollins, 2004), pp. 135–6.
[56] Patricio Navia, 'Neo-Liberal and Socialist: Lessons from the Ricardo Lagos Government for Leftist Leaders in Latin America', unpublished paper, Instituto de Ciencias Sociales, Universidad Diego Portales, 1 April 2005.

Lagos's unique willingness is not, of course, a consequence of his brief employment by UNDP or of the longer period of his 'recycling' through the United Nations. It has more to do with the complexities of Chile's uniquely long democratic experience before 1973. In countries without that experience, Gutierrez's innovation may still serve a democratic purpose.

Pointing to UNDP's exhaustive research, in 2004 Dante Caputo worried, deeply, about the fragility of the region's democracy. The average Latin American has seen no improvement in her economic condition for over a generation and the region remains the most inegalitarian in the world. This is the foundation on which authoritarian populism can be built:

> The main question we have to answer [is], 'How long can a democratic system resist this level of poverty and this level of inequality?' So, are we ready to solve those problems? . . . Otherwise, you know, people will say that they will accept an authoritarian régime, will accept some level of corruption. Because we have found that, a very surprising answer, thirty percent of the population in Latin America is ready to support a régime which is corrupted.[57]

This is one of the main lessons UNDP has learned about development and democracy.

Bernard Aronson, the man who had been in charge of the United States' Latin American policy in the late 1980s, took part in the same discussion. He recognized the region's economic problems, but said that they could be explained by the unwillingness of most Latin American governments to embrace the 'Washington Consensus' formula of economic laissez-faire (discussed in the next section). The one exception, Aronson argued, had been Chile's military government of the 1970s and 1980s. That was why, he said, Chile had been the one Latin American country to experience sustained economic growth.

Caputo demurred. If Aronson's account was accurate, then why had UNDP discovered that public support for the market economy to be lower in Chile than anywhere else in Latin America? Caputo said that he

---

[57] Dante Caputo interviewed by Tom Ashbrook, 'Latin America's Dance with Democracy', the 18 Aug. 2004 edition of the radio programme, *On Point*. The hour-long programme was directed towards an audience in the United States. The other participants included Carol Williams, *Los Angeles Times* correspondent in Caracas, and Mark Weisbrot of the Center for Economic and Policy Research in Washington, D.C. http://www.onpointradio.org/shows/2004/08/20040818_a_main.asp (accessed 1 Nov. 2005).

had raised this surprising lack of support with Ricardo Lagos at one of the many public dialogues about the UNDP findings. Summarizing the old professor's complex response, Caputo noted that few champions of the 'Washington Consensus' really understood the details of the Chilean case. Chile, Lagos said, has a strong, well-developed, capable state. Both before the 1973 coup and after the restoration of democracy, Chile's governments had been able to regulate the market and tame the social destructiveness of the forces that an uncontrolled market can release. Therefore UNDP's polls probably just indicated the public's support for the mixed political economy that Chile actually had.

All Latin Americans, Caputo emphasized, need to understand such complexities. They need to understand the real lessons of the past. Otherwise, unreflective advocates of a radically market-oriented 'neoliberalism' will be tempted to support military governments 'tough' enough to impose what they believe (incorrectly) were the policies that accounted for Chile's relative economic success. Alternatively, Caputo argues, the dispossessed may turn to unreflective populists who will bring back the policies that were in place before the laissez-faire 'Washington Consensus', older policies with just as dismal a record of failure.

Africa and structural adjustment

While RBLAC was learning to search for this middle path towards economically sustainable democracy, UNDP's Africa Bureau was helping sub-Saharan governments to learn to overcome an economic crisis even more acute than Latin America's stagnation. From the mid-1970s onwards, African countries and their governments faced devastating problems, beginning with the drought and famine that so engaged Brad Morse's sympathy. The oil crises of 1974 and 1979 raised the price of essential imported fuel to unprecedented levels, ultimately forcing most governments to increase foreign borrowing. Then, at the end of the decade, skyrocketing global interest rates and falling commodity prices (which were both, in large part, consequences of the policies that developed countries adopted to deal with the problems of the 1970s) made Africa's foreign debts unsustainable. Beleaguered governments turned to the World Bank and the International Monetary Fund (IMF) for new loans. Those organizations were ready to help as long as Africans adopted a specific set of domestic policies that were meant to force the economies of debtor nations to adjust to the new structure of the world economy as a whole. In 1989 international macroeconomist John

Williamson retrospectively christened these ten policies 'the Washington Consensus', in part because they were the 'structural adjustment' prescription of the Washington-based Bretton Woods multilateral organizations as well as of the Reagan administration. Paul Krugman, the celebrated international economist whose first major experience of the developing world came as a UNDP expert in the Philippines,[58] adds that Williamson was referring to 'all those institutions and networks of opinion leaders centred in the world's de facto capital', including 'think tanks, politically sophisticated investment bankers, and world finance ministers, all those who meet each other in Washington and collectively define the conventional wisdom of the moment'.[59]

Within the new global structure, supporters argued, development still could be possible, but only through (i) balanced budgets, achieved by (ii) cutting support for infant industries and redistributive social policy and (iii) tax reform; (iv) financial, (v) monetary, and (vi) trade liberalization; (vii) welcoming foreign investment; (viii) denationalizing state enterprises and (ix) 'ensuring secure property rights' (taking away the state's power to renationalize); and (x) wholesale deregulation. These policies were self-reinforcing. Once an old-style populist development state gave up one policy tool, the others became costly burdens. Once a government had denationalized, it made sense to cut the support for infant industries (since that money was now just going into private hands) and to welcome foreign investment needed to replace the local firms in the sectors decimated by the other policy shifts.[60]

From the beginning, critics argued that the policy package would be devastating to the poor. Tanzania's President Julius Nyerere demanded, 'Must we starve our children to pay our debts?'[61] For the World Bank, the new orthodoxy reversed the anti-poverty commitments made under Robert S. McNamara.[62] In part, this change reflected the influence of the US Reagan administration, which came to power in 1981 with a commitment to withdraw from any multilateral institutions that failed to transmit its policy preferences. Surprisingly (to some), the first targets

---

[58] Paul Krugman, interview with CNM, 9 Sept. 2004.
[59] Paul Krugman, 'Dutch Tulips and Emerging Markets', *Foreign Affairs*, 74, 4 (1995): 28.
[60] John Williamson, *Latin American Adjustment: How Much Has Happened?* (Washington, D.C.: Institute for International Economics, 1990).
[61] Quoted in Maggie Black, *Children First: The Story of UNICEF, Past and Present* (New York: Oxford University Press, 1996), p. 157.
[62] Devesh Kapur, John B. Lewis, and Richard Webb, *The World Bank: Its First Half-Century* (Washington, D.C.: Brookings Institution Press, 1997), pp. 22–5.

of the administration's pressure were the IMF and the Bank, which had already begun to move towards the administration's neo-liberal perspective.[63] For example, a famous 1981 World Bank report, by market-oriented economist Eliot Berg, overlooked external shocks and questions of distribution to put most of the blame for Africa's economic crisis on African governments' support of public ownership and regulated markets.[64]

Yet even at the beginning of the 1980s optimists believed that, through the engagement with African governments over structural adjustment, the IMF and the World Bank would 'learn to interest themselves in distributional issues'. This was the thrust of Gerald K. Helleiner's presidential address to the Canadian Association of African Studies in May 1982. Helleiner, a friend of Nyerere, had long been one of the economists most involved in the engagement between the UN system and Africa. He spoke favourably of an alternative vision for socially oriented structural adjustment programmes articulated by the Economic Commission for Africa (ECA) and he anticipated UNICEF's later call for 'adjustment with a human face'.[65]

Helleiner seems to have been right: as early as 1989 (ironically, in the year that Williamson gave 'the Washington Consensus' its name), the World Bank began to call for a different approach in Africa, the 'human-centred development strategy made by the ECA and UNICEF'.[66] Action by the Bank, the IMF, and major donor countries followed, even if incompletely and long after the change in rhetoric.[67]

---

[63] Craig N. Murphy, *Global Institutions, Marginalization, and Development* (London: Routledge, 2005), pp. 127–8. John Williamson contrasts the decidedly market-oriented 'Washington Consensus' with the more radical 'neoliberal' 'market fundamentalism' of the Reagan administration and others: 'A Short History of the Washington Consensus', paper presented at a conference, 'From the Washington Consensus towards a new Global Governance', Barcelona, 24 Sept. 2004.

[64] Kapur, Lewis, and Webb, *World Bank*, p. 23. The 'Berg Report' is World Bank, *Accelerated Development in Sub-Saharan Africa: An Agenda for Action* (Washington, D.C.: World Bank, 1981).

[65] A slightly less sanguine version of the address was published as Gerald K. Helleiner, 'The IMF and Africa in the 1980s', *Canadian Journal of African Studies*, 17, 1 (1983): 17–33; the quotation is from p. 28. Giovani Andrea Cornia, Richard Jolly, and Frances Stewart, eds., *Adjustment with a Human Face: Protecting the Vulnerable and Promoting Growth* (New York: Oxford University Press, 1987).

[66] Barber B. Conable, President of the World Bank, 'Foreword', in World Bank, *Sub-Saharan Africa: From Crisis to Sustainable Growth* (Washington, D.C.: World Bank, 1989), p. xii.

[67] Adebayo Adedeji, 'The ECA: Forging a Future for Africa', in Yves Berthelot, ed., *Unity and Diversity in Development Ideas: Perspectives from the UN Regional Commissions* (Bloomington, Ind.: Indiana University Press, 2004), pp. 285–6.

Some call these changes the victory of 'UNICEF and the ECA' over the World Bank in the 'Battle for the African Mind'.[68] Moreover, they fault UNDP for failing to use the bully pulpit of the Programme's central position in the UN development network to lead a concerted, public, global campaign for what Hans Singer calls the United Nations' socially oriented 'New York Dissent' from the Washington Consensus.[69]

UNDP followed a different strategy, the one Helleiner had anticipated, of 'learning through engagement'. UNDP contributed to the Bretton Woods institutions' new perspective by increasing the capacity of African governments to design something more appropriate than the 'shelf-model' programmes that the World Bank had originally offered.[70] In retrospect, it seems likely that both strategies – UNICEF/ECA's pounding on the bully pulpit and UNDP's engagement – were essential.

UNDP's contribution began in 1980, when the ECA and the Organization of African Unity (OAU) were working on a response to the continent's economic crisis – the 'Lagos Plan of Action', the programme favoured by Nyerere and Helleiner. Arguably, without UNDP, the plan would never have been formulated. UNDP 'financed a series of symposia, courses and seminars . . . in preparation for the Lagos Plan of Action, which assembled prominent African personalities with the aim of identifying the elements of a viable development strategy'.[71]

The debate about Africa's future continued to centre on the World Bank and the ECA/OAU visions – on 'the Lagos Plan versus the Berg Report' – for many years, and UNDP continued to provide the major financial backing for all the ECA/OAU studies of how the Lagos Plan could be implemented.[72]

One of the 'African personalities' in the early Lagos Plan discussions was a charismatic economist from Burkina Faso, Pierre-Claver Damiba. At the age of 28, he had become his country's minister in charge of

---

[68] Adedeji, 'The ECA', p. 266, coined the phrase.

[69] Hans Singer, interview with CNM, 8 July 2005. Richard Jolly, interview with CNM, 19 May 2004. Adedeji, 'The ECA', pp. 275–86.

[70] Kapur, Lewis, and Webb's description of the early 1980s Bank programmes, *The World Bank*, p. 24.

[71] Ngila Mwase, 'The UNDP Representation to the African Union and Liaison Office with the Economic Commission for Africa (RAULOE): Achievements during the Period 1977–2004', unpublished paper, UNDP Maputo, March 2005, p. 3.

[72] Ibid., p. 4. Some representative studies of the debate include Robert S. Browne and Robert J. Cummings, *The Lagos Plan of Action vs. the Berg Report: Contemporary Issues in African Economic Development*, 2nd edn (Lawrenceville, Vir.: Brunswick Publishing Company, 1985), and Timothy M. Shaw, ed., *Alternative Futures for Africa* (Boulder, Colo.: Westview Press, 1982).

economics, planning, agriculture, and public works. A few years later, he became the first president of the West African Development Bank, and then briefly went to the World Bank as Executive Vice President of the International Finance Corporation, the affiliate that works with the private sector. That is where Brad Morse found Damiba and convinced him to take over UNDP's Africa Bureau, in 1982, to bring it 'new thinking and new blood'.[73]

Morse's own commitment to Africa ended up leaving Damiba very much in charge. From 1984 to 1986, his last year at UNDP, Morse worked almost full-time in a second position as head of the UN Office of Emergency Operations in Africa, the coordinating mechanism for the UN system's responses to the drought of the first part of that decade, a crisis similar to the one that had engaged him when he first came to the United Nations in the 1970s. In the new project Morse was assisted by a Canadian, Maurice Strong, who would continue to play a major role in UN development work. At the end of Morse's tenure, in 1986, a special session of the General Assembly was held on the critical economic situation in Africa. Another Canadian, the country's UN ambassador, Stephen Lewis, drafted the resulting 'UN Programme of Action for African Economic Recovery and Development, 1986–90' that called for additional outside assistance to the continent of more than US$10 billion each year. That level of funding was not forthcoming, but the General Assembly resolution became an additional source of guidance for UNDP's policy alongside the Lagos Plan and the OAU's 'Africa Priority Programme'.[74]

Faced with those guidelines, Damiba's overarching goal was to make UNDP more than 'a house of procedures' for managing development projects that had been thought up by others. He initiated major evaluations of national programmes of technical assistance and then later convinced Bill Draper and Arthur Brown to let him recruit more than thirty economists who could work with African governments. The economists would help to ensure that the critically important injections of foreign assistance that all African governments received, often from many different sources, would be coordinated in overall economic plans. UNDP would help to improve each country's autonomous capacity to develop coherent macroeconomic policies. That meant strengthening the capacity of African governments to 'start thinking by themselves about

---

[73] Pierre-Claver Damiba (recalling Brad Morse's words), interview with CNM, 12 Jan. 2005.
[74] Garth ap Rees, electronic mail to CNM, 21 Dec. 2005.

what should be done to adjust economies' rather than 'wait for the World Bank and the IMF to tell them'. It meant training

> civil servants so that when negotiating with the World Bank and the IMF and bilaterals on adjustment, they can say, 'Look, we have social programmes to mitigate the devastating impact.'[75]

The starting point of UNDP's new approach in Africa was the National Technical Cooperation Assessments and Programmes Project (NATCAP), begun in 1986 under the leadership of Sakiko Fukuda-Parr and Carlos Lopes. As Damiba argues, from the very beginning the major point of technical assistance had been to build the capacity of local institutions and of individuals – that was the reason for all those 'national counterparts' in the original EPTA projects of the 1950s, but, by the 1980s, in many places, this emphasis had been lost. Many African governments looked to technical cooperation as just another source of revenue, 'which it was; in some countries its value dwarfed earnings from the major export crop'.[76] Fukuda-Parr explains the project this way:

> Everyone agrees that capacity is the weakest link. Everyone realizes that expatriate 'experts' descend and get the job done but without leaving behind lasting capacity, and that people go for training and don't come back. Everyone realizes that there is a need for better, more effective methods of capacity development but donors are not prepared to address the root causes of this ineffectiveness . . . As far as UNDP's role in Africa was concerned, doing something about capacity and addressing the need for reform in technical cooperation were part of the 'structural adjustment agenda' we were pushing for. The initiative led to countries debating these issues, developing national policy frameworks, and building programmes so that the money being spent would be used rationally and effectively.[77]

The individual national studies led many governments to reduce their reliance on expatriates in many fields at the same time that they convinced some governments of the desirability of working with some of UNDP's new economists to design appropriate responses to the dilemma of structural adjustment.

Beyond just helping African governments design alternatives to the 'shelf-model' programmes from Washington, Damiba also worked to put UNDP at the negotiating table when many of its African partners faced their major donors. This was particularly important because, in

---

[75] Pierre-Claver Damiba, interview with CNM, 12 Jan. 2005.   [76] Ibid.
[77] Sakiko Fukuda-Parr, electronic mail to CNM, 27 Dec. 2005.

the early 1980s, the United States, some other major bilateral donors, and the Bretton Woods institutions had strengthened a set of 'policy dialogue' mechanisms whose goal was to use the combined leverage of all the foreign assistance coming into a country to press for the adoption of the whole Washington package.[78] Damiba convinced the Administrator to give UNDP the skilled personnel needed to make the regular 'Round-Table' discussions between donors and national governments the effective locus of such dialogue. UNDP had been mandated to carry out such meetings for the poorest (the 'least-developed') developing countries, but even for Burkina Faso the first did not take place until 1991.[79] According to Fukuda-Parr, when the early Round Tables did take place, they tended to be 'undisciplined project fairs', anathema to anyone who wanted to set priorities in 'resource-constrained situations'.[80] By 1990, with its new capacity, UNDP did become the coordinator of 'policy dialogue' with most African countries, beginning with Burkina, Lesotho, Mali, and Malawi. This meant chairing meetings in Geneva every two to three years with the countries and their donors, assisting governments in preparing their necessary strategy papers, and helping with 'resource mobilization', that is to say, persuading the donors to contribute. In these situations, Damiba argues, UNDP never made a public frontal assault on the Bank's orthodoxy, but simply helped governments committed to the Lagos Plan to convince the donors that their preferred policies would be more effective than the Bank's 'shelf-model'.[81]

Richard Jolly (who spearheaded the UNICEF push for 'adjustment with a human face' and would later direct UNDP's Human Development Report Office) is convinced that Damiba's strategy came at too high a cost: 'The rest of the United Nations wanted UNDP to take on the role of confronting the Bank.' UNDP had experience – as a coordinator of the other multilateral agencies and through its continuous, extensive involvement on the ground in every developing country – that no other

---

[78] Enrico Augelli, 'Il "dialogo politiche" secondo Washington', *Politica Internazionale* 14, 1 (1986): 188–211.

[79] Harouna Ouedrago (a UNDP economist who worked on structural adjustment and related issues), interview with CNM, 13 Jan. 2005. Arthur Holcombe, *Running on Two Tracks* (no city [probably New York]: UNDP, n.d. [probably 1998]), pp. 40–1, recalls, 'The United Nations Conference on Least Developed Countries in 1981 entrusted UNDP with responsibility for organizing Donor Round Table Meetings (RTMs) intended to mobilize additional resources for the 36 poorest developing countries.'

[80] Sakiko Fukuda-Parr, electronic mail to CNM, 27 Dec. 2005.

[81] Pierre-Claver Damiba, interview with CNM, 12 Jan. 2005.

agency, not even the World Bank, could match.[82] UNDP's low profile left the job of directing the public battle of ideas to UNICEF.[83]

Damiba is unapologetic about the policy he pursued. It was just realistic, he argues, given that African states needed the levels of financing that only the Bretton Woods institutions could provide:

> My position was the following: we have the sub-Saharan African countries, weak vis-à-vis the World Bank. If we [UNDP] start to fight the World Bank, the African countries will fight us, because they will go by all means with the World Bank. I had to say . . . [to] heads of state . . . 'Look, I disagree with World Bank adjustment. It is why UNDP will work with you to strengthen your capacity to challenge the World Bank one day.' It is a selfish position, not a tactical position . . . They said, 'Damiba, stay with us. One day, the World Bank will come eat from our hands.'[84]

Damiba may have been right about governments going with the Bank. In Pakistan a very highly respected Resident Representative, Hans von Sponeck, followed the different strategy of leading all the UN agencies in promoting a social action programme to give a 'human face' to the country's era of structural adjustment. Unfortunately, the relationship between the Bank and UNDP 'became very acrimonious for many years. Money became decisive rather than substance.' Despite the almost universal esteem in which Sponeck was (and still is) held by Pakistani authorities, and despite UNDP's long and more complex involvement in the country, the government chose the World Bank to be the lead agency for the social action programme, even though many told Sponeck that 'structural adjustment . . . would have had the more human face with UNDP'.[85]

In contrast, Anne Forrester, who served in Ghana in the late 1980s when the country began its major structural adjustment drive, followed Damiba's strategy. As Resident Representative she offered the support of UNDP economists, helped to set up a 'national consultancy régime' to make the expertise of the country's three universities available to the government, and helped to finance the locally designed programme to mitigate the social cost of adjustment. Forrester suggested that

---

[82] Richard Jolly, interview with CNM, 8 July 2005.   [83] Black, *Children First*, pp. 155–62.

[84] Pierre-Claver Damiba, interview with CNM, 12 Jan. 2005.

[85] The quotations are from Hans von Sponeck, interview with NR, 3 Nov. 2004; Sartaj Aziz, interview with CNM, 10 Dec. 2004. Almost everyone we interviewed in Pakistan expressed unusually high regard for Sponeck. The same was true in India, where he also served as Resident Representative.

Ghanaian NGOs be appointed to distribute the aid for those displaced after losing their civil service employment, and then provided capacity-building assistance to those organizations, something that created further institutional support for Ghana's version of 'adjustment with a human face'.[86]

Unlike Pakistan, where the positive macroeconomic results of structural adjustment were slow to emerge and the social action plan largely failed,[87] Ghana quickly became a showcase for the World Bank, one of the very few African examples where adjustment seemed to 'work', where the government did not sink further into a trap of foreign debt and where the worst social horrors that many had anticipated did not take place.[88] A few years later, however, even analysts sympathetic to structural adjustment programmes noted Ghana's growing debt and nearly unchanged levels of poverty, but these conditions still reflected one of the best records on the continent.[89] Nevertheless, even if we have yet to learn how to achieve effective 'adjustment' in Africa, Ghana helped to convince the World Bank that the laissez-faire prescriptions of the early 1980s were not enough. Moreover, the African examples emboldened the rest of UNDP to take a stronger role in promoting a focus on social and distributional issues in countries facing structural adjustment and in the world at large, a role consistent with Bill Draper's embrace of 'advocacy'.

Away from the field, back in New York and Washington, UNICEF and the ECA's engagement in the battle of ideas also had its effect. On 10 May 1989, a local (African) truce was reached at a kind of summit of the leaders of the 'Washington Consensus' and the 'New York Dissent'. The Bank's president, chief economist, and African executive directors and representatives of the IMF joined the heads of the ECA, the OAU, and the African Development Bank and Richard Jolly, Pierre-Claver Damiba, Arthur Brown, and Bill Draper. They affirmed that, in Africa at least, 'adjustment must . . . take full account of the human dimension' and

[86] Anne Forrester, interview with NR, 16 Feb. 2005.
[87] See Christopher Candland, 'Institutional Impediments to Human Development in Pakistan', in Amita Shastri and A. Jeyaratnam Wilson, eds., *The Post-Colonial States of South Asia: Democracy, Development, and Identity* (London: Curzon Press, 2001), pp. 264–80.
[88] See, e.g., Robert P. Armstrong, *Ghana Country Assistance Review: A Study in Development Effectiveness* (Washington, D.C.: World Bank, 1996).
[89] Commonwealth Business Council, *Commonwealth Insight 2003: Ghana Investment Conference Report* (London: Commonwealth Business Publications, 2004), p. 17. From a more critical perspective, see Susan George, 'Rethinking Debt', paper presented at the North–South Roundtable on Moving Africa into the 21st Century: An Agenda for Renewal, Johannesburg, 18 Oct. 1995.

'substantial debt relief measures are needed, since the external debt burden remains a severe constraint on African development'.[90]

It would be years before all parties would translate those affirmations into action. (It took until 2005 before the World Bank and the IMF joined in a major agreement to relieve Africa's foreign debt.[91]) Yet the new learning-oriented UNDP increasingly contributed to others' understanding of Africa and the critical issues there. The NATCAP project resulted in a 1993 book, *Rethinking Technical Cooperation in Africa, Reforms for Capacity Building*, that Damiba attributes almost entirely to Fukuda-Parr.[92] She in turn recalls, 'The World Bank bought up several hundred copies! [However,] UNDP external relations told me to burn every copy because it was politically dangerous, being too critical of donors and of ourselves and of our core business.'[93]

Despite the new level of agreement about the African crisis, many left the 1989 summit convinced of the need to continue the global battle of ideas. Richard Jolly carried on his work with Mahbub ul Haq (Sponeck's most important government partner in Pakistan, and Draper's key appointee to UNDP), Barbara Ward (ul Haq's 'mentor since Cambridge days'), and others through an annual 'North–South Roundtable' that

> brought together leading progressive economists of the North and South . . . for open debate on global policy challenges and policy choices . . . Central to these debates was the idea that development was about people, and that improvements in human living conditions and life chances can be made quite dramatically and rapidly even in poor countries through properly targeted social intervention.[94]

Jolly recalls meeting near the University of Sussex at an inn frequented by Thomas Paine, the revolutionary author of *The Age of Reason* and *The Rights of Man*, and feeling a real continuity between the Roundtable and Paine's work to expand human freedom, two centuries before.[95]

---

[90] ECA and World Bank, 'Joint Statement on Africa's Long-Term Development', meeting on Structural Adjustment in Sub-Saharan Africa, Washington, D.C., 10 May 1989.

[91] Edmund L. Andrews, 'Rich Nations Reach Deal to Drop the Debt of Poor Ones', *New York Times*, 25 Sept. 2005.

[92] Pierre-Claver Damiba, interview with CNM, 12 Jan. 2005. Nevertheless, the book is usually found under the name of a consultant involved in the project. It is a sign of the new era of cooperation that he was Eliot Berg; see UNDP and Berg, *Rethinking Technical Cooperation: Reforms for Capacity Building in Africa* (New York: UNDP, 1993).

[93] Sakiko Fukuda-Parr, electronic mail to CNM, 27 Dec. 2005.

[94] Sakiko Fukuda-Parr and Selim Jahan, 'Haq, Mahbub ul (1934–1998)', in David A. Clark, ed., *The Elgar Companion to Development Studies* (Cheltenham: Edward Elgar, forthcoming).

[95] Jolly, interview with CNM, 8 July 2005.

Meanwhile, before leaving UNDP in 1991, Damiba convinced the Programme, the Bank, and the African Development Bank to create the African Capacity Building Foundation (ACBF) 'to build and strengthen sustainable indigenous capacity for macroeconomic policy analysis and development throughout sub-Saharan Africa'.[96] Gerald Helleiner, Kwesi Botchwey (the minister responsible for Ghana's socially oriented structural adjustment programme), and others connected to UNDP's African initiatives in the 1980s have been central to ACBF's programmes that train African economists and work to reverse the brain drain.

The lessons that the Africa Bureau's capacity-building economists of the 1980s brought to UNDP complemented those coming to the Programme through RBLAC's support of democratization and UNIFEM's focus on the role of women in development. It would take more than a decade before these separate lessons would be woven together into a single design for UNDP's work. Yet, even by the end of the 1980s, the Capacity Study's fears of a brainless and doomed Programme had, perhaps serendipitously, been proved wrong. UNDP had developed multiple brains and they were not the centres of expertise within the Specialized Agencies that Muchkund Dubey and 'the Consensus' had attempted to preserve. They were, instead, institutionalized in such entities as RBLAC's band of social scientists and the Bureau's intimate connections with the regions' democratic régimes, in UNIFEM's engagement with the global women's movement and its role as innovator and advocate throughout the UN system, and in the Africa Bureau's economists and their capacity-building work that reached down into governments and civil society and outwards to UNDP's multilateral and bilateral partners.

There were certainly many problems with this new, widely distributed 'brain', problems beyond the initial lack of connections among its various centres. Damiba points out that, in Africa, giving life to this new brain meant killing off the old one. In an era when UNDP's real resources were shrinking, putting more money into the 'upstream' work of building the capacity of governments to understand and manage their economies meant cutting funds that otherwise might have gone to sectoral projects administered by the Specialized Agencies. Therefore UNDP lost its (albeit limited) connection to the Agencies' expertise in agriculture, education, health, labour, and other fields. Moreover, the Africa Bureau's new cadre of professional economists often clashed with the broadly trained

---

[96] African Capacity Building Foundation, *Annual Report 2000* (Harare: ACBF, 2000), p. 2.

generalists who had always been at the core of UNDP's field presence. 'Some economists started to say, "Look, it will be better if we were Resident Representatives. We want to be in the driving seat."'[97]

Creating a unified focus for UNDP's work, coping with the increasingly competitive relationship between the Programme and other parts of the UN development system, and managing a fundamental change in UNDP's professional culture would prove to be some of the organization's major challenges in the 1990s.

[97] Pierre-Claver Damiba, interview with CNM, 12 Jan. 2005.

9

'Bottoms up' development helps make UNDP a mammal

It was in 1989 – right after the UN–World Bank truce on structural adjustment in Africa – that I first thought a great deal about UNDP. What I thought was that the Programme's time had passed. At the time, I was using public sources to put together a data set of the regular activities of all the global-level intergovernmental organizations going back to their beginning in the mid-nineteenth century.[1] UNDP and its predecessors accounted for about 4 per cent of all those activities. One of the most perceptive books then available said that UNDP had once played a crucial, dialectical role: strengthening the authority of governments throughout the developing world, while increasing the dependence of most of their citizens on them. [2]

Yet, in mid-1989, it was easy to believe that the Programmes' glory days were over. UNDP's engagements with revolutionary states and movements were unknown to me and most other observers (the engagements took place away from the public eye), and other organizations had begun to eclipse UNDP in its traditional fields. By then, most UN agencies carried out development projects funded from their regular budgets and many had their own representatives throughout the developing world. Moreover, compared with most of its competitors, UNDP had little focus – a complaint I later heard from scores of staffers. Hamid Ghaffarzadeh, who began working for UNDP in the mid-1980s, for example, says that he rarely contradicted his wife when she said that he 'worked for UNICEF; at least that made a picture in people's minds'.[3]

True, back in the late 1980s, one could have started with people like Kwesi Botchwey, Gabriel Valdés, and Peg Snyder and trace three critically

---

[1] Craig N. Murphy, 'Data on the Civil Activities of World Organizations', in *International Organization and Industrial Change: Global Governance since 1850* (Cambridge: Polity Press, 1994), pp. 285–92.

[2] Susan A. Gitelson, *Multilateral Aid for National Development and Self-Reliance: A Case Study of UNDP in Uganda and Tanzania* (Kampala: East African Literature Bureau, 1975), pp. 174–5.   [3] Hamid Ghaffarzadeh, interview with the author (CNM), 7 March 2005.

important global policy networks: one adding a social dimension to structural adjustment, the second strengthening new democracies, and the third empowering women. But these networks did not belong to any *one* organization; instead, they were what scholars of international relations had started to call 'epistemic communities' – informal associations linked by knowledge.[4] UNDP provided one home for all three of the networks, but they had other homes as well; for example, as an economist who was part of UNDP's programme to strengthen African capacity notes, many of those hired came from the World Bank or the International Monetary Fund (IMF).[5]

I was very wrong. UNDP continued to have a unique role to play. At the same time that I was working on an obscure data set, much more creative social scientists were doing work that would give the organization a new, globally significant, purpose. Mahbub ul Haq and his small group of UNDP colleagues were working on the first *Human Development Report*. Ul Haq's friend and colleague, Amartya Sen, remembers

> the phone calls that came repeatedly from Mahbub in summer 1989, with his explaining to me what is going to happen (and why I should join in this 'vitally important' crusade) . . . What must have appeared to many in the United Nations system as a rather eccentric plan of an independent-minded Pakistani economist has become a central component of critical attention in the world of communication and public discourse.[6]

Ul Haq's project was only one part of a change that Brad Morse's successor, Bill Draper, brought to UNDP in the late 1980s. Another of ul Haq's colleagues – fellow economist and *Human Development Report* collaborator, Paul Streeten – says that people are either molluscs or mammals. Molluscs are hard on the outside, but mushy underneath. Mammals are soft and warm, but firm inside – they have a backbone. Ul Haq, Streeten says, was the quintessential mammal.[7] And, today, so is UNDP, largely due to the backbone, the mission, brought to the Programme by Draper with the incomparable help of ul Haq and his friends.

---

[4] Peter M. Haas, 'Introduction: Epistemic Communities and International Policy Coordination', *International Organization*, 46, 1 (winter 1992): 1–37.

[5] Harouna Ouedraogo, interview with CNM, 13 Jan. 2005.

[6] Amartya Sen, 'A Decade of Human Development', *Journal of Human Development*, 1, 1 (2000): 17.

[7] Sakiko Fukuda-Parr and Selim Jahan, 'Haq, Mahbub ul (1934–1998)', in David A. Clark, ed., *The Elgar Companion to Development Studies* (Cheltenham: Edward Elgar, forthcoming).

Draper

William H. Draper III, who replaced Morse in 1986, is still a controversial figure among UNDP old-timers. He was a straightforward, enthusiastic American businessman nominated by Ronald Reagan at the suggestion of Draper's old friend, Vice-President George H. W. Bush. The new Administrator seemed as distant from the traditional UN culture and as different from the circle of understated, old-style democratic socialists recruited by David Owen, as one could be. Draper had no abiding interest in strengthening Third World governments and was greatly suspicious about increasing citizens' dependence upon them. It must have been disconcerting to many staffers, he admits, to have an Administrator 'dedicated and passionate about the private sector' and its potential as an agent for positive change.[8]

In public, Draper could be awkward and undiplomatic – very much *not* the UN style. Margaret Joan Anstee, who had risen high in the Secretariat proper before Draper's arrival, recalls,

> Whenever I would meet him on the street – I was an Under-Secretary General [the only woman at that rank], the same level he was – he would just slap me on the back and say, 'Hiya kiddo', and I would always want to say . . . 'What other Under-Secretary General do you do this to?'

Perhaps even worse, he would sometimes botch major public speeches; on one occasion, Anstee remembers, Draper called the kind of development he advocated, 'the bottoms up approach'.[9]

To top everything off, says Richard Olver (whose knowledge of the organization goes back to when his father, John Olver, joined in 1946), Draper just 'didn't respect us' – the international civil servants who had built the Programme and committed their lives to it. 'He didn't have the capacity to understand the institution as it was.'[10] Some staffers were convinced that 'Draper knew nothing about development when he arrived.'[11]

Some headquarters stalwarts also faulted Draper for being a poor empire-builder, incompetent at the cut-throat internal politics of the UN system. For example, Draper let the UN Fund for Population Activities

---

[8] William H. Draper III, interview with CNM, 29 Sept. 2004.
[9] Margaret Joan Anstee, interview with CNM and Elizabeth Mandeville (EM), 6 July 2005.
[10] Richard Olver, interview with CNM, 3 June 2004.
[11] Sarah Papineau Marshall recalls this widespread assumption. Interview with CNM, 23 Nov. 2004.

(UNFPA) become autonomous from UNDP, both administratively and financially,[12] thus violating the first rule of bureaucracy, 'Keep all you have'.[13]

There is no question that, initially, Draper hoped to divorce UNDP from the UN proper. He envisioned a 'World Development Organization' that would not have to deal with the UN's 'terribly cumbersome' bureaucracy.[14] Richard Olver believes that, as a consequence, after Arthur Brown's retirement in 1989, Secretaries-General have assigned UNDP Associate Administrators from the Secretariat proper, to serve as the Administrator's 'minder from the UN side'.[15] Although, in fact, this assessment could not be applied to Brown's immediate successor, Andrew Joseph, who was recruited to the Technical Assistance Board by David Owen in 1963.

Moreover, the man who eventually replaced Brown, Luis Maria Gomez, paints a very different picture of Brad Morse's successor. Draper, Gomez argues, is undoubtedly a genius. A few months into Gomez's job as Associate, the two men took part in a senior management retreat. Everyone had to take the same battery of tests: 'Draper beat me at every test, in perception, IQ, intelligence, etc.'[16] This was not surprising, perhaps, for someone who had been one of the most successful venture capitalists, a business that requires a variety of different kinds of intelligence and instincts.

Moreover, contrary to the perception of many UNDP old-timers, Draper knew a great deal about development, and even more about the principle of solidarity on which UNDP had been founded, and he knew it from as early an age as Olver did. Draper's father, General William H. Draper Jr, helped to lead recovery efforts in both Germany and Japan, and was the man with Paul Hoffmann when he received the call to take over administration of the Marshall Plan.[17] The elder Draper also had been, along with Owen, Hoffmann, and Richard Symonds, one of the pioneers promoting family planning in developing countries, which was one reason why the younger Draper very much wanted UNFPA to be able to leave the

---

[12] Ibid. However, UNDP and UNFPA remain under the same governing board of state members.   [13] According to the British television comedy, *Yes, Minister*.

[14] William H. Draper III, interview with CNM, 28 Sept. 2004.

[15] Olver, interview with CNM, 3 June 2004.

[16] Luis Maria Gomez, interview with Neysan Rassekh (NR), 12 Dec. 2004.

[17] William H. Draper Jr, oral history interview with Jerry N. Hess, Truman Presidential Museum and Library, 11 Jan. 1972, http://www.trumanlibrary.org/oralhist/draperw.htm# 57 (accessed 27 Nov. 2005).

incubator that UNDP had initially provided.[18] Immediately before coming to UNDP, Draper had served as head of the US Export-Import Bank, an organization that, despite contrary pressures from Reagan's budget office, had retained some of the development focus and culture of the 'Good Neighbor' policy era when it was founded.[19] It was at the Ex-Im Bank, and when considering the situation on the ground in Africa, that Draper developed his deep convictions about the centrality of women in development.[20]

Önder Yücer, one of the youngest Res Reps at the time the new Administrator arrived, says that those who highlight Draper's occasional verbal clumsiness fail to see that he was just disinclined 'to talk about things that he doesn't believe in'. Draper, Yücer emphasizes, believed in UNDP, and in the necessity of the Administrator taking personal responsibility for maintaining and increasing its resources. Yücer recalls the first time he heard his new boss on that subject, 'Draper simply transformed himself from a fisherman into an apostle. It was incredible . . . This awkward man was able to touch the right nerves or buttons to raise resources.' Not surprisingly, Draper increased UNDP's core funding to the highest levels, in real terms, ever achieved, before or since.[21]

Draper muses that staff members who thought he did not respect them failed to understand how exciting the organization's 'culture of commitment to helping your fellow man' was for him,

> I probably wasn't the kind of businessman they thought I was at the time . . . I asked a lot of questions because that was my style, to make sure of the quality of the people I was asking and if they had good answers . . . The people you select and delegate to are the ones who end up making it a success or a failure.

In part to illustrate the point, he talks about one of the things he truly admired about Ghana's Jerry Rawlings, the military officer who ran the country throughout its celebrated structural adjustment programme. 'What I loved about him,' Draper says, 'was how he'd get halfway into a subject and then say, "Tell him",' and then the minister involved 'would very eloquently tell the rest of the story.' This man who had had more impact on Ghana than anyone since Nkrumah, 'would always cut himself off after he got the thing started', making it clear that he completely trusted those under him, those who would make his work a success or

---

[18] Sarah Papineau Marshall, interview with CNM, 23 Nov. 2004.

[19] William H. Becker and William M. McClenahan Jr, *The Market, the State, and the Export-Import Bank of the United States, 1934–2000* (Cambridge: Cambridge University Press, 2003), p. 28.   [20] William H. Draper III, interview with CNM, 28 Sept. 2004.

[21] Önder Yücer, interview with CNM, 7 Dec. 2004.

9.1 Draper (left) signs an agreement to cooperate to fight AIDS with UN Director-General for Development and International Economic Co-operation Jean Ripert and the WHO's Halfdan Mahler (right), 29 March 1988

failure.[22] Yücer describes a similar situation with African leaders gathered in Namibia, but with Draper leading *his* team, 'He was a *UNDP leader* and was very *proud* of his young managers around – advisors, assistants – and that's how he wanted *us* to be.'[23]

Many of those young managers around Draper were women. Sarah Papineau Marshall, who served in Draper's office from 1988 to 1991, points out that, despite the casual sexism of his greeting to Anstee, Draper's trust in women is unquestionable, 'He did an amazing job of elevating women, making more women Res Reps' than all those who had come before him.

> He had a deep belief that women were good managers [and] deep instincts about people [in general]. Because he had been a venture capitalist, the thing he knew how to do best was to judge people. He took huge risks putting 'odd' people in 'odd' jobs in 'odd' places, and it really worked out well. I saw him do this with many women.[24]

[22] William H. Draper III, interview with CNM, 28 Sept. 2004.
[23] Önder Yücer, interview with CNM, 7 Dec. 2004.
[24] Sarah Papineau Marshall, interview with CNM, 23 Nov. 2004.

Of course, Draper's confident choices for many senior positions proved controversial, but no more controversial than the new mechanism he invented for deciding whether proposed projects would be funded or his creation of what Arthur Holcombe describes as UNDP's 'second track': the promotion of particular visions of development, what UNDP calls 'advocacy'.[25]

Draper arrived at a time when the power of the heads of UNDP's regional bureaux – 'the barons' – was at its height. While some of the bureaux were dynamic – the creative parts of an emerging 'learning organization' – in the late 1980s there was little cross-fertilization, insufficient learning from one bureau to the next. In part to rectify that, Draper set up an 'Action Committee'. He met every Wednesday morning at 9 a.m. with the regional directors and relevant desk officers to review and approve the larger projects.

Sarah Papineau Marshall recalls that, initially, 'the barons' thought that the meetings 'were a waste of time'. They would 'send in pretty girls, anything to get these projects approved'.[26] That proved to be a particularly unproductive strategy. In fact, Trevor Gordon-Somers recalls, the best thing about the meetings that they 'obliged us all to take into consideration issues of gender'. If you could not point to a project's positive impact on women, Draper was unlikely to approve it, which was, 'on balance, a good thing'.[27]

It was thoughtful and committed answers to questions about a project that assured Draper's approval. Patrick Shima recalls being sent to defend one of the first projects heard by the Committee. At the end of the presentation Draper asked, 'What is the economic return?' Shima (and, he believes, others in the room) were dumbfounded. It may have been the first time that an economist's standard question about opportunity costs – about whether something was the most productive way that resources could be used – had been asked at that level within UNDP.[28] Moreover, it turned out that Draper was not looking for some sort of rote calculation of rate of return – the sort of thing essential to the development banks, which have to worry about the 'bankability' of projects, but not to an agency in the business of giving grants. Draper wanted to hear that Shima

---

[25] Arthur Holcombe, *Running on Two Tracks* (no city [probably New York]: UNDP, n.d. [probably 1998]), pp. 52–62.
[26] Sarah Papineau Marshall, interview with CNM, 23 Nov. 2004.
[27] Trevor Gordon-Somers, interview with EM, 12 April 2005.
[28] Margaret Joan Anstee disagrees: 'Draper was not the first to introduce the concept of opportunity costs. We did this routinely in the early days', letter to CNM, 31 Jan. 2006.

had thought about alternative uses of all the resources that would be committed to the project – the grant money, the time of government officials who were executing the project, the patience and goodwill of the people it was supposed to benefit – and that Shima was convinced that *this* use would benefit people the most.[29]

The Committee did provide more cross-fertilization; the entrepreneurial barons certainly proved willing to copy successful projects initiated in other regions. Yet, Gordon-Somers notes, there was one significant downside:

> When you are in a multicultural, multilingual organization and you run up to the highest internal committee and you're a young person coming up to defend a particular project and you have to do it in English [the meetings' working language], it puts you at a disadvantage.

This is especially true when you may be given only fifteen minutes to make your case.[30]

Draper's avoidance of UNDP's other official languages (French and Spanish), Papineau Marshall says regretfully, made him subject to the anti-American stereotypes still shared by many UN staffers.[31] The same image of 'the ignorant American' initially kept some staffers from seeing the sense of the most important questions that Draper initially asked them. They were, to paraphrase, 'Doesn't UNDP *believe* in anything? And, if so, shouldn't we be *advocating* what we believe in?'

One response was, 'Of course [unspoken thought: you ignoramus] we believe in something. We believe in supporting the *different* development paths chosen by each of our programme countries. We are impartial. We do not discriminate. Our grants are not subject to conditionalities. That is why we do not advocate any one thing.'[32]

Still, UNDP's strong internal culture meant that its staff members – all those descendents of David Owen – also tended to believe in many other things. Most were values shared by Draper as well: the desirability of democracy, the priority of improving the lives of the least advantaged, and, increasingly, the importance of raising the status and

---

[29] Patrick Shima, interview with CNM, 3 Sept. 2004.
[30] Trevor Gordon-Somers, interview with EM, 12 April 2005.
[31] Sarah Papineau Marshall, interview with CNM, 23 Nov. 2004.
[32] These are all manifestations of one of what Patrick Shima calls 'UNDP's auto-genocidal beliefs', 'Core resources belong to the recipient.' See his 'Twenty-Five UNDP Auto-Genocidal Beliefs and Practices: UNDP Cultural Norms, Positive in Intent, Disastrous in Effect', unpublished paper, 1997.

participation levels of women in society. Draper's embrace of 'advocacy' allowed those values to be put forward and made part of the staff's official remit. At the same time Draper's advocacy themes, listed below, began to give UNDP the kind of focus and direction it lacked. It made it possible for Hamid Ghaffarzadeh to tell his wife, 'Just say, "He's working to save the environment; that's one of four or five things that his employer, UNDP, does".'

Eventually, in 1990, the Governing Council would direct the Programme to focus on one version of the themes. 'Human development' was described as the overriding priority. UNDP's particular focus would be on 'poverty eradication' (and, within that theme alone, 'grassroots participation'). The other focuses would be the environment, 'management development', 'technical cooperation among developing countries', the transfer of technology, and 'women'.[33] Traditionalists could describe these as an extension of the themes introduced as part of I. G. Patel's 'New Dimensions',[34] but, with the exception of the technology issues, they had much more to do with the agenda that Draper brought to UNDP in 1986: promoting the private sector, women, the non-governmental organizations (NGOs) of 'civil society', and the environment.

Arthur Holcombe provides representative examples of the early impact of Draper's agenda throughout Asia. In countries responding to the pressure of structural adjustment, the private sector initiative allowed UNDP to support governments that developed coherent policies for privatizing key industries without creating inordinate hardship for their workers and the poor. In Pakistan Hans von Sponeck coordinated a review of all UN agency experience 'accommodating WID (Women in Development) concerns' and 'followed up with assistance . . . intended to strengthen the appraisal, monitoring, and evaluation of national development programmes from the standpoint of women's interests'. And UNDP began actively supporting NGOs involved in the environment through one of Draper's innovative small grants programmes. Projects included 'tree planting through Mosque societies', urban environmental improvements in some of Asia's largest cities, and regional workshops on the advantages of greater collaboration between governments, NGOs, and donors.[35]

---

[33] UNDP, *Report of the Governing Council: Thirty-seventh Session (28 May–23 June 1990)*, 90/34.
[34] Richard Olver, interview with CNM, 3 June 2004.
[35] Holcombe, *Running on Two Tracks*, pp. 54–8.

Ul Haq

Long before approaching the Governing Council to approve the greater focus that he was bringing to the UNDP, Draper looked outside the UN 'to get some intellectual support for what we were doing'.[36] He turned to Mahbub ul Haq, who had deeply impressed Draper when they had been introduced by General Zia ul Haq, the Pakistan military ruler for whom the economist had worked in the 1980s. To top it off, Arthur Brown, 'the finest, most capable person' Draper had ever known, said that Mahbub ul Haq was the man for the job.[37]

The story of ul Haq's recruitment to UNDP actually begins thirty years earlier, in autumn 1958, when a young University of Manchester student of economics from East Pakistan travelled to Cambridge to hear what would become a celebrated series of lectures by an American economist, W. W. Rostow, on 'The Stages of Economic Growth'.[38] Her supervisor, the prolific Canadian trade economist, Harry Johnson, was sitting next to her; behind them was a Cambridge economist whom Johnson knew, Amartya Sen. Johnson introduced his two south Asian colleagues:

'Khadija', Sen said, 'you are from Pakistan? Would you like to have dinner with me?'

Johnson looked back, 'You are not going to win my best student.'

'OK, would you like to have tea?'

'Sen, don't bother my best student!'

Sen persisted, 'Do you know ul Haq?', apparently some young man who had been at Cambridge.

'No.'

'You are the kind of girl he is looking to marry, the rare combination of brains and beauty, that is what Mahbub is looking for.'

Khadija and Amartya did not have tea, but they became friends anyway. Two years later, Khadija, back in Pakistan, finally met Mahbub, her assigned supervisor at her new job with the Pakistan Institute of Development Economics. Within a short time they were married and a few weeks after that they ran into Sen, who said, 'Mahbub, I was sure you would get married to Bani [Khadija's pet name]!'

'But,' ul Haq asked, 'how did you know?'

Fast forward to the end of 1988: Khadija Haq is considering a job offer

---

[36] William A. Draper III, interview with CNM, 28 Sept. 2004.

[37] William A. Draper III, interview with CNM, 29 Nov. 2005.

[38] This account is from Khadija Haq, interview with CNM, 7 Dec. 2004.

from Jim Grant, UNICEF's legendary director in the days of 'adjustment with a human face'. To take it would mean moving to New York. Mahbub decided, 'I will follow you. You have a job. I will do something.'

Shortly after they arrived in New York, friends began telling ul Haq, 'Bill Draper has been looking for you. We don't know why, but he's been looking for you.'

Draper wanted ul Haq to join UNDP and he was willing to let the economist decide not only what his job would be, but also on the terms under which he would serve. Ul Haq wanted to write a report, a kind of 'state of the human condition', and he wanted complete editorial independence – complete intellectual freedom. That was just fine with Draper, although it was unprecedented for the UN.

Mark Malloch Brown muses over the 'several theories about why Bill allowed this report to be established' and finally settles on the conclusion that Draper was

> one of the wisest, cleverest, wryest of people who knew exactly what he was doing, and, behind a façade of pretending that he didn't, was delighted to launch such a subversive publication on the world.

Ul Haq's first *Human Development Report* (HDR) and all the reports that followed, Malloch Brown argues, created 'an extraordinary advocacy tool' whose strength derives from the way it 'benchmarks progress' with a set of clear indicators,[39] beginning with the Human Development Index, one of the major innovations in the 1990 report, *Concept and Measurement of Human Development.*[40]

With the publication of ul Haq's first report, Draper encouraged the weaving together of the various strands of advocacy: the goals that he had brought to UNDP, those that had long been part of the organization's culture, and the learning achieved by the Programme's relatively autonomous parts. Moreover, the very independence of the report – which ensured that every report would disturb at least some UN member governments – was part of a causal chain that led many NGOs and political parties in the developing world, which had long advocated those goals, to embrace the human development framework and suggest further ways in which it could be refined. This helped to turn UNDP from being an organization that increased the dependence of people on their governments to one that also helped to keep governments accountable to their citizens.

[39] Mark Malloch Brown, 'Welcome' address to the First Global Forum on Human Development, New York, 29 July 1999.
[40] UNDP, *Human Development Report 1990: Concept and Measurement of Human Development* (New York: Oxford University Press for UNDP, 1990).

Human development and the global reports

When I think about 'human development', one thing that regularly comes to mind is a speech by the US presidential candidate, Bobby Kennedy, shortly before his assassination in 1968:

> Too much and too long, we seem to have surrendered community excellence and community values in the mere accumulation of material things. Our gross national product . . . if we should judge America by that – counts air pollution and cigarette advertising, and ambulances to clear our highways of carnage. It counts special locks for our doors and the jails for those who break them. It counts the destruction of our redwoods and the loss of our natural wonder in chaotic sprawl. It counts napalm and the cost of a nuclear warhead, and armored cars for police who fight riots in our streets . . . Yet, the gross national product does not allow for the health of our children, the quality of their education, or the joy of their play. It does not include the beauty of our poetry or the strength of our marriages, the intelligence of our public debate or the integrity of our public officials. It measures neither our wit nor our courage; neither our wisdom nor our learning; neither our compassion nor our devotion to our country. It measures everything, in short, except that which makes life worthwhile.[41]

The connection is far from coincidental: both Kennedy and ul Haq were deeply influenced by Barbara Ward – the collaborator with Arthur Lewis and Sartaj Aziz on the Pearson Commission Report, friend of the Kennedy administration, and wife of Sir Robert Jackson. Khadija Haq says that as far as 'human development' goes, 'Ward was guru of all of us' – herself, her husband, Amartya Sen, and Richard Jolly, who took over the Human Development Report Office after ul Haq's return to Pakistan in 1995. Ul Haq's concept, his wife argues, can be traced back to Ward's warning to the developed countries in the economic boom years of the 1950s, 'Our physical capacity has gone beyond our ethical capacity'; there was more to being a human being, Ward argued, than producing wealth.[42] Amartya Sen remembers discussions with ul Haq in their undergraduate digs in 1953, talking about life expectancy and literacy and other measurable things beyond money that might provide a better indication of whether people have been given a chance for a complete human life.[43]

---

[41] Robert F. Kennedy, speech at the University of Kansas, Lawrence, Kan., 18 March 1968. A recording of the excerpt can be found at http://www.angelfire.com/pa4/kennedy4/gross.html (accessed 28 Nov. 2005).   [42] Khadija Haq, interview with CNM, 7 Dec. 2004.
[43] Amartya Sen, interview with CNM, 8 Dec. 2005.

Modestly, Khadija Haq does not mention that the first major publication on the concept of human development was a volume that she and UNDP's Üner Kirdar edited from papers at the 1986 North–South Roundtable in Islamabad.[44] Her husband's research throughout the 1980s further convinced him that, while income growth might (in the long run) be necessary for people to enjoy 'long, healthy, and creative lives',[45] economic growth did not by itself *ensure* such 'human' development. For example, in the late 1980s Saudi Arabia's per capita gross national product (GNP) was fifteen times that of Sri Lanka, where literacy – an indicator of the educational preconditions for a full, human life – was much higher.[46] The differences between this and similar pairs of countries had to do with the distribution of resources, especially the strength of social systems excluding whole categories of people (for example, women) from access to the human relationships and things that allow full humanity.

Nevertheless, ul Haq's emergent approach could not be reduced to adding attention to distribution to an overall concern with income growth. The concept of human development recognized that, as human beings, we value a multitude of things – many of which have no market price. Our sources of fulfilment are many, and the potential impediments to our fulfilment just as varied. The philosopher Martha Nussbaum (who, along with Amartya Sen, has developed the more complex philosophical underpinning of the human development approach) explains that the approach's central question

> is not, 'How satisfied is this woman?' [or] 'How much in the way of resources is she able to command?' It is, instead, 'What is she actually able to do and to be?' The core idea seems to be that of the human being as a dignified free being who shapes his or her own life, rather than being passively shaped or pushed around the world in the manner of a flock or herd animal.[47]

[44] Khadija Haq and Üner Kirdar, *Human Development: The Neglected Dimension* (Islamabad: North–South Roundtable, 1986). The book's role is identified by Asuncion Lera St Clair, 'The Role of Ideas in the United Nations Development Programme', in Morten Bøås and Desmond McNeill, eds., *Global Institutions: Framing the World?* (London: Routledge, 2003), p. 184.

[45] The first definition of 'human development', provided in the body of *Human Development Report 1990*, p. 9.

[46] Mahbub ul Haq, 'United Nations Role in Human Development', paper presented at the North–South Roundtable, Uppsala, 6 Sept. 1989.

[47] Martha Nussbaum, 'Capabilities and Social Justice', *International Studies Review*, 4, 2 (2002): 123.

The epigraph of this paper by Nussbaum reinforces the point. It comes from Karl Marx's *Economic and Philosophical Manuscripts*, the writings of a young radical democrat:

> In place of the *wealth* and *poverty* of political economy come the *rich human being* and *rich human need*. The rich human being is . . . the human being *in need of* a totality of human life-activities.[48]

Some critics of ul Haq (and of Sen, Nussbaum, Jolly, and others who embrace and build on his ideas) see an emphasis on the richness of human needs as a recipe for policy gridlock. With a vast array of impediments to human development what should be our first priority? Yet there are actually some indisputable material enemies of human development that demand attention. The first is absolute poverty. Ashis Nandy (the social psychologist whose ideas about the cultural impact of colonialism were introduced in chapter 4) notes that even though most societies have recognized some form of elective poverty – the poverty of Saint Francis or of Gandhi – as contributing to the deepest kind of humanity, there is no disagreement about the absolute misery of basic physiological needs not being met.[49] The plight of the one in five or one in six of us in that condition must be a priority.

In fact, the annual *Human Development Report* has helped to make it a priority. It has had an almost immediate impact on the allocation of development funds, especially donor funds, shifting them towards the priority concerns of poverty reduction and social welfare. In part, this was because the first reports coincided with the end of the cold war, a moment when a shift from military spending was possible.[50] It was also because the persuasiveness of the report's analysis convinced a self-reinforcing cascade of development agencies to change their priorities. UNICEF's Jim Grant, for example, used it to pressure the Development Assistance Committee (the coordinating body of the major bilateral donors) to begin reporting the percentage of their aid allocations going to human development priority areas.[51] In the mid-1990s

---

[48] Karl Marx, *Early Writings*, ed. and trans. T. B. Bottomore (New York: McGraw-Hill, 1964), pp. 164–5, quoted in Nussbaum, 'Capabilities and Social Justice'.

[49] Ashis Nandy, 'The Beautiful, Expanding Future of Poverty: Popular Economics as a Psychological Defense', *International Studies Review*, 4, 2 (2002): 107–21.

[50] Mahbub ul Haq, 'Policy Impact of the 1991 *Human Development Report* on the Donor Community', unpublished report, UNDP New York, 30 Aug. 1991.

[51] Letter from Jim Grant to Alexander R. Love, Chairman of the Development Assistance Committee, 6 Aug. 1991, included as an annex to ibid.

Draper's successor, Gus Speth, worked with two Secretaries-General and the heads of all the UN programmes and funds to make sustainable human development their shared goal, and to establish in-country and global mechanisms for supporting that goal.[52] At the bottom of the cascade, at the 1998 memorial service for ul Haq, stood the World Bank's president, James Wolfensohn. Sarah Papineau Marshall recalls his words:

> If Mahbub is flying around up there around my head, if he is, he'll be laughing, because I have one thing to say to him, 'Mahbub – you were right!'[53]

To some extent, Wolfensohn's deeds matched his words. While conducting research for this book I met more people from the World Bank with the title 'Human Development Officer' than I did men and women charged with that portfolio in UNDP offices, and, in late 2005, there were almost as many Internet pages about 'human development' on the World Bank site as there are on UNDP's.[54]

Yet the two organizations together account for less than 3 per cent of the 2,000,000 pages that mention at least one *Human Development Report* – ten times the number of Internet references to the 'Washington Consensus'. And if you try to find all the references to the concept alone,[55] you get about as many pages as when you search for the Beatles – *Variety* magazine's 'icons of the century'.[56] Ul Haq's concept has indeed become a central feature of the global intellectual and policy landscape.

The global HDRs have been produced every year since 1990. The Programme's commitment began modestly; Ul Haq wrote out the first HDR by hand at a table in a 'little room at the UNDP where the supply stuff was kept'. His immediate collaborators were his wife (unofficially), a secretary, and Inge Kaul – a UNDP veteran with advanced degrees in sociology and economics who, initially, had just stopped by and volunteered.[57] In addition, Kaul says, there was a small group of notable 'core

---

[52] See chapter 10, below.
[53] Sarah Papineau Marshall, interview with CNM, 23 Nov. 2004.
[54] The Google search engine found 82,000 as compared with 108,000 on 29 Nov. 2005. The remaining comparisons were also made using Google and at the same time.
[55] Searching for 'human development' but eliminating pages that refer to 'embryology' and 'psychology'.
[56] 'Icons of the Century', *Variety*, October 2005, http://www.variety.com/index. asp?layout=variety100&content=jump2&jump=iconIndex (accessed 1 Dec. 2005).
[57] Khadija Haq, interview with CNM, 7 Dec. 2004.

consultants' – Amartya Sen, Paul Streeten, Frances Stewart, Gus Ranis, and Meghnad Desai.[58]

The leadership of the HDR Office changed little over the next fifteen years (Sakiko Fukuda-Parr succeeded Inge Kaul in 1995, working first with ul Haq and then with Richard Jolly when he replaced ul Haq in 1996; after Jolly left in 2000, and was not replaced, Fukuda-Parr remained for another five years), but the work behind the global reports became increasingly elaborate. In the 2005 report, the first under Kevin Watkins (the former policy director at the global development NGO, Oxfam), he acknowledges no fewer than 250 people with substantive involvement.[59]

One reason for the ever-expanding network at the core of the global HDRs is that most reports focus on one or another new dimension, a new side, of the wealth of relationships and current policy choices that determine the degree to which every human being can enjoy a full life – for example, income inequality, poor governance, restrictive gender relations, and over- and under-consumption. This series of policy applications, this refraction of the core concept into an entire spectrum of relevant policy realms, has required the report's authors constantly to expand the range of experts involved in their production. Each of the new dimensions explored have, in turn, helped to maintain the vitality of the larger human development research programme and of the concept itself. Sen summarizes ul Haq's justification for this methodology:

> He wanted to build on agreement (what Cass Sunstein, the Chicago legal theorist, calls 'an incompletely theorized agreement'). Such agreements may emerge pragmatically, on quite diverse grounds, after a general recognition that many things are important. Mahbub . . . told the world: 'Here we have a broad framework; you want something to be included in the list . . . tell us *what*, and explain *why*. We *will* listen.'[60]

Three of the reports that opened up especially significant debates were those in 1992, in 1995 (*Gender and Human Development*), and in 2004 (*Cultural Liberty in Today's Diverse World*).

The 1992 HDR included a chapter on political freedom that provided some preliminary measures and argued that freedom and human

[58] Inge Kaul, 'Choices that Shaped the Human Development Reports', in Sakiko Fukuda-Parr and A. K. Shiva Kumar, eds., *Readings in Human Development*, 2nd edn (New Delhi: Oxford University Press, 2003), p. 85.

[59] This does not include those acknowledged only for their editorial assistance, *Human Development Report 2005 – Aid, Trade, and Security in an Unequal World* (New York: UNDP, 2005), pp. vii–ix.   [60] Sen, 'A Decade of Human Development', 22.

development moved in tandem. This was particularly controversial with those UN member states that saw its arguments about human rights, democratization, and the importance of independent NGOs as raising questions about internal governance that should be outside the purview of international organizations. Sally Timpson recalls Draper having insisted that ul Haq include a 'Human Freedom Index' after 'the US did not appear at the top' in the first HDR.[61] Amartya Sen believes that controversy would have been much more muted if the question of measuring political freedom had been better thought through. 'The last thing I want', he says, 'is a single index for "democracy".' His dissatisfaction with the original index was the basis for 'The one big fight with Mahbub' in their lives.[62]

Nevertheless, the 1992 chapter began a more careful consideration of political freedom by UNDP that has continued ever since.

This work could be seen as acknowledging the validity of the criticism of the UN development system first raised in the context of the UN Relief and Rehabilitation Administration (UNRRA): a system of practical solidarity among states would make more sense in a democratic world, one where recipient states were held accountable to their people. That criticism (which had often been made by donor country politicians who were sceptical of the UN) mattered a great deal to UN Secretary-General Boutros Boutros-Ghali, who saw the UN's peace and development mandates as inseparable. The 1993 global HDR helped to convince him that democracy was a prerequisite for both, an argument he made in his article, 'Democracy: A Newly Recognized Imperative', in early 1995. In his last act as Secretary-General, he attempted to make the promotion of democratic governance a co-equal UN goal by publishing his *Agenda for Democracy*, which followed his earlier *Agenda for Peace* and *Agenda for Development*.[63]

The 1995 HDR carefully documented that women contributed more than half of the global economic output, but received only a quarter of the rewards. At the same time, even though the gaps between women and men on a host of measures – literacy, school enrolment, and even

---

[61] Sarah Timpson, letter to CNM, 20 Jan. 2006.

[62] Amartya Sen, interview with CNM, 8 Dec. 2005.

[63] Boutros Boutros-Ghali, 'Democracy: A Newly Recognized Imperative', *Global Governance*, 1, 1 (1995): 3–11. I was one of the co-editors of this new journal and worked with the Secretary-General and his staff on the various drafts of the article. Boutros-Ghali discusses his work in his *Unvanquished: A US–UN Saga* (New York: Random House, 1999), pp. 318–20, 334–5.

income – were narrowing, most women's access to positions of power – in government and in the private sector – remained blocked. (This finding is one reason why many feminists question the Millennium Development Goals – which focus on that first set of indicators – and say that they represent an insufficient and out-of-date understanding of the problem.) The 1995 report played a major role in the debates at the Beijing World Conference on Women and led to the regular preparation of national estimates of the previously unmeasured economic contributions of women as well as to tools for assessing the impact of macroeconomic policies on women.[64]

The 2004 global report, the last during Sakiko Fukuda-Parr's long tenure, focused on issues as controversial as the promotion of substantive democracy. In much of the world people's freedoms are severely restricted by governments that make it impossible for some citizens to be educated in their own language, practise their own religion, or otherwise choose their own identity. The problems that come with the denial of cultural freedom are relatively easy to identify, even if many governments would prefer that specific, concrete examples be suppressed (for example, the vilification of the Roma, the suppression of the Kurds, the denial of native rights throughout the Americas). Perfect solutions are much more difficult to find, but the report aimed, at least, to expand the range of policy options. For example, many African governments have dealt with the linguistic fractionalization of their countries by continuing to use the language of the former colonizer. The report points to a possible alternative: standardizing the orthography and vocabulary of the fifteen 'core languages' spoken in 85 per cent of African households and using them.[65]

Choosing among such imperfect solutions is far from easy. Amartya Sen emphasizes that, within the larger logic underlying the human development approach (the theory of human capabilities that he, Nussbaum, and others have elaborated), substantively democratic procedures provide the only reasonable means to do so. Democracy also provides a logically consistent solution to the potential for policy gridlock created by the realistic recognition by the human development approach of the multiplicity of human ends. In the words of the Kenyan popularization of Sen's ideas introduced in chapter 1, if we want to identify the most salient impediments to

---

[64] Mahbub ul Haq, *Reflections on Human Development* (New York: Oxford University Press, 1995), pp. 208–9; and see Caren Grown, Diane Elson, and Nilufer Cagatay, eds., 'Growth, Trade, Finance, and Gender Inequality', special issue, *World Development*, 28, 7 (July 2000).

[65] UNDP, *Human Development Report 2004: Cultural Liberty in Today's World* (New York: UNDP, 2004), pp. 62–3.

human development we need 'just ask', but we have to ask 'everybody'. In the end, 'Free political participation and basic education are not only conducive to development, it can't happen without them',[66] which is why, in 1995, Boutros Boutros-Ghali called democracy an 'imperative'.[67]

Regional, national, and local reports

The same logic also means that some office at UNDP headquarters in New York could never be the final word on what should be 'included in the list' of human development concerns. This is why UNDP has supported regional, national, and local reports focused on the impediments to human development that are most salient to people in each country or locality. Normally, these reports are completed by teams approved by the national government yet ensured the same independence granted to ul Haq and his successors. More than 500 separate reports have been published over the years; they cover the vast majority of developing nations and former Leninist countries. The New York office provides a network of training workshops and the regional bureaux often provide financial and logistical support, but the reports are designed and executed by networks of local scholars, often among the most distinguished social scientists in that part of the world.

Ella Libanova, the deputy director of Ukraine's National Institute of Demography, explains some of the most basic advantages of the many national reports: the main indicators used in the global reports are very rough measures of the complex concept of human development, and national teams often can do better. The indicator that is most often reported in the media, the original Human Development Index (HDI) began as a simple aggregate of GNP per capita, adult literacy, and life expectancy, indices of access to economic choices, knowledge, and longevity for which there is data from most countries.[68] Ukraine has a long history of collecting quite sophisticated data on production, housing, health care, and many other aspects of human life. It also has very sophisticated and creative statisticians ('Probably more than we need!') capable of designing and analyzing complex surveys in order to

---

[66] Anantha Kumar Duraiappah, Flavio Comim, Davinder Lamba, and Terry Hirst, *There is a Better Way! An Introduction to the* Development as Freedom *Approach* (Nairobi: International Institute for Sustainable Development and the Mazingira Institute, 2003), pp. 4–5.   [67] Boutros-Ghali, 'Democracy'.

[68] Mahbub ul Haq, 'The Birth of the Human Development Index', in Fukuda-Parr and Kumar, *Readings in Human Development*, p. 127.

develop more sophisticated measures of each of these dimensions of human development.[69] Moreover, in Ukraine, and in most other countries, national HDR teams have gone beyond the HDI and the other innovative measures introduced in the global reports to design measures that are particularly relevant to their own countries.

In Brazil, the additional variables added to national reports combine with the reports' much finer detail (state-to-state comparisons in the national report down to even neighbourhood-to-neighbourhood comparisons in some reports done for individual cities) to create an indispensable tool for policy makers. In the late 1990s the reports shaped the budget allocations of poverty programmes both at the national level and within major cities such as Rio de Janeiro.[70]

In other parts of Latin America the impacts of the national reports have been different. Chapter 8 mentions the version of the recent Argentine HDR that the authors wrote for secondary schools, but neglects to explain that the national reports – and the separate reports on the overwhelmingly dominant Province of Buenos Aires – have helped to shape the public debate about the fairest way to respond to the belt tightening needed after the most recent financial crisis.[71] In Chile the better economic conditions enjoyed by Ricardo Lagos's government have allowed a different focus. Culture was the topic of the 2002 report, which briefly became a national bestseller and played a significant role in the legislative debate over settling 'the cultural deficit that accumulated during the military régime'.[72]

A different history has dictated a different focus in eastern Europe and the former Soviet Union. Bulgaria's 2001 report focused on substantive democratization, on 'the need for a transition from "individuals" to "citizens"'. The report led to constitutional and institutional changes – the introduction of proportional representation, legislation to establish a national Ombudsman (concerned primarily with issues of human rights), and significant political decentralization.[73] In Armenia the 2000

---

[69] Ella Libanova, interview with CNM, 10 March 2003.

[70] Elena Martínez, interview with CNM, 3 June 2004. The key study was *Human Development Report for Brazil 1996*, http://www.undp.org.br/HDR/Hdr96/rdhbin.htm (accessed 30 Nov. 2005).   [71] Carlos Felipe Martínez, interview with CNM, 3 Aug. 2004.

[72] Chilean Government, 'A Cultural Explosion' http://www.chileangovernment.cl/index.php?option=displaypage&Itemid=56&op=page&SubMenu= (accessed 24 Nov. 2005). UNDP Evaluation Office, 'NHDRs as Instruments of Change: Good Practices in Policy Impacts', 15 Dec. 2004, pp. 3–4.

[73] UNDP Evaluation Office, 'NHDRs as Instruments of Change', p. 5; Boriana Katzarska, interview with CNM, 4 May 2005.

HDR focused on human rights policies and is used to introduce the concepts in public secondary schools throughout the country. In Russia the impact has been less universal, but may eventually prove deeper: four universities have begun MBA (Master of Business Administration) programmes in human development.[74]

In Africa, the HIV/AIDS crisis has been a major focus of the national HDRs. In socially conservative Botswana, one of the countries most seriously affected, the national reports 'catalysed the Government to introduce a publicly funded programme of universal access to anti-retroviral therapy' and a student version of the report, in both English and Setswana, has been published in numbers that should allow it to reach every secondary school student in the country. Mozambique's 2000 report, *Education and Human Development*, had a similar impact in a different cultural context: a national curriculum on HIV/AIDS for primary school pupils.[75]

Throughout Asia national HDRs often focus on the structure of national development policy as a whole. Vietnam's 2001–10 development plan includes 'a substantial improvement in Vietnam's Human Development Index'. The government distributed the 2001 report, *Doi Moi Process and Human Development*, to all members of the National Assembly and to the Plenum of the Communist Party's Central Committee, where it was the basis for the main development strategy discussion.[76] In Buddhist Bhutan, the first national HDR introduced a very different indicator of human development, *Gross National Happiness*. The report became the basis for Bhutan's long-term development strategy as well as a draft constitution that will transform the small Himalayan country from a paternalistic, closed monarchy into a relatively open democracy, albeit one that provides no guarantees of linguistic or religious rights to its large Nepalese, Hindu minority.[77]

Assuring equal opportunity, opening a closed society, and creating substantive democracy have been the themes of the HDRs that have recently received the most attention, globally, the successive volumes of the annual *Arab Human Development Report*, first published in 2002. Rima Khalaf Hunaidi, the Jordanian economist and former planning minister whom Mark Malloch Brown brought in to run the Arab Bureau,

---

[74] UNDP Evaluation Office, 'NHDRs as Instruments of Change', p. 9.
[75] Ibid., pp. 2, 4, 9.   [76] Ibid., p. 9.
[77] Brent Hurd, 'Bhutan Experiments in Democracy', *ASEAN News Network*, 29 April 2005, http://www.aseannewsnetwork.com/2005/04/bhutan-experiments-in-democracy.html (accessed 24 Nov. 2005).

was, in Fukuda-Parr's words, 'the visionary and intellectual' behind the report, the person who developed its 'conceptual framework and political message'.[78]

In its 'Person of the Year' issue, *Time* magazine called the first report, 'perhaps the most important volume published in 2002'.[79] The article highlighted one key passage from this independent assessment by the broad group of leading Arab intellectuals brought together by Hunaidi:

> The wave of democracy that transformed governance in most of Latin America and East Asia in the 1980s and Eastern Europe and much of Central Asia in the late 1980s and early 1990s has barely reached the Arab states . . . More than half of Arab women are still illiterate. Only 0.6% of the population uses the Internet. The quality of public institutions is low. One out of every five people lives on less than $2 per day. Poor or unavailable health care or opportunities for a quality education, a degraded habitat: all are widely prevalent in Arab countries.[80]

The 2004 report emphasized that the proximate causes of the region's poor record were the policy decisions of repressive Arab governments. Moreover,

> the failure of democracy . . . is not cultural in origin. It lies at the convergence of political, economic, and social structures that have suppressed or eliminated organized social and political actors capable of turning the crisis of authoritarian and totalitarian régimes to their advantage.[81]

The sources of that failure, argues the lead author of the reports, Egyptian sociologist Nader Fergany, are external as well as internal. 'I do not think that the current US administration wants democracy in the region. I think they are used to dealing with oppressive governments',[82] is his unsubtle, off-the-cuff summary of the problem that the report itself deals with in a much more nuanced way. It outlines conditions under which both external and internal powers might be convinced to act on their higher, often truly democratic, aspirations rather than acting

---

[78] Sakiko Fukuda-Parr, letter to CNM, 2 Jan. 2006.

[79] Michael Elliot, 'The Trouble with Saving the World', *Time*, 160, 27 (30 Dec. 2002): 108–12.

[80] Quoted in this way in the *Time* article. However, the separate sentences are in fact dispersed throughout the 'Overview' section of UNDP, *The Arab Human Development Report for 2002: Creating Opportunities for Future Generations* (New York: UNDP, 2002), pp. 1–11.

[81] *The Arab Human Development Report 2004: Towards Freedom in the Arab World* (New York: UNDP, 2005), p. 11.

[82] Speaking at a public conference in Alexandria; reported in Fatemah Farag, 'Facing Up to Failed Development', *Al-Ahram Weekly*, 687 (22–28 April 2004) (http://weekly.ahram.org.eg/2004/687/eg6.htm, accessed 24 Nov. 2005).

habitually or reactively and, as a consequence, reinforcing the major sources of 'unfreedom'.

Each of the Arab HDRs has been unpopular with many people in every Arab capital, even some who work in UNDP country offices with their necessarily close relations with the national government. When I asked one seasoned staffer in Cairo to speculate about why the people who helped so much with my schedule there did not arrange for me to meet with Fergany, I got an earful about scholars involved with the reports being old, disgruntled 'Sorbonne Marxists trying to relive Paris in 1968'.

'That's OK', I said, 'I had dinner with him last night.'

Fergany had studied in the 1970s with many of the people who then taught me a few years later, but Ricardo Lagos was about as French and Marxist as the faculty in North Carolina got in those years. (Well, he was a man of the left – although adamantly not a Marxist – and he did turn to France for help in designing the Ministry of Culture that grew from the 2002 Chilean HDR.)

After remembering common acquaintances, Fergany helped me to understand why he and the other Arab HDR authors were willing to endure the controversy over each report. It was late April 2005 and the 2004 report, finished more than six months earlier, had just been published. Since September the Arab and international media had been speculating that the United States and some important Arab governments had been trying to suppress the report. (The United States because the 2004 HDR pointed to the occupations of Iraq and Palestine as having major adverse effects on human development.) Yes, Fergany said, he was sure that there had been pressure, including threats to withdraw contributions to UNDP, but he knew of no documents or smoking gun.

The immediate source of the delays had been the many suggestions from the reports' Readers Group and Advisory Board.[83] Mark Suzman, Malloch Brown's right-hand man (Suzman, Malloch Brown says, combines 'the best qualities of Friedrich Engels and Sancho Panza'[84]) and a superb writer, later explained that many involved common problems of translation, phrases in English that sounded more 'heated' than in the original Arabic.[85] Fergany never doubted that the book would be

---

[83] Nader Fergany, interview with CNM, 26 April 2005.
[84] Mark Malloch Brown, *Mark Malloch Brown at the United Nations Development Programme: Statements, Speeches, and Commentary: 1999–2005* (New York: UNDP, 2005), p. xxii.
[85] Mark Suzman, interview with CNM, 21 Oct. 2005.

published. Even if the Administrator abrogated the agreement on independence that went back to Draper and ul Haq, 'We'd find another publisher. Every year, I've always had "the other book" ready.'

'So, what difference does the UNDP sponsorship make?'

It is not just the funding. UNDP shares the burden with regional funders, and Fergany and his colleagues would be successful with many global foundations. For the group producing the Arab HDR, it is not the training offered by the HDR Office; the Arab social scientists are as sophisticated as any of the consultants New York could provide. It is the 'UN stamp'. If the first report had appeared with just the names of the distinguished authors and the mark of a respectable academic publisher on the cover, it would have been read 'only by people like you' – academics, regional specialists, and maybe a few others who liked some of the earlier work done by one or another of the authors. In contrast, as it is, even though the reports are decidedly *not* reflections of 'official' UN policy, the UN's sponsorship, the endorsements by UN officials, the fact that people can most easily access the HDRs by going to a UN website, give the ideas contained in the reports greater authority, and greater impact, than they otherwise would have.[86]

The same considerations affect all of the hundreds of other groups of scholars and policy analysts responsible for the growing library of HDRs.

In India, where a panoply of HDRs – global, South Asian, national, and local – play an important role in public debate, the sources of power of the HDRs are particularly clear. Dr Sanjaya Baru, the media advisor to Prime Minister Manmohan Singh, points out that, since the beginning, the annual HDRs have made a huge media splash at least once a year, when they are first published. That is the power of the UN stamp. Yet the HDRs have also had more continuous and enduring impact due to the quality and power of the analysis, the separate HDR brand. 'Unlike other UN reports, *Human Development Reports* are read by students and the academic community' and through them the ideas filter into the political system at large, so that now (in 2004) improving human development 'has come to be accepted across parties as a given'.[87]

Sarah Burd-Sharps, who runs the New York office supporting national human development reports, worries that India's Planning Commission has taken over the process and mandated state-level reports, potentially undermining the independence that has helped make the reports so

[86] Nader Fergany, interview with CNM, 26 April 2005.
[87] Sanjaya Baru, interview with CNM, 11 Dec. 2004.

9.2 Sonia Gandhi and the winners of the 2000 ul Haq Memorial School Debate Competition, that each year has students throughout India address a different aspect of human development

authoritative.[88] K. C. Pant, the Commission's deputy chairman and the man who promoted the state reports, sees it as less problematic because, even if initiated by the government in New Delhi, the task of writing the state reports 'was given to prestigious institutions outside the government because they are independent'. Pant sees no sign that the state reports have played a role in recent elections, even if the issues they address have been relevant; 'In qualitative terms, all these issues are already there in the political debate.' The state HDRs only added the 'quantitative aspect'.[89]

Former Prime Minister I. K. Gujral, one of India's most respected voices on foreign affairs, a man whose experience with UNDP goes back more than thirty years, paints a more complex picture:

> The NGO movement in India has grown fast . . . Consciousness is growing very fast . . . People do judge political parties on their performance . . . In the most backward states, they issue an HDR. One by one, every state is thinking it's important . . . Whenever a [head of government] appears before parliament, he's always confronted with it – 'how many points you've slipped', and 'what will you do about it'.

[88] Sarah Burd-Sharps, interview with CNM, 4 June 2004.
[89] K. C. Pant, interview with CNM, 13 Dec. 2004.

Elections, Gujral says, 'are decided by local situations'. (Indian elections, he says, 'are different from the West in that way', although, as Brad Morse's friend Tip O'Neill used to say, 'All politics is local politics.') In the last election the 'people in power thought they'd done everything, that the sun was bright . . . but the people said, "No, it wasn't".'[90]

Sanjaya Baru, the spokesman for the unexpected winner in the 2004 national elections, emphasizes that, despite government rhetoric,

> In the 1990s . . . we were not investing in human development. This election and [the new] government's political platform was entirely that – we need to combine policies for growth with policies for equity and social justice . . . I think this has become widely accepted.[91]

Continuing impact and UNDP's ambiguous edge

Hafiz Pasha, the distinguished Pakistani economist brought in by Malloch Brown to direct the Asia bureau, expects that the human development records of governments will continue to be an important standard of measure for citizens, but he worries that, since the days of his creative compatriot, UNDP has nurtured no further major conceptual breakthroughs. As far as new research in development economics goes, the World Bank, with its much larger budget, has regained its pre-eminence.[92] Inge Kaul (who directed UNDP's Office of Development Studies), Ruben Mendez, and Kaul's collaborators have done innovative work on 'global public goods' and 'international public finance',[93] but their audience has been primarily academic; their concepts have not come to pervade public debate.

Perhaps the most disappointing aspect of the human development research programme – and an area in which UNDP could have a major intellectual impact in the future – involves applications of the concept to wealthy nations. The 2000 report, *Poverty in Plenty: A Human Development Report for the UK*, was both the first 'national HDR to focus on an industrialised country' and the first produced solely by an NGO, without UNDP

[90] I. K. Gujral, interview with CNM, 11 Dec. 2004.
[91] Sanjaya Baru, interview with CNM, 11 Dec. 2004.
[92] Hafiz A. Pasha, interview with CNM, 7 Oct. 2004.
[93] Inge Kaul, Isabelle Grunbeg, and Marc A. Stern, eds., *Global Public Goods: International Cooperation in the 21st Century* (New York: Oxford University Press, 1999); Ruben P. Mendez, *International Public Finance: A New Perspective on Global Relations* (New York: Oxford University Press, 1992); Inge Kaul and Pedro Conceição, eds., *The New Public Finance* (New York: Oxford University Press, 2006).

sponsorship. Perhaps because it did not have the UN stamp, it did not receive the widespread attention granted to other national HDRs (or, for example, to IMF reports on the British economy) even though it was well received by scholars and some in the NGO community.[94]

Potentially more significant is the *Arctic Human Development Report*, commissioned while Iceland held the rotating chair of the international organization linking the eight Arctic states.[95] The report covers only the northern parts of five wealthy Arctic countries (Canada, Finland, Norway, Sweden, and the United States), but its conceptualization and organization have implications for the way in which influential HDRs can be produced in the wealthy countries. Like UNDP HDRs, the report was produced by some of the leading scholars of the region – whose own prestige added to that of its intergovernmental sponsor.[96] It also included fundamental conceptual innovations, including the idea of 'fate control', a version of 'control over one's own destiny', a virtue usually attributed to substantive democracies. However, in the context of the sparsely populated Arctic, the concept has special meaning for native peoples who have long dominated the region, but who are now small minorities in much more populous nations.

It may be that, as time goes on, the regional and local reports will provide the greatest opportunities both for conceptual breakthroughs and real impact. Nader Fergany, for example, argues that, recently, the Arab HDR has had more global impact than the global reports themselves.[97] Yet Burd-Sharps worries that agenda setting in New York may weaken the ability of local HDR teams to respond appropriately and creatively to local conditions. All the country offices are under great pressure to produce periodic reports on the achievement of the Millennium Development Goals (MDGs), causing talent and funds to be diverted away from the HDRs. Moreover, while the standards of measurement provided by the MDGs may be more complex than the original HDI (the eight MDGs involve at least eleven indicators rather than three), they still provide only a partial account of the diverse dimensions of human development and they ignore the foundations of human agency and freedom, the dimensions that distinguish the human development approach from other approaches.

---

[94] Jane Seymour, ed., *Poverty in Plenty: A Human Development Report for the UK* (London: Earthscan Publications, 2000).

[95] *Arctic Human Development Report 2004* (Akureyri, Iceland: Stefansson Arctic Institute, 2004). [96] Oran Young, interview with CNM, 6 Sept. 2005.

[97] Nader Fergany, interview with CNM, 26 April 2005.

Conceivably, the more complex goals and standards of measurement provided by the range of HDRs could at least guide UNDP's own strategies, especially within countries, as is the case in India. However, this is only true in countries where the paradigm has been so widely embraced.

In fact, much of the significance of the reports comes from the way in which they push governments to go beyond what they are willing to do at the moment. That is why ul Haq demanded independence, and that is why Draper recognized that the reports could not serve as strict guides for UNDP programming. After the publication of the first report, the Malaysians, who disliked ul Haq's conclusions and had tried unsuccessfully to suppress the report, walked out of the Governing Council. 'So what?' Draper responded.[98] Yet, of course, if a clear majority of the Council opposed any of the advocacy recommendations of the reports, UNDP would be prevented from acting on them, making it just as useful to the Administrator as it is to HDRs' authors to say that 'The analysis and policy recommendations of this Report do not necessarily reflect the views of the United Nations Development Programme.'

Yet, paradoxically, Draper's 'second track', that of 'advocacy' – the backbone he gave to UNDP – survives due to the Governing Council's 1990 decision that human development was the overriding priority and objective of all UNDP assistance.[99] This has both justified the continuing support of all the 'unofficial' reports that clarify the meaning of the otherwise ambiguous concept and have served as cover for successive Administrators, Regional Directors, and Res Reps who have used such clarifications as action guides and as welcome prods to NGOs and political parties who embrace the goals that UNDP advocates more than do its government partners.

The 'UNDP' that has those more controversial advocacy goals, the organization that is 'ahead of' and that nudges forward governments, is not the one you will find by picking up an official phone directory and looking at the names and job titles of most of the people with desks in the New York headquarters or the country offices. It is, instead, the decentralized complex of relatively autonomous people and organizations that make up the larger, looser, UNDP. It includes the 10,000 or more people working on this year's *Human Development Reports*, from ul Haq's successor all the way down to the research assistants of the lecturer writing a

[98] Sarah Papineau Marshall, interview with CNM, 23 Nov. 2004.
[99] UNDP, *Report of the Governing Council: Thirty-Seventh Session (28 May–23 June 1990),* 90/34.

background paper that will be summarized in a single box in a single national HDR.

One of the things that I found the most amusing (and yet most telling) as I studied UNDP was just how fuzzy its boundaries are. I have at least thirty business cards that say 'UNDP' given to me by people described as decidedly '*not* part of UNDP' by officials in the national or New York headquarters. Some cards are from NGO leaders who have managed UNDP projects for five or more years. Others – the largest part of those that I collected – come from those long involved in HDRs that UNDP has sponsored and funded. Frequently I received two cards – one emphasizing a UNDP affiliation, the other identifying a university, an NGO, or a consulting company – one emphasizing the UN stamp, the other demonstrating the bona fides of independence. (I, too, carried both kinds of card, and for the same reason.) Paradoxically, to be the kind of organization with backbone that Bill Draper wanted to create – and yet to retain the trust of the developing world and the attention of the media that gave it much of its power – UNDP has *had* to present such a soft and fuzzy exterior.

Draper left UNDP in July 1993, after a term three years shorter than Brad Morse's and only half as long as Hoffman's UN tenure. Yet the impact of the Draper years on UNDP's future was profound; it ensured that the Programme would have a future.

Sadly, Draper's last years at UNDP, and those immediately afterwards, were marked by tragedies involving those on whom he had come to rely. In March 1993 the dear friend of both Draper and his wife, Arthur Brown, died after a painful struggle with cancer. Shortly afterwards Brown's wife was killed by someone attempting to rob their Kingston home. Then one of the men on whom Draper had most come to rely after Brown's retirement left UNDP under a cloud, a charge of sexual harassment: 'a clear sign of the "better atmosphere" for women within UNDP', said some. 'In this instance, an unfair frame-up that left a huge void', say others. Earlier, another key person, Pierre-Claver Damiba, in his last months with the UNDP began to act erratically, 'quirky and nervous' (in Draper's words), as if temporarily possessed by an unpredictable demon. Draper was not upset when the director of the Africa Bureau left to mount his unsuccessful bid for the Burkina presidency.

Out of all these tragedies, only the last, for Draper, had any redeeming feature. The evidence suggests that Damiba eventually recovered and his replacement was, Draper believes, one of the best appointments he ever made: Ellen Johnson-Sirleaf, a Liberian economist, banker, and former finance minister, the first woman in such a high position within UNDP. Johnson-Sirleaf maintained UNDP programmes to increase the capacity of African states to deal with structural adjustment on their own terms, experimented with decentralization, and put in place the foundational programmes that would allow a human-development-oriented UNDP to work effectively in the continent where human development was the most challenged. Draper was pleased, but far from surprised[100] when in November 2005 Johnson-Sirleaf was elected president of Liberia, the first woman elected to head any African government.

Elena Martínez, one of the women to follow Johnson-Sirleaf as a regional director, fears that near the end of his term Draper became frustrated even in carrying out those parts of the job he cared about most. Balancing the different demands of the donors was increasingly difficult; at the end of the Reagan era, 'Some Nordic countries didn't want to see Draper in their capitals.' Yet 'despite Draper's friendship with Bush [senior]', even his relationship with Washington had become a little uneasy. 'There was a guy in the State Department named John Bolton', remembers Martínez, 'who was in charge of international organizations and he was from the *right* right.'[101] He was forceful and controversial, disliked by some in the US press and some in Congress, but the hero of others. It proved controversial for UNDP to work with various US conservative groups that Bolton argued should become new UNDP partners; it proved equally controversial to ignore his suggestions.[102]

In many ways, Draper was lucky to leave UNDP when he did, shortly after the end of the cold war. It was a time when most UN members admired his conviction that the Programme should stand for something, and only a few tried to use UNDP to pay back cronies or score points by attacking any friend of Ronald Reagan or George H. W. Bush who filled a high UN post – a time when Draper had to deal more with other mammals than with snakes.

There is one widely told story about the respect that Draper enjoyed for his convictions in those years.[103] It was spring 1990, and Draper was a guest at dinner at the Res Rep's house in Havana, along with Fidel Castro.

---

[100] William A. Draper III, interview with CNM, 29 Nov. 2005.
[101] Elena Martínez, interview with CNM, 3 June 2004.
[102] Ian Williams, "Why the Right Loves the UN," *The Nation*, 13 April 1992, http://www.globalpolicy.org/reform/williams.htm (accessed 22 March 2006), written by one of Bolton's detractors, gives a sense of the new level of controversy that UNDP faced.
[103] It was told most vividly by Draper himself, interview with CNM, 29 Sept. 2004

'Immediately, we hit it off', Draper says, even though all the old UNDP hands were cringing at Draper's undiplomatic comments about anti-government demonstrations in the streets of Moscow and Cuba's human rights record.

But Castro gave as good as he got, lambasting Draper for US sanctions and betting him that President Daniel Ortega, the leader of the left-wing FSLN (the Sandinistas) that had been the target of the United States' secret and ultimately unsuccessful war in Nicaragua, would handily win the upcoming Nicaraguan elections.

That, in fact, was what the polls predicted, but Draper would have none of it: 'I'll take Chamorro [the conservative candidate, backed by Reagan], and I'll bet you twenty bucks.' Draper pulled out a twenty. Castro took two ten-peso notes from an assistant, waited to see if Draper would complain about the difference in market value, and, when he didn't, whipped out a pen and signed both notes, and smiled.

'Of course, they went up in value like this', Draper points to the sky. 'So he gives them to me and I give him the twenty (which I signed, which didn't change the value one bit!).'

Draper won the bet. Afterwards, when Cuban delegates came to visit Draper in New York – often looking for help for an economy wracked by its forced adjustment to the end of the Soviet era – 'They would pre-empt me, saying, "Castro knows he owes you twenty bucks".' Draper, for his part, pledged the Programme to help Cuba achieve Castro's development goals, at least in those ways that UNDP could within its, now more coherent, mandate.

Working for 'a holy man' after the cold war

So what kind of mammal did UNDP become?

Shortly after Ukraine's Orange Revolution, Klavdia Maksimenko, one of the people in the Kiev office working late each night to backstop the new government, pulls up a photograph on her computer screen. It is of a drawing made by a group of young UNDP officers from around the world gathered together at a management retreat. They had been asked to imagine UNDP as an animal. The Programme was long-lived, gregarious, and compassionate; 'It had to be an elephant.' The glasses are 'because it is wise'. Cesar Silang-Cruz from the Bureau of Crisis Prevention and Recovery, who held the pen, gave it the face of Gandhi, or maybe that of the favourite of Hindu deities, Ganesh, 'the remover of obstacles'. Of course, the elephant is also doing the impossible. It is flying, or at least attempting to.

I showed the drawing to a friend, a professor of international environmental policy, who instantly recognized it, 'Oh, it's Gus Speth!'

'Speth', Önder Yücer says of the man who became Administrator after Bill Draper, 'to me, he's like a holy man, very shy, very cerebral . . . with an innocent soul . . . very different from Draper.'[1]

Yet it was Draper who recommended that his old friend, the US president George H. W. Bush, nominate Speth.[2] As it turned out Bush lost his 1992 bid for a second term as US president, and Bill Clinton was the one who nominated his fellow 'New South' Democrat. Speth is an environmentalist who, like Clinton, followed a stint as a Rhodes Scholar at Oxford with a law degree at Yale. Then Speth founded the World Resource Institute (WRI) and built it into one of the world's leading research organizations in the field of environmental policy. Ruben Mendez, one of UNDP's significant contributors to international public policy analysis, says, 'Speth brought an intellectual caliber to the

[1] Önder Yücer, interview with the author (CNM), 7 Dec. 2004.
[2] William H. Draper III, interview with CNM, 29 Sept. 2004.

10.1 UNDP as a flying elephant

leadership of UNDP not seen since the days of Arthur Lewis and I.G. Patel.'[3]

Speth's face did, in a sense, become that of UNDP. He created coherence and unity out of Draper's innovations and the intellectual support that Draper had received from ul Haq. He worked to make human development (with an additional focus on environmental and institutional sustainability) the operational framework of UNDP's programmes. Under Speth, UNDP became an organization dedicated to just one thing: 'sustainable human development', SHD. With a scholar's thoroughness, Speth attempted to make the organization a coherent instrument of this one purpose. That required adding new capacities to deal with the

[3] Ruben P. Mendez, 'United Nations Development Programme', http://www.yale.edu/unsy/ UNDPhist.htm (accessed 2 Dec. 2005).

10.2 James Gustave Speth

environment, extreme poverty, and those crises that rob people of the opportunity to pursue human development. Sakiko Fukuda-Parr, who at the time was a manager overseeing programmes in eleven of the poorest African countries, recalls the exhilaration she and many other officers felt as a result, 'I had something to work with, a purpose that should be driving all the country programmes.'[4]

In many ways, the 1990s were favourable to this unified vision. Environmentalism was on the rise, spurred by the 1992 'Earth Summit' in Rio de Janeiro, which helped UNDP to initiate and maintain a substantial and innovative environmental programme. The Soviet Union collapsed in December 1991, and the successor governments of the former Soviet republics and those throughout central and eastern Europe embraced the democracy and markets that UNDP continued to affirm as central contributions to human development. Conflict-ridden, post-cold war Africa – the site of some of the UN security system's most abysmal failures – gave UNDP ample scope to prove its ability to avert crises and deal with their consequences. Throughout the decade, many times, the elephant really did fly.

During those years I often worked with an Italian diplomat, Enrico Augelli, who made a real difference in some difficult places, including

---

[4] Sakiko Fukuda-Parr, letter to CNM, 2 Jan. 2006.

Somalia and the Sahel. Yet Enrico always credited his partnerships with others as the reason for his successes;[5] 'Remember,' he said, 'Antonio Gramsci [the great Italian social theorist] said that the qualities of intellectual leadership and political leadership are rarely combined in a single individual.'[6]

My friend believed that Speth combined both qualities, but in unequal parts, 'More the Sraffa [the economist friend of both Gramsci and Keynes] than the Mussolini.' Unsupported by the hortatory political skills of a Hoffman or a Morse, UNDP's new unified purpose went unnoticed by much of the rest of the development community. For example, Nafis Sadik, the UN Population Fund (UNFPA) head believes that 'Until Mark Malloch Brown arrived, UNDP . . . didn't know what its role was. No one could give a straight answer to exactly what was its mandate.'[7]

Önder Yücer considers remarks like Sadik's to be explicable, if absurd. For Yücer, the sadder story was Speth's lack of success at fund-raising in an environment in which it was becoming increasingly difficult. Aid levels dropped at the end of the cold war. The charming, but inconsistent, US president did poorly by UNDP. Some other traditionally large donors were just as bad; when Sweden (along with Austria and Finland) entered the European Union (EU) in 1995, the obligation to channel some funds through the EU seemed to have 'a direct effect on contributions to UNDP'.[8] In the resulting atmosphere in which raising local resources became the major way to expand programmes, entrepreneurial regional bureaux and country offices would sometimes disregard Speth's quietly articulated vision.

Yücer (who is Turkish) and Speth (from South Carolina) had a friendship based, in part, on cultural similarities between their very different homelands. Yücer remembers, wistfully, that sometimes they would

> just look at each other and smoke. He was definitely aware of the fact that on resource mobilization, he'd failed. I didn't know whether he'd admit it, but some offices that could be very opportunistic would try to hit on this sore point, and once, while we were puffing on cigars, he privately agreed.[9]

---

[5] One journalist called him 'Machiavelli' in contrast to the American 'Rambo' who headed the UN's Somalia mission. Frances Kennedy, 'In Somalia: Machiavelli vs. Rambo', New York Times, 22 July 1993.

[6] Antonio Gramsci, Selections from the Prison Notebooks, ed. and trans. Quentin Hoare and Geoffrey Nowell Smith (London: Lawrence & Wishart, 1971), pp. 57, 170.

[7] Nafis Sadik, interview with Neysan Rassekh (NR), 2 Nov. 2004.

[8] Sarah Timpson, letter to CNM, 20 Jan. 2006.

[9] Önder Yücer, interview with CNM, 7 Dec. 2004.

Internal reforms

It is more than sad that some of the people whom Speth considered to be 'the last great concentration of idealists on the planet' would come to undercut his vision. Speth speaks fervently about having travelled more than any other Administrator before or since, just to be with his staff and to try 'to keep morale high'.[10] Beyond sharpening UNDP's mission, his major goals included giving the country offices greater autonomy and diffusing expertise more broadly throughout the organization, in part by establishing local knowledge centres – SURFs (sub-regional resource facilities) – in part by investing in staff skills and training, all the while maintaining UNDP's commitment to 'bottom-up, country-driven programming of development assistance resources without conditionality'.[11]

In his first year, Speth led staff to articulate a unified statement of mission that reemphasized UNDP's link to the United Nations and identified the Programme with the quest for SHD: human development that would not compromise the natural environment on which future generations must rely. In June 1994 the Executive Board (UNDP's newly renamed governing body) affirmed the mission and some of the structural changes Speth had enacted to support it.[12] In 1998 the Board made a second key decision, narrowing the focus of the Programme in response to the mission. The decision was not written with the clarity that a professor might demand, but with Speth's help,[13] it can be translated into common language:

The Board committed UNDP to helping countries achieve SHD and listed three 'basic goals'. The first – to 'serve as a major substantive resource on how to achieve' the vision – meant sponsoring the *Human Development Report*. The second – helping the UN 'family become a unified and powerful force' for sustainable human development – referred to the UNDP Res Reps' role as UN Resident Coordinators and to the Administrator's new role as chair of regular meetings of the heads of

---

[10] James Gustave Speth, interview with CNM, 24 Sept. 2004.

[11] Bruce Jenks, *UNDP in the 1990s: The Story of a Transformation* (New York: UNDP, 1999), provides the best concise account of the process and results. 'Reform in Action', *UNDP Today*, April 1998, is a concise discussion of the results.

[12] UNDP, *Report of the Executive Board (6–16 June 1994)*, 94/14.

[13] Memorandum re UNDP's SHD Programming Framework: New Guiding Principles and Current Major Development Services (with attachments), from James Gustave Speth to Resident Representatives and others, 5 June 1998, and interview with CNM, 24 Sept. 2004.

all UN development agencies. The third goal's slightly convoluted wording committed the Programme's own resources to protecting the environment, encouraging good governance, advancing women, and fighting poverty.

Speth recalls that only one of these four areas, 'good governance' – a stalking horse for the human development concern with accountability and the building of democratic institutions and a strong civil society – was difficult to sell to the Board.

> We – both me personally and UNDP – spent a lot of time and energy making 'good governance' a legitimate theme . . . and then building it up as a major focus of country programming . . . including the big issues of corruption and human rights.[14]

'Just do it', Speth's closest advisors told him; just make 'good governance' a central part of UNDP's work, and the Board will come along.[15]

Speth's Associate Administrator, Rafeeuddin Ahmed, who had known UNDP and its governing boards for more than thirty years, helped to move the unified vision forward, using political skills that partially complemented Speth's own: 'a delightful personality, uncanny ability to find compromise wordings, and realism'.[16] Still, the match-up between the two men was far from perfect. Robert England recalls that Rafee Ahmed's 'external communications skills were less impressive than Gus's own', and, near the end of their service together, both men proved less adept at the cut-throat internal politics of the UN system than some others in similar positions in other organizations.[17] Nonetheless, when Ahmed moved on (shortly before Speth left to become dean of Yale's environment school), the Administrator expressed his 'profound appreciation' for 'Rafee's remarkable capacity to find elegant solutions to complex issues'.[18]

The environment and new sources of funding

In establishing his signature programmes on the environment, Speth benefited from another kind of political leadership, one that had put

[14] James Gustave Speth, annotation on documents sent to CNM, 18 Dec. 2004.
[15] James Gustave Speth, interview with CNM, 24 Sept. 2004.
[16] Chuck Lankester, interview with NR, 9 Nov. 2004.
[17] J. K. Robert England, letter to CNM, 10 Jan. 2006.
[18] 'Administrator Praises Outgoing Associate Administrator Rafeeuddin Ahmed's Outstanding Contributions to UNDP', UNDP Press Release, New York, 12 Jan. 1999.

the funding mechanisms for his vision in place before he arrived. Nonetheless, Speth's summary of his part – 'We initiated UNDP's programmes in the environment after the good start at Rio'[19] – is actually too modest.

Before he joined UNDP, Speth helped establish the institutions that would allow the Programme to take on its new mandate. The 1992 Rio conference (officially, the UN Conference on Environment and Development) stood at the end of two decades in which environmentalists put the connection between development and the environment on the global agenda. Speth was at the centre of that initiative, as was another man who would play a central role in attempts to reform the UN development system throughout the 1990s: Maurice Strong.

Strong had been a successful Canadian businessman before heading his country's foreign aid programmes in the 1960s. He also worked with Lester Pearson to create the International Development Research Centre, a public corporation dedicated to the application of science to problems of poorer nations and one of the major sources of new, sustainable technologies used throughout the developing world. In 1972 Strong chaired the first of the global environmental conferences, which was held in Stockholm, and he became the first Executive Director of the organization created to carry on the conference's work, the UN Environment Programme (UNEP).

As a concession to the developing world, the General Assembly placed UNEP's headquarters in Nairobi, Kenya. Nonetheless, most of the concerns of the developing world remained off the global environmental agenda for many years. Multilateral forums paid little attention to the opportunity costs that would have to be borne by industrializing countries if global and regional environmental crises were to be averted. Southern governments wondered why, if Europe, North America, and Japan all sacrificed their air, forests, and waters to rapid industrial development, the rest of Asia, South America, and Africa should be expected to do any differently.

In 1987, two major studies began envisioning ways to overcome this problem: Northern finance could be provided for Southern activities to preserve the environment. One report came from Norwegian Prime Minister Gro Harlem Brundtland's independent Commission on Environment and Development (one of a long sequence of bodies modelled on the Pearson Commission); the suggestions reflected the views of

<hr />

[19] Speth, annotation on documents sent to CNM, 18 Dec. 2004.

one of the Commission's most active members, Maurice Strong. The other report came from Speth's WRI, in collaboration with UNDP.[20]

In the same year governments crafted the first major global climate treaty, the Montreal Protocol, which was designed to phase out the use of chemicals that destroy the atmosphere's radiation-screening ozone layer. In 1990 the treaty's signatories added a 'Multilateral Fund' to ease the burden on those developing countries that stop using ozone-depleting chemicals. In 1993 the Fund became a permanent institution, with UNDP, the World Bank, UNEP, and the UN Industrial Development Organization sharing responsibility for its governance.

The structure of the Fund was repeated in the larger Global Environment Facility (GEF) established in 1991. Initially Draper, advised by Maurice Strong, hoped to keep GEF solely within UNDP, where, Strong believed, GEF's environmental goals would prove more acceptable to the developing world than they would if the Facility were run by the Bank, due to UNDP's history of solidarity, in contrast to the World Bank's tradition of conditionality.

Donors had a different idea. This was the end of the Reagan era and the North–South conflict of the 1970s was far from forgotten. In the words of Tim Rothermel (then working closely with the Administrator), 'One day we were in the driver's seat, the next we were happy to ride in the back.'[21]

Despite the qualms of Strong, Draper, and the developing world, GEF's shared leadership (which mirrored the highly successful CGIAR – the Consultative Group on International Agricultural Research) had not upset Speth. (WRI had even clashed with Draper when UNDP initially had hoped to be solely responsible.) Draper quickly came to respect Speth's point of view. After the GEF agreement was in place, Draper's attention moved back to the private sector, women, and NGOs (non-governmental organizations), but he had come to think of Speth as someone to take over UNDP when the time came, 'Because Speth was dedicated and passionate about the environment as I had been . . . about the private sector . . . He had a lot of things I didn't have.'[22]

In 1992 Maurice Strong cajoled leaders at the Earth Summit to think about further North–South agreements – on biodiversity, climate change, and desertification. Each, he argued, would require additional

[20] Helen Sjoberg, From Idea to Reality: The Creation of the Global Environment Facility, GEF Working Paper 10 (Washington, DC: GEF,1994), pp. 4–5.

[21] Quoted in ibid., p. 14.

[22] William A. Draper III, interview with CNM, 29 Sept. 2004.

tranches of funding. Strong received commitments for a new fund to build the capacity of developing countries to meet the sustainable development goals contained in the conference's final declaration, 'Agenda 21'. This created a third source of money for UNDP initiatives on the environment.

Speth's first year as Administrator was also the first that the entire range of environmental funds – from the Montreal Protocol, GEF, and 'Capacity 21' – were available for UNDP's use. They amounted to more than US$150 million, three times the core funding of the autonomous programmes then embedded within UNDP (including the Capital Development Fund, UNIFEM, and UN Volunteers); at the time, the regular contributions of UN member states amounted to only $920 million.[23] Thus environmental issues would quickly become a major part of UNDP's portfolio.

The impact of these new programmes has been felt in almost every part of the world. Hamid Ghaffarzadeh, the Iranian whose wife used to find it easier to say that he worked for UNICEF, explains that UNDP/GEF provided the impetus for setting up the institution that may save the Caspian Sea from the kind of devastation that has taken place in the smaller Aral Sea to its east. The five states that share the Caspian (Azerbaijan, Iran, Kazakhstan, Russia, and Turkmenistan) used a series of grants to conduct a scientific diagnostic analysis, which led to a set of regional and national action plans to protect biodiversity, control toxic emissions, and create sustainable fisheries and environmentally sensitive coastal communities.

Ghaffarzadeh asked me if I knew about the research on how international agreements were reached to help save the Mediterranean. Yes, I knew the widely cited book that talks about it as a largely science-driven process, a story of the power of epistemic communities.[24] 'Think about Iran', still reeling from its long war with Iraq, and the other countries plunged into economic chaos after the break-up of the Soviet Union. Someone had to pay for the science and 'bring together the community', and UNDP was there.[25]

[23] Memorandum re Five Key Goals for UNDP in the Coming Year, from James Gustave Speth to Strategy and Management Committee Members and Resident Representative, 3 April 1995.

[24] Written by someone who would later be one of Gus Speth's collaborators, Peter M. Haas, *Saving the Mediterranean: The Politics of International Environmental Cooperation* (New York: Columbia University Press, 1990); see James Gustave Speth and Peter M. Haas, *Global Environmental Governance* (Washington, D.C.: Island Press, 2006).

[25] Hamid Ghaffarzadeh, interview with CNM, 7 March 2005.

10.3 (a&b)   Bernard Lédéa Ouedraogo and his work

In Ghana Jonathan Allotey, the executive director of the Environmental Protection Agency, explains that UNDP's Montreal Protocol funding, along with some clever work by his agency, has led to a more than 70 per cent reduction in Ghana's use of ozone-depleting chemicals, putting it far ahead of the 50 per cent target it was supposed to reach in 2005.[26] Allotey's compatriot, Adisa Yakubu, speaks more dramatically about the impact of GEF funding on local projects designed to help people to establish sustainable livelihoods. 'Remember, the environment is the *religion* of the people' throughout most of rural Ghana. These projects let us 'tackle environmental degradation as a religious issue' as well as one of science. Roads have been built too close to the farms. There is runoff. Crops fail. We talk about it. The popular solution and the scientific one are the same. 'Raise the road. Tell the earth. And bring back the god.'[27]

Directly to the north of Ghana, in Burkina Faso, Bernard Lédéa Ouedraogo has been helping farmers maintain sustainable livelihoods since Yakubu was a little girl. Naam, the rural people's movement

[26] Jonathan Allotey, interview with CNM, 18 Jan. 2005.
[27] Adisa Yakubu, interview with CNM, 17 Jan. 2005.

Ouedraogo helped establish in the 1960s, is now one of the largest in Africa, with hundreds of thousands of members maintaining a dozen credit banks and hundreds of grain storage facilities, wells, and mills. A larger group that grew from Naam, SixS (Se servir de la saison sèche en Savane et au Sahel – in English, 'using the dry season in the Savannah and the Sahel'), unites small farmers across West Africa. Many analysts credit it with disseminating the local knowledge that has helped turn back the desert.

Ouedraogo sits beneath his 1978 Paul G. Hoffman Award and recalls that Brad Morse was master of the ceremonies for another prestigious prize Naam received a decade later. He is grateful for UNDP's help over more than forty years (and, pointedly, for UNICEF's as well). GEF and Capacity 21 have just made it much easier for groups with similar goals to get started in other countries, and, he says, there are always new technologies to try, pointing to a double-walled adobe building rising outside his window, a giant 'solar' refrigerator. If it works, another six months of potatoes, beans, 'anything', could be stored by cooperatives throughout the Sahel. Maybe many power plants will never have to be built, preserving the sky and the trees as well as the farmers.[28]

In many places, UNDP–GEF projects have focused on preserving biodiversity by protecting a species at the top of a food chain. To do so requires protecting an entire local ecology. As with the tiger projects mentioned in chapter 2, many of the projects have involved creating sustainable livelihoods for poor people who must share their habitat with a charismatic animal. The headline of one press release about a UNDP project in Pakistan reads, 'Day Farmers Let a Leopard Go Free'. Another press release, 'Rescuing Pakistan's Blind Dolphins', is about fishermen on the Indus, whose own efforts at saving an endangered species have provided the model for a more comprehensive UNDP programme.

The charismatic mammals – snow leopards blessed by the Dalai Lama and the dolphins, who are ancient Indus River animal gods, as much as any tiger – encourage complicated partnerships with global donors. The World Conservation Union, the World Wide Fund for Nature, the Aga Khan Rural Support Programme, the International Fund for Agricultural Development, the European Union, the United Kingdom, and the Netherlands all joined UNDP in mediating the relationship between Pakistani farmers and their endangered neighbours. Moreover, the central GEF secretariat, which sits at the World Bank's headquarters in

---

[28] Bernard Lédéa Ouedraogo, interview with CNM, 15 Jan. 2005.

Washington and shares the Bank's aggressive attitude towards public relations, hired a superb development journalist, former Guyanan diplomat Frank A. Campbell, to provide regular updates on such projects for interested news outlets around the world.[29]

Some of the impacts of UNDP conservation projects are so commonplace that they have never made it into the news, even if they are particularly remarkable. I recently replaced the light bulb above my desk with a 'warm white compact fluorescent' that, on sale, cost only 99 cents; the package promises a US$45 savings in electricity over incandescent bulbs like the one that had just burned out. The savings will come courtesy of UNDP, at least in this sense: the bulb was made in China and the Chinese compact fluorescent industry began with a series of UNDP projects that both increased demand and lowered the cost of production.

In this case, the initial problem in the early 1990s was a projected shortfall in Chinese electricity production. The bulbs, which use a quarter of the energy of those they replace, promised to fill much of the gap. Unfortunately, in the beginning, the fluorescents cost Chinese consumers 140 yuan (US$17). 'Therefore', Yu Cong, of the Energy Research Institute of China's National Development and Reform Commission explains, 'we tried to introduce the idea [to consumers] and have a Chinese factory learn how to produce a high quality product at a low price.' When the UNDP projects ended a few years later, a massive education campaign had convinced consumers (especially businesses) that eventually the high-priced bulbs would pay for themselves. More significantly, studies of foreign factories, improvements made in China, and the new economies of scale achieved through the popularity of the bulbs had lowered the cost to Chinese consumers to 20 yuan (US$2.50). Of course, the US, British, Dutch, and German companies that used to dominate the global market had been forced to drop their prices as well, often by moving production to China. In 2005, my 99-cent bulb was 'manufactured in China' for an old US company for whom foreign production was relatively new.

The story is an example of what most of UNDP's new environmental projects were meant to do: have a disproportionate impact (in this case, on global energy consumption) through carefully selected interventions

[29] Frank A. Campbell, 'The Day Farmers Let a Leopard Go Free', and 'Rescuing Pakistan's Blind Dolphin', http://www.gefweb.org/ResultsandImpact/Results_at_a_Glance/Project_Stories/project_stories.html (accessed 12 Dec. 2005).

(creating a virtuous circle of Chinese consumer interest while lowering the cost of production). Fundamentally there was nothing new to this strategy. UNDP had triggered similar innovations before, even relative to energy conservation. In the mid-1970s, for example, Singapore faced a similar gap in the capacity to produce electricity for its growing economy. A small UNDP project with the National Productivity Board funded the development of the first electricity key system for hotels – the cards that guests must take with them in order to get back into their room and that also must be placed in a slot by the door to engage electricity when the room is occupied, thus preventing electricity in the room being wasted while the guest is away with the key.[30] In the 1990s, the only things new were UNDP's broad commitment to conservation projects in every country where the Programme worked and the availability of funds to carry them out.

Crisis work and promoting good governance

UNDP's other major innovations of the 1990s relied less on new sources of funding than on a shift away from the old UNDP's pre-investment surveys and funding of small projects in every economic and social sector. In early 1997, looking back over project expenditures in 1994 and 1995, Speth was pleased to find that a third had gone to projects 'in the area of governance'.[31] This was partially a consequence of the integral connection between democratization and human development, but it also reflected the impact on UNDP of new demands placed on it after the fall of the Soviet Union and the outbreak of the violent conflicts in the years immediately after the end of the cold war.

UNDP's involvement in both of these fields has been so extensive that those who attempt to look at every case cannot go beyond statistical summaries. The linked conflicts in Africa throughout the 1990s engaged more than two dozen countries and UNDP was involved either in crisis prevention or peace-building work (or both) in all of them. Under Draper, from 1991 to early 1993 (Speth arrived in July of that year) UNDP welcomed the former Soviet republics as recipient countries, took steps to establish links with all parts of disintegrating Yugoslavia, and

---

[30] Chow Kit Boey, Chew Moh Leen, and Elizabeth Su, *One Partnership in Development: UNDP and Singapore* (Singapore: United Nations Association of Singapore, 1989), p. 39.

[31] James Gustave Speth, 'Challenges for Sustainable Human Development: Good Governance and Democratization', address to the Bruno Kriesky Forum for International Dialogue, Vienna, Austria, 15 April 1997, p. 2.

deepened its involvement in the rest of eastern Europe.[32] Before Speth left UNDP in July 1999, the Programme had provided electoral assistance in sixty-eight countries – forty-three in Africa, six in eastern Europe and the former Soviet Union, and many of the rest in countries where the end of the cold war had opened opportunities for democratic change.[33]

Much of this complex picture can be understood by considering the larger political goals UNDP hoped to serve and then looking at just three countries: Ukraine, Bulgaria, and Rwanda. They are all special cases: Ukraine, the Soviet republic whose history is most closely linked to Russia's, Bulgaria, once Moscow's most loyal ally in eastern Europe, and the African country where, in the 1990s, things went most wrong. They are very different countries, but conditions in each are much better now than in 1994. Their transformation has been remarkable only because the initial conditions were so unfavourable. Those stark initial conditions also make the differing roles played by UNDP relatively easy to discern.

Goals: democracy and human security

In many speeches Gus Speth would make the link between 'good governance' and substantive democratization completely explicit, as he did in 1997:

> In the end, we at UNDP have no choice but to provide democratization assistance . . . Democratization, by whatever name, down whatever path, is one of the pillars of sustainable human development . . . The *Human Development Report* has said that human development is development 'of the people, by the people, for the people'. Is it possible, over time, to achieve human development without government of the people, by the people, and for the people? . . . So, however messy and complex individual situations become, we in the larger international assistance community have no choice but to support responsible democratization initiatives, not just because we

---

[32] 'Technical Cooperation in the Transformation of Eastern European Economies', *Report of the Governing Council: Thirty-Eighth Session (3–25 June 1991)*, 91/24; 'Preparations for the Fifth Programming Cycle: Belarus, Estonia, Latvia, and Ukraine', *Organizational/Special Session Meeting (10–14 Feb. 1992)*, 92/8; 'UNDP Programme in Former Yugoslavia' and 'Matters Relating to the Programming Cycles: Azerbaijan, Kazakhstan, Kyrgyzstan, the Republic of Moldova, the Russian Republic, and Uzbekistan', *Thirty-Ninth Session (4–29 May 1992)*, 9/27 and 92/29; ' Matters Relating to the Programming Cycles: Bosnia and Herzegovina, the Czech Republic, Georgia, the Slovak Republic, Slovenia, and Tajikistan', *February Special Session (19 Feb. 1993)*, 93/3.

[33] Richard Ponzio, 'UNDP Experience in Long-Term Democracy Assistance', in Edward Newman and Roland Richard, eds., *The UN and Democracy Promotion: From Rhetoric to Reality* (Tokyo: UN University Press, 2004), p. 214.

have been asked, but because such initiatives align our work with one of the greater human struggles of our time – the struggle for social justice in a world that is fundamentally unfair, and increasingly so.[34]

At the time Speth spoke, former UN Secretary-General Boutros-Ghali had become anathema to the Americans, who had originally supported him, as well as to many other UN members who believed that he had cleaved too close to US policy. Yet Speth continued to credit and repeat the message from *An Agenda for Democratization*, one of the most forceful statements linking development and democracy until the publication of Amartya Sen's *Development as Freedom* in 1999. Speth chose a paragraph from the *Agenda* to be his speech's climax:

> Non-democratic States, over time tend to generate conditions inimical to development: politicized military rule; a weak middle class; a population constrained to silence; prohibitions on travel; censorship; restrictions on the practice of religion or imposition of religious obligation; and pervasive and often institutionalized corruption . . . The reality is that no State can long remain just or free, and thus have the potential to pursue a successful and sustainable development strategy, if its citizens are prohibited from participating actively and substantially in its political processes . . . Increasingly, it is from this perspective that democracy is being seen today – as a practical necessity.[35]

Finally, reflecting on the increasing demands placed on the UN immediately after the cold war, Speth argued for an increasing role for development agencies in times of crisis, 'a seamless transition from efforts aimed at dealing with peacekeeping, to political and humanitarian affairs, and development'.[36] If the real enemies of human self-realization are the destitution, insecurity, and the political inequality that leave so many without control over the major decisions that affect their lives, then promoting human development demands treating the three sets of issues as one. Our fundamental security needs – the needs felt during natural disasters, humanitarian emergencies, periods of social crisis, and war – should not be placed to the side, as if they were something to be addressed separately. Mahbub ul Haq called this combined UN agenda a concern for 'human security'.[37]

---

[34] Speth, 'Challenges for Sustainable Human Development', p. 3.
[35] Ibid., quoting paragraph 25 of Boutros Boutros-Ghali, *An Agenda for Democratization*, 17 Dec. 1996, http://www.library.yale.edu/un/un3d3.htm (accessed 7 Dec. 2005).
[36] Speth, 'Challenges for Sustainable Human Development', p. 7.
[37] Mahbub ul Haq, 'New Compulsions of Human Security', address to the NGO/DPI Annual Conference, New York, 8 Sept. 1993.

Ukraine: giving voice

Speth remains fascinated by the extent to which so many of the post-Soviet states took on the agenda of sustainable human development. That is why the newly created Regional Bureau for Europe and the Commonwealth of Independent States (RBEC) was the first to support national human development reports.[38]

Yet, for many of the successor governments, one aspect of human development – democracy – seemed anything but 'a practical necessity'. It was increasingly an irritant to Leonid Kuchma, the former Soviet rocket scientist elected to the presidency of the newly independent Ukraine in 1994 on a platform of maintaining close ties with Moscow. Kuchma oversaw a decade of failed economic reforms, growing intolerance of the press, and state complicity in violence against his political opponents. When Kuchma took power, Ukraine was still suffering the consequences of the world's greatest single environmental catastrophe (the meltdown of the Chernobyl nuclear reactor in 1986), and the country faced a complex set of potentially violent conflicts including those involving ethnic Tatars from the Crimean peninsula.

The country also had a two-year-old UNDP office that had helped with the 1994 elections. From the beginning, the office had defined its goal as 'promoting human security'.[39] Stephen Browne, the Resident Representative who opened the office, lists three major accomplishments in its first decade: helping deal with the aftermath of Chernobyl, a Crimea Integration and Development Programme, and some innovative, low-cost work setting up Internet connections, not only for the UN office, but for Ukrainian citizens at large.[40]

Yet the documents Browne sent me about Chernobyl seem a little thin. They look like a PR job rather than anything substantive: there is a 1996 photograph of a concerned-looking Rafee Ahmed with the UN's then Under-Secretary-General for Humanitarian Affairs, Yasushi Akashi, standing in front of the sarcophagus of the sealed nuclear plant.

'You may be wrong', says Serhiy Kurykin, the Environment Minister in the Orange Revolution government and a leader of the European Federation of Greens, 'look at what the UN said'. Ahmed and Akashi emphasized the villagers' desire to return to the land and the pain of

---

[38] Speth, annotation on documents sent to CNM, 18 Dec. 2004.
[39] Stephen Browne, 'The United Nations in Ukraine, 1992–2005: A Glance into the Future', unpublished paper, Kiev, May 1995, p. 7.
[40] Stephen Browne, interview with CNM, 5 Nov. 2004.

social dislocation, and Akashi turned the villagers' complaints into something universal by quoting the inscription on the Hiroshima monument about never committing the same mistake again. 'Real sustainability must be based on democratic principles', Kurykin says. 'In words as well as deeds', UNDP lives those principles, and not *just* by acting as a global megaphone for Chernobyl's disenfranchised:

> Compare UNDP with USAID [the United States' main bilateral development agency]. Many USAID projects are compatible with UNDP priorities [the human development priorities that Kurykin endorses]. But USAID proposes its own vision of local problems and its own model. UNDP is much more flexible; [everything is] done in active contact with local people. This creates a more effective programme.[41]

I am probably too easily convinced by the Green politician. We are of the same generation and share similar political views, and he has been recommended to me by a friend whose book on environmental politics in the former Soviet Union is a model of critical scholarship.[42]

I am less likely to be taken in by Refat Chubarov, the giant, emphatic Tatar leader.[43]

He explains how Stalin deported more than 200,000 Crimean Tatars and another thirty or forty thousand Crimean Armenians, Bulgarians, and Greeks to other parts of the Soviet Union. When the Soviet Union disintegrated, their descendents found that if they headed home to Crimea they were unable to establish themselves as legal citizens of Ukraine. In addition, the refugees found that they could access few public services – no housing, no water for their squatter settlements, and only one out of twenty schools taught in the Tatar language. Moreover the hostility of many Crimean residents was palpable. The warm peninsula had become a preferred place of retirement for many officers from the old Soviet military. They had the legal rights that the returning minorities did not have and they provided a ready cadre of leaders for a larger anti-refugee movement.

The ten-year story of crisis avoidance, beginning in 1993, is one of 'proactivism and goodwill of the Tatars' working with a UNDP office that was 'rather subjective' and incoherent at the beginning, but that 'listened to [Tatar] NGOs' (at a time when minorities were still disenfranchised)

[41] Serhiy Kurykin, interview with CNM, 11 March 2005.
[42] Jane I. Dawson; see her *Anti-Nuclear Activism and National Identity in Russia, Lithuania, and Ukraine* (Durham, N.C.: Duke University Press, 1996).
[43] Refat Chubarov, interview with CNM, 11 March 2005.

and knew how to make connections to other donors. UNDP pulled together eight bilateral donors (including the Vatican), other multilateral institutions, and the government in Kiev to provide water, build clinics and schools, teach tolerance and encourage public dialogue, and, perhaps most significantly, change local and national laws in order to secure citizenship and cultural rights for all.[44]

To me, the whole package seems like what UNDP has done in Palestine. Chubarov dismisses that view: UNDP had to learn what to do 'in Ukraine'; luckily, it was open to learning and had good teachers. Even then, it took years for them to recognize that you 'could not just give water to the Tatars'; to prevent conflict, improvements had to be seen in everyone's lives.

The proof that something worked lies in the comparison with cases in other parts of the Soviet Union. In 1992 many observers thought that Crimea was as much a candidate for violent conflict as Chechnya. Chubarov summarizes the three differences, no one of which would, by itself, have been decisive: there was the leadership of the disadvantaged groups (a polite way of pointing, among other things, to his own role), the openness and commitment of the central government to a peaceful settlement, and the presence of an international partner that learned quickly and that could bring in a host of other donors.

I am no expert on the region, but, to me, Chubarov's explanation sounds plausible.

Stephen Browne himself is a major source of information about the third activity that he believes had significant, positive impact. In December 1994 the office opened the UN-operated Kiev FreeNet, the country's first Internet provider, which was, indeed, free to users due to partnerships with George Soros's International Science Foundation, the Eurasia Foundation, the US Library of Congress, the Canadian Bureau of International Education, and a European consortium that had installed a satellite dish on UNDP's roof. Users registered for dial-up connections at the UN office or else came into the office's business centre to use the free computers there. The plan, according to Rafal Rohizinski, the UNDP officer in charge, was to spin off an independent, non-governmental service provider, a 'unique, very Ukrainian vision of the Internet'.[45]

---

[44] UNDP, *Crimea Integration and Development Programme: Conflict Prevention in Action* (Simferopol: CIDP, 2000) describes the programme.

[45] Quoted in 'Kiev FreeNet Now Up and Running', *Ukrainian Business Journal* (February 1995), p. 2.

The overall goal, Browne says, was to break through the country's 'information barrier. Not an Iron Curtain, exactly, but a serious intellectual one.'[46] Soon not only were government offices and UN projects throughout the country linked in a single network, students, NGOs, and private companies were linked to one another and to a wider world. Kurykin was in daily conversation with Green activists throughout Europe. Chubarov could maintain links with minority leaders and refugees throughout the entire Commonwealth of Independent States. And an entire new network of electronic media, often deeply critical of the government, began to grow. By 2002 the BBC reported claims by those involved in Ukraine's flourishing Internet community that they had 'become the target of abuse and harassment' from Kuchma's government.[47]

It is best to leave the story here, at least for the moment. When I visited Ukraine in 2005, shortly after the democratizing 'Orange Revolution' replaced Kuchma with Viktor Yushchenko (one of the victims of the old régime's violence, now recovering from his slow poisoning by Dioxin), many people spoke about the role of the Internet in linking a complex opposition during the weeks of public demonstrations over the first elections that the government had rigged. Few credited a Russian argument that 'you could see the hand of the US' in Yushchenko's victory because George Soros and UNDP had been behind FreeNet from the beginning. (*Wikipedia*, the online encyclopaedia, repeats the extravagent claim, pointing to UNDP-supported FreeNets that copied the model in Ukraine and that then facilitated 'colour revolutions' in Kyrgyzstan and elsewhere.[48]) Nevertheless, many Ukrainians agreed that, without UNDP, the country's dense Internet network would have taken many more years to develop and they contrasted government control of the web in China with the uncensored system that grew from FreeNet, which was essential to the revolution.

Beautiful Bulgaria and beyond

As was the case in Ukraine, UNDP's unique role in Bulgaria reflected the personality of a key Resident Representative. Ukraine's Stephen Browne

---

[46] Stephen Browne. 'The World Wide Web: A Story of Mice and Menus', *Logon* (Newsletter of the UNDP Division of Administrative and Information Services), 26 April 1995, pp. 19–20.

[47] Steven Eke, 'Profile: Leonid Kuchma', *BBC News: World Edition*, 26 Sept. 2002, http://news.bbc.co.uk/2/hi/europe/2283925.stm (accessed 20 Dec. 2005).

[48] 'Color Revolution', *Wikipedia*, http://en.wikipedia.org/wiki/Color_revolution (accessed 20 Dec. 2005).

is a well-recognized scholar of development – a bit like an English Gus Speth. (Hans Singer wrote the preface to Browne's latest book.[49]) Browne modelled Ukraine's FreeNet on the near-zero-cost link-ups to the original Internet backbone made by hundreds of universities long before most UN offices had heard of the World Wide Web.[50] Antonio Vigilante, the elegantly dressed and explosively energetic Italian who served as Res Rep in Bulgaria, found different sources of inspiration.

Vigilante reminds me of my late friend, Enrico Augelli. One beautiful spring afternoon when we were walking around Rome's Piazza Navona, eating ice cream and debating some thing like 'human security', Enrico pointed up to Bernini's stunning fountain and the lovely buildings behind:

> You see, *this* is development: having small luxuries [raising his ice cream cone] in a beautiful place doing things that matter – talking politics, making love [eyes towards a couple embracing]. I want *everyone* in Mogadishu or Ouagadougou to have something like this [arms encompassing the entire, uniquely beautiful scene].

For years, I would joke with my students about Enrico's fantasy, until I visited Sofia and saw something like it made real.

The story[51] begins in October 1996, in the depths of Bulgaria's post-Soviet economic crisis. The new Res Rep, his wife and daughters, and two visiting consultants from his wife's home country, Bolivia, are sitting in the family apartment trying to think of anything that the UN could do in this hopeless situation: rampant unemployment, triple-digit inflation, the rapid deterioration of social services, infrastructure, and housing, and hopelessness – worst of all, hopelessness. The eight-year-old complains, 'No hay color [there's no colour].' If only the dirt on the buildings, in the streets, in the parks, could be cleaned up. The UNDP office had little it could offer – a few people, barely enough to keep up with the bureaucratic demands from New York, and a US$300,000 annual budget – but 'perhaps it would be possible to find a little money for paint'.

Slowly, the idea emerged: the city or neighbourhood groups – someone – would identify a building or a few buildings of real emotional importance. UNDP and various partners – they would have to be found – would provide paint and materials, and funds to pay the workers. This could encourage small private companies to be formed – construction, restoration, these are fields where it is easy to start small and the companies can

---

[49] Hans Singer, Preface to Stephen Browne, *Beyond Aid: From Patronage to Partnership* (Aldershot: Ashgate, 1999), pp. ix–x.   [50] Browne, 'World Wide Web', pp. 19–20.
[51] As recounted by Antonio Vigilante, interview with CNM, 20 April 2005.

grow very large. These are also labour-intensive fields; they can employ many people. Yet such jobs never disappear, no matter how industrial or post-industrial a society becomes.

The result was 'Beautiful Sofia', started in 1998, and then 'Beautiful Bulgaria', which has restored the historic centres of over 100 towns and created tens of thousands of jobs – mostly for the unskilled (most of them from the long-term unemployed), many of them in the Roma minority. Beyond training thousands and encouraging hundreds of viable new businesses, the programme has stimulated much broader urban revivals and has spurred tourism. In part this is because, despite the dirt and the Stalinist greyness, Bulgaria has an astonishing architectural richness – from Roman amphitheatres and Ottoman mosques to workshops and houses built with the organic simplicity of the nineteenth-century 'National Revival', which took place at the leading edge of the global Arts and Crafts movement (a movement that John A. Hobson was thinking of when he wrote, in 1902, 'Nationalism is the plain highway to internationalism'[52]). Even brutal post-war schools and apartment blocks become beautiful when painted using the palette of the mountains, sky, and countryside around them.[53]

'Beautiful Bulgaria' attracted at least a dozen other donors and has been replicated in Serbia, Romania, and other countries, but the greatest impact has been in Bulgaria itself. It stimulated or reinforced a host of other partnerships with UNDP including the Job Opportunities through Business Support Project (JOBS), that maintains more than forty self-sustaining regional business centres, which have helped to establish more than 1,000 small private companies by providing consultancy services, access to credit, information technology, and low-cost, newly renovated premises.[54] JOBS has provided the same impetus to the textile, wood products, handicraft, tourism, and organic farming sectors that 'Beautiful Bulgaria' gave to renovation and construction.

Similarly, the restoration of buildings from the National Revival led to a reevaluation and transformation of one of its most important institutions, the *chitalishte*, or 'reading houses', one of the few pre-communist, non-governmental institutions that survived throughout the country.

---

[52] John A. Hobson, *Imperialism: A Study* (New York: James Pott & Co., 1902), p. 9.
[53] Two bilingual books of photographs document the hundreds of restorations; *Beautiful Bulgaria* (Sofia: Ministry of Labour and Social Policy, 2001) and *Beautiful Bulgaria*, 2nd rev. edn (Sofia: Ministry of Labour and Social Policy, 2003).
[54] Elena Panova, interview with CNM, 4 May 2005. Ministry of Labour and Social Policy and UNDP, *Jobs* (Sofia: UDSP, 2003).

10.4 *Beautiful Bulgaria*: the cover of the 2003 book

With the help of UNDP (which brought in the Dutch and the US aid agencies) more than 200 of these local libraries and cultural centres have been transformed into local information technology centres, places for teaching and learning about ecologically sustainable livelihoods, studios, and galleries, and even day-care centres and clubs for people with disabilities.[55]

Ultimately, the greatest impact of 'Beautiful Bulgaria' and the projects that grew from it has been psychological. Like the projects of the Expanded Programme for Technical Assistance that contributed to the 'decolonization of the mind' fifty years before, UNDP projects have helped to make Bulgarians confident that they could shape their future 'the way we see it in our dreams'.[56] Vigilante puts it this way, 'Beautiful Bulgaria has become a symbol of a country profoundly renovating

---

[55] Maria Zlatareva, interview with CNM, 4 May 2005. *The Bulgarian Chitalishte: Tradition Meets the Future* (Sofia: UNDP, 2004).

[56] Ivan Neikov, Minister of Labour and Social Policy, Preface to *Beautiful Bulgaria*, p. i.

itself while taking pride in its history and identity.' It restored citizens' faith in and affection for their cities. It is 'a development programme with a soul'.[57]

What does this have to do with countries in crisis and with governance? The paint, the colours, the restoration of the memory of a nineteenth-century nationalism that was inclusive and internationalist – one that embraced synagogues, mosques, as well as churches, Turks and Roma as well as Slavs – were all part of the creation of a new civic culture and a new identification with a larger, democratic Europe. Newspaper editorials, transcripts of radio talk shows, responses to the open-ended questions on a 2000 Gallup poll, and almost everyone I spoke to when visiting Bulgaria in spring 2005, say that 'Beautiful Bulgaria', and what followed from it, gave the country the confidence, the experience, and the remembrance of its own past, to strive to become part of the European Union.

Ivan Neikov, the minister who helped make 'Beautiful Bulgaria' a reality, says that Antonio Vigilante must be there on the day of Bulgaria's EU accession in 2007 or 2008: 'Antonio is the mother of this.' At Bulgaria's darkest point, everyone was 'looking for the piece that will make it move. We didn't have time to analyse, have feasibility studies, needs assessment, etc.' Vigilante (and his family) found the piece that could unblock Bulgaria's economic, political, and psychological logjam. Since then the movement has been inexorable.[58]

The world's failure and Rwanda's reconstruction

There is no way to make the story of what happened in Rwanda sound like those of eastern Europe – or like more than a dozen stories of UNDP support for democratization in Africa during the Speth era that resemble those of eastern Europe.[59] Rwanda was the worst of another set of cases in the 1990s that included Somalia and Angola.[60] In 100 days from April to July 1994 almost a million people, including at least three-quarters of the entire Tutsi population of Rwanda, were systematically slaughtered, despite a widely ratified UN Genocide Convention and ample early warning provided to the UN Secretariat and the Security Council by its

---

[57] Quoted in ibid., p. iii.   [58] Ivan Neikov, interview with CNM, 4 May 2005.
[59] Parts of two of those stories are highlighted in chapter 12.
[60] In Angola, Margaret Joan Anstee recalls, 'International indifference in not stopping the renewal of the war in 1993 cost as many lives as in Rwanda, though unpublicized and over a longer period', letter to CNM, 31 Jan. 2006.

own officers in the field. Some fault the Clinton administration, which had the knowledge and capability to respond, but which had suffered a public relations blow the previous October when eighteen US soldiers in Somalia had been killed in front of television cameras.[61] Other analyses of the aetiology of the genocide blame not only the UN Secretariat, the Security Council and its permanent members, but also the entire international aid community – public and private – which for twenty years nurtured a deeply aid-dependent régime that increasingly incited ethnic hatred and violence.[62]

The consequences of the failure to avert the genocide have mounted from year to year. The predominantly Tutsi military government that seized power to stop the slaughter went on to trigger a cascade of wars across central Africa that eventually involved, 'some one-fifth of African governments and armies from across the continent . . . as well as perhaps a dozen or more armed groups', according to the Organization of African Unity's Panel of Eminent Personalities to Investigate the 1994 Genocide in Rwanda and the Surrounding Events. The group, chaired by Stephen Lewis (the Canadian diplomat who worked with Maurice Strong and Brad Morse framing the UN's response to the African crises in the 1980s), goes on to say,

> The alliances between and among these groups, with their varied and conflicting interests, have been bewildering. The situation is further endlessly complicated by . . . enormous mineral resources – an irresistible lure for governments, rogue gangs and powerful corporations alike – and by the continuing problem of arms proliferation sponsored by governments throughout the world as well as a multitude of unscrupulous private hustlers.[63]

In the lead-up to the genocide, UNDP was just as silent as other donors. However, immediately afterwards it helped to set up refugee camps in neighbouring Tanzania for those fleeing from the new Tutsi government and helped Rwandan refugees, some who had been in exile for more than

---

[61] As one officer said, 'We are doing our calculations back home and one American casualty is worth about 85,000 Rwandan dead.' Quoted in Samantha Power, 'A Problem from Hell': America and the Age of Genocide (New York: Basic Books, 2002), p. 382. Power is particularly critical of the United States.

[62] Peter Uvin, Aiding Violence: the Development Enterprise in Rwanda (West Hartford, Conn.: Kumarian Press, 1998); Michael Barnett, Eyewitness to a Genocide (Ithaca, N.Y.: Cornell University Press, 2001); Villa Jefremovas, Brickyards to Graveyards: From Production to Genocide in Rwanda (Albany: State University of New York Press, 2002); International Panel of Eminent Personalities to Investigate the 1994 Genocide in Rwanda and the Surrounding Events, Rwanda: The Preventable Genocide (Addis Ababa: Organization of African Unity, 2000).

[63] International Panel, Rwanda: The Preventable Genocide, pp. ES57–8.

thirty years, to return home.[64] (Some of those fleeing the new government were members of the militia group implicated in the genocide. They attempted to gain control of refugees and threaten Rwanda's new peace.) Shaharyar M. Khan, the Pakistan diplomat who served as the Special Representative of Secretary-General Boutros-Ghali after the genocide, says that UNDP was the first UN agency willing to return. 'I was very glad,' Khan says, 'because we were the peacekeepers, but someone had to rebuild this devastated country. We formed a good partnership to start with.' Khan's military forces helped to keep the peace in areas not yet controlled by the new Tutsi military government, while UNDP Res Rep Ahmed Rhazaoui coordinated an ever growing UN presence, with the World Food Programme (WFP) playing a particularly critical role, sustaining more than a million people in late 1994 and 1995. UNDP, Khan remembers, pledged to 'build the bridges, start up the schools, prepare the roads, rebuild the airports, get signals for aircraft to come in, etc.'[65]

It proved not to be that simple, Khan recalls. A few months later there were still only a few cars and telephones working throughout the country. All the UN agencies certainly wanted to help – no doubt feeling the horror of the failure of the international community to act before the genocide – but it was hard to maintain a unified programme. Rhazaoui left quickly, and his successor, Sukehiro Hasegawa, seemed to Khan to spend an inordinate amount of time trying to assert UNDP supremacy over the other UN agencies; Khan remembers complaints from the other agencies and his own attempt to convince Speth to find a better 'team player'.

It is unclear whether the real problem was the impossibility of the job or the impossibility of the time. My friend Enrico Augelli, who ran the Italian mission in Somalia and was the last foreign diplomat there in mid-1994, remembered Hasegawa as one of the most effective and cooperative diplomats in Mogadishu the year before. Hasegawa remembers the whole period as an especially trying one for anyone in UNDP who had experience in crisis countries. They were rapidly pulled from place to place – in his case, Somalia, Rwanda, Cambodia, and, eventually, Timor Leste.[66]

In 1998, when Stephen Browne took over as Res Rep in Rwanda, none of his 'six or seven' immediate predecessors had served as much as two years. There was no chance that a single Res Rep could make the overwhelming kind of difference in Rwanda that Browne and Vigilante had

---

[64] J. Victor Angelo, interview with CNM, 8 Jan. 2005.

[65] Shaharyar M. Khan, interview with CNM, 10 Dec. 2004. See Khan's *The Shallow Graves of Rwanda* (London: I. B. Tauris, 2000).

[66] Sukehiro Hasegawa, interview with CNM, 2 June 2005.

made in eastern Europe. Nevertheless, Omar Bakhet, who served immediately before Browne (and who moved on to become director of UNDP's
Emergency Response Division), did something close to that. He set in
place a relatively coherent programme aimed at restoring essential government functions, rebuilding the judicial system, re-establishing essential institutions (such as schools, hospitals, and banks), and building
some fundamentally new institutions such as an engineering college and
a management school.

Even though some coherence had been achieved, the string of short-
lived country office heads had been overseeing what Browne describes as
'a massive spending spree'. When he arrived the UN had already spent
over a billion dollars since the genocide, UNDP by itself somewhere from
US$100–200 million. The agencies were scaling down, but there were still
160 people in the UNDP office and hopes (never fulfilled) of finding
(perhaps from the Japanese) the six or seven billion dollars that the
country office felt that Rwanda really needed.[67]

With the money it was able to spend under the various Res Reps, UNDP
mounted a peace-building programme that looked like a combination of
the UN's earliest technical assistance in the 1950s with the new governance
work in eastern Europe. UN Volunteers helped to reconstruct the National
University in Butare and worked to train a new generation of teachers. In
1997 UNDP (along with the Dutch, Germans, and Japanese) began
helping the government to construct the Kigali Institute of Science,
Technology and Management, the country's first engineering school and
an essential part of the new government's vision for the future. The
Programme has helped to train a new generation of economic and social
planners, providing much of the economic expertise available to the government. In addition, UNDP has helped Rwandans to draft a new constitution, hold local and national elections, and train a new police force,
members of parliament, and judges. UNIFEM has taken on the task of
creating gender units in both the legislative and judicial branches.[68]

What has been the long-term impact? Well, Rwanda has a higher percentage of women in parliament than any other nation, but that may be
the only measure on which the country is outstanding. The elected leader,

---

[67] Stephen Browne, interview with CNM, 5 Nov. 2004.
[68] An oddly retrospective 'Ten Years On: Helping Rebuild a Nation, the United Nations in
Rwanda', www.unrwanda.org/undp/genocide.pdf (accessed 2 Dec. 2005), outlines these
programmes. The interviews with UN officers provided more detail, as does Memorandum
report re UNDP 1999–2005, Accomplishments and Remaining Challenges from Mark
Malloch Brown to Kemal Dervis, August 2005.

Paul Kagame, the military man whose rebel forces ended the genocide, brooks no dissent. Peter Uvin, the development analyst and sometime UNDP consultant who documented the international aid community's knowledge of, and silence about, the preconditions of the genocide, believes that 'We now may be where we were fifteen years ago [in 1990] – and that makes me worried.' Half of government resources and nine-tenths of civil society resources come directly from development aid. (Of course, that situation is similar to that in many other African countries.)

'Easily 25 to 45 per cent of all aid going to Rwanda is going to governance.' This, Uvin admits, reflects a change that he has promoted, but it also means that there is very little money going to poverty alleviation (that missing six or seven billion dollars). 'Rwanda', Uvin argued in 2005,

> in practice, is one of the major places where this approach [a focus on good governance] has been applied. In many ways, I think, the overwhelming insight is that capacity to make these things happen according to our own ['Western'] ideas and principles is amazingly small.[69]

Stephen Browne largely agrees with Uvin:

> Rwanda is now in a full phase of post-conflict reconstruction, for which short-term assistance can be essential. But aided rehabilitation must lead to an early restoration of normal development processes and encourage a mentality of self-sufficiency rather than dependence, which aid agencies are often disinclined to do.

There is one, more positive, indication, according to Browne: 'It is the *Government* which has recently stated its intention to reduce dependence on aid in the future.'[70]

Nevertheless, *caveat lector*; Browne wrote this in 1999.

Poverty, women, UN reform, and the unfilled tin cup

Rwanda was not the only place where funds for alleviating poverty disappeared in the 1990s. The decade after the cold war was one in which aid in general began to dry up. Global contributions to development assistance fell by a quarter in real terms during the Speth years.[71] The decline in

---

[69] Faculty Profile, Peter Uvin, Henry Leir Professor of International Humanitarian Studies and Director, Institute for Human Security, the Fletcher School, http://fletcher.tufts.edu/profilesfaculty/uvin.shtml (accessed 12 Nov. 2005).

[70] Browne, *Beyond Aid*, p. 173 (emphasis added).   [71] Calculated from ibid., p. 33.

contributions to UNDP was much larger. In real terms UNDP's core
funding dropped nearly 60 per cent; due to the expansion of programmes
in eastern Europe, in Africa, the world's poorest region, core resources fell
by 70 per cent. In 1999, fifty UNDP country offices – many of them in the
poorest countries – were spending more on administering the office than
on actual programmes.[72]

Not surprisingly, in terms of poverty alleviation UNDP's major
accomplishments of the period have to do with coordinating funding and
using it more effectively. In 1995, at the World Summit for Social
Development (held in Copenhagen shortly before the Beijing Conference
on Women), governments agreed to push for regular national poverty
assessments 'with rigorous attention to the gendered dimension of
poverty'. In 1999 these assessments became the indicative plans, or
Poverty Reduction Strategy Papers (PRSPs), required by the World Bank.
This was, Speth says, work 'launched and initiated' by UNDP.[73]

In the same year in which the Bank began the PRSPs, it joined the
International Monetary Fund, the UN, and the organization of the major
bilateral donors in supporting a list of seven sustainable development goals
derived from the 1995 global meetings and the earlier Rio summit.[74] The
1999 agreement provided the basis for the eight, slightly less ambitious,
Millennium Development Goals (MDGs), adopted at the global summit in
2000. (The MDGs abandoned earlier commitments to reproductive health
services for all and to reversing environmental decay – major blows to
women's groups and to environmentalists.) Speth points out that the 1999
goals were first discussed in the UN Development Group, the regular meetings of UN development programmes, funds, and agencies that he chaired.
They had begun in 1997 as part of a larger reform package.

That package 'was my baby', Speth says, 'and I think she has grown up
well. It is hard to imagine how much effort it took to get this in place and
then off to a good start.'[75]

The reforms involved six elements: (i) the coordinating Group itself;
(ii) a UN Development Assistance Framework (UNDAF) for each

---

[72] UNDP 1999–2005: Accomplishments and Remaining Challenges, p. 1.
[73] Speth, annotation on documents sent to CNM, 18 Dec. 2004; UNDP Policy Paper,
'Poverty Eradication: A Policy Framework for Country Strategies', New York, 1995,
pp. 24–42.
[74] A Better World for All: Progress towards the International Development Goals (Washington,
D.C., Paris, and New York: International Monetary Fund, Organisation for Economic Cooperation and Development, United Nations, and World Bank, 2000).
[75] Speth, annotation on documents sent to CNM, 18 Dec. 2004; UN Development Group,
A Framework for Change (New York: United Nations, 1997).

country to link the whole range of UN development activities to common objectives within a single time-frame; (iii) a commitment to having UN offices share common premises, 'UN Houses'; (iv) helping governments to follow up on global conferences and the goals set there, thus, for example, establishing the procedures to monitor the MDGs; (v) strengthening the UN Resident Coordinators and opening up greater opportunities for officers outside UNDP to take on that role; and (vi) reinforcing collaboration with the Bretton Woods agencies and with the UN's mechanisms for dealing with violations of human rights.

Looked at from the perspective of the entire history of UN development work, these reforms may not seem that startling. In David Owen and Paul Hoffman's day, Speth's predecessors had been the men on whom the first Secretaries-General relied to coordinate the development work of the entire UN family. In the best of cases, for example in Singapore, there really had been government indicative plans into which every element of UN (and bilateral) support had been coherently integrated – this had been Arthur Lewis's vision going back to his first report for the Fabian Society – and UNDAF would just pull things back towards a consistency that in some countries had been lost and in others had never been established. Following up on the global conferences was a bit new, although even the goals of the First Development Decade had been monitored by New York. Asserting the role of UNDP's (or, earlier, the Technical Assistance Board's) Resident Representative as each country's chief UN officer has been a regular issue in UNDP's history. And managing the sometimes troubled relationship with the powerful Bretton Woods agencies is a recurring theme.

In the 1990s, though, achieving even the reaffirmation of these principles may have been remarkable because shrinking development resources made reform increasingly important, yet the coalition pushing for such reform was inherently dysfunctional. In 1995 Stephen Browne captured the need for reform, and part of the dysfunction, especially well. Despite all the claims about the inadequacy of development assistance, he wanted to assert, as strongly as possible, that

> the UN System is over-aided. Anyone who has any doubts about this should ask whether, in some of our individual programme countries, it is justified to have a dozen or more separate UN agency reps – each with separate offices – jostling for influence and where different agency missions are treading on each other's coat-tails. Even in a new country like Ukraine, there have been instances of blatant duplication, which are easy to spot in an

integrated office through which everything passes. Even UNDP's own small departments sometimes compete with each other.[76]

Similarly, part of the horror of Somalia in the early 1990s – and then repeated in some other crisis countries – was that aid agencies, in their rush to be in the most newsworthy disaster area of the day, bid up prices of housing, transportation, and other services. The international community thereby helped to impoverish some of the few Somalis who had been spared the famine and to put money into the hands of warlords, who perpetuated the violence.[77] With aid budgets shrinking and the demand for services growing – as it did throughout the post-cold war decade, maintaining the UN's multiple, competing development units seemed, at the very best, absurd.

Yet initial attempts to rationalize the UN's work proved difficult. In summer 1996 Boutros-Ghali asked Maurice Strong to take on the job (with the support, on development matters, of Speth), and a few months later Boutros-Ghali's successor, Kofi Annan, asked Strong to stay on as Under-Secretary General for UN Reform. UNFPA's Nafis Sadik explains,

> The initial proposal was that there should be one development programme, and that UNICEF, and UNFPA, and the development part of WFP should be all merged into UNDP. Obviously, we resisted very strongly for very obvious reasons in that UNDP was not very well established and its funding was going down. Even Maurice Strong said that UNICEF and UNFPA were brand names and therefore they had to be preserved because they were well known – especially UNICEF is very well known – and UNDP was not known at all, in spite of its fifty years of existence.[78]

This is an odd comment. UNDP was certainly well known in the developing world, although not necessarily as well known as UNICEF among citizens in the donor countries. UNDP was certainly 'well established'. Moreover, as a glance at any multinational corporation would reveal, it is quite easy to maintain multiple brand names under a single administration. General Motors finds it easy to sell both Opels and

---

[76] Browne, 'The United Nations in Ukraine', p. 9 (emphasis in original).

[77] Enrico Augelli and Craig N. Murphy, 'Lessons of Somalia for Future Multilateral Humanitarian Peace Operations', *Global Governance*, 1, 3 (1995): 341–63. Pankaj Mishra saw the same pattern in Afghanistan a decade later, 'The Real Afghanistan', *New York Review of Books*, 52, 4 (10 March 2005) 44–8.

[78] Nafis Sadik, interview for the UN Intellectual History Project, 20–21 May 2002, Graduate Center, City University of New York.

Cadillacs (and dozens of other brands) within a single corporate struc-ture. The real problem that Maurice Strong would face was the vested interests of all the redundant offices that any comprehensive reform would have abolished.

The leaders of each of the organizations that Strong hoped to merge had allies within the funding nations, and, as the saying goes, 'He who has the gold, makes the rules.' Or perhaps in this case, 'She who has the gold'. Carol Bellamy, who was then UNICEF chief, points out that Speth's major rivals – Sadik, herself, and Catherine Bertini of WFP (like Bellamy, an American) – all had direct lines into the US Congress and the White House, 'a lot of women'.[79] In Washington, Bill Clinton seemed to insist on the kind of rationalization that Strong and Boutros-Ghali pro-posed. Congressional leaders had been demanding such belt-tightening for more than a decade and, because such reform had not been forth-coming, refusing to pay part of the dues the United States owed to the UN. On the other hand, Hillary Clinton – the president's wife and a political force in her own right – had her own agenda. Roy Morey, who served as Speth's Washington liaison, recalls her 'speaking at a UNFPA forum, right at the time a budget was going to be submitted in Congress'. He is certain of, but

> can't prove, direct tit-for-tat. Twenty-five million dollars [about one-third of the US's contribution] taken out of the request for UNDP and given to UNFPA. [Hillary] made the announcement at a big meeting in Europe, rubbing the noses of rather conservative members of Congress

who disliked UNFPA's support for women and reproductive health.[80]

In the meantime, according to a Nordic newsletter for development insiders, 'Sweden, the largest Nordic donor, told Bellamy frankly that if UNICEF remained outside the reform process this would have conse-quences for UNICEF's funding'.[81] Yet, Bellamy is sympathetic to the reformers who had to navigate among the UN organizations and their donor allies. She is especially sympathetic to Speth, 'He was trying to be reasonable.' Unfortunately his professorial manner, his quiet attempts to explain that 'This is a good direction', often proved ineffective. Bellamy does not say so directly, but perhaps, like many professors no matter how

---

[79] Carol Bellamy, interview with Elizabeth Mandeville (EM), 9 Aug. 2005.
[80] Roy Morey, interview with EM, 4 April 2005.
[81] 'Move by UNICEF Chief to Dilute UN Reform Plan May Backfire', *Development Today: Nordic Outlook on Development Assistance, Business, and the Environment*, 7, 11–12 (23 July 1997): 4.

kind and well intentioned, Speth may have come across as arrogant and condescending. On the other hand, Bellamy agrees, Speth's reforms, including the UN Development Group, were a reasonable compromise because they accepted the autonomy of the different programmes and funds while creating frameworks in which their shared interests could come to the fore. 'It is,' Bellamy says, 'for the principals of the core agencies to make the thing work, and if they don't . . . then that's the choice you make.'[82]

As far as Speth's reassertion of UNDP as the UN's coordinator within each developing country goes, Bellamy (unlike Sadik) sees little to complain about. Nevertheless, she points out that this reassertion turned out to be a lot less than it seemed. Beginning in the 1990s, in dozens of countries (usually crisis countries) the Resident Coordinator (and UNDP Res Rep) has been pushed to the side when a 'Special Representative of the Secretary-General' (SRSG) was put in charge of the UN presence:

> The lack of understanding and respect, not for UNICEF, but for the development process and the country teams . . . in a lot of these SRSGs or whoever the hell they were, was much more worrisome than an occasional boring, pompous, Resident Coordinator.[83]

In the end the UN development system may have been as under-coordinated and 'over-aided' at the end of the post-cold war decade as it had been at the beginning.

In 2004, thinking back on the limited results of the 1990s reforms, a successful (private) development fund-raiser who had worked in UNDP under Draper says that some in her field believe that 'Speth just didn't know how to shake the tin cup'. To be more accurate, she explains, he faced the most difficult fund-raising environment ever experienced by any Administrator with fund-raising skills that were probably no better than those of his predecessors.[84] Certainly Speth would have had more credibility in the reform process had donors been increasing their contributions to UNDP. Sadik's dismissal of the Programme ('its funding is going down') would have had little bite.

Yet the most tragic impact of the declining donor commitment may not have been on UN reform, but on the unified purpose that Speth had finally brought to UNDP. The Programme's budget actually remained relatively stable throughout the 1990s. Much of the drop in donor contri-

---

[82] Carol Bellamy, interview with EM, 9 Aug. 2005.
[83] Ibid.   [84] Sarah Papineau Marshall, interview with CNM, 23 Nov. 2004.

butions was offset with funds from 'cost-sharing' projects. These gave UNDP some administrative overhead that could be used to pursue its own goals, but undermined a unified, strategic vision.

Throughout the 1990s Eduardo Gutierrez, the major innovator of cost-sharing projects in Argentina, worried about the perverse consequences of headquarters urging country offices in Asia and Africa to follow the Latin American lead.[85] When I began my research one of the retirees who first offered to help, Patrick Shima, advised that, when visiting country offices, I ask experienced staff members, 'What are the key factors you believe UNDP Headquarters uses in judging the performance of this office?' This would provide 'a true insight . . . as to what drives country office operations, which most agree is the heart of UNDP'.[86] I followed the advice, and heard 'the volume of resources we raise locally' much more often than 'the consistency of our country programme with UNDP's overall goals'.

Önder Yücer shakes his head at comments like that by Nafis Sadik in 1999 that UNDP 'didn't know what its role was', but he recognizes the truth behind them. An independent assessment of possible futures for UNDP, more than 400 pages long, written a year earlier for the German Development Institute, could come up with five plausible scenarios, only one of which involved the 'substantive focusing' that Speth had attempted. Equally plausible was UNDP simply becoming a contractor for others.[87] As Speth's successor, Mark Malloch Brown, told the man who succeeded him, 'In chasing after business of all sorts, UNDP had become a jack-of-all-trades but seemed the master of none. Any kind of development project in any sector you could imagine, UNDP was doing somewhere in the world.'[88] As a result, Malloch Brown, whose leadership strengths combine the political and intellectual, but emphasize the political, would face a very different set of issues than those that had engaged the 'holy man' he followed.

---

[85] Eduardo Gutierrez, interview with CNM, 3 Aug. 2004.

[86] Patrick Shima, electronic mail to CNM, 28 July 2004.

[87] Stephan Klingebiel, *Effectiveness and Reform of the United Nations Development Programme* (London: Frank Cass, 1999), pp. 283–90.

[88] UNDP 1999–2005: Accomplishments and Remaining Challenges, p. 2.

11

'Fabian socialists do not make the cut'

Mark Malloch Brown was a new kind of Administrator. Most strikingly, he was not from the United States.

In 1999, with the real US financial contribution to UNDP dropping (and with the United States owing more than a billion dollars in back dues to the UN proper), European governments pressed Kofi Annan to choose Speth's successor from a more reliable donor country. John Bolton, the former Reagan administration official, complained that Bill Clinton's refusal to demand that an American have the job showed that the Democrat was 'spineless' and 'without vision', but it had been congressional Republicans who led the effort to reduce US contributions and hold back part of its dues for more than a decade. Clinton tended to defer to them on UN-related issues, saving his political capital for what he saw as bigger battles. The *New York Times* even reported, 'Washington had given up the post in hopes of further reducing its contribution to United Nations development aid.'[1]

The Secretary-General ended up bypassing the candidates pressed on him by donor governments, and went instead for a man he had respected for two decades, a UK citizen with an advanced degree in political science from the University of Michigan and a long career in public communication. Annan and Malloch Brown had been colleagues at the Office of the UN High Commissioner for Refugees in the 1980s. Afterwards, Malloch Brown founded *The Economist Development Report*, worked for a private firm that had advised a host of leaders of the new democratic movements of the late 1980s and early 1990s, and then, in 1994, took over external affairs at the World Bank.

Given his experience, Annan's friend may have been the first Administrator to understand UNDP's peculiar form of organization from the day that he arrived. Malloch Brown recognized that the Programme had always really been about persuasive communication, about 'coordinating and cultivating'. He called UNDP 'a network of smart ideas [and] talented

---

[1] Judith Miller, 'Outgoing UN Development Chief Berates US', *New York Times*, 1 May 1999.

people' focused on 'advocacy and advice, pilots and partnerships'.[2] Yet the new Administrator believed that, for UNDP to continue to do its quintessential job, its organizational culture needed to change.

Malloch Brown's strategies for achieving that cultural change included bringing different perspectives to the top of the organization. He gave part of that task to Joan Dunlop, whose International Women's Health Coalition had a twenty-year track record as one of the most effective international non-governmental organizations (NGOs) in almost all the global development policy debates.[3] Dunlop acted as a headhunter. Her job was to find a new kind of leader to fill open positions at the top of the Asian and eastern European bureaux. 'My sense', Dunlop says, was that Malloch Brown 'wanted someone with senior government experience . . . a first class economist who is also a social reformer. People comfortable with a free market economy who had management experience.' With that in mind, she wrote in one of her recruitment letters, 'Hence, those who are second or third generation trained by Fabian socialists do not make the cut.' (They will not get the job.)[4] The new Administrator, who admired Bill Draper, wanted to alter the self-replicating mix of people chosen by the UN network's *first* British leader, David Owen, more than fifty years before.

Malloch Brown did change UNDP, although perhaps not as dramatically as he had hoped to. He put the Programme back on a solid financial footing and raised its global profile. In his final year as Administrator, *Time* magazine placed Malloch Brown (and, pointedly, *not* Kofi Annan) on its list of the world's '100 most influential people'. In addition, there, at the top of those categorized as 'scientists and thinkers', was Jeffrey Sachs, the economist whom Malloch Brown had brought in to be sort of his own Mahbub ul Haq. The list contained other UNDP partners and friends: Singapore's Lee Kuan Yew, the Orange Revolution's Viktor Yushchenko, Kenya's Wangari Maathai, and Stephen Lewis, the Canadian diplomat now coordinating the UN's HIV/AIDS efforts in Africa.[5]

Of course, as with any significant organizational change, Malloch Brown's revolution came at a cost. In securing funding and raising the

[2] Mark Malloch Brown, 'Statement to the Executive Board', 19 June 2000, in *Mark Malloch Brown at the United Nations Development Programme: Statements, Speeches, and Commentary, 1999–2005* (New York: UNDP, 2005), p. 167.

[3] Ole Jacob Sending, 'Policy Stories and Knowledge-Based Règimes: The Case of International Population Policy', in Morten Bøås and Desmond McNeill, eds., *Global Institutions and Development: Framing the World?* (London: Routledge, 2004), p. 65.

[4] Joan Dunlop, interview with Elizabeth Mandeville (EM), 18 Aug. 2005.

[5] 'The *Time* 100: The Lives and Ideas of the World's Most Influential People, 2005', http://www.time.com/time/2005/time100/ (accessed 6 Jan. 2006).

11.1 Mark Malloch Brown

Programme's profile, Malloch Brown left UNDP with a slightly less coherent purpose than Gus Speth's sustainable human development (SHD).
UNDP went back to Draper's strategy of 'running on two tracks'. UNDP
provided each government with a set of services (within the Programme's
mandate) tailored to the country's own development priorities. At the same
time UNDP maintained a 'second track' of advocacy, advocating both
human development and, increasingly, the Millennium Development
Goals (MDGs), potentially contradictory frameworks united under a
common concern for democratic governance. Malloch Brown gave prominence to the MDGs, arguing that they reflected a global consensus on
targets, even if they rested on no widely shared understanding about the
nature of development or how it could be achieved. Similarly, the critical
issues facing many governments led UNDP to take on new tasks without
really placing them conceptually under the SHD framework. The most significant of these, that of combating HIV/AIDS, was something that no
other UN development organization was willing to address in the same way.

By the end of Malloch Brown's tenure in 2005, UNDP was, undoubtedly, a more legitimate organization in the eyes of many developing
nations and of most major donors than it had been at the beginning.

It was also, in many ways, a much more professional organization. Malloch Brown's last official words as Administrator were these:

> I'm very, very glad that Kemal Dervis [the former Middle East Technical University economist] comes to succeed me . . . [A]fter dinner as I was just leaving, Kemal got into a real debate with Hafiz Pasha and Kalman Mizsei [the regional bureau chiefs recruited by Dunlop] and Rima [the visionary economist behind the *Arab Human Development Reports*] and others about the real economic costs of trade and free trade. And they started talking about curves that I vaguely remember from my very simple 101 training in economics, and calculations of benefit that I couldn't keep up with, and I was able to stand up and say, I'm leaving. I'm leaving because this organization has now reached an intellectual level where I can't keep up! It's time to go.[6]

It was more legitimate, more professional, and in the words of the Carter Center's Ed Cain (who spent much of his career with UNDP), an organization whose understanding of its own purpose was as close to 'the role it was designed to play from the beginning'[7] as it ever had been.

Solvency and reform

When he arrived, Malloch Brown clearly understood the immediate crisis that UNDP faced: the shrinking development assistance pie, and UNDP's shrinking proportion of it. When he spoke about the problem, he talked about a deep global consensus on development that many others did not see and he emphasized only the nobler motivations of donors. Nevertheless, the reforms instituted by the new Administrator were realistic and they worked. They endeared UNDP both to donor governments and to many other development organizations. This allowed UNDP to build a more complex system of partnerships and, through them, become a more viable organization.

In 1999 UNDP had programmes in over 160 countries, but fewer than one in ten were based on 'sustainable business models'.[8] Most country offices, and the UN coordination role that they performed, were threatened by the continuing drop in core support; this decline was taking place at a much faster rate than was the overall drop in international aid throughout the 1990s.

[6] Malloch Brown, 'Farewell', 13 July 2005, in *Mark Malloch Brown at the United Nations Development Programme*, p. 584.
[7] Recall Edmund Cain's statement, interview with the author (CNM), 8 Sept. 2004.
[8] Memorandum report 'UNDP 1999–2005, Accomplishments and Remaining Challenges', from Mark Malloch Brown to Kemal Dervis, August 2005, p. 2.

In 2005 Malloch Brown told his successor that UNDP's particular problem had been a consequence of its success, of other organizations adopting the human development approach. 'What do you do', Malloch Brown wrote, 'when you have done such a good job of persuading others that you have the right ideas that they are doing them as well now, and on a much bigger scale with a lot more resources?'[9]

An alternative explanation of UNDP's problem is that donors found other organizations' *interpretations* of 'human development' more attractive than that of UNDP. Sakiko Fukuda-Parr points out that the World Bank's operationalization of 'human development' involved little more than renaming its departments concerned with education and health:

> It is another thing to go one step further, and espouse the entire paradigm, that development is about improving the lives of each individual and a process that involves individuals being able to improve their own lives and make a difference in society . . . [T]hat requires redefining a whole spectrum of development policy analysis that goes beyond spending more on education and health.[10]

It means tackling deeply rooted problems of social justice.

Some critics are even less charitable. They see not only a simplifying-through-disaggregation of ul Haq's central concept in other organizations, but also a deradicalization of the policy analysis that other agencies apply to each of the separate elements. For the Bank and for some bilateral organizations, 'poverty alleviation' is still often reduced to 'growth', 'crises of human security' become opportunities to restructure societies to reinforce the global status quo, and 'good governance' becomes little more than 'protecting private property'.[11] (These organizations are also, of course, ones where major donors have great influence over how the

---

[9] Ibid., p. 3.   [10] Sakiko Fukuda-Parr, letter to CNM, 2 Jan. 2006.
[11] Recall that the Bank's historians, Devesh Kapur, John B. Lewis and Richard Webb, *The World Bank: Its First Half-Century* (Washington, D.C.: Brookings Institution Press, 1997), p. 54, reiterate the theme that the Bank has consistently seen growth as the primary way to reduce poverty. Paul Cammack, 'The Mother of All Governments: The World Bank's Matrix for Global Governance', in Rorden Wilkinson and Steve Hughes, eds., *Global Governance: Critical Perspectives* (London: Routledge, 2002), pp. 36–54, discusses the ways in which Bank security crises and governance programmes work to institutionalize a particular form of political economy, as do a number of the authors in Isabella Bakker and Stephen Gill, eds., *Power, Production, and Social Reproduction* (Houndmills: Palgrave Macmillan, 2003). Bakker and a number of the other authors have worked for UNDP. Romilly Greenhill and Patrick Watt, *Real Aid: An Agenda for Making Aid Work* (Johannesburg: Action Aid International, 2005), outline similar difficulties with both Bank and bilateral programmes nominally concerned with 'human development'.

money is spent and what they gain in return.) In contrast, UNDP considers political reform to be as important as economic reform not because it accelerates growth, but because it helps to secure justice.

UNDP's largest problem in the 1990s was not just that others had embraced human development. It was that only a portion of all foreign aid goes to the things that UNDP considered important. Nigeria's UN ambassador, Joseph Garba, put one part of the problem succinctly, 'The Cold War is over, and Africa lost.'[12] With the fear of the spread of communism in the developing world diminished, aid to the poorest continent, he argued, began to dry up as soon as the competition between the superpowers ended. What donor interest remained, Garba maintained, was largely focused on the nations of the former Soviet bloc, some of them newly democratic or newly independent, many of them newly poor and newly conflict-ridden. Of course, Africa still gained from the portion of aid that supports the international system of solidarity embodied in the UN's development network. The international NGO ActionAid estimates that portion – what they call 'real aid' – as only 40 per cent of the aid granted in 2003.[13]

Since the 1950s UNDP and its predecessors have been very successful in cultivating the donor countries whose foreign assistance contains the highest proportion of 'real aid'. Nine of the ten countries with the best records, according to ActionAid, are regularly among the top fifteen contributors to UNDP (Denmark, Finland, Ireland, Japan, the Netherlands, Norway, Sweden, Switzerland, and the United Kingdom). Taken together, they are responsible for the majority of the Programme's core resources. Therefore maintaining their support is what the management schools call a 'critical success factor' for UNDP. Yet equally important is maintaining the support of one of the donors with one of the worst 'real aid' records, the United States. The US contribution to UNDP's core has acted as an informal upper limit to the contributions of other important donors. For example, many in tiny Norway – whose population is quite a bit less than the average of the US states – believe that giving more to UNDP than does the superpower would have unfortunate political consequences, both at home and in its relations with its powerful ally.[14]

---

[12] Quoted in John Maxwell Hamilton, 'Lessons for the Media from Foreign Aid', *Media Studies Journal*, 13, 3 (1999): 103.

[13] Greenhill and Watt, *Real Aid*, p. 17.

[14] As was forcefully brought home to me by many with whom I spoke at the Norwegian Institute of International Affairs, 28 Oct. 2005.

Given those constraints, to maintain core funding levels during a period
when overall aid was dropping and US aid was dropping even more
rapidly, UNDP had to be able to attract an *increasing* percentage of all the
'real aid' that the United States offered. UNDP also had to maintain or
increase its percentage of the aid budgets of the larger group of key donors.
This was a difficult task when each country's bilateral agency had the same
fundraising goals, and better access to its national legislature.[15] Moreover,
as Roy Morey, who was Speth's man in Washington, points out, all of the
organizations of the UN network were also competing for the same money
and, in the United States at least, an accident of politics made some much
more successful than UNDP. When conservative Republicans gained
control of the House of Representatives, they would have preferred to cut
off the UN entirely, but, Morey says, 'They didn't want to be accused of
hating everybody in developing countries . . . [so they] threw in their lot
with children' and substantial US funding was transferred to UNICEF.[16]

Beyond the 'real aid' that the United States gives, in part to UNICEF and
UNDP, it gives much more aid – ActionAid says six times as much – for
other purposes, including as direct support for its national security policies. Many other donors at the bottom of the 'real aid' chart do the same.
Not withstanding self-interested motivation for giving such funds, it is
often used in ways that improve the lives of people in the countries that
receive it. When the wealthy countries discovered new (post-cold war)
security concerns, UNDP was remarkably effective in capturing some of
the newly available resources, especially after the '9/11' 2001 terrorist
attacks on the World Trade Center and the Pentagon (the US Department
of Defense headquarters). By 2004 Afghanistan, where the United States
and its allies had removed the government that had sheltered the 9/11 terrorists, had become the country where (in financial terms) UNDP delivered
the most. Iraq, the site of the second war begun under a new US security
doctrine, was UNDP's number six. The total of the increase in funding just
to those two countries accounted for about 25 per cent of the 80 per cent
increase in overall funding achieved during Malloch Brown's tenure.[17]

Tapping into new streams of security-oriented aid would not, by itself,
have maintained the integrity of the Programme. To ensure that UNDP
did not become what the eminent scholar of international affairs, Robert

[15] Approximately US$100 million of the US$2.3 billion in 'real aid' estimated by Greenhill
and Watt, *Real Aid.* p. 31.   [16] Roy Morey, interview with EM, 4 April 2005.

[17] Calculated from 'UNDP 1999–2005', pp. 54–9, and UNDP, *Annual Report 2005: A
Time for Bold Ambition: Together We Can Cut Poverty in Half* (New York: UNDP, 2005),
p. 40.

W. Cox, called a mere system of 'global poor relief and riot control',[18] Malloch Brown had to prove to donors that UNDP could achieve the traditional goals of 'real aid' – building Northern solidarity with the people of the developing world' – as efficiently and as effectively as any other organization. It therefore would prove fortunate that Speth had brought a new level of professionalism to the UN network, including tools to allow multi-year planning of country programmes and avoid duplication from one UN organization to another. Within UNDP Speth established a system of 'Results Oriented Annual Reports' (ROARs) that would link the inputs the Programme provided to national goals and allow evaluation based on real outcomes.[19] Malloch Brown would be the implementer and beneficiary of all these innovations, but, initially, he had to focus elsewhere. To avoid financial crisis in a Programme built around a network of people meant finding a way to cut staff.

To do so, Malloch Brown turned, in part, to Brian Gleeson, an Australian human resources expert who had worked on Kofi Annan's initial reform project and for former Norwegian Prime Minister Gro Brundtland when she restructured the administration of the World Health Organization (WHO).

UNDP began a process of 'reprofiling' all the jobs within the organization, first at headquarters in New York, then in the country offices. The aim was to cut the number of people in New York by 25 per cent (in part by sending some to the field) and then cut the core budget of each field office by 15 per cent. That meant working out the actual range of functions that needed to be carried out in each part of the organization, eliminating unnecessary tasks, combining functions into new job descriptions, assessing the fit between the skills of existing staff and the new jobs, reassigning many people, and 'letting others go', often with a separation package. 'We all had to apply for our jobs again', is how most people in the country offices put it.

This was a process fraught with opportunities for disaster, but it largely worked, in part simply because the initial situation in many parts of the organization was such a mess and reprofiling at least shook things up. Gleeson estimates that

> Fifty per cent of the country offices that I visited had a dysfunctional leadership team . . . the Res Rep in charge, or the deputy . . . not being in sync with

---

[18] Robert W. Cox, 'Critical Political Economy', in Björn Hettne, ed., *International Political Economy: Understanding Global Disorder* (London: Zed Books, 1995), p. 41.

[19] UNDP, 'Annual Report of the Administrator for 1998', 23 April 1999, p. 4.

staff. Sad to see. International staff in these countries disempowering
national staff with cultural bias, lack of cultural sensitivity, harassment, violence . . . Many of these people had never seen anyone from headquarters
. . . All the real stories came out.

In one country, 'there was a guy running a sex Internet business from his
office', but his Res Rep defended him, ' "Come on, he's been here sixteen
years and has children, I can't get rid of him." Within a few months',
Gleeson adds, 'both he and the Res Rep were gone.'[20]

At least four aspects of the implementation of the plan reinforced the
boost in morale that came from this simple attention to long-neglected
problems. First, people within the organization, not outside consultants,
did the exercise. A large group, over 400, received training and a subset
carried out the process. This both gave many people new skills and made
the exercise much more like one of peer review. Second, the whole thing
was kept transparent. With everything on an open website, it was relatively easy to work out what you needed to do to keep your job, what your
options were, and whether there was any favouritism going on. Third, the
Programme simultaneously instituted an annual, confidential Global
Staff Survey, asking everyone for feedback on about 100 questions
ranging from the effectiveness of their immediate superior to the coherence of UNDP's overall mission. Such surveys have become commonplace in effectively managed companies, but were unheard of and
considered 'very risky in the UN', according to Gleeson.[21]

Finally, UNDP provided severance packages to more than 1,000 of
those it let go. At their best, the packages were part of a reorganization of
work – an outsourcing of non-essential tasks to more efficient private
companies – that fitted with Malloch Brown's overall business plan.
Joseph Tetteh, who spent most of his adult life as a UNDP driver in
Ghana's country office was the beneficiary of one of these packages. He
used the severance money to buy an elegant used black BMW – a truly
classic car with butter-soft leather seats, polished wood, and the ability to
cut out all the noise coming from Accra's busy streets. The car moves
much more swiftly through the city's white-water rapids of traffic than
any of the lumbering SUVs that now seem to be the vehicle of choice in
UN country offices.

[20] Brian Gleeson, interview with CNM, 2 June 2004.
[21] Ibid. Margaret Joan Anstee disagrees: 'We were doing it in Vienna in late 1980s–1990, as
part of a general UN process. People just keep reinventing the wheel and claiming that
nothing happened before they came on the scene!' Letter to CNM, 26 Feb. 2006.

The hope was that the country office would give up its fleet of blue-logoed cars and contract out to private companies like Tetteh's when there was the occasional visiting dignitary who needed transportation, thus continuing to provide former staff like Tetteh with work for the organization. And, in fact, when the Secretary-General is in town, he is quite happy to ride in the beautiful old car with Tetteh, who is Kofi Annan's contemporary and from the same region of the country. But, of course, a lot of people in the Accra office still feel they need their UN vehicle on immediate call – especially if someone else at their same level has one – so the corps of drivers has not shrunk that much. Tetteh, a very generous and gentle man, is philosophical about all that. He feels that UNDP has done well by him. His adult children have been educated all over the world, thanks to the money he was able to save, both when he was an employee and now that he has his own business, and he still relishes the opportunity to meet so many interesting people who are doing so many good things. 'But there is always room to grow', to do better, 'for me, maybe for UNDP.'[22]

In many country offices I kept hearing that one of the best recent reforms had been a new selection programme for Resident Coordinators and other senior officers. The *Financial Times* explained one aspect of this system for finding the most effective leaders:

> The United Nations Development Programme . . . has developed a surprisingly cut-throat solution. Send all your senior officials to a fantasy developing country, confront them with venal leaders, obstructive agitators, and manipulative reporters, throw in a few surprises and tell them their career depends on the outcome. If they perform well, they stay. But if they flounder, they can kiss the job goodbye (or, in the UNDP's more diplomatic language, 'identify which skills need further development').[23]

Many of the rest of the Malloch Brown-era efforts focused on turning UNDP into a learning organization. A first step was to keep increasing the percentage of the budget going to staff development, something that began under Speth. Then there was the matter of ensuring that appropriated funds were used effectively. This included a shift of emphasis from staff travel to an electronic, 'Virtual Development Academy', accessible to staff members around the world. Finally, there was the issue of making the knowledge produced throughout the vast organization more accessible and useful to everyone within it. The key has been the Internet, something quite a bit faster and accessible to more people than Bill Draper's

---

[22] Joseph Tetteh, interview with CNM, 19 Jan. 2005.
[23] Mark Turner, 'A Game of Management Survival', *Financial Times*, 4 Aug. 2003.

Action Committee ever was. By 2005, about 5,000 of UNDP's more than 7,000 core employees and another 1,000 people on the organization's fuzzy edge of external experts took part in one or more of sixteen 'knowledge networks', most built around specific practices like 'democratic governance' or 'poverty reduction'. The electronic bulletin board systems allow staffers across the globe to raise questions and share answers at any time of day or night. These days, when UNDP is supporting, on average, one election every two weeks somewhere in the world, a typical question might be about registering voters in a country where most public records have been destroyed in a war. The typical flood of answers would yield five or six possible solutions, each with known costs and benefits.[24]

More controversial among staff members, but with just as great impact on the organization's capacity, has been a web-based business system called 'Atlas' (as in 'holding up the world'). In 2004, it replaced some twenty-one separate, incompatible systems used in different parts of the organization – as well as a great deal of work done only on paper. Atlas is essentially an extremely complex project management and accounting system that allows each of the business activities within UNDP to be tracked from any office. It has markedly increased transparency, speeded up decision making and the disbursal of funds, allowed rapid and more thorough cost–benefit analysis, and helped to transfer management experience from one part of the organization to another.[25]

Any organization that introduces a new integrated information technology system faces anger and resistance. A staffer from Finland working in a remote office that lacked the Internet bandwidth that Atlas really required grumbled to me that Jan Mattsson, the Bureau of Management Director who brought the system in, was 'a real Hemulen!' – one of the benignly authoritarian beings introduced in the quintessentially Finnish 'Moomintroll' stories. 'The Hemulen', the stories' author tells us, 'isn't outstandingly intelligent and easily becomes a fanatic.'[26] In 2004 and 2005 there were certainly lots of stories of individuals throughout UNDP becoming unproductive for months as they slowly learned new ways to do their work, people who felt that Atlas had been designed by someone who was both a little dense and a little crazy.

---

[24] UNDP Knowledge Services Team, 'UNDP Knowledge Networking', presentation to the UNESCAP-Knowledge Management Workshop, Bangkok, Thailand, 7 March 2005.

[25] Jens Wandel, Jan Mattsson, and Georges van Montfort, 'Realigning the UNDP', unpublished paper, August 2005.

[26] Tove Jansson, The Exploits of Moominpappa, trans. Thomas Warburton (London: Puffin Books, 1969), p. 21.

Nevertheless, in the end, even some of the most fanatical aspects of the system have paid off. Anyone with access to the Programme's internal Internet site can see up-to-date and historical reports on every office, sources of funding, and even some information on every employee. (One day, when surfing those files, I was pleased to find, for example, that UNDP's 'Goodwill Ambassadors', including the football greats, Ronaldo and Zidane, all have relatively high honorary UN grades – sort of the equivalent of being two-star generals – but I was surprised that, despite the reforms, UNDP still had so many 'brigadiers' on the books.) More significant are uses like this one reported by the Res Rep in Rwanda:

> When I first arrived . . . one of the major challenges was the US$60 million in unaccounted programme and trust funds, some going back ten years. We had over 100 unclosed/unaudited projects that were not running. Donors had stopped giving new money to the Country Office and were very vocal in their displeasure at the state of affairs. Today, owing to the Atlas-driven auditing and accounting process, we have cleared up the entire backlog and accounted for all the money . . . all the donors have come back on board as we have continued to demonstrate transparency in our accounting and in our programmes.[27]

By 2005 a half-decade of these and other reforms had paid off. Donors came back and UNDP funding grew more rapidly than overall aid increased in the years after 9/11. A series of internal and external evaluations help to explain why. The Global Staff Surveys have shown across-the-board improvements since 2000, including on issues where the Programme originally scored very poorly, such as 'in UNDP, administrative tasks get handled in a timely manner'. In 1999 only one out of six staffers agreed. In 2004 it was one out of two. In the same year about 90 per cent of UNDP's partners agreed that the Programme's projects reflected national priorities and 90 per cent said that they truly involved beneficiaries in their design and execution, up from under 80 per cent and about 60 per cent respectively two years earlier. Reports by the 'Multilateral Organizations Performance Assessment Network' (MOPAN) – largely made up of the donors that give the highest proportion of 'real aid' – handed UNDP high marks.[28] Finally, in 2005, a much more comprehensive British study, ranked UNDP, other UN agencies, and the multilateral development banks on a variety of measures of capacity, especially the capacity to identify and learn from results. UNDP had the best record of the entire group.

[27] Quoted in 'UNDP 1999–2005', p. 66.   [28] UNDP, *Annual Report 2005*, pp. 37–9.

Table 11.1. *Organizational effectiveness (percentage of maximum possible score)*

Agency	Internal performance	Country-level results	Partnership focus	Total scores
UNDP	**96**	**98**	**98**	**97**
World Bank	86	86	91	88
World Health Organization	68	65	70	68
World Food Programme	75	76	84	78
European Union	79	84	93	85
Average over all 23 agencies studied	**81**	**74**	**83**	**80**

Unfortunately, as my grandmother used to say, 'No good deed goes unpunished.' External observers largely credited Mark Malloch Brown with the organizational reforms that produced these results (hence his position on *Time* magazine's list of global influentials). At the end of 2004, with the United Nations wracked by the continuing scandals over the Oil for Food Programme that the Secretariat had managed as part of the Security Council's sanctions on Iraq, Kofi Annan asked his friend to leave UNDP and become, effectively, his number two. Malloch Brown did so in 2005, but with some misgivings. What he had done at UNDP, Malloch Brown says, self-effacingly, was to finish the process that Draper and Speth had started – of moving the organization's business practices at least from 'the 1950s to the 1980s', but the UN Secretariat was even 'further back', organizationally, than UNDP.[29]

Poverty and the MDGs

Some stories in the development press made it sound as if one of Malloch Brown's major accomplishments for Kofi Annan in this new role involved saving the MDGs (one part of the Secretary-General's larger reform agenda) from John Bolton. George W. Bush had named Bolton as US ambassador to the UN shortly before the September 2005 summit that Annan had hoped would back his plans. The US ambassador was, in fact,

[29] Mark Malloch Brown, interview with CNM, 21 Oct. 2005.

a major ally in pursuing many of the goals Annan had outlined in his March reform report,[30] but the US administration disliked fixed targets like those that had been agreed to by Bill Clinton at the Millennium Summit in 2000. As Stephen Krasner, the State Department's Director of Policy Planning, puts it, the United States has, increasingly, 'a different attitude toward international obligations, more interest based rather than aspirational, as opposed to Europe', which, in a variety of cases, 'will not come close to meeting their targets, but the Europeans like the targets nevertheless'.[31]

In fact, it was precisely the 'benchmark' quality of the MDGs that made them so appealing to Malloch Brown and many of their supporters; that was why, in 2002, he happily accepted the roles of 'scorekeeper and campaign manager' of the MDGs for himself (as chair of the UN Development Group) and for UNDP. He argued that UNDP would build on the benchmarking experience gained through the *Human Development Report* (HDR), citing Brazil's allocation of anti-poverty funds to its fourteen states with the lowest Human Development Index and the similar programme in Madhya Pradesh, which (until it was split in 2000) had been the largest of the Indian states, with a destitute population as great as that in all of Brazil.[32]

Some in UNDP felt that this conclusion reflected a misunderstanding of the *major* function of the HDRs. Fighting poverty, ending destitution, is *one* thing that must be done to foster human development, but it is only a part of a much larger picture. Sakiko Fukuda-Parr writes, 'MDG reports are monitoring tools and national HDRs are more analytical and longer-term frameworks.' Things that cannot be measured easily cannot be included in the MDGs: democracy, equity, social justice, and human rights. The MDGs are potentially excellent tools for democratic accountability; 'people can post these in village halls and demand action', but they do not cover every aspect of human development.[33]

The MDGs certainly were not meant to demote 'human development', even though, when Malloch Brown first came to UNDP, he used the tag line 'Partnerships to Fight Poverty' as the description of UNDP's work,

[30] Kofi Annan, 'In Larger Freedom: Towards Development, Security, and Freedom for All', Report of the Secretary-General to the General Assembly, 21 March 2005.
[31] Stephen D. Krasner, electronic mail to CNM, 5 Sept. 2005.
[32] Malloch Brown, 'New Direction, A New Relationship: Poverty Reduction Strategy Papers and the Millennium Declaration Goals', 19 March 2001, in *Mark Malloch Brown at the United Nations Development Programme*, p. 240.
[33] Sakiko Fukuda-Parr, letter to CNM, 2 Jan. 2006.

believing that, to the public at large, Speth's 'Sustainable Human
Development' evoked no clear image.[34] Nonetheless, Malloch Brown
links fighting poverty and the democratic-capacity-building work that
was one of the major innovations of the Speth and Draper eras. In the
major speech where he pointed to the benchmarking role played by some
HDRs, Malloch Brown embraced the World Bank's 'poverty reduction
strategy papers' (PRSPs) as the key tool that governments and donors
would use to help countries to achieve their anti-poverty goals. He
pledged UNDP's support to civil society dialogues and other means of
helping to ensure that the plans reflected the priorities of the public at
large. At the same time, UNDP would provide technical assistance to help
countries to identify the widest range of alternative strategies that could
be used to achieve those of the MDGs that were achievable.

In the poorest continent, Africa, this pledge, in practice, meant something of a return to the Damiba-era provision of economic expertise to
national governments negotiating with a powerful World Bank and other
donors which have long-standing (and sometimes effective) methods of
coordinating their policy, and, of course, a return to a kind of policy that
the UN network began in the 1950s. When the process works well, the
results can be very significant. In Ghana, the government that came to
power in the 2000 elections that ended Jerry Rawlings's long rule used
UNDP funds to bring an expatriate economist, George Yaw Gyan-
Baffour, back to work on Ghana's first PRSP. Then there was an updated
'GPRS' (Ghana Poverty Reduction Strategy, an outward and visible sign
of an inward and committed national ownership), and, finally, the
country's MDG report. Gyan-Baffour talks about the importance of the
public dialogues that have 'brought about a consciousness' that public
policy can have an impact on poverty and he praises the way in which the
informal network of economists working on MDG issues in different
countries (brought together by UNDP) has encouraged both their creativity and their discipline.

The former Howard University professor (educated at the Helsinki
School of Economics and the University of Wisconsin, and long-time resident of Geneva and Washington, D.C.) is conscious of the irony of his
UNDP role. We spoke in a room he occupied in the same Flagstaff House
compound where Robert Jackson and Arthur Lewis worked almost fifty
years before. (The furniture looks as if it might have been scratched by
Jackson's Siamese cats.) Gyan-Baffour's indicative planning job is almost

---

[34] Mark Malloch Brown, interview with CNM, 4 June 2004.

the same as Lewis's. 'UNDP', the planner says, 'has a history of staying at the forefront, yet behind the scenes. This is an oxymoron, but that's the way it is.'[35]

The difference, this time, is the public involvement of the expert that the UN Programme provided – part of the job of the new UNDP style of support for the PRSPs. The public dialogues convinced Gyan-Baffour and his family to move back to Ghana so that he could contest a parliamentary seat in the rural district where he was born. This fits with Malloch Brown's usual argument about the connection between UNDP's anti-poverty work and its concern with democratic governance. It is the argument that Dante Caputo and Ricardo Lagos have made about Latin America: if the political debate in poor democratic countries comes to focus on concrete development issues and real solutions (through local HDRs, the promotion of the MDGs, public dialogues about the PRSPs, or any other mechanism), democracy is much more likely to be preserved. Moreover, UNDP has been involved in some very dramatic cases of self-reinforcing cycles in which national dialogues about addressing poverty have reinforced democratization, and new stages of democratization have led to more direct attention to poverty. Bolivia, over the last decade, is a case often cited by people within the Programme.[36] Gyan-Baffour's move from economic advisor to legislator is a small, personal example of the same process.

Before I leave, my Ghanaian colleague wants to talk about the 'superstars' that UNDP has brought in to help this work. Most prominent is Jeffrey Sachs, once the bad-boy development economist hated by progressives in central and eastern Europe and Latin America for the social costs of the 'shock therapy' he recommended to countries facing structural adjustment, but now transformed, in part by the perspective on poverty that his wife, a physician, gave him when she joined his international missions. Did I agree that Sachs's new report on practical steps to achieve the MDGs was brilliant?[37] Yes, actually, I did, but I doubted that we would see the donor funding needed for the 'massive scale-up' of pilot projects in those countries (probably including Ghana) where lack of aid was, now, the main impediment to rapid gains. Sachs should have

---

[35] George Gyan-Baffour, interview with CNM, 18 Jan. 2005.

[36] UNDP Evaluation Office, Evaluation of UNDP's Role in the PRSP Process, vol. 1 (New York: UNDP, 2003), p. 29. Antonio Vigilante, interview with CNM, 20 April 2005.

[37] UN Millennium Project 2005. Investing in Development: A Practical Plan to Achieve the Millennium Development Goals (New York: UNDP, 2005). On Sachs's understanding of poverty see Sonia Erlich Sachs and Jeffery D. Sachs, 'Too Poor to Stay Alive', in Kyle D. Kauffmann and David L. Lindauer, eds., AIDS and South Africa: The Social Expression of a Pandemic (New York: Palgrave Macmillan, 2004), pp. 1–16.

had political scientists (or maybe some politicians) on his team to give the analysis a bit more realism. Gyan-Baffour smiles.

The other superstars are UNDP's football-playing Goodwill Ambassadors, Ronaldo and Zidane, who have probably done more to publicize the MDGs through their television spots and 'Matches Against Poverty' than all the rest of the MDG promoters combined. Jeff Sachs's involvement with UNDP's position could be attributed to Malloch Brown, but Speth deserves much of the credit for Ronaldo and Zidane. It was on Speth's watch, in 1998, that UNDP appointed its first Goodwill Ambassadors, Hollywood's Danny Glover and Nadine Gordimer, the South African Nobel literature laureate.

Crisis prevention and recovery, the bureau and beyond

In late 2004 Glover left UNDP to become a Goodwill Ambassador for UNICEF, explaining that he had a growing concern for children, who are increasingly the direct or indirect victims of war.[38] When Nigeria's Joseph Garba said that Africa had 'lost' at the end of the cold war, he was not just referring to shrinking aid. The 1990s plunged many of the world's poorest countries into cycles of violent internal conflict marked by warlordism and shadowy 'private' armies of self-described 'rebels' supported by the guns and money of foreign governments. Humanitarian agencies – both public and private – ended up with the responsibility for helping victims to cope with the resulting physical and psychological devastation. Many agencies began to complain that they were becoming tools of insensitive Northern governments trying to maintain international order on the cheap. An angry *Annual Report* of the International Federation of Red Cross and Red Crescent Societies referred to the resulting intergovernmental and non-governmental 'colonialism' and the 'pimp talk' that pervaded the reports of all the organizations seeking to satisfy the shifting charitable whims of the major donors.[39] It was in this context that Robert W. Cox worried about the UN becoming a system of 'poor relief and riot control' for an increasingly unequal world.[40]

UNDP took on some of this post-cold war burden as part of its overall SHD agenda. Inside the organization you regularly hear the calculation

[38] UNICEF Transcript, Danny Glover Press Conference, Addis Hilton, 27 Nov. 2004.
[39] International Federation of Red Cross and Red Crescent Societies, *World Disasters Report* (Oxford: Oxford University Press, 1997), pp. 14, 21.
[40] Robert W. Cox, 'Critical Political Economy', in Björn Hettne, ed., *International Political Economy: Understanding Global Disorder* (London: Zed Books, 1995), p. 41.

that about one-third of the countries where UNDP works are either facing crises or recovering from them. When Malloch Brown arrived, even before receiving Executive Board approval, he put this work – which had grown dramatically in the Speth era – under a new 'Bureau for Crisis Prevention and Recovery' (BCPR) – elevating the task to the same level as that of UNDP's long-powerful regional bureaux. He hired Julia Taft, an American with significant experience in international humanitarian work, to be the new 'baron'. Part of Malloch Brown's goal was to have Taft and the Bureau act as 'a Trojan horse for internal change'. Their job would be to attract a young, dynamic new staff and new funding to some of UNDP's least-active field offices, many of them, tragically, in countries where the need was greatest.[41]

Afghanistan would prove to be one of the major successes of this plan. When Malloch Brown arrived, the office was 'still the old Asia Bureau at its worst'. Community development projects right out of the 1950s were still the name of the game in a country torn apart by two decades of war. With 'Julia kicking them every day for a year', the Afghanistan country office became one of the most dynamic in the world.[42] After the fall of the Taliban régime that had supported the 9/11 attacks, the Bureau quickly delivered the equipment – desks, computers, vehicles, and phones – to set up the new government. It helped to provide salaries and training for police and civil servants, supported the constitution-making process, set up the electoral system, trained more than 100,000 election officers, helped to create a new justice system, disarmed tens of thousands of soldiers, and helped to rebuild infrastructure throughout the country.[43]

In Afghanistan, as in many of the other countries in which the Bureau works, much of UNDP's funding came through special arrangements with especially interested donors. Thus, in Afghanistan in 2005, 17 per cent of the funds expended came from the United States, 15 per cent from Japan, and 13 per cent from the United Kingdom. In much of Africa the major funding partners are, more typically, other UN entities, the development banks, and countries that give a great deal of 'real aid'. Norway, for example, was the largest national donor to UNDP's programmes in Rwanda in 2005.[44] Similar funding arrangements, and the rapid

---

[41] Mark Malloch Brown, interview with CNM, 4 June 2004.
[42] Ibid.
[43] Julia Taft, interview with CNM, 6 Oct. 2004. *UNDP in Afghanistan 2005* (Kabul: UNDP, 2005).
[44] Figures taken from the web-based Atlas 'Executive Snapshot' on UNDP's internal network.

accumulation of professional experience within the BCPR, have assured UNDP a role in almost all of the world's conflict and post-conflict countries.

Unfortunately the unevenness of donor interest ensures that some places still lack even 'poor relief and riot control'. Pekka Hirvonen, a social and economic historian in the Finnish Foreign Ministry, paints the larger picture:

> Many European donors favour countries in . . . Europe's own restless back-yard . . . Much of this aid is motivated by domestic political concerns, above all fears of uncontrolled immigration from crisis-stricken countries . . . Other European countries favour their old colonies where European companies often have a strong presence . . . Much of the recent increase in US development assistance has gone to funding state-building and reconstruction projects in regions that have been directly involved in US-led military operations . . . As for other donors to Iraq and Afghanistan, the picture is even uglier . . . money going to these two countries has been taken – at least in part – from existing aid programmes . . .

. . . to countries with equal needs.[45] Given that background, it may be remarkable that UNDP has been able to do as much work as it has in countries that are not so favoured: demobilizing former combatants in Liberia, Sierra Leone, and elsewhere and helping to remove landmines or destroy other weapons there and in Angola, Eritrea, the Solomon Islands, and other countries.

Sometimes, though, even a quick read through the project documents makes me wonder how well the 'recovery' and 'prevention' sides of UNDP's work have been integrated. Most of the individual projects in UNDP's large programme for the resettlement and reintegration of former combatants in Sierra Leone involved rebuilding prisons, police barracks, and an occasional magistrate's court. The palpable fear in a country so long in turmoil seems to be reflected in line after line: 'Improvements to Kono Prison . . . Reconstruction of Female Ward & Perimeter Fence, Kailahun Prison . . . Production of Low Cost Building Materials for Construction of Police Officers Quarters'.[46] Perhaps it is too much to expect people who have lived so long with fear to see other solutions, but these appear to be purely *government* priorities. They do not

---

[45] Pekka Hirvonen, 'Stingy Samaritans: Why Recent Increases in Development Aid Fail to Help the Poor', Global Policy Forum Policy Paper, August 2005.

[46] Government of Sierra Leone and UNDP, 'Support to Resettlement and Reintegration Programme (SRRP-SIL/02/09) Annual Progress Report, 1 Jan.–31 Dec. 2003, pp. 1–9.

reflect the desires for passable roads, rebuilt schools, and new clinics that I heard from ex-combatants camped along Freetown's roads and filling the grounds of churches and mosques.

Yet people from every part of UNDP (not just BCPR) can be extremely effective in dramatically improving the lives of some of the world's most disadvantaged people while simultaneously quelling some of the post-9/11 fears of the largest donors. In the anxious days immediately after the World Trade Center fell, the United States, Norway, and other countries closed down the remittance companies that transferred almost one billion dollars a year into stateless Somalia from its many countrymen who work abroad. The host countries feared that the unregulated companies could be used to funnel money to terrorists, but their response destroyed Somalia's most vital link to the rest of the world. Andrea Tamagnini, the Somalia Country Director, and Abdusalam Omer, an expert on international fund transfers, quickly pulled together a team to visit the United States, the United Kingdom, Norway, and the United Arab Emirates (UAE) to meet with regulatory agencies, legislators, the Somali community, and private banks to find ways to open new channels for funds to flow into each country. The ultimate solutions differed from host country to host country, but the channels reopened quickly, which would not have happened without UNDP. Moreover, the UN intervention spurred local-level dialogues in Oslo, Minneapolis, and other cities, events that helped to dismantle the wall of distrust that isolated many Muslim immigrants immediately after 9/11.[47]

Much of UNDP's effectiveness comes from its good relations with governments (in the remittances case: with some major donors and with the UAE) and from UNDP's positive reputation among the development *cognoscenti*. (Luckily some important leaders of the Somali diaspora are professors in different development fields.) Therefore UNDP officers at the centre of a particular network (people such as Tamagnini) are often those who can best play the conflict prevention role.

Adama Guindo, the dynamic Malian serving as Res Rep in Madagascar in 2002, also exemplifies the pattern. The country had at the time two men who said they were president. Didier Ratsiraka, the

[47] 'Terror Slur Threatens Somali Cash Lifeline', *BBC*, 18 Oct. 2002. Andrea Tamagnini and Abdusalam Omer, 'Back to Office Report, Mission to Promote a Better Understanding of Remittances', 5–27 Oct. 2002. Abdusalam Omer, 'A Report on Supporting Systems and Procedures for the Effective Regulation and Monitoring of Somali Remittance Companies (Hawala)', Prepared for UNDP Somalia, n.d. Andrea Tamagnini, 'The Somalia Remittance (Hawala) Initiative', n.d. Ahmed Samatar, interview with CNM, 21 May 2005.

twenty-year incumbent, had been declared the victor in the December 2001 elections, but by a body that he had appointed. His opponent, Marc Ravalomanana, disagreed. Many in the local diplomatic community wanted to avoid the dispute, but Guindo, whose UN experience included the then recent horrors of the Liberian civil war, convened the major ambassadors (of France, the United States, and Germany) and began to make contact with Ravalomanana's major backer in civil society, Madagascar's Council of Churches. 'Most of the time', Guindo says,

> UNDP has to be close to government, but, in all these kinds of situations, I think it's also important that you cultivate good relationships with civil society . . . They should trust you, should see you as neutral, as a broker, instead of siding only with government. It's a very difficult equilibrium to obtain . . . In the case of Madagascar, fortunately, we had a lot of grass-roots activities, so I used to go out of the capital city, talking to people, and so people knew me. They knew me, . . . so when the crisis started, no one questioned the neutrality of UNDP.[48]

Through the civil society groups, Guindo convinced Ravalomanana to accept mediation by Senegal's president; Guindo even accompanied Ravalomanana to Dakar, the Senegalese capital, where the two competing presidents agreed to form a government of national unity pending a recount.

When, as expected, Ravalomanana won the recount and Ratsiraka tore up the Dakar agreement, Guindo's focus changed to working with Madagascar's major donors to convince the old president to give up the fight. A brief military crisis followed. (The two men are from different regions and their backers split somewhat along ethnic lines, so that some regional governors and military men initially failed to accept the recount.) Nevertheless, within two months Ratsiraka was gone, in self-exile to Paris. UNDP then began to support Ravalomanana's anti-corruption drive and programme of 'rapid and durable development'.

We asked Guindo whether what he did to avert a conflict was really 'development' work.

'They both go together', he says, 'because, unless we have a sound governance system in place, you cannot perform the traditional UNDP work, you cannot do anti-poverty work.' UNDP should ask everywhere, 'How do you make sure that the governance of a country is right to prevent crises that can deepen the poverty situation?'

[48] Adama Guindo, interview with EM, 18 July 2005.

Fortunately – for the UN if not for UNDP – many of the Res Reps who share Guindo's approach and his political skills get pulled into the conflict work of the United Nations proper. Some become Special Representatives of the Secretary-General. (They are not among the SRSGs that UNICEF's Carol Bellamy accused of lacking understanding and respect 'for the development process and the [UN] country teams'.) Throughout my research, I kept hearing the names of two of the men pulled into a slightly different political role in Speth's day – Denis Halliday and Hans von Sponeck. (We have met them before, doing some of the most creative work of the old Asia Bureau in Singapore, Iran, and Pakistan.) Younger officers, deeply concerned about the future of the UN, often spoke about them with awed respect, sometimes with sadness.

Halliday and von Sponeck served successive terms as UN Humanitarian Coordinator in Iraq. Both resigned in protest over the *in-humanitarian* consequences of the Oil for Food Programme and the UN Security Council's unwillingness to 'carry out its mandated responsibilities to assess the impact of sanctions policies on civilians'.[49] The Oil for Food Programme restricted food and humanitarian supplies coming into Iraq, and funnelled what did come in through the country's increasingly brutal government. The consequences included a massive increase in infant mortality, one of those instances of children becoming the indirect victims of war. In July 2000 Halliday told a reporter for Egypt's *Al-Ahram*, 'The UN is still responsible for killing 6,000 to 7,000 Iraqis per month. And these aren't my figures, they're UN figures, UNICEF figures.'[50]

Halliday and von Sponeck opposed the 2003 US and British-led invasion of Iraq that ended the sanctions policy. The former UNDP officers argued, in part, that the policies of the great powers would ensure a continuing decimation of Iraq's civilian population.

Since the war in Iraq began, Halliday and von Sponeck have often spoken out against it, often questioning the role of the UN. That role has been exceedingly difficult to carry out since August 2003, when a bomb at UN headquarters in Baghdad killed twenty-three people, including Sergio Vieira de Mello, the head of the UN mission and Malloch Brown and Kofi Annan's friend of twenty-five years. Malloch Brown had the excruciating task of flying to the region to represent the Secretary-

---

[49] Denis Halliday and Hans von Sponeck, 'The Hostage Nation', *Guardian,* 29 Nov. 2001.
[50] Amira Howeidy, 'Death for Oil: An Interview with Dennis [*sic*] Halliday, Ex-UN Assistant Secretary-General Heading the UN Humanitarian Mission in Iraq', *Al-Ahram Weekly,* 19 July 2000.

General to survivors and family members. Back in New York, speaking to
the Executive Board, less than three weeks after the tragedy, he said,

> Until we restore a national, regional and global consensus for the direction
> of change in Iraq more men and women – Iraqi, American, UN and others
> will lose their lives in a fight that may have begun as the last stand of a failed,
> and ugly, régime but is becoming a clash of approaches to our new century
> . . . [a fight whose] outcome will not be settled in the military dimension of
> the war against terrorism, but in the hearts and minds of young Iraqi men
> and women – and those identifying with them across the world – as they
> judge who will give them a stake in their own future.[51]

Towards that end UNDP has taken a central role in preparing for the
three rounds of Iraqi elections, training local journalists, and supporting
Iraq's new Ministry of Human Rights, court system, and Bar Association.

Will the UN be judged as having helped to give the Iraqi people a stake
in their own future? In 2003, Halliday told Scotland's *Sunday Herald* that
the Baghdad bombing had been a consequence of the UN having been
'taken over and corrupted by the US and UK'. He warned that 'further
collaboration' between the UN and the United States and Britain 'would
be a disaster for the United Nations as it would be sucked into supporting
the illegal occupation of Iraq'.[52] Two years later, Halliday spoke of such
UN support as a fact,[53] while von Sponeck said that his former colleagues
had failed when faced by the challenge 'to show that, ultimately, conscience was superior to obedience'.[54]

I honestly do not know what I think about the UN's – and UNDP's –
role in Iraq since the beginning of the war. (And I know that, up close,
even organizations and people who, from a distance, look like saints,
always have a few warts; for example, the independent group investigating
the Oil for Food scandals faulted the UN for having no post-employment
conflict of interest safeguards that would have prevented von Sponeck
from seeking funds for his anti-sanctions work from firms trying to obtain

[51] Malloch Brown, 'Statement to the Executive Board', 8 Sept. 2003, in *Mark Malloch Brown at
the United Nations Development Programme*, p. 436.

[52] Neil McKay, 'Former UN Chief: Bomb Was a Payback for Collusion with US', *Sunday
Herald*, 29 Jan. 2006.

[53] Denis Halliday, 'The UN and Its Conduct During the Invasion and Occupation of Iraq',
Testimony to the World Tribunal on Iraq, 3 July 2005, http://www.globalresearch.ca/
index.php?context=viewArticle&code=HAL20050703&articleId=627 (accessed 29 Jan.
2006).

[54] Hans von Sponeck, 'The Conduct of the UN before and after the 2003 Invasion', Testimony
to the World Tribunal on Iraq, 24 June 2005, available at http://www.globalpolicy.org/
security/issues/iraq/unrole/2005/0624unconduct.htm (accessed 29 Jan. 2006).

contracts with the Iraqi government, which he had done.[55]) Chapter 12 takes up another recent case – post-Aristide Haiti – where UNDP's role has been similar to its role in Iraq. It is a place about which, after leaving UNDP for UNICEF, Danny Glover said, 'For those with even an iota of conscience, there is no alternative. Haiti must be returned to its people.'[56] The question in both crisis countries, in the end, may not be whether UNDP's crisis work has truly fostered democracy. It may be whether UNDP has improved a situation that otherwise would have been worse.

Democratic governance and ICT

In the next chapter Haiti is one of two short geographic diversions from interconnected stories about crises and democratic governance that take place in south-east Asia – in Indonesia and Timor Leste – stories that illustrate many of the most recent innovations in UNDP's governance work. Here I concentrate on one aspect of an evolving governance agenda that, in the end, did not become as important to UNDP as its support for elections, judicial reform, and the strengthening of parliaments: the use of information and communication technology (ICT) to improve the efficiency of governments and make them more accountable.

Many historians lament that, while high-speed computers and the Internet encourage the creation of innumerable documents – the grist to the historian's mill – most of those e-mails, web pages, and downloadable files are ephemeral. Every regular update wipes out part of the record. This has made something called 'the Wayback Machine'[57] critically important. It lets us see at least the top level of many websites back to their beginning.

By looking at the first copy of UNDP's website for each year, we can see the evolution of the Programme's goals under Speth, Malloch Brown, and Dervis. Every page includes a list of UNDP's 'focus' or 'practice' areas. (Originally, these foci were somewhat aspirational. Despite the addition of new terms, recall that the UNDP of 2005 was actually much more focused than the Programme eight or ten years earlier, at the beginning of the long process of reform.) At least three things are interesting about the changes in the list during the Malloch Brown era. One is the fact that, as of 2001,

---

[55] Independent Inquiry Committee into the United Nations Oil-for-Food Programme, 'Manipulations of the Oil-for-Food Programme by the Iraqi Règime', 27 Oct. 2005, pp. 507–9.

[56] Danny Glover, 'There Are Times when One Must Simply Take a Stand', *Haiti Progress*, 8 Dec. 2004, p. 1.

[57] Available at http://www.archive.org/web/web.php (accessed 29 Jan. 2006).

UNDP was finally open about its support of *democratic* governance. The other is the appearance and disappearance of an ICT practice area.

In mid-2001 Malloch Brown made the case for the centrality of ICT to UNDP's work, arguing that democracy could only be sustained with 'strong, accountable institutions, a culture of participation and democratic respect and openness'. He pointed to the Internet's promise 'from being a platform for a new investigative media to increasing direct participation' and emphasized benefits of 'e-governance' that would streamline and improve 'government services and institutions by making them cheaper, more efficient and more accessible'.[58]

Much of the technology needed to extend these benefits throughout the world could come from developing countries, due, in part, to work that UNDP had started more than thirty years before. India's National Informatics Centre, the core of one of the largest and most sophisticated e-governance networks in the world, began as a series of small UNDP projects in the 1970s. Many of the projects provided hardware – one of those things that traditionalists had considered so unprecedented and questionable about I. G. Patel's 'New Dimensions' (see chapter 6). N. Vijayaditya, the University of North Carolina Ph.D. in electrical engineering who now directs the Centre, explains that UNDP had initially been reluctant to fund his first experiment, but later the expert who recommended against the project was gracious enough to say, 'I'm glad you didn't take my advice.'[59]

The Centre now has 3,500 technicians who are constantly creating new applications to add to India's fully computerized system for issuing passports and tracing records, smart card system for registering vehicles, pilot national identity card programme, largely paperless method of obtaining import and export licences, computerized election management applications, and an Atlas-like system for running government offices, 'a boon for transparency'.[60] These examples only begin to scratch the surface of the Centre's work; it affects almost everyone in India, every day, by guiding power across the national grid, monitoring water and sewerage systems in many cities, making land ownership records easily accessible to those trying to sell or buy, and in a dozen other ways.[61]

---

[58] Malloch Brown, 'Democracy and the Information Revolution', 27 June 2001, in *Mark Malloch Brown at the United Nations Development Programme*, p. 250.

[59] N. Vijayaditya, interview with CNM, 13 Dec. 2004.   [60] Ibid.

[61] The many applications are discussed throughout National Informatics Centre, *ICT Solutions for Good Governance* (New Delhi: Ministry of Communications and Information Technology, 2004).

Table 11.2. *UNDP's focus lists, 1998–2006.*

1998	1999	2000	2001	2002	2003	2004	2005	2006
Poverty	Poverty	Poverty	Democratic governance	Democratic governance	Democratic governance	Democratic governance	MDGs	Democratic governance
Environment	Gender	Gender	Pro-poor policies	Poverty reduction	Poverty reduction	Poverty reduction	Democratic governance	Poverty reduction
Gender	Environment	Environment	Crisis prevention and recovery	Crisis prevention and recovery	Crisis prevention and recovery	Crisis prevention and recovery	Poverty reduction	Crisis prevention and recovery
Governance	Governance	Governance	ICT	Energy and environment	Energy and environment	Energy and environment	Crisis prevention and recovery	Energy and environment
			Energy and environment policy	ICT	ICT	HIV/AIDS	Energy and environment	HIV/AIDS
			HIV/AIDS	HIV/AIDS	HIV/AIDS		HIV/AIDS	Women's empowerment
			Human Development Report					

Vijayaditya estimates that there is some '60,000 man-years of knowledge we have created' in the Centre's hardware and software. He is proud of the ever increasing number of countries that have asked for India's help in setting up similar systems, including some countries that are only now beginning to develop political cultures of openness, including Laos and Mongolia. Vijayaditya even wonders if some of this experience might be useful back in the country where he received his doctorate, since the United States seems recently to be having much more trouble with its systems for registering and verifying voters and for counting their ballots than does India.[62]

Egypt's Hisham El Sherif tells a somewhat similar story, but about a country without India's unique democratic tradition. El Sherif's doctorate in management and engineering came from the Massachusetts Institute of Technology (MIT), where he formed a vision of using ICT to help to improve government decision making and accelerate socioeconomic development throughout the developing world. He returned to Egypt, and, with the help of UNDP, delivered his first 'dream', an Information and Decision Support Centre for the Egyptian cabinet. Then, from 1988 to 1991, El Sherif worked with UNDP, the Arab Fund for Economic and Social Development, and various Arab governments to think through the problem of developing the whole range of Arabic language software. In January 1992, RITSEC – the Regional Information Technology and Software Engineering Centre – was established in Cairo. It added a training institute a year later. Since then, the Centre has been involved in an astonishing range of software projects, including digital documentation of the artistic and literary treasures of Egypt and the entire Islamic world. It has also trained hundreds of thousands of ICT users and tens of thousands of managers in government and the private sector.[63]

Given UNDP's record, and the support of partners like Vijayaditya and El Sherif, world-renowned leaders in the field who were grateful for the catalytic role that the Programme had played in their own countries, the ICT practice area seemed like a natural step. Yet the very development of sophisticated ICT capacity in parts of the Third World may have made a large programme in this field impracticable. Moreover, the timing could not have been worse. In autumn 2001, immediately after 9/11, Malloch Brown announced the creation of a Trust Fund for ICT for Development, with an initial contribution of US$5,000,000 from the Japanese

---

[62] N. Vijayaditya, interview with CNM, 13 Dec. 2004.
[63] Hisham El Sherif, interview with CNM, 27 April 2005.

government.[64] Unfortunately, the trust fund never attracted large donations. A period of global economic uncertainty followed the terrorist
attacks, and aid priorities shifted in the way in which Pekka Hirvonen
describes. Large transfers of government funds, which might (indirectly)
have helped to make Third World companies even more competitive with
the Information Age leaders in the First World, were not forthcoming.
Potential UNDP partners, including El Sherif, found it much easier to
obtain foundation grants or World Bank backing for their next round of
projects, such as RITSEC's Global Development Learning Centre, which
provides distance learning to decision makers all over the world.[65] UNDP,
not surprisingly, folded its ongoing ICT work back into its other practice
areas.

William J. Drake, president of Computer Professionals for Social
Responsibility and a senior associate at the International Centre for Trade
and Sustainable Development in Geneva calls the 'gutting of [UNDP's]
ICT work . . . pretty sad, especially with so little elsewhere to take its
place'.[66] Yet El Sherif advises UNDP to 'Set priorities. Do not overdo the
things that others can do.' Does this mean let long-time partners like
himself and Vijayaditya lead the ICT for development drive? Probably.

He adds at the end of our conversation, 'I am ready, with my own
money, to work with UNDP to bring these cases [the whole range of
Egyptian experience] to the presidents of every country across Africa and
across the Middle East.' The ability to facilitate such South–South partnerships may, in the end, prove to be UNDP's one comparative advantage
in this field.

Influencing policy on HIV/AIDS

Even in the worst of Cairo traffic, it takes less than an hour to get from El
Sherif's conference room – crowded with the equipment, computer disks,
and magazines that you would find in an MIT professor's office – to the
serene, uncluttered halls of Al-Azhar University. I am jealous of the rapt
attention that students give to the middle-aged man who is softly speaking in their midst. For a few seconds I let myself indulge in the fantasy that
I am witnessing an ancient form of education, one unconnected to the
modern chaos outside the walls of this 1,000-year-old building. Yet I am

---

[64] UNDP Press Release, 'Government of Japan and UNDP Launch ICT Trust Fund with $5
Million Contribution from Japan, UNDP Administrator Visits Japan', 31 Oct. 2001.
[65] Hisham El Sherif, interview with CNM, 27 April 2005.
[66] William J. Drake, electronic mail to CNM, 15 April 2004.

here to talk about something much more recent, and more much treacherous than the automobiles careening along Sharia Muiz al-Din Allah,
the main street of medieval Cairo: HIV/AIDS. This was a field where
UNDP could do something that others really could not do.

Malloch Brown added the continuing practice area in 2001 – the same
year that ICT temporarily became a UNDP focus. Unlike with ICT, which
was more of a top-down response to global trends, UNDP's HIV/AIDS
focus responded to pressure from the front line, from country offices.
Since 1990 Garth ap Rees and the Regional Bureau for Africa (RBA) had
been pushing WHO, the International Labour Organisation, and World
Bank officials throughout the continent to focus on the issue, 'It was a
constant uphill battle with the odds stacked against us, but in my time
RBA as a whole never gave up trying.'[67] The arguments for the centrality
of the disease to UNDP's own anti-poverty goals were overwhelming in
countries where the epidemic had already drawn in almost every extended
family. Yet, given UNDP's unique capabilities, equally strong arguments
could be made for having an HIV focus in regions where the epidemic was
only beginning, including the Arab world. UNDP does not have the
medical expertise of the WHO or the knowledge of reproductive health
issues of the UN Population Fund, but it has the *combination* of connections with policy makers, nationally and regionally, and with potentially
concerned NGOs that some of the other relevant members of the UN
family do not have. In fact, the first scholarly evaluations of the UN
system's response to the disease (which first appeared in the early 1980s)
deeply criticized the UN's lack of involvement on the ground; the first
major multinational evaluative study, in 1995, did not even include a field
component, because there was so little UN country-level work on
HIV/AIDS to consider.[68]

UNDP's tradition of advocacy gave the organization the willingness to
press even the most socially conservative governments on this critical
issue. The Programme's traditions of neutrality and national ownership
made it an effective advocate, as we have already seen in cases in which
national human development reports focusing on the epidemic helped to
shift government policy in Botswana, Mozambique, and other countries.
In Africa the combination of strategies UNDP used – mobilizing NGOs,

---

[67] Garth ap Rees, letter to CNM, 21 Feb. 2006.
[68] See Leon Gordenker, Roger A. Coate, Christer Jönsson, and Peter Söderholm, *International
Cooperation in Response to AIDS* (London: Pinter Publishers, 1995), and Peter Söderholm,
Global Governance of AIDS: Partnerships with Civil Society (Lund: University of Lund
Press, 1997).

11.2 The country office in Sierra Leone

engaging the public media, identifying previously untapped sources of foreign funding – differed from country to country.

The same was true in the Arab world. The same range of interventions – involving NGOs, the media, and government, have been used – with the important addition of a programme involving Muslim and Christian religious leaders from throughout the region.[69] Working with a group of Christian and Muslim leaders in Cairo who had become concerned when the disease reached worshippers in their own churches and mosques, UNDP organized two large regional colloquia in 2004. The first was in Damascus and the second in Cairo, and there were follow-ups in other countries throughout the following year. The meetings took

---

[69] I am grateful to Amy B. Kay, Khadija T. Moalla, and all the religious leaders to whom they introduced me for teaching me about this remarkable programme.

religious leaders through a process of learning about the disease, based on the assumption that 'knowledge shapes attitudes and attitudes shape action'.[70] Each meeting introduced people living with the disease. *Al-Ahram* reported,

> A former sex worker who came from a background of poverty and struggle for survival shared her testimony about living with HIV/AIDS. Following this woman's moving story, a hardline imam from Morocco tried to comment but his words were broken by an onset of tears. Other imams asked this woman to forgive them and pray for them.[71]

At the end of the Cairo conference, in December 2004, eighty leaders, including the Sheik El Azhar (the head of Cairo's oldest university), Dr Said Tantawi, the Coptic Pope, the director of Ullamas in Sudan, Shia leaders from Lebanon, and leading figures from the different Orthodox churches in Palestine signed the remarkable 'Cairo Declaration of Religious Leaders in the Arab States in Response to the HIV/AIDS Epidemic'. The declaration has been the main text of Friday and Sunday sermons throughout the region, and the centrepiece of training for tens of thousands of ministers, imams, and priests.

In the sixteen-paragraph document, two paragraphs stand out. One affirms that 'abstinence and faithfulness are the two cornerstones of our preventive strategies'. The next reads:

> We view as impious anything that may cause infection through intention or negligence – as a result of not using all preventive means available, in accordance with heavenly laws.[72]

I come from the most religious of the industrialized countries, one of the places where the AIDS epidemic began. Like most Americans, I have been very close to people who have lived with the disease, and with people who have died from it. Despite our longer experience, and our supposed modernity and compassion, in my country it would be difficult to convince eighty of the most prominent religious leaders to agree to the second paragraph, even though they would affirm the first. I doubt that the religious leaders of the Arab world have greater

---

[70] Khadija T. Moalla, interview with CNM, 19 April 2005.
[71] 'Compassion and AIDS in the Arab World', *Al-Ahram Weekly*, 20 Oct. 2005.
[72] The Cairo Declaration of Religious Leaders in the Arab States in Response to the HIV/AIDS Epidemic, at http://www.undp.org/dpa/pressrelease/releases/2004/december/Cairo%20 DeclarationEnglish.doc (accessed 31 Jan. 2006).

11.3 Debating the Cairo Declaration on HIV/AIDS, 2004

compassion or intelligence than those in the United States. The difference has to do with the collective learning that the Arab leaders engaged in through the help of UNDP. The Damascus and Cairo meetings involved much the same open-ended training that UNDP has organized in many parts of the developing world, albeit rarely with as distinguished participants. Stephen Lewis, the Secretary-General's special envoy for HIV/AIDS in Africa, writes about a similar process in rural Ethiopia:

> The results of the Community Conversations supported by UNDP in the South are highly improbable but startling. It is astonishing to witness the communities talk about the sensitive elements of their culture and society and see behavioural changes happening in such a short time.[73]

My grandmother, the same one who warned about good deeds going unrecognized in this world, used to quiz her grandchildren about what deeds we would be able to cite to Saint Peter to get us into the Christian heaven. If Malloch Brown were asked that question

[73] 'UNDP 1999–2005', p. 26.

about his time at UNDP, he could point to work in the AIDS practice area. In the long run, and even today in many parts of the world, other UN organizations will take on the major field role, sharing medical information, testing vaccines, scaling up successful low-cost treatment programmes. UNDP's role has been to persuade people of the gravity of the problem, and to build the capacity of national leaders to deal with it.

It is not only among the religious leaders of the Arab world and some socially conservative places in Africa that UNDP's persuasive communication has made a difference. Roy Morey recounts a long story of UNDP trying to convince the Chinese of the importance of the global epidemic, a story filled with strong personalities, a quiescent WHO representative, and lots of denial. ('AIDS is a problem of homosexuals. We don't have homosexuals in this country. Therefore, we appreciate your interest, but we don't have a problem.') The end of the story has senior figures in the government, long-time partners of UNDP, identifying HIV/AIDS as the greatest threat to China's development.[74] It is the first issue Long Yong Tu cites when I ask about UNDP's role in the country over the next five years, 'China did not recognize it as a serious issue . . . Now we realize we do not have sufficient control.' UNDP can give China a global perspective. 'For example, how have the Scandinavians, etc. faced this?'[75] It is another case where UNDP can help reveal the stones that will let China cross a particular river.

UNDP's impact is indirect, but its HIV/AIDS work has still saved lives and will save many more. The Programme's roles – influencing governments at all levels, helping to build their capacity, and starting high-level dialogues within civil society – are things that very few other organizations would have been able to do. Either they would have lacked the trust of powerful, socially conservative groups that were just coming to grips with the crisis, or else they would have lacked access to the knowledge that would eventually give those groups the capacity to deal with the problem with reason and compassion.

Malloch Brown also made sure that UNDP would be able to take on other new tasks in the future. His reforms made UNDP a model (among international development organizations, at least) of efficiency and effectiveness, which was why it could navigate so skilfully through the rapidly changing 'winds and currents' of donor preferences in the troubled years after 9/11. Robert W. Cox's image of the effective executive

---

[74] Roy Morey, interview with EM, 4 April 2005.
[75] Long Yong Tu, interview with CNM, 1 Dec. 2004.

head with excellent 'sailor's skills' certainly applies to Malloch Brown, even if it is not yet clear just how far he has been able to shift the interests and aspirations of the most hidebound of states.

Ironically, though, despite Malloch Brown's self-image as an organizational revolutionary, he brought UNDP back to be much closer to the institution created in the 1940s and 1950s. Fabians might not need apply, but the new kind of people and the new ideas that Malloch Brown brought into the UNDP mix just made the organization a more modern version of the one shaped by David Owen and W. Arthur Lewis. As Basem Khader puts it, 'Perhaps at the end of the day UNDP still needs a few Fabians to steer the ship beyond "efficiency" to "equity".'[76] Malloch Brown's organization was more open about its advocacy – of democracy, of the MDGs, and of many strands of human development – but, like Owen's organization, it supported governments in their pursuit of their own agendas, even when their priorities differed from those that would have been set by Jeffrey Sachs or by an extraordinarily knowledgeable Res Rep.

UNDP's commitment to this original principle was driven home to me when visiting the UAE, the economically successful congeries of city-states where the UNDP of the 1980s and 1990s is spoken of in the same reverent tones that many Singaporean officials use for the UN programmes of the 1950s and 1960s. For years UNDP was the only accredited UN agency in the country. It helped to build the Emirates' world-class civil aviation system, supported urban planning, and helped to establish the country's first university.[77] More recently UNDP has helped the country to develop a national strategy for the advancement of women and a national environmental action plan, as well as to improve public administration and help local companies meet internationally recognized global quality and business process standards such as ISO 9000. Of course, notably absent from the UNDP portfolio in the UAE are projects promoting democratic governance, or even any direct attention to the economic conditions of the vast army of foreign workers who commute each day from isolated barracks-like communities to build the luxury apartments, offices, and hotels that make the country's ever growing skyline. (Although studies of how workers might gain rights as

---

[76] Basem Khader, letter to CNM, 13 Feb. 2006.
[77] I joined Neysan Rassekh (NR) at the end of his research trip to the UAE, 26 Feb.–2 March 2005. The information comes from his interviews with Nadir Hadj-Hammou, Khalfan Ali Musbbeh Al Mehairi, Amin Mohammed Yusuf, Ahlam Allamki, Khalid Al Bustani, Dhalhi Khalfan Tamin, Ahmad Al Banna, and Frederick Hare.

citizens had been done by UNDP in the 1980s.) Some current UNDP staffers see a deep contradiction between the principles the Programme advocates and its close relationship with the Emirates' benevolent, but absolute, rulers. Yet that relationship just reflects adherence to the UN network's *first* principle, to serve all UN member governments.

Malloch Brown reaffirmed that connection when the organization was 'rebranded' in 2002. A symbolic part of that exercise brought back the UN symbol (the olive branches surrounding a map of the world) and the blue colour that had been abandoned by Draper and Speth. To reinforce the point, the new logo placed the first two letters of the acronym above the second. In English (increasingly the Programme's dominant language) that placement stressed: we are the *UN's* Development Programme.

Not surprisingly, Malloch Brown's rebranding grew out of the strategy of persuasive communication that it also affirms. Part of that strategy has been with the Programme from the start: solidarity and neutrality breed trust. In the Emirates, UNDP is deeply trusted. That is why UNDP could call on the country to help with the problem of remittances to Somalia after 9/11 and why the UAE was willing to host the first meeting of donors to war-torn Iraq held within the region in February 2004, at a time when many Arab states remained deeply opposed to the occupation of the country. It is why Dubai has built its own programmes of development assistance and established its award recognizing best practices to improve the living environment throughout the world; they are ways for a now-wealthy UAE to carry out its responsibilities to countries whose peoples are less advantaged. (It is consistent with the original UN development principle that the award winners include many whose views differ markedly from those of Dubai's rulers, Argentina's radical 'Red Solidaria', a network highlighting the plight of the marginalized, for example.)[78] Moreover, as I kept hearing in the UAE (just as I kept hearing in China) if anyone is going to convince the country's rulers to embrace *all* the principles that UNDP advocates, it will be UNDP.[78]

[78] Qassim Sultan Al Banna, interview with CNM and NR, 2 March 2005.

12

'Ploughing the sea'? UNDP and the future of global governance

Many of Kemal Dervis's early speeches as Administrator argued that UNDP's coordinating role and its early recognition of the imperative of UN reform would put it at the centre of an imminent process that was inseparably linked to a larger task of building effective, increasingly democratic global governance. Dervis told a January 2006 meeting of Res Reps,

> Please don't treat this as, 'Yeah, we've heard it before, they keep talking about UN reform, but it's business as usual.' I don't think it will be business as usual over the next two to three years. You, the Resident Coordinators, will be in the middle of all this . . . hopefully with the help of all the agencies and agency management behind you.[1]

The next day Dame Margaret Anstee, co-author of the Capacity Study (see chapter 6) and champion of a more rational United Nations for more than fifty years, wrote to say, 'Anyone who believes that logical, overall reform is feasible is ploughing the sea!' She later added, 'But I DO think that reform is essential and urgent but that the only way of making headway is by some individual and important changes that would have a multiplier effect.'[2]

The recurrent impediments to comprehensive UN reform are the deep conflicts that fracture the state system and, therefore, are played out within intergovernmental organizations. A classic study of the early 1960s pointed to the persistence of at least four separate divisions within the UN, including the cold war, East–West conflict, and the North–South conflict, questions of 'supra-nationalism' or respect for the UN per se, and the conflict over the fate of Palestine.[3] While the cold war is over, the

[1] Kemal Dervis, Opening Statement, Global Management Team Meeting, The Hague, 30 Jan. 2006.

[2] Margaret Joan Anstee, letters to the author (CNM), 31 Jan. and 15 Feb. 2006.

[3] Hayward R. Alker, Jr, and Bruce M. Russett, *World Politics in the General Assembly* (New Haven: Yale University Press, 1963).

other divides remain. In early 2006, many observers worried that the North–South conflict would end up derailing Secretary-General Kofi Annan's ambitious agenda for his final year.

Scholars of international organizations have long looked for models of reform in those few institutions that have been able to overcome one or more of the deep conflicts. This makes UNDP's past particularly relevant, not only for those whose ultimate goal is substantively democratic global governance, but also for those concerned with making 'individual and important changes in the United Nations' today. UNDP has a strong track record of helping states to become more democratic at the same time as encouraging UN members to focus on global interests rather than on the conflicts that divide them.

The reasons for UNDP's success can be illustrated in just a few inter-connected stories in South-East Asia, beginning at the time of the Asian financial crisis and ending with the Indian Ocean tsunami, while other simultaneous stories – including the recent history of the UN in Haiti, the place where the story of UN development assistance began – can high-light the limits of what any intergovernmental organization can do. Those stories make up this final chapter, which ends back on the coast of West Africa in a place where the UN development network has operated almost as long as it has in Haiti, but with very different results.

Democracy against the odds

UNDP has a significant capacity to promote democracy, especially in periods of political crisis. Recall an argument, and a person, introduced in chapter 1: the argument is that the UN Resident Coordinator is often the only person able to convene all the key people in a country experiencing political turmoil; the person is Ravi Rajan, who made that argument based on his own experience in a crisis when UNDP facili-tated the democratization of Indonesia, one of the world's most popu-lous and largest countries, and, with it, the liberation of one of the world's last colonies.

I first learned about Rajan from an academic colleague, Christopher Candland, a professor of comparative politics with wide experience in South and South-East Asia (someone who once worked for UNDP's Hafiz Pasha). In 2001 Candland and his wife, Siti Nurjanah, a journalist and non-governmental organization (NGO) leader, published a study with the British Royal Institute of International Affairs in which they argued that the Indonesian democratic process that began in 1998 could easily be sidetracked.[4] By early 2004, as Indonesia prepared for its second multiparty election, they were a little less doubtful about the country's democratic future due to a sequence of events in whose entirety UNDP had been involved.

The events began with the 1997 financial crisis that undermined Suharto's long-lived, authoritarian régime. The austerity measures that the Bretton Woods organizations required in exchange for their help meant sharp increases in the cost of food, fuel, and basic education. Faced with growing public discontent and waning international support, Suharto resigned in May 1998 in favour of his deputy, Jusuf Habibe. Rajan helped to convince Habibe that 'no one would recognize an election that he won'; the new president agreed to call the first free elections in more than forty years.[5] With the donor community having no further interest in propping up the government, Rajan went to NGO leaders to ask them to form political parties and to act as conduits of international relief:

> Suddenly, you had money going directly, outside of the national treasury, from the international community to these NGOs. This was a no-no before. When a democratically elected government came in, they [the government] wanted us to stop. ('We don't need you now.') We said, 'We're not contesting your legitimacy, but it works . . . You can stop it from going to these organizations, but I don't think it will go to you.' The new government accepted that and money is still flowing.[6]

Of course, UNDP played a role in the 1999 elections, which brought that reasonable new government to power.

The country office coordinated the funding and technical assistance needed to help the parliament draft new election laws, supported Indonesia's new independent electoral commission, gave grants to scores of NGOs that provided voter education and election monitors, coordinated the training of nearly two million poll workers, and, in Rajan's words, 'bought gallons and gallons and gallons of ink'. It eventually covered more than 100 million fingers with the purple evidence of having cast a ballot. International monitors, led by Jimmy Carter, judged the remarkably peaceful election to be free and fair.

Rajan muses, 'What to do for an encore?' Well, he says, UNDP still could help with two things.

---

[4] Christopher Candland and Siti Nurjanah, 'Indonesia after Wahid: The New Authoritarianism', Royal Institute of International Affairs Briefing Paper, New series, no. 28, December 2001.

[5] Ravi Rajan, interview with CNM, 4 June 2004.   [6] Ibid.

First, bringing the World Bank back in. The Bank refused loans to the democratic government until Indonesia began to 'address a pervasive culture of corruption', but the NGOs that shared the Bank's newfound concern distrusted any of the Bank's plans to address it. No wonder, Rajan argues: the Bank 'had been in bed with Suharto', ignoring his corruption for decades. UNDP provided an essential bridge between the potential allies, creating a 'Partnership for Governance' with the Bank that enlisted the NGOs that had the eyes and ears necessary to make any anti-corruption policy successful.

Second, UNDP set up programmes to train the new parliamentarians, bringing counterparts from Rajan's native India to explain their understanding of the role both of the governing parties and those in opposition. Rajan remembers conversations before the state visit to India made by President Abdurrahman Wahid (popularly known as 'Gus Dur'), the liberal religious leader of Indonesia's largest NGO, which had been convinced to form a party to contest the 1999 elections. Gus Dur was a frail man who wanted to minimize the strain of the sixteen-day foreign tour. Certainly, he pleaded, it would be enough to meet India's president and the conservative prime minister, Atal Bihari Vajpayee. The Indian parliamentarian whom UNDP had brought to Jakarta to train the new legislators insisted, 'If you're visiting our country and you are meeting the prime minister, you have to meet the opposition.'[7] Gus Dur acquiesced, saving his health by refusing 'the customary inspection of the honour guard' and getting to know Sonia Gandhi, with whom he seemed to have a great deal more in common than he had with India's then prime minister.[8]

In a similar way Rajan relied on other UNDP partners in the developing world to introduce Indonesia's new leaders to the idea that in a large, multi-ethnic nation, federalism can make a great deal of sense, an idea that had long been anathema because the Dutch had used federal structures to divide the independence movement. UNDP ignored the Dutch and US models that still dominated Indonesian textbooks: we 'sent them to South Africa to meet [Nelson] Mandela and see how they had set up a constitutional convention'.[9]

UNDP continued to support post-election civic education in Indonesia, encouraged legislative and civil service reform at all levels, worked to help resolve many of the potentially violent conflicts that

---

[7] Ibid.
[8] Kornelius Purba, 'Abdurrahman Visits RI's Cultural Kin', *Jakarta Post*, 9 Feb. 2000.
[9] Ravi Rajan, interview with CNM, 4 June 2004.

divide the complex country, and supported the 2004 elections, which most observers see as another critical step towards the consolidation of democracy over a significant part of the world.

Candland and Nurjanah's concern about the reemergence of authoritarianism reflects an insight shared by political scientists around the world: governments that rely on the support of – and, therefore, that need to nurture – only a small part of their population are actually often much easier to maintain than democratic régimes that must provide collective goods to support the broadly based coalitions that support them. That is why, in many developing countries, a single free election (frequently, immediately after decolonization) has been followed by the consolidation of a cosy authoritarianism: a government that uses all the instruments of the state, and the systems of international aid, to extract resources for its small but powerful core constituency.[10] The consolidation of democracy requires that most of a country's potential political contenders become convinced that their long-term interests are best served by relying on, and supporting, a broad popular constituency – using political power to create the social services and booming economy that will endear them to a wide electorate.

How can potential contenders be convinced that the democratic path is in their interest? It helps to have a broadly based, and empowered, network of NGOs and a deep and complex civil society. Independent electoral bodies (unlike the presidential cronies that Adama Guindo originally found in Madagascar) are also very important. (Among other things, the transparency that such bodies establish can help to convince respected and active civil society leaders to go into electoral politics.) Finally, it is important to develop a civic culture that differs from the 'winner take all' philosophy that becomes entrenched in many societies that have long been under autocratic rule; parties have to become convinced that they will have a respected role to play whether they win the elections or whether they lose. UNDP's work in Indonesia, on all these issues – like its work in Madagascar and in many other countries – helped to turn a political crisis into an opportunity to move from one kind of political system to another.

---

[10] A recent, important theoretical and empirical elaboration of this insight is Bruce Bueno de Mesquita, Alastair Smith, Randolph M. Siverson, and James D. Morrow, *The Logic of Political Survival* (Cambridge, Mass.: MIT Press, 2003). One view of the implications of this research for international development assistance is spelled out in Bruce Bueno de Mesquita and George W. Downs, 'Democracy and Development', *Foreign Affairs*, 84, 5 (September/October 2005): 77–86.

UNDP's role is frequently not just a matter of having the right strategy. The unique position of the Res Rep/UN Resident Coordinator gives UNDP the ability to take on such work. Part of the position's power comes from the prestige of being the centre of the UN team. Perhaps an even larger part comes from the strong connections that the most active Res Reps develop not only with the government, but also with the most active parts of civil society – the places from which political alternatives arise. Finally, there is UNDP's larger, global experience in supporting democratic governance, on which every Res Rep can draw.

When the odds seem insurmountable

It is hard to overstress the commitment to democratic change found at all levels within UNDP. In the months leading up to Ukraine's Orange Revolution, at a time when democracy seemed unlikely, UNDP's east European bureau chief, Kalman Mizsei, devoted himself to working with an independent commission to draw up an agenda for the transformation of Ukraine into a fully open society should Viktor Yushchenko happen, miraculously, to be allowed to win planned elections.[11] During Sierra Leone's 2002 elections, one of the drivers in the Freetown office, Francis Davis, not only risked his life carrying cash to remote parts of the country to see that election officials were paid, he also organized all the drivers to be volunteer observers in places that international observers had overlooked or were afraid to go to.[12]

Nevertheless, there are situations that no amount of creativity and commitment can fully transform, as I learned in Port-au-Prince in June 2004, a few months after Adama Guindo, the then Res Rep in Haiti, played a role similar to the one he had played in Madagascar two years before. In February Guindo had helped to convince Haiti's elected president, Jean-Bertrand Aristide, to board a plane that would take him into exile after his country, already reeling from a three-year cut-off of aid, had been plunged into turmoil by armed insurgents crossing into the country from staging grounds in the Dominican Republic.

Shortly after I met Guindo, Louis Saint-Lot, a businessman who was unusual in his willingness to maintain warehouses in Port-au-Prince's Cité Soleil slum, Aristide's stronghold, told me not to be naïve about the cause of the president's departure. Bill Clinton supported Aristide. US

---

[11] Blue Ribbon Commission for Ukraine, *Proposals for the President: A New Wave of Reform* (Kiev: UNDP, 2005).   [12] Francis Davis, interview with CNM, 10 Jan. 2005.

policy changed after George Bush's election. Yes, elite Haitian-Americans in Florida – an increasingly powerful group in a state governed by the US president's brother – made a difference, Saint-Lot said, but *most* of the Haitian elite had come to despise the radical champion of the poor and even many Haitian democrats worried that Aristide was on the road to becoming a dictator.[13] Robert Fatton, a leading scholar of Haitian politics who is sympathetic to the left, argues that Aristide

> armed young unemployed thugs, the *Chimères*, to intimidate the opposi-
> tion . . . While voicing a radical rhetoric, he followed the neoliberal stric-
> tures of structural adjustment. In addition, his régime was incapable of
> resisting the temptations of corruption, . . . high cadres contributed to the
> perverse persistence of the 'narco-state' inherited from the military dicta-
> torship. Not surprisingly, Aristide lost the unconditional popular support
> he once enjoyed and some of his own *Chimères* turned against him.[14]

Louis Saint-Lot counts himself among the democrats. After all, his father, Emile, was the UN representative who co-authored the Universal Declaration of Human Rights and helped to ensure that Haiti was the first developing country to receive a comprehensive UN technical assistance mission. The younger Saint-Lot was, himself, angry that Aristide's party 'rigged [the November 2000 Haitian Senate] elections that they were going to win anyway'. Of course, because we are sitting on a plane taking the short hop from Port-au-Prince to Miami, he recalls that there were other problematic elections at that time in this part of the world.[15]

Paul Farmer, the celebrated physician who works among Haiti's poor and who wondered how the 'international community' can have had so little effect in the country, emphasizes the external factors that contributed to the turmoil. He points out that in 2001 the new US admin-istration cut off aid and convinced the development banks to stop loans in protest over the eight contested Haitian Senate seats. He writes that it 'would take an intrepid investigative reporter, rather than a physician like myself' to determine whether the United States did anything more to undermine the elected president.[16] Ahead of a new round of UN-backed Haitian elections, two *New York Times* reporters provided an

[13] Louis Saint-Lot, interview with CNM, 1 Aug. 2004.
[14] Robert Fatton, Jr, 'The Fall of Aristide and Haiti's Current Predicament', paper presented at the Conference on Canada in Haiti: Considering the 3-D Approach, Center for International Governance Innovation, Waterloo, Ontario, 3 Nov. 2005, p. 11.
[15] Louis Saint-Lot, interview with CNM, 1 Aug. 2004.
[16] Paul Farmer, 'Who Removed Aristide?', *London Review of Books*, 15 April 2004.

answer: going well beyond the economic sanctions, at least part of the US foreign policy apparatus had worked to ensure Aristide's rapid removal.[17]

Almost everyone I met in Port-au-Prince told me that Adama Guindo, faced with the inevitable, had tried as hard as he could to do well by the Haitian people. After Aristide's departure, the Res Rep sat at the centre of the small group that chose an interim prime minister. Guindo convinced the former UNDP expert, Gérard Latortue, to stand for the job, thus providing a credible alternative to men who were all-too-strongly promoted by major powers.[18] Aristide's former prime minister, Yvon Neptune (the man Latortue replaced) put it to me this way: even after Aristide was forced out, 'Mr Guindo displayed a real disposition to be on the side of Haiti, and always on the side of the poor'.[19]

Neptune was dressed in a dirty string vest and shorts. He offered me the only place to sit in his sweltering unlit cell in Port-au-Prince's central prison. He and another former minister had been held there, without charge, since Aristide's departure. They were rarely allowed to speak to anyone but close family members. However, UNDP was involved with a remarkably humane project, Assistance à la Réforme de L'Administration Pénitentiaire, and I had been able to step away from the discussion of accurate record keeping, bathing water, wider bunks, shade, and latrines to spend twenty minutes with this man who, Saint-Lot said, was especially frightening to many wealthy Haitians. (After Neptune's widely publicized hunger strike, Latortue's government finally charged him with organizing murderous attacks during the turmoil before Aristide's departure.) It was startling: Neptune and his jailers agreed about nothing except the positive role of Guindo and of UNDP.

Like Sisyphus in the ancient Greek myth slowly pushing his rock up the hill, Guindo and the whole UN development team keep trying to do good in Haiti, but, so often, the rock starts rolling away. The humane new infrastructure and careful records of the central penitentiary disappeared in a February 2005 armed attack that some newspapers reported as an (ultimately unsuccessful) attempt to set Neptune free. A year later, the new elections (with all the usual UN support) took place. Perhaps Guindo and the Secretary-General's Special Representative, Juan Gabriel Valdés (son of the Chilean foreign minister who was UNDP's first Latin American bureau chief) looked with some relief at the outcome – the

[17] Walter Bogdanich and Jenny Norberg, 'Democracy Undone: Back Channels vs. Policy; Mixed US Signals Helped Tilt Haiti towards Chaos', *New York Times*, 29 Jan. 2006.
[18] Adama Guindo, interview with CNM, 30 July 2004.
[19] Yvon Neptune, interview with CNM, 31 July 2004.

victory of another of Aristide's former associates, René Préval: a candidate supported by Haiti's impoverished majority yet acceptable to the United States. (As I left UNDP headquarters on the evening the results were declared, I passed a knot of about fifty jubilant Haitian flag-waving Préval supporters who had gathered spontaneously across the street from the Secretariat building to thank the organization for its continuing commitment.) Nevertheless, Valdés looked resignedly forward to 'decades' of extensive UN involvement in the country,[20] an involvement that may continue to be the kind that Robert Cox considers to be 'global poor relief and riot control'.[21]

At the college where I work, the first person to teach both international organization and what we now call 'development' was Emily Greene Balch, someone who received the Nobel Peace Prize for her scholarship and her activism. In 1926 Balch led a multi-sectoral team that investigated the US occupation of Haiti – a team very much like that first UN technical assistance team a quarter of a century later. Balch and her colleagues looked at finance, agriculture, labour, health, transport, and communication. She wrote, 'The whole situation is a tragic impasse. Each group stalemates the other. The Haitians are not willing to accept American control . . . The Americans, who hold the purse strings', refuse to let Haitians really manage themselves.[22] It is not ill-will (of the United States towards Haiti or of Haitians towards the United States) that leads to the recurrent impasse. It is rather what the Mormon ethicist and business consultant Steven R. Covey calls the problem of matching one's 'circle of influence' with one's 'circle of concern', a problem that exists in all situations of great inequality: those who, by luck or misfortune, can influence more people than they can fully understand ultimately have to delegate their influence – we might say, allow complete democracy – in order to achieve their own deepest moral goals, yet the very powerful rarely recognize that fact.[23]

---

[20] Quoted in James Harding, 'In Haiti, the Vote Isn't Nearly Powerful Enough', *Washington Post*, 16 Oct. 2005.

[21] Robert W. Cox, 'Critical Political Economy', in Björn Hettne, ed., *International Political Economy: Understanding Global Disorder* (London: Zed Books, 1995), p. 41.

[22] The passage refers specifically to education policy, but could summarize the entire report, Emily Greene Balch, ed., *Occupied Haiti: Being the Report of a Committee of Six Disinterested Americans Representing Organizations Exclusively American, Who, Having Personally Studied Conditions in Haiti in 1926 Favor the Restoration of the Independence of the Negro Republic* (New York: The Writers Publishing Company, Inc., 1927), p. 104.

[23] Stephen R. Covey, *The Seven Habits of Highly Successful People* (New York: Simon & Schuster, 1990), pp. 81–91.

Nevertheless, as Juan Gabriel Valdés knows, sometimes the recognition *does* take place, the political impasses *are* overcome. Valdés became an exile after the military coup that aborted Chile's democracy in 1973. Even though the United States had backed the coup, by 1987 – as part of that larger Reagan, George H.W. Bush, and Clinton policy of actively supporting liberal democracy – Washington was promoting free elections in Chile.[24] Haitians worry that the incredibly steep gradient of power between their country and their neighbour makes a long-term reversal of their country's recurrent impasse unlikely. Fatton, in words like Farmer's, concludes that 'the so-called "international community" has neither the will, nor the interest in effecting the transformations required for establishing an equitable and democratic Haiti'.[25] Yet, there are examples to the contrary. One is Timor-Leste.

In December 1975, the same US policy makers who had backed Chile's generals gave Indonesia's Suharto the green light to take over the impoverished and powerless Portuguese colony of East Timor, then in the process of gaining its independence after Portugal's own democratic revolution.[26] After twenty-four years of brutal Indonesian rule – including the deaths of at least 200,000 in a country with a population that is, today, still under one million – the pressures associated with the Asian financial crisis – and a change of US policy – led Jusuf Habibe to accept UN-managed elections in August 1999. The East Timorese voted overwhelmingly for independence, but the Indonesian military instituted a final 'scorched earth' policy, focused on the colony's capital, Dili, killing tens of thousands and destroying much of the colony's infrastructure. The carnage stopped only after the military intervention of neighbouring Australia and the imposition of a UN peacekeeping force. Sovereignty passed temporarily to the United Nations, and Kofi Annan and Mark Malloch Brown's close friend, Sergio Vieira de Mello, served as the country's ultimate authority until Timor-Leste's independence in May 2002.

Vieira de Mello recruited people from all over the world to govern the country during his brief period of direct administration. Pakistan's Saeed Qureshi talks about their bewildering range of tasks, from holding 'really

---

[24] William I. Robinson, *Promoting Polyarchy: Globalization, US Intervention, and Hegemony* (Cambridge: Cambridge University Press, 1996), p. 173.

[25] Fatton, 'Fall of Aristide', p. 15.

[26] William Burr and Michael J. Evans, 'East Timor Revisited: Ford, Kissinger, and the Indonesian Invasion, 1975–76', National Security Archive Electronic Briefing Book no. 62, 6 Dec. 2001, http://www.gwu.edu/~nsarchiv/NSAEBB/NSAEBB62/ (accessed 4 Feb. 2006).

very basic, but very necessary' classes on how to start a small business, to identifying and developing skilled Timorese counterparts. (The national who replaced Qureshi in his economic policy role, Mari Alkatiri, became the country's first prime minister.)[27] Yet, despite hard work and good intentions, the UN's direct rule generated deep resentment among the Timorese.

The most important role played by anyone from UNDP during this time was probably that of Francis M. O'Donnell, who led a series of missions to evaluate the UN's government of the colony. O'Donnell (who later became Res Rep in Ukraine and served during the Orange Revolution) recalls how UN staffers in Dili told him how 'unqualified' and 'unready' the Timorese were to run their own affairs after more than 450 years of colonialism, 'Forgetting', he says, 'how this might sound to an Irish ear'.[28] The paternalistic views of the first group of UN officers were particularly galling to Timorese economic planner, Emilia Pires, because many of the rapidly recruited foreign nationals were so clearly unqualified for *their* jobs:

> I think the UN was not ready to administer the country . . . [T]o administer, you actually need administrators. You need public servants, bureaucrats, because they are the ones who know how to do it . . . [I]f they were supposed to set up a judicial system, then they should have been people from the judicial system. If they were supposed to set up an agriculture ministry, then they should have been that type of people, or from the public service, etc., etc., because you need or require different skills.[29]

O'Donnell took a simple message back to Kofi Annan: 'Nobody can tell people that they are not ready for independence.'

Timorese Nobel peace laureate José Ramos-Horta then met with the Secretary-General and demanded a fixed date for the UN's departure.[30] A joint UN–Timorese administration, elections, and independence soon followed.

Throughout that rapid transition, UNDP began to take on a more central role, not only supporting the elections, but also building the capacity of the new state. The Programme worked with the UN

---

[27] Saeed Qureshi, interview with CNM, 8 Dec. 2004.

[28] Francis M. O'Donnell, interview with CNM, 11 March 2005.

[29] Emilia Pires, interview with Kym Smithies, 11 May 2004, for the film *United Nations Country Team, Timor-Leste*, Dili, June 2004. This part of the interview was not included in the film.

[30] Jarat Chopra, 'The UN's Kingdom of East Timor', *Survival*, 42, 3 (2000): 33. The article is an excellent analysis of the failures of the UN's direct administration.

12.1 East Timor: welcoming a long-delayed election

administration and the Timorese to identify and fill a few hundred key positions within the government that would benefit from qualified, temporary external counterparts. UNDP set up training programmes for the new parliament and the judiciary system, engaging in complicated negotiations among all the stakeholders in order to establish a working system of legislative oversight and for courts from the magistrate through to the appellate level. And other UNDP officers began creating a variety of programmes to reintegrate former combatants and map out a long-term economic strategy for the new country.

The problems confronted by Timor-Leste, and by UNDP, were far from straightforward. Consider just the issue of valid laws, which exist in four languages: Portuguese (colonial law and the law of the newly independent legislature), Tetun (the local language), Indonesian (the language of the last twenty-five years of colonialism), and English (in which the UN administration had worked). Most of the Timorese law graduates who would be the most likely to become magistrates or judges had been educated in Indonesian or English. They were the *least* comfortable in Portuguese, the primary language of the new state and the language preferred by the anti-colonial leadership, many of whom had become involved in the struggle as young men and women when Portugal still ruled. For UNDP to have any success required an ability to recruit a group of experts with an unusual combination of skills, not only administrative, but linguistic.

José Ramos-Horta, who became Timor-Leste's first foreign minister, says that getting the right people was, in part, a matter of having the resources on hand to pay the people with the right combination of skills. He credits the direct involvement of Annan and Malloch Brown with getting 'the donor community to deliver most of what they promised'.[31] Moreover, Gus Dur, someone whom Ramos-Horta considers to be a democratic leader of global stature, made rapid reconciliation with Indonesia possible.[32] That, in turn, encouraged the return of Timorese professionals who would be able to keep close ties to Indonesia where they had businesses, family, schoolmates, and friends. The government was able to recruit a dedicated and highly qualified temporary staff from Portugal, Brazil, Macao, lusophone Africa, Australia, Indonesia, and many other parts of the world to help build the new state.[33] When I was in Timor-Leste, in June 2005, many of the advisors were, perhaps precipitously, in their last few months. Hazem Galal, UNDP's thirty-something Egyptian head of the major capacity-building project, was looking forward to visiting family in Brazil and taking up a new job with Price Waterhouse Coopers' government consultancy practice in the United Arab Emirates, where Ramos-Horta also asked him to set up shop as Timor-Leste's honorary consul in the Middle East.[34]

Transferring skills, changing attitudes

Even if all of the impasses preventing the emergence of effective, democratic governments in every nation were to disappear, we would still live in a world of great inequality, a place where accidents of birth will determine most of our fates. When the unprecedented 26 December 2004 tsunami crushed the coasts of Indonesia, Thailand, Sri Lanka, India, and a half-dozen other countries the unequal geography of fate seemed

---

[31] Jose Ramos-Horta, interview with Kym Smithies, n.d., for *United Nations Country Team, Timor-Leste.*

[32] Jose Ramos-Horta, interview with Ray Suarez, 'Nation Building', *News Hour with Jim Lehrer* transcript, broadcast 19 May 2000.

[33] Haoling Xu, 'Timor-Leste – A New Nation's Path to Sustainable Development', unpublished paper, Dili, UNDP, n.d., and Augusto Barreto Soares, Hazem Galal, and Toshi Nakamura, 'Capacity Development at the World's Newest Nation: Timor-Leste, Challenges and Lessons Learned from the Program Approach', Dili, Government of RDTL and UNDP, April 2005, provide good summaries of this experience.

[34] Hazem Galal, interview with CNM, 2 June 2005.

unusually stark. One hundred and thirty thousand died in Indonesia alone, and one million were displaced. In South Asia, primarily India and Sri Lanka, another million were displaced, and another 50,000 died.

Yet the disaster was less hideous than it might have been, in small but significant part due to UNDP. In the hours immediately after the first reports of the calamity, experts everywhere worried about the greater tragedy that could come from a lack of clean water and the spread of bacteria from decomposing bodies and the inconceivable amounts of rubbish and wreckage that would spread cholera and other diseases. That did not happen in India and Sri Lanka because disaster recovery institutions were in place. Nor did it happen in Aceh – the Indonesian province where the destruction was greatest – due to rapidly designed, effective clean-up programmes. UNDP played a role in both these processes.

UNDP's role in India came through its consistent, decade-long support of an increasingly complex system of national, state, and local disaster management institutions. The Ministry of Home Affairs, with UNDP support, had built a system to ensure immediate interdepartmental collaboration and had trained a cadre of disaster management professionals who understood the specific 'cultural settings' of every part of the country. The Indian disaster preparedness group had more than 170 national UN Volunteers (UNVs) ready to provide technical and administrative support. Many were physicians, trained 'to actively monitor the unfolding health scenario wherever any disaster strikes'.[35]

In 2003, seven Indian national UNVs had also gone to Sri Lanka to begin replicating the Indian experience, establishing a national disaster recovery system and developing local strategies. G. Padmanabhan, in UNDP's New Delhi office recalls, 'They worked very well with the authorities there. One of them was immediately recruited as an international UNV and asked to stay back' to work with the prime minister's office to create a permanent system of emergency coordination.[36]

When the tsunami hit, Sri Lanka received assistance from the entire world; only a small part of it came from UNDP, but the skills earlier passed on through UNDP and UNV made a difference in the effective use of the aid that the country received. India refused any international assistance, arguing that the tragedy was less severe than the

---

[35] UN Volunteers, India, *Helping People Cope: UN Volunteers Support Disaster Mitigation in India* (New Delhi: UNV, 2003), p. 20. I learned about the development of the UNDP disaster relief programme in India from G. Padmanabhan in an interview on 11 Dec. 2004, shortly before the tsunami took place.

[36] G. Padmanabhan, interview with CNM, 11 Dec. 2004.

Gujarat earthquake just three years earlier. Instead, the country sent helicopters and warships to help with the clean-up and to distribute food, tents, and medicine to Sri Lanka and the Maldives. Both India's self-reliance and its ability to use its capacity to aid its neighbours grew from work in which UNDP had been involved for a decade.

Aceh did not have the benefit of a decade of attention to potential natural disasters. The province was the site of a long-standing low-level war against the old authoritarian government in Jakarta. However, beginning in 2001, UNDP had a Crisis Prevention and Recovery Unit operating with the new government to work on long-term peace-building measures in Indonesia's multiple secessionist regions. That allowed the country office to have relevant professionals in the field in less than forty-eight hours. UNDP immediately began hiring tsunami survivors to clean up debris, at first around Banda Aceh's hospitals and other public buildings.[37] Less than three weeks after the disaster, Douglas Keh, a former advisor to the Crisis Bureau's Julia Taft, told reporters, 'Empowering victims to help themselves is much more important than cash. No one likes to get handouts forever. They would get depressed. It's pure therapy to get people to work.'[38]

Five months later, Normala, a thirty-four-year-old mother who saw most of her village of Dusun Tonkol sweep past her out to sea, made the same point. As long as aid supervisors treated the Acehnese with dignity (some, unfortunately, did not) the continuing clean-up not only provided cash, it gave hope that the community would return, even though more than 1,000 people died in her village alone.[39]

Perhaps even more important, the training that UNDP could provide, the rubber gloves, the speed with which the cleanup got started, and its persistence over so many months, helped to ensure that disease did not spread among the 400 people from Dusun Tonkol who survived. Ahmad Human Hamid, head of the Aceh Recovery Forum, who is deeply critical of much of the international effort, says, 'Thank God, there was no outbreak of disease', and the immediately established cash-for-work programmes were responsible for that. Nevertheless, he wants me to be clear that just cleaning the streets and staffing the dumps is 'doing nothing for the long-term livelihood' of people like Normala.[40]

[37] George Conway, interview with CNM, 24 May 2005.
[38] Quoted in Cindy Sui, 'In Indonesia, a Struggle to Help Tsunami Survivors Gain Livelihood', *Agence France-Presse*, 13 Jan. 2005.
[39] Normala, interview with CNM, 27 May 2005.
[40] Ahmad Human Hamid, interview with CNM, 27 May 2005.

12.2 Street cleaning in Banda Aceh after the December 2004 tsunami

Another NGO leader, Teuku Ardiansyah, makes the point a little more broadly: only truly successful aid work can turn 'guests' into 'friends'. That has not happened with those who have come to Aceh and started acting like an 'owner' or a 'master'.[41] The (non-UNDP) cash-for-work programme boss of Normala's friend, Nurlaili, is an example. Nurlaili left her job after he asked her to scavenge a meal from food that aid workers had discarded.[42] For the cynical supervisor, the five-month-old programme had become nothing more than a stream of never-ending handouts.

More generally, for solidarity to be built between those who are more and less powerful, development cooperation has to show results. If every case were like Haiti's, with so little to see for sixty years of international involvement, perhaps all that we could expect from powerful donor countries is a self-interested cynicism about the developing world, even if donor policies are part of the explanation of the failures. When people offering skills or resources can see both immediate and long-term results, as the Indian UNV in Sri Lanka, Rita Missal, did, it reinforces their determination to help their neighbours. You willingly become, Missal says, 'very alert so as not to make any mistakes at all'.[43] That is undoubtedly the

[41] Teuku Ardiansyah, interview with CNM, 28 May 2005.
[42] Nurlaili, interview with CNM, 27 May 2005.
[43] UN Volunteers, India, *Helping People Cope*, p. 29.

attitude that US Secretary of State Condoleezza Rice hoped that Americans aiding the tsunami victims in Aceh would have when she spoke to the US Senate about the opportunity for better relations between the United States and the Islamic world created by the tragedy.

UNDP's learning and the value of openness

This self-reinforcing aspect of *effective* international cooperation makes the capacity of a knowledge-oriented organization like UNDP particularly critical.

In the late 1980s Ernst B. Haas, one of the most eminent scholars of international organizations since their beginning, argued that UNDP and the Special Fund *had been* effective learning organizations in Paul Hoffman's day, but that things had changed with the compromises made after the Capacity Study.[44] Haas's research on UNDP was only a very small part of a larger study, and he missed evidence that would have led him to a different conclusion. He wrote before the publication of the first *Human Development Report* in 1990, and at a time when UNDP kept its engagements with China and the Palestinian leadership very quiet.

If we bear in mind the evidence that he did not have, it is clear that UNDP continued to learn, even if measured only by ideas taken on board by other organizations. The evidence of that is not just the popularity of the human development concept or the frequency with which the Programme is cited as being on the leading edge of UN reform; it also is in UNDP's frequent place in the stories other organizations tell about their own learning. The World Bank's historians, for example, point to Brad Morse's role in the Bank's self-critical reassessment of its grand regional development projects centred on large dams, something that took place in the mid-1990s, long after similar issues had been raised inside UNDP.[45]

Today, UNDP has all but one of the characteristics that Haas identified as those of other intergovernmental organizations with an unusual capacity to learn. UNDP lacks the close attachment to a scientific

---

[44] Ernst B. Haas, *When Knowledge is Power: Three Models of Change in International Organization* (Berkeley: University of California Press, 1990), p. 157.

[45] Devesh Kapur, John B. Lewis, and Richard Webb, *The World Bank: Its First Half-Century* (Washington, D.C.: Brookings Institution Press, 1997), p. 1203. Sanjeev Khagram, *Dams and Development: Transnational Struggles for Water and Power* (Ithaca, N.Y.: Cornell University Press, 2004), uses the case that Morse was asked to evaluate for the Bank to explore the global rise and fall of big dam projects.

community – the medical doctors of the World Health Organization or the neoclassical economists of the International Monetary Fund (IMF) – that can continuously bring new knowledge into the organization. Instead, UNDP's history reveals another mode of organizational learning, one that needs only that 'incompletely theorized agreement', which, as Amartya Sen says, 'may emerge pragmatically, on quite diverse grounds, after a general recognition that many things are important'.[46] This makes UNDP particularly relevant for those considering the future of global governance. In the fields closest to the deep conflicts that fracture the state system, 'incompletely theorized agreements' are the *best* that we can expect.

UNDP's capacity to learn in such an 'incompletely theorized' field has been forged, in part, by the tension between its commitment to serve the various goals and plans of the UN's many developing country members, and the Programme's equal commitment to the egalitarian principles that have given UNDP both its distinctive organizational culture and its 'backbone'. If UNDP were 'running on one track' *only* – either acting simply as a service provider to the governments of developing countries or as an advocate of a particular development theory – its staff, country offices, and bureaux would have had less cause to be creative. Similarly, to maintain the Programme's resources in an increasingly competitive environment, successive Administrators had to navigate between the organization's solidarity with its developing country clients and the changing agendas of their major donors, a tension that provided another spur to innovation.

For these tensions to be sufficient to ensure innovation, UNDP also needs to remain very open to the communities in which knowledge is generated, even though it is tied to no single 'epistemic community'. Unfortunately, like a traditional bureaucracy (which it is not), UNDP has a host of mechanisms that insulate it from new information coming from the outside. I saw telling examples of this in Indonesia and Timor-Leste, where UNDP let me hire Siti Nurjanah, the popular local journalist and NGO leader who had earlier worried about the consolidation of Indonesian democracy, to help with the research. My more permanent UNDP colleagues twice invited me to meetings without including her. What happened at both meetings seemed to suggest that Nurjanah's non-inclusion was part of the communication strategy that Mark D. Alleyne,

---

[46] Amartya Sen, 'A Decade of Human Development', *Journal of Human Development*, 1, 1 (2000): 22.

the leading scholar in the field, sees as typical of the UN Secretariat,[47] one of trying to control information, especially the dissemination of 'negative' information, even at the cost of organizational learning.

Sometimes this means drawing attention away from other organizational difficulties. One of the meetings was a staff discussion of the Programme's work in Aceh. Shortly after the tsunami, Mark Malloch Brown had promised that New York would act on requests for funds from the field within two days. Five months later, approval times had slowed to two weeks, a repetition of a general failing within the organization that was being tackled, worldwide, through reforms such as the adoption of Atlas. Nevertheless, there was still a long way to go, especially when confronted by an unprecedented crisis and a great outpouring of generosity. In the six months after the tsunami, UNDP delivered only US$35 million of the US$122 million that it had available to spend.[48]

The other meeting revealed some of the pathologies of UN coordination and concerns about showing a good face to donors. Fourteen people sat in the cramped local UN headquarters. Each of them had a critical job to do administering the programme of one or another UN agency, but all wanted to be part of the decision about a single site, near the airport, that UN tsunami envoy Bill Clinton could visit in the thirty minutes that he had to spend with the Indonesian victims of the disaster. One of the four original criteria for choosing the site was that it be one where 'every agency has a project to showcase'. (Quite reasonably, this was the first goal to be dropped.) The rest of the meeting was about security and managing information per se, with the ultimate goal of encouraging the generosity of northern donors. Clinton could not be taken to the recycling centre – 'the dump' – even though it was the final stage of the project through which the UN had, unequivocally, saved lives. The smell was too strong. Similarly, while the UN wouldn't want 'to set up a Potemkin village',[49] perhaps additional displaced people might be invited to the camp nearest the airport and some cosmetic work done to give reporters a better story.

[47] Mark D. Alleyne, *Global Lies? Propaganda, the UN and World Order* (Houndmills: Palgrave Macmillan, 2003), p. 178.

[48] Memorandum report re UNDP 1999–2005, Accomplishments and Remaining Challenges, from Mark Malloch Brown to Kemal Dervis, August 2005, p. 51. Earlier, on p. 49, Malloch Brown writes, 'If there is an "Achilles Heel" of UNDP at the moment – something which could drag down all the other successes – it is the organizational incapacity to deliver on a scale commensurate with its mission.'

[49] The elaborate fake villages constructed by Catherine the Great's minister, Grigori Potemkin, to hide the squalor when she toured Ukraine in 1787.

There is something naïve and a little old-fashioned about the orientation to information reflected here. As Alleyne puts it, it rests on a view of
the world as a place where 'ideas can take hold of and impose a discipline
that would otherwise not exist' and where various 'authorities', including
popular journalists and experienced scholars truly 'control' information
flows, and those people, in turn, can easily be influenced by a respected
body such as the UN.[50]

These days, available sources of information are just much too great
for such a strategy to work. For example, Nurjanah had already heard
about the UNDP's slowing delivery (and that of other UN agencies) from
Yanty Lacsana, Oxfam's liaison manager in Banda Aceh, and we could
have learned about it from a host of local partners.[51] Moreover, even if
parading the attractive success of the dozen UN agencies behind Bill
Clinton would bring in more donor dollars (and that seems questionable), the goal seemed a little irrelevant when the agencies were having
trouble spending the money they already had.

The ingenuousness of this orientation to information suggests that it is
a matter of habit, of organizational culture, rather than a strategy based
on deep reflection. It is a habit found in most bureaucracies that are
subject to neither the discipline of the electorate nor that of the market,
including bureaucracies at the intergovernmental level.[52]

In organizations with strong ties to a specific scientific profession –
organizations in which almost everyone is trained within the knowledge
field – the habit of *two-way* interaction with knowledge makers – of
always trying to learn as well as trying to inform – is much more commonplace.

UNDP's fuzzy surface of experts gives the Programme access to new
knowledge in many fields. Yet that 'epistemic' surface only partially pene-
trates an organizational core, which, like the Secretariat proper, is linked to
the profession of diplomacy, and, understandably, the UN's own professional diplomats constantly try to find words acceptable to their 191
members with their dozens of incompatible worldviews. Ernst Haas
implored the staff of international organizations to search for compromise

---

[50] Alleyne, *Global Lies?*, p. 182.   [51] Yanty Lacsana, interview with CNM, 27 May 2005.
[52] Michael Barnett and Martha Finnemore, *Rules for the World: International Organizations in
Global Politics* (Ithaca, N.Y.: Cornell University Press, 2004), pp. 40–1. Barnett and
Finnemore see it as one aspect of the greatest pathologies that have ever affected international organizations, a small contributing factor to disasters such as the Rwandan genocide
or the involuntary repatriation of refugees.

wording that preserves truth and maintains the organization's transparency and openness, but often it seems that the diplomatic task is more easily accomplished by obfuscation that alienates the external knowledge communities on which any organization has to rely in order to learn.[53]

Beyond the standard communities committed to expanding knowledge – the professional scientists, social scientists, and journalists – another great source of knowledge for the progressive transformation of global governance has always been NGO activists. In fact, the story of Brad Morse's role in the World Bank's reassessment of large dams is largely one of reinforcing and translating the sustained advocacy of conservationists, environmentalists, and human rights groups into terms understood by the Bank.[54] Unfortunately, despite the active reaching out to civil society that has been a goal of UNDP since Draper's day, some of the UN's current organizational constraints keep the Programme from truly mutual, two-way engagements with parts of civil society as well.

In Banda Aceh NGO leaders kept telling me that my colleagues and I were 'the first people from UNDP' to come visit them in their own offices. That was due, in part, to UNDP's understaffing; it is easier to do as much work as possible from the regional office in order to minimize time lost in travel. A larger problem was security: UN rules prevented staff from taking part in casual meetings in a place that was still, in many ways, a war zone.

The same could not be said in the then very safe city of Dili, where the major NGO involved in evaluating the work of the entire donor community in Timor-Leste, La'o Hamutuk, is close to UNDP headquarters, and the staff of both organizations cannot help running into each other in dozens of public gatherings. Yet, La'o Hamutuk's Mericio Akara claims that some people in UNDP try to keep the relationship at arm's length, largely due to the independent, critical approach that his organization takes.[55] Sukehiro Hasegawa, the long-experienced Special Representative of the Secretary-General sighed a bit when we mention the NGO. He spoke about how one of the hardest jobs as a Res Rep (or someone in his

---

[53] Haas, *When Knowledge is Power*, p. 209.

[54] See Khagram, *Dams and Development*. The larger historical record is discussed in Craig N. Murphy, 'Social Movements and Liberal World Orders', in *Global Institutions, Marginalization, and Development* (London: Routledge, 2005), pp. 54–72; parts of the argument rely heavily on John Braithwaite and Peter Drahos, *Global Business Regulation* (Cambridge: Cambridge University Press, 2000).

[55] Mericio Akara, interview with CNM, 2 June 2005. The report in question was 'Observations Regarding the RESPECT Program in East Timor', *The La'o Hamutuk Bulletin*, 5, 5–6 (December 2004): 1–6.

current position) involves developing the people who serve under you. Most of those on the UNDP staff in Dili would have no trouble learning from someone like Akara, as he knew what we knew after meeting Hazem Galal and his colleagues. There are others who worry a great deal about deference and about the reputation of the UN (not a bad thing, of course). They need to learn, by example and by experience, the benefits that can come with greater openness.[56]

There is one important lesson from UNDP's history for the immediate task of UN reform; it is probably the same one that Haas championed more than fifteen years ago: opening the organization further – encouraging 'knowledgeable critique' – and using the example of UNDP's relative openness to encourage other parts of the UN system to pursue greater transparency and two-way involvement with knowledge makers (scholars, journalists, reflective activists) and with civil society at all levels. Increased openness, as Haas argued, is 'likely [to] increase trust and respect for what is being attempted, to encourage understanding for lack of success, and to make international officials less defensive'.[57]

This, I believe, is the *major* reason that governments across the North–South divide should embrace the institutionalization of greater transparency and openness that Kofi Annan placed at the centre of his reform agenda. Doing so is the key to preserving UNDP's ability to learn and extending it to other parts of the United Nations. It is definitely one those 'individual and important changes that would have a multiplier effect'.

Remembering our shared history

Even though I am from the United States, I recognize that one of the least persuasive arguments for a greater commitment to openness is the one made by the US House of Representatives in a letter to the Group of 77 (the Third World alliance) at the beginning of 2006:

> Reform of the UN hinges upon greater transparency and accountability to the people of the world, especially to the citizens of those few nations who bear the burden of financing UN programmes, many of which benefit nations belonging to your caucus.[58]

[56] Sukehiro Hasegawa, interview with CNM, 2 June 2005.
[57] Haas, *When Knowledge is Power*, p. 210.
[58] Quoted in Thalif Deen, 'US Legislators Cross Swords with UN Bloc', Inter Press Service News Agency, 16 Feb. 2006, http://www.ipsnews.net/news.asp?idnews=32193 (accessed 16 Feb. 2006).

Everything from the word 'especially' on was unnecessary. Such implied threats reinforce the North–South conflict, the deep international fissure that UNDP has helped to transcend.

While it is true that, sixty years on, we may not be that much closer than the founders of the UN were to knowing how to achieve 'development' (how to overcome the global inequality that has grown over the last two centuries), we *are* closer to agreeing on what development really is. We also have good reasons to believe that the 'Way' of conducting international affairs invented by the wartime generation is really 'Better' than what existed before. Throughout the world, most people and their governments believe that it *is* desirable to feel material responsibilities towards countries where people are not as fortunate. Even in my own country, where the strong public support of the United Nations that existed for more than fifty years has fundamentally eroded since 2000 (and where people who are the most knowledgeable about the UN have become the most sceptical),[59] the commonsense support of this larger principle – as evidenced by the outpouring of concern after the 2004 tsunami – remains high.

I often wish that Paul Hoffman's vision of UNDP operating everywhere, including in the 'developed' world (including 'Mississippi, if asked') had become a reality. The experience of both receiving and giving multilateral support changes people's understanding of their past as well as their future. I saw a striking example of that in Ghana, shortly after the tsunami hit on the other side of the world. On my last day in the country, much of the UN office drove for half the day from the capital to Cape Coast Castle, which was built for the slave trade by the Portuguese in the 1480s, a generation before the occupation of Timor and the birth of Philip II. It was later rebuilt and occupied, successively, by the Dutch, the Swedes, and the British. It was being used on that day in January 2005 by one of Ghana's ancient traditional rulers, the King of Elmina, whose dynasty may be bit older than that of the Kings of Denmark or the Emperors of Japan. He was there to honour UNDP's Res Rep, Alfred Sallia Fawundu, by naming him a traditional chief, 'Nana Yaw Abayie', 'His Excellency Far-Travelling [i.e., born on Thursday] and Respected' or, more precisely, 'The Chief whose Coming Augurs Well for the Future'.

Those who have read this book through from the beginning will find the specific things that Fawundu accomplished somewhat commonplace.

---

[59] The Pew Research Center for the People and the Press and the Council on Foreign Relations, *America's Place in the World 2005* (Washington, D.C.: The Pew Center, 2005), pp. 13, 37.

The linguists (the King's spokespeople) alluded to his role in convincing Ghana's charismatic long-time strongman, Jerry Rawlings, not to impede a free election that transferred power to the opposition. They spoke about small things, like Fawundu bringing *New York Times* pundit and globalization cheerleader Thomas L. Friedman to Ghana, something that mattered a lot because Friedman's enthusiasm about the prospects for the country within the global market proved infectious. Then there were the immediate things: examples of giving rather than receiving. Just hours after the first reports of the tsunami, tens of thousands of Ghanaians were asking how to contribute support. Friends came to Fawundu asking for help getting money to Asia. Within days, he had worked with the major cell-phone providers to set up a system for people to make small donations, a few cedis (Ghana's national currency) every time they called. Shortly afterward, a webpage appeared, www.ghanatsunamirelief.com, to take credit card donations that went to the UN office to be distributed through UN programmes in countries throughout the Indian Ocean region.

Most of the speakers dwelt on the longer history of the UN's involvement in Ghana, at least fifty years, going back to Sir Robert Jackson and W. Arthur Lewis, and, when I spoke with the King, he emphasized that the main purpose of the ceremony was to use Fawundu's planned departure in 2005 to honour all that the UN had done for the country for half a century.

The UN's history and the Res Rep's most recent work led one speaker back to a longer history: three hundred years before, the Dutch had taken men from Elmina as soldiers to crush rebellions in Java, so near to where the waves had just swept over Dusun Tonkol. To the Dutch, the Cape Coast men had been terrible disappointments: they fought poorly and took local wives, bringing them back to Cape Coast, along with the technique for making Javanese cloth, now ubiquitous across sub-Saharan Africa – one of the two types of traditional cloth in the African dress worn that day.

Elmina's history and the events that day reminded many of us of the problem that UNDP was meant to solve, as well as a basic mechanism of its solution. Over the last generation, scholars around the world in the field that has come to be known as 'macro-' or 'big history', have converged on a single explanation of the inequality that is characteristic of the modern world. It began at the end of the fifteenth century, in places like Elmina and Dili, when (primarily as a matter of the luck of geography) people living on the western edge of Europe gained privileged access

12.3 A ceremony at Cape Coast Castle

to the wealth of the Americas and united a global economy. The 'hub' of the world economy (the place where people, ideas, and wealth flowed most freely), which had long been in South-West Asia, moved to the edges of the North Atlantic, and places like Elmina and Dili became outposts, siphoning all sorts of advantages towards the hubs. After more than two centuries of slow transformation, quantitative changes led to a qualitative break, the Industrial Revolution; a fundamentally new economic system appeared on the edges of the North Atlantic and the world was transformed.[60]

There is an almost axiomatic understanding about inequalities of power that appears in the political philosophy written in almost every part of the world: when the powerful wish to maintain their advantage (which, fortunately, they do not always want to do), they work to divide the less powerful from each other and to make them forget the history that links them to each other and to the powerful themselves. This means that the tools of the less powerful always include building *unity* and

---

[60] An excellent version of this account appears in David Christian, *Maps of Time: An Introduction to Big History* (Berkeley: University of California Pres, 2004), pp. 334–439.

reviving *memory*. All the cell-phone clicks made by so many of the people in Ghana for so many months afterward – all those cedis flying on their way to Aceh – and the history that was remembered in Elmina while hon-ouring the Res Rep are, in that sense, part of a larger historical process of transforming the divisions of the world.

So too, is the unity fostered by UNDP – an institution 'far travelling and respected' just like the man Ghanaians chose to represent the whole. Has UNDP made a great difference in the larger historical task for which it was created? It is probably too soon to know. If, a continent away, Latin America's Liberator, Simón Bolívar, when readying himself for exile and preparing to die, could have looked forward 175 years to the region today, I doubt that he would have said that his life, devoted to liberation and to unity, had been so much 'ploughing the sea'. Similarly, if they could live another century, those who despair that the UN development network has not accomplished its loftiest aims – who despair that the poverty Paul Hoffman expected to be gone by 2000 is still with us and the UN is becoming 'more and more marginal' – might think differently. Those who gave the honours in Elmina may turn out to be right that UNDP's work augurs well for the future.

INDEX